Annaeus Seneca

Moral Essays & Dialogues

Translated by
On the Shortness of Life: JOHN W. BASORE
All Other Works: AUBREY STEWART

ISBN: 1541308034
ISBN-13: 978-1541308039

CONTENTS

On the Shortness of Life *(De Brevitate Vitæ)*	1
Of a Happy Life *(De Vita Beata)*	31
Of Providence *(De Providentia)*	69
On the Firmness of the Wise Man *(De Constantia Sapientis)*	85
Of Anger *(De Ira)*	
Book I	111
Book II	141
Book III	183
Of Leisure *(De Otio)*	231
Of Peace of Mind *(De Tranquillitate Animi)*	243
Of Clemency *(De Clementia)*	
Book I	277
Book II	313
On Benefits *(De Beneficiis)*	
Translator's Preface	324
Book I	329
Book II	348
Book III	387
Book IV	428
Book V	471
Book VI	504
Book VII	553

On the Shortness of Life

I

The majority of mortals, Paulinus, complain bitterly of the spitefulness of Nature, because we are born for a brief span of life, because even this space that has been granted to us rushes by so speedily and so swiftly that all save a very few find life at an end just when they are getting ready to live. Nor is it merely the common herd and the unthinking crowd that bemoan what is, as men deem it, an universal ill; the same feeling has called forth complaint also from men who were famous. It was this that made the greatest of physicians exclaim that "life is short, art is long;" it was this that led Aristotle, while expostulating with Nature, to enter an indictment most unbecoming to a wise man—that, in point of age, she has shown such favour to animals that they drag out five or ten lifetimes, but that a much shorter limit is fixed for man, though he is born for so many and such great achievements. It is not that we have a short space of time, but that we waste much of it. Life is long enough, and it has been given in sufficiently generous measure to allow the accomplishment of the very greatest things if the whole of it is well invested. But when it is squandered in luxury and carelessness, when it is devoted to no good end, forced at last by the ultimate necessity we perceive that it has passed away before we were aware that it was passing. So it is—the life we receive is not short, but we make it so, nor do we have any lack of it, but are wasteful of it. Just as great and princely wealth is scattered in a moment when it comes into the hands of a bad owner, while wealth however limited, if it is entrusted to a good guardian, increases by use, so our life is amply long for him who orders it properly.

II

Why do we complain of Nature? She has shown herself kindly; life, if you know how to use it, is long. But one man is possessed by an avarice that is insatiable, another by a toilsome devotion to tasks that are useless; one man is besotted with wine, another is paralyzed by sloth; one man is exhausted by an ambition that always hangs upon the decision of others, another, driven on by the greed of the trader, is led over all lands and all seas by the hope of gain; some are tormented by a passion for war and are always either bent upon inflicting danger upon others or concerned about their own; some there are who are worn out by voluntary servitude in a thankless attendance upon the great; many are kept busy either in the pursuit of other men's fortune or in complaining of their own; many, following no fixed aim, shifting and inconstant and dissatisfied, are plunged by their fickleness into plans that are ever new; some have no fixed principle by which to direct their course, but Fate takes them unawares while they loll and yawn—so surely does it happen that I cannot doubt the truth of that utterance which the greatest of poets delivered with all the seeming of an oracle: "The part of life we really live is small. For all the rest of existence is not life, but merely time. Vices beset us and surround us on every side, and they do not permit us to rise anew and lift up our eyes for the discernment of truth, but they keep us down when once they have overwhelmed us and we are chained to lust. Their victims are never allowed to return to their true selves; if ever they chance to find some release, like the waters of the deep sea which continue to heave even after the storm is past, they are tossed about, and no rest from their lusts abides. Think you that I am speaking of the wretches whose evils are admitted? Look at those whose prosperity men flock to behold; they are smothered by their blessings. To how many are riches a burden! From how many do eloquence and the daily straining to display their powers draw forth blood! How many are pale from constant pleasures! To how many does the throng of clients that crowd about them leave no freedom! In short, run through the list of all these men from the lowest to the highest—this man desires an advocate, this one answers the call, that one is on trial, that one defends him, that one gives sentence; no one asserts his claim to himself, everyone is wasted for the sake of another. Ask about the men whose names are known by heart, and you will see that these are the marks that distinguish them: A cultivates B and B cultivates C; no one is his own master. And then certain men show the most senseless indignation—they complain of the insolence of their superiors, because they were too busy to see them when they wished an audience! But can anyone have the hardihood to complain of the pride of another when he himself has no time to attend to himself? After all, no matter who you are, the great man does sometimes look toward you even if his face is insolent, he does sometimes condescend to listen to your words, he permits you to appear at his side; but you never deign to look upon yourself, to give ear to yourself. There is no reason, therefore, to count anyone in debt for such services, seeing that, when you performed them, you had no wish for another's company, but could not endure your own.

III

 Though all the brilliant intellects of the ages were to concentrate upon this one theme, never could they adequately express their wonder at this dense darkness of the human mind. Men do not suffer anyone to seize their estates, and they rush to stones and arms if there is even the slightest dispute about the limit of their lands, yet they allow others to trespass upon their life—nay, they themselves even lead in those who will eventually possess it. No one is to be found who is willing to distribute his money, yet among how many does each one of us distribute his life! In guarding their fortune men are often closefisted, yet, when it comes to the matter of wasting time, in the case of the one thing in which it is right to be miserly, they show themselves most prodigal. And so I should like to lay hold upon someone from the company of older men and say: "I see that you have reached the farthest limit of human life, you are pressing hard upon your hundredth year, or are even beyond it; come now, recall your life and make a reckoning. Consider how much of your time was taken up with a moneylender, how much with a mistress, how much with a patron, how much with a client, how much in wrangling with your wife, how much in punishing your slaves, how much in rushing about the city on social duties. Add the diseases which we have caused by our own acts, add, too, the time that has lain idle and unused; you will see that you have fewer years to your credit than you count. Look back in memory and consider when you ever had a fixed plan, how few days have passed as you had intended, when you were ever at your own disposal, when your face ever wore its natural expression, when your mind was ever unperturbed, what work you have achieved in so long a life, how many have robbed you of life when you were not aware of what you were losing, how much was taken up in useless sorrow, in foolish joy, in greedy desire, in the allurements of society, how little of yourself was left to you; you will perceive that you are dying before your season!" What, then, is the reason of this? You live as if you were destined to live forever, no thought of your frailty ever enters your head, of how much time has already gone by you take no heed. You squander time as if you drew from a full and abundant supply, though all the while that day which you bestow on some person or thing is perhaps your last. You have all the fears of mortals and all the desires of immortals. You will hear many men saying: "After my fiftieth year I shall retire into leisure, my sixtieth year shall release me from public duties." And what guarantee, pray, have you that your life will last longer? Who will suffer your course to be just as you plan it? Are you not ashamed to reserve for yourself only the remnant of life, and to set apart for wisdom only that time which cannot be devoted to any business? How late it is to begin to live just when we must cease to live! What foolish forgetfulness of mortality to postpone wholesome plans to the fiftieth and sixtieth year, and to intend to begin life at a point to which few have attained!

IV

You will see that the most powerful and highly placed men let drop remarks in which they long for leisure, acclaim it, and prefer it to all their blessings. They desire at times, if it could be with safety, to descend from their high pinnacle; for, though nothing from without should assail or shatter, Fortune of its very self comes crashing down.

The deified Augustus, to whom the gods vouchsafed more than to any other man, did not cease to pray for rest and to seek release from public affairs; all his conversation ever reverted to this subject—his hope of leisure. This was the sweet, even if vain, consolation with which he would gladden his labours—that he would one day live for himself. In a letter addressed to the senate, in which he had promised that his rest would not be devoid of dignity nor inconsistent with his former glory, I find these words: "But these matters can be shown better by deeds than by promises. Nevertheless, since the joyful reality is still far distant, my desire for that time most earnestly prayed for has led me to forestall some of its delight by the pleasure of words." So desirable a thing did leisure seem that he anticipated it in thought because he could not attain it in reality. He who saw everything depending upon himself alone, who determined the fortune of individuals and of nations, thought most happily of that future day on which he should lay aside his greatness. He had discovered how much sweat those blessings that shone throughout all lands drew forth, how many secret worries they concealed. Forced to pit arms first against his countrymen, then against his colleagues, and lastly against his relatives, he shed blood on land and sea.

Through Macedonia, Sicily, Egypt, Syria, and Asia, and almost all countries he followed the path of battle, and when his troops were weary of shedding Roman blood, he turned them to foreign wars. While he was pacifying the Alpine regions, and subduing the enemies planted in the midst of a peaceful empire, while he was extending its bounds even beyond the Rhine and the Euphrates and the Danube, in Rome itself the swords of Murena, Caepio, Lepidus, Egnatius, and others were being whetted to slay him. Not yet had he escaped their plots, when his daughter and all the noble youths who were bound to her by adultery as by a sacred oath, oft alarmed his failing years—and there was Paulus, and a second time the need to fear a woman in league with an Antony. When he had cut away these ulcers together with the limbs themselves, others would grow in their place; just as in a body that was overburdened with blood, there was always a rupture somewhere. And so he longed for leisure, in the hope and thought of which he found relief for his labours. This was the prayer of one who was able to answer the prayers of mankind.

V

Marcus Cicero, long flung among men like Catiline and Clodius and Pompey and Crassus, some open enemies, others doubtful friends, as he is tossed to and fro along with the state and seeks to keep it from destruction, to be at last swept away, unable as he was to be restful in prosperity or patient in adversity—how many times does he curse that very consulship of his, which he had lauded without end, though not without reason! How tearful the words he uses in a letter written to Atticus, when Pompey the elder had been conquered, and the son was still trying to restore his shattered arms in Spain! "Do you ask," he said, "what I am doing here? I am lingering in my Tusculan villa half a prisoner." He then proceeds to other statements, in which he bewails his former life and complains of the present and despairs of the future. Cicero said that he was "half a prisoner." But, in very truth, never will the wise man resort to so lowly a term, never will he be half a prisoner—he who always possesses an undiminished and stable liberty, being free and his own master and towering over all others. For what can possibly be above him who is above Fortune?

VI

When Livius Drusus, a bold and energetic man, had with the support of a huge crowd drawn from all Italy proposed new laws and the evil measures of the Gracchi, seeing no way out for his policy, which he could neither carry through nor abandon when once started on, he is said to have complained bitterly against the life of unrest he had had from the cradle, and to have exclaimed that he was the only person who had never had a holiday even as a boy. For, while he was still a ward and wearing the dress of a boy, he had had the courage to commend to the favour of a jury those who were accused, and to make his influence felt in the law-courts, so powerfully, indeed, that it is very well known that in certain trials he forced a favourable verdict. To what lengths was not such premature ambition destined to go? One might have known that such precocious hardihood would result in great personal and public misfortune. And so it was too late for him to complain that he had never had a holiday when from boyhood he had been a trouble-maker and a nuisance in the forum. It is a question whether he died by his own hand; for he fell from a sudden wound received in his groin, some doubting whether his death was voluntary, no one, whether it was timely.

It would be superfluous to mention more who, though others deemed them the happiest of men, have expressed their loathing for every act of their years, and with their own lips have given true testimony against themselves; but by these complaints they changed neither themselves nor others. For when they have vented their feelings in words, they fall back into their usual round. Heaven knows! such lives as yours, though they should pass the limit of a thousand years, will shrink into the merest span; your vices will swallow up any amount of time. The space you have, which reason can prolong, although it naturally hurries away, of necessity escapes from you quickly; for you do not seize it, you neither hold it back, nor impose delay upon the swiftest thing in the world, but you allow it to slip away as if it were something superfluous and that could be replaced.

VII

But among the worst I count also those who have time for nothing but wine and lust; for none have more shameful engrossments. The others, even if they are possessed by the empty dream of glory, nevertheless go astray in a seemly manner; though you should cite to me the men who are avaricious, the men who are wrathful, whether busied with unjust hatreds or with unjust wars, these all sin in more manly fashion. But those who are plunged into the pleasures of the belly and into lust bear a stain that is dishonourable. Search into the hours of all these people, see how much time they give to accounts, how much to laying snares, how much to fearing them, how much to paying court, how much to being courted, how much is taken up in giving or receiving bail, how much by banquets—for even these have now become a matter of business—, and you will see how their interests, whether you call them evil or good, do not allow them time to breathe.

Finally, everybody agrees that no one pursuit can be successfully followed by a man who is busied with many things—eloquence cannot, nor the liberal studies—since the mind, when its interests are divided, takes in nothing very deeply, but rejects everything that is, as it were, crammed into it. There is nothing the busy man is less busied with than living: there is nothing that is harder to learn. Of the other arts there are many teachers everywhere; some of them we have seen that mere boys have mastered so thoroughly that they could even play the master. It takes the whole of life to learn how to live, and—what will perhaps make you wonder more—it takes the whole of life to learn how to die. Many very great men, having laid aside all their encumbrances, having renounced riches, business, and pleasures, have made it their one aim up to the very end of life to know how to live; yet the greater number of them have departed from life confessing that they did not yet know—still less do those others know. Believe me, it takes a great man and one who has risen far above human weaknesses not to allow any of his time to be filched from him, and it follows that the life of such a man is very long because he has devoted wholly to himself whatever time he has had. None of it lay neglected and idle; none of it was under the control of another, for, guarding it most grudgingly, he found nothing that was worthy to be taken in exchange for his time. And so that man had time enough, but those who have been robbed of much of their life by the public, have necessarily had too little of it.

And there is no reason for you to suppose that these people are not sometimes aware of their loss. Indeed, you will hear many of those who are burdened by great prosperity cry out at times in the midst of their throngs of clients, or their pleadings in court, or their other glorious miseries: "I have no chance to live." Of course you have no chance! All those who summon you to themselves, turn you away from your own self. Of how many days has that defendant robbed you? Of how many that candidate? Of how many that old woman wearied with burying her heirs? Of how many that man who is shamming sickness for the purpose of exciting the greed of the legacy-hunters? Of how many that very powerful friend who has you and your like on the list, not of his friends, but of his retinue? Check off, I say, and review the days of your life; you will see that very few, and those the refuse. have been left for you. That man who had prayed for the fasces, when he attains them, desires to lay them aside and says over and over: "When will this year be over!" That man gives games, and, after setting great value on gaining the chance to give them, now says: "When shall I be rid of them?" That advocate is lionized throughout the whole forum, and fills all the place with a great crowd that stretches farther than he can be heard, yet he says: "When will vacation time come?" Everyone hurries his life on and suffers from a yearning for the future and a weariness of the present. But he who bestows all of his time on his own needs, who plans out every day as if it were his last, neither longs for nor fears the morrow. For what new pleasure is there that any hour can now bring? They are all known, all have been enjoyed to the full. Mistress Fortune may deal out the rest as she likes; his life has already found safety. Something may be added to it, but nothing taken from it, and he will take any addition as the man who is satisfied and filled takes the food which he does not desire and yet can hold. And so there is no reason for you to think that any man has lived long because he has grey hairs or wrinkles; he has not lived long—he has existed long. For what if you should think that that man had had a long voyage who had been caught by a fierce storm as soon as he left harbour, and, swept hither and thither by a succession of winds that raged from different quarters, had been driven in a circle around the same course? Not much voyaging did he have, but much tossing about.

VIII

I am often filled with wonder when I see some men demanding the time of others and those from whom they ask it most indulgent. Both of them fix their eyes on the object of the request for time, neither of them on the time itself; just as if what is asked were nothing, what is given, nothing. Men trifle with the most precious thing in the world; but they are blind to it because it is an incorporeal thing, because it does not come beneath the sight of the eyes, and for this reason it is counted a very cheap thing—nay, of almost no value at all. Men set very great store by pensions and doles, and for these they hire out their labour or service or effort. But no one sets a value on time; all use it lavishly as if it cost nothing. But see how these same people clasp the knees of physicians if they fall ill and the danger of death draws nearer, see how ready they are, if threatened with capital punishment, to spend all their possessions in order to live! So great is the inconsistency of their feelings. But if each one could have the number of his future years set before him as is possible in the case of the years that have passed, how alarmed those would be who saw only a few remaining, how sparing of them would they be! And yet it is easy to dispense an amount that is assured, no matter how small it may be; but that must be guarded more carefully which will fail you know not when.

Yet there is no reason for you to suppose that these people do not know how precious a thing time is; for to those whom they love most devotedly they have a habit of saying that they are ready to give them a part of their own years. And they do give it, without realizing it; but the result of their giving is that they themselves suffer loss without adding to the years of their dear ones. But the very thing they do not know is whether they are suffering loss; therefore, the removal of something that is lost without being noticed they find is bearable. Yet no one will bring back the years, no one will bestow you once more on yourself. Life will follow the path it started upon, and will neither reverse nor check its course; it will make no noise, it will not remind you of its swiftness. Silent it will glide on; it will not prolong itself at the command of a king, or at the applause of the populace. Just as it was started on its first day, so it will run; nowhere will it turn aside, nowhere will it delay. And what will be the result? You have been engrossed, life hastens by; meanwhile death will be at hand, for which, willy nilly, you must find leisure.

IX

Can anything be sillier than the point of view of certain people—I mean those who boast of their foresight? They keep themselves very busily engaged in order that they may be able to live better; they spend life in making ready to live! They form their purposes with a view to the distant future; yet postponement is the greatest waste of life; it deprives them of each day as it comes, it snatches from them the present by promising something hereafter. The greatest hindrance to living is expectancy, which depends upon the morrow and wastes to-day. You dispose of that which lies in the hands of Fortune, you let go that which lies in your own. Whither do you look? At what goal do you aim? All things that are still to come lie in uncertainty; live straightway! See how the greatest of bards cries out, and, as if inspired with divine utterance, sings the saving strain:

> The fairest day in hapless mortals' life
> Is ever first to flee.

"Why do you delay," says he, "Why are you idle? Unless you seize the day, it flees." Even though you seize it, it still will flee; therefore you must vie with time's swiftness in the speed of using it, and, as from a torrent that rushes by and will not always flow, you must drink quickly. And, too, the utterance of the bard is most admirably worded to cast censure upon infinite delay, in that he says, not "the fairest age," but "the fairest day." Why, to whatever length your greed inclines, do you stretch before yourself months and years in long array, unconcerned and slow though time flies so fast? The poet speaks to you about the day, and about this very day that is flying. Is there, then, any doubt that for hapless mortals, that is, for men who are engrossed, the fairest day is ever the first to flee? Old age surprises them while their minds are still childish, and they come to it unprepared and unarmed, for they have made no provision for it; they have stumbled upon it suddenly and unexpectedly, they did not notice that it was drawing nearer day by day. Even as conversation or reading or deep meditation on some subject beguiles the traveller, and he finds that he has reached the end of his journey before he was aware that he was approaching it, just so with this unceasing and most swift journey of life, which we make at the same pace whether waking or sleeping; those who are engrossed become aware of it only at the end.

X

Should I choose to divide my subject into heads with their separate proofs, many arguments will occur to me by which I could prove that busy men find life very short. But Fabianus, who was none of your lecture-room philosophers of to-day, but one of the genuine and old-fashioned kind, used to say that we must fight against the passions with main force, not with artifice, and that the battle-line must be turned by a bold attack, not by inflicting pinpricks; that sophistry is not serviceable, for the passions must be, not nipped, but crushed. Yet, in order that the victims of them nay be censured, each for his own particular fault, I say that they must be instructed, not merely wept over.

Life is divided into three periods—that which has been, that which is, that which will be. Of these the present time is short, the future is doubtful, the past is certain. For the last is the one over which Fortune has lost control, is the one which cannot be brought back under any man's power. But men who are engrossed lose this; for they have no time to look back upon the past, and even if they should have, it is not pleasant to recall something they must view with regret. They are, therefore, unwilling to direct their thoughts backward to ill-spent hours, and those whose vices become obvious if they review the past, even the vices which were disguised under some allurement of momentary pleasure, do not have the courage to revert to those hours. No one willingly turns his thought back to the past, unless all his acts have been submitted to the censorship of his conscience, which is never deceived; he who has ambitiously coveted, proudly scorned, recklessly conquered, treacherously betrayed, greedily seized, or lavishly squandered, must needs fear his own memory. And yet this is the part of our time that is sacred and set apart, put beyond the reach of all human mishaps, and removed from the dominion of Fortune, the part which is disquieted by no want, by no fear, by no attacks of disease; this can neither be troubled nor be snatched away—it is an everlasting and unanxious possession. The present offers only one day at a time, and each by minutes; but all the days of past time will appear when you bid them, they will suffer you to behold them and keep them at your will—a thing which those who are engrossed have no time to do. The mind that is untroubled and tranquil has the power to roam into all the parts of its life; but the minds of the engrossed, just as if weighted by a yoke, cannot turn and look behind. And so their life vanishes into an abyss; and as it does no good, no matter how much water you pour into a vessel, if there is no bottom to receive and hold it, so with time—it makes no difference how much is given; if there is nothing for it to settle upon, it passes out through the chinks and holes of the mind. Present time is very brief, so brief, indeed, that to some there seems to be none; for it is always in motion, it ever flows and hurries on; it ceases to be before it has come, and can no more brook delay than the firmament or the stars, whose ever unresting movement never lets them abide in the same track. The engrossed, therefore, are concerned with present time alone, and it is so brief that it cannot be grasped, and even this is filched away from them, distracted as they are among many things.

XI

In a word, do you want to know how they do not "live long"? See how eager they are to live long! Decrepit old men beg in their prayers for the addition of a few more years; they pretend that they are younger than they are; they comfort themselves with a falsehood, and are as pleased to deceive themselves as if they deceived Fate at the same time. But when at last some infirmity has reminded them of their mortality, in what terror do they die, feeling that they are being dragged out of life, and not merely leaving it. They cry out that they have been fools, because they have not really lived, and that they will live henceforth in leisure if only they escape from this illness; then at last they reflect how uselessly they have striven for things which they did not enjoy, and how all their toil has gone for nothing. But for those whose life is passed remote from all business, why should it not be ample? None of it is assigned to another, none of it is scattered in this direction and that, none of it is committed to Fortune, none of it perishes from neglect, none is subtracted by wasteful giving, none of it is unused; the whole of it, so to speak, yields income. And so, however small the amount of it, it is abundantly sufficient, and therefore, whenever his last day shall come, the wise man will not hesitate to go to meet death with steady step.

XII

Perhaps you ask whom I would call "the engrossed "? There is no reason for you to suppose that I mean only those whom the dogs that have at length been let in drive out from the law-court, those whom you see either gloriously crushed in their own crowd of followers, or scornfully in someone else's, those whom social duties call forth from their own homes to bump them against someone else's doors, or whom the praetor's hammer keeps busy in seeking gain that is disreputable and that will one day fester. Even the leisure of some men is engrossed; in their villa or on their couch, in the midst of solitude, although they have withdrawn from all others, they are themselves the source of their own worry; we should say that these are living, not in leisure, but in busy idleness. Would you say that that man is at leisure who arranges with finical care his Corinthian bronzes, that the mania of a few makes costly, and spends the greater part of each day upon rusty bits of copper? Who sits in a public wrestling-place (for, to our shame I we labour with vices that are not even Roman) watching the wrangling of lads? Who sorts out the herds of his pack-mules into pairs of the same age and colour? Who feeds all the newest athletes? Tell me, would you say that those men are at leisure who pass many hours at the barber's while they are being stripped of whatever grew out the night before? while a solemn debate is held over each separate hair? while either disarranged locks are restored to their place or thinning ones drawn from this side and that toward the forehead? How angry they get if the barber has been a bit too careless, just as if he were shearing a real man! How they flare up if any of their mane is lopped off, if any of it lies out of order, if it does not all fall into its proper ringlets! Who of these would not rather have the state disordered than his hair? Who is not more concerned to have his head trim rather than safe? Who would not rather be well barbered than upright? Would you say that these are at leisure who are occupied with the comb and the mirror? And what of those who are engaged in composing, hearing, and learning songs, while they twist the voice, whose best and simplest movement Nature designed to be straightforward, into the meanderings of some indolent tune, who are always snapping their fingers as they beat time to some song they have in their head, who are overheard humming a tune when they have been summoned to serious, often even melancholy, matters? These have not leisure, but idle occupation. And their banquets, Heaven knows! I cannot reckon among their unoccupied hours, since I see how anxiously they set out their silver plate, how diligently they tie up the tunics of their pretty slave-boys, how breathlessly they watch to see in what style the wild boar issues from the hands of the cook, with what speed at a given signal smooth-faced boys hurry to perform their duties, with what skill the birds are carved into portions all according to rule, how carefully unhappy little lads wipe up the spittle of drunkards. By such means they seek the reputation of being fastidious and elegant, and to such an extent do their evils follow them into all the privacies of life that they can neither eat nor drink without ostentation. And I would not count these among the leisured class either—the men who have themselves borne hither and thither in a sedan-chair and a litter, and are punctual at the hours for their rides as if it were unlawful to omit them, who are reminded by someone else when they must bathe, when they must swim, when they must dine; so enfeebled are they by the excessive lassitude of a pampered mind that they cannot find out by themselves whether they are hungry! I hear that one of these pampered people—provided that you can call it pampering to unlearn the habits of human life—when he had been lifted by hands from the bath and placed in his sedan-chair, said questioningly: "Am I now seated?" Do you think that this man, who does not know whether he is sitting, knows whether he is alive, whether he sees, whether he is at leisure? I find it hard to say whether I pity him more if he really did not know, or if he pretended not to know this. They really are subject to forgetfulness of many things, but they also pretend forgetfulness of many. Some vices delight them as being proofs of their prosperity; it seems the part of a man who is very lowly and despicable to know what he is doing. After this imagine that the mimes fabricate many things to make a mock of luxury! In very truth, they pass over more than they invent, and such a multitude of unbelievable vices has come forth in this age, so clever in this one direction, that by now we can charge the mimes with neglect. To think that there is anyone who is so lost in luxury that he takes another's word as to whether he is sitting down! This man, then, is not at leisure, you must apply to him a different term—he is sick, nay, he is dead; that man is at leisure, who has also a perception of his leisure. But this other who is half alive, who, in order that he may know the postures of his own body, needs someone to tell him—how can he be the master of any of his time?

XIII

It would be tedious to mention all the different men who have spent the whole of their life over chess or ball or the practice of baking their bodies in the sun. They are not unoccupied whose pleasures are made a busy occupation. For instance, no one will have any doubt that those are laborious triflers who spend their time on useless literary problems, of whom even among the Romans there is now a great number. It was once a foible confined to the Greeks to inquire into what number of rowers Ulysses had, whether the Iliad or the Odyssey was written first, whether moreover they belong to the same author, and various other matters of this stamp, which, if you keep them to yourself, in no way pleasure your secret soul, and, if you publish them, make you seem more of a bore than a scholar. But now this vain passion for learning useless things has assailed the Romans also. In the last few days I heard someone telling who was the first Roman general to do this or that; Duilius was the first who won a naval battle, Curius Dentatus was the first who had elephants led in his triumph. Still, these matters, even if they add nothing to real glory, are nevertheless concerned with signal services to the state; there will be no profit in such knowledge, nevertheless it wins our attention by reason of the attractiveness of an empty subject. We may excuse also those who inquire into this—who first induced the Romans to go on board ship. It was Claudius, and this was the very reason he was surnamed Caudex, because among the ancients a structure formed by joining together several boards was called a caudex, whence also the Tables of the Law are called codices, and, in the ancient fashion, boats that carry provisions up the Tiber are even to-day called codicariae. Doubtless this too may have some point—the fact that Valerius Corvinus was the first to conquer Messana, and was the first of the family of the Valerii to bear the surname Messana because be had transferred the name of the conquered city to himself, and was later called Messala after the gradual corruption of the name in the popular speech. Perhaps you will permit someone to be interested also in this—the fact that Lucius Sulla was the first to exhibit loosed lions in the Circus, though at other times they were exhibited in chains, and that javelin-throwers were sent by King Bocchus to despatch them? And, doubtless, this too may find some excuse—but does it serve any useful purpose to know that Pompey was the first to exhibit the slaughter of eighteen elephants in the Circus, pitting criminals against them in a mimic battle? He, a leader of the state and one who, according to report, was conspicuous among the leaders of old for the kindness of his heart, thought it a notable kind of spectacle to kill human beings after a new fashion. Do they fight to the death? That is not enough! Are they torn to pieces? That is not enough! Let them be crushed by animals of monstrous bulk! Better would it be that these things pass into oblivion lest hereafter some all-powerful man should learn them and be jealous of an act that was nowise human. O, what blindness does great prosperity cast upon our minds! When he was casting so many troops of wretched human beings to wild beasts born under a different sky, when he was proclaiming war between creatures so ill matched, when he was shedding so much blood before the eyes of the Roman people, who itself was soon to be forced to shed more. he then believed that he was beyond the power of Nature. But later this same man, betrayed by Alexandrine treachery, offered himself to the dagger of the vilest slave, and then at last discovered what an empty boast his surname was.

But to return to the point from which I have digressed, and to show that some people bestow useless pains upon these same matters—the man I mentioned related that Metellus, when he triumphed after his victory over the Carthaginians in Sicily, was the only one of all the Romans who had caused a hundred and twenty captured elephants to be led before his car; that Sulla was the last of the Roman's who extended the pomerium, which in old times it was customary to extend after the acquisition of Italian but never of provincial, territory. Is it more profitable to know this than that Mount Aventine, according to him, is outside the pomerium for one of two reasons, either because that was the place to which the plebeians had seceded, or because the birds had not been favourable when Remus took his auspices on that spot—and, in turn, countless other reports that are either crammed with falsehood or are of the same sort? For though you grant that they tell these things in good faith, though they pledge themselves for the truth of what they write, still whose mistakes will be made fewer by such stories? Whose passions will they restrain? Whom will they make more brave, whom more just, whom more noble-minded? My friend Fabianus used to say that at times he was doubtful whether it was not better not to apply oneself to any studies than to become entangled in these.

XIV

Of all men they alone are at leisure who take time for *philosophy*, they alone really live; for they are not content to be good guardians of their own lifetime only. They annex every age to their own; all the years that have gone before them are an addition to their store. Unless we are most ungrateful, all those men, glorious fashioners of holy thoughts, were born for us; for us they have prepared a way of life. By other men's labours we are led to the sight of things most beautiful that have been wrested from darkness and brought into light; from no age are we shut out, we have access to all ages, and if it is our wish, by greatness of mind, to pass beyond the narrow limits of human weakness, there is a great stretch of time through which we may roam. We may argue with Socrates, we may doubt with Carneades, find peace with Epicurus, overcome human nature with the Stoics, exceed it with the Cynics. Since Nature allows us to enter into fellowship with every age, why should we not turn from this paltry and fleeting span of time and surrender ourselves with all our soul to the past, which is boundless, which is eternal, which we share with our betters?

Those who rush about in the performance of social duties, who give themselves and others no rest, when they have fully indulged their madness, when they have every day crossed everybody's threshold, and have left no open door unvisited, when they have carried around their venal greeting to houses that are very far apart—out of a city so huge and torn by such varied desires, how few will they be able to see? How many will there be who either from sleep or self-indulgence or rudeness will keep them out! How many who, when they have tortured them with long waiting, will rush by, pretending to be in a hurry! How many will avoid passing out through a hall that is crowded with clients, and will make their escape through some concealed door as if it were not more discourteous to deceive than to exclude. How many, still half asleep and sluggish from last night's debauch, scarcely lifting their lips in the midst of a most insolent yawn, manage to bestow on yonder poor wretches, who break their own slumber in order to wait on that of another, the right name only after it has been whispered to them a thousand times!

But we may fairly say that they alone are engaged in the true duties of life who shall wish to have Zeno, Pythagoras, Democritus, and all the other high priests of liberal studies, and Aristotle and Theophrastus, as their most intimate friends every day. No one of these will be "not at home," no one of these will fail to have his visitor leave more happy and more devoted to himself than when he came, no one of these will allow anyone to leave him with empty hands; all mortals can meet with them by night or by day.

XV

No one of these will force you to die, but all will teach you how to die; no one of these will wear out your years, but each will add his own years to yours; conversations with no one of these will bring you peril, the friendship of none will endanger your life, the courting of none will tax your purse. From them you will take whatever you wish; it will be no fault of theirs if you do not draw the utmost that you can desire. What happiness, what a fair old age awaits him who has offered himself as a client to these! He will have friends from whom he may seek counsel on matters great and small, whom he may consult every day about himself, from whom he may hear truth without insult, praise without flattery, and after whose likeness he may fashion himself.

We are wont to say that it was not in our power to choose the parents who fell to our lot, that they have been given to men by chance; yet we may be the sons of whomsoever we will. Households there are of noblest intellects; choose the one into which you wish to be adopted; you will inherit not merely their name, but even their property, which there will be no need to guard in a mean or niggardly spirit; the more persons you share it with, the greater it will become. These will open to you the path to immortality, and will raise you to a height from which no one is cast down. This is the only way of prolonging mortality—nay, of turning it into immortality. Honours, monuments, all that ambition has commanded by decrees or reared in works of stone, quickly sink to ruin; there is nothing that the lapse of time does not tear down and remove. But the works which philosophy has consecrated cannot be harmed; no age will destroy them, no age reduce them; the following and each succeeding age will but increase the reverence for them, since envy works upon what is close at hand, and things that are far off we are more free to admire. The life of the philosopher, therefore, has wide range, and he is not confined by the same bounds that shut others in. He alone is freed from the limitations of the human race; all ages serve him as if a god. Has some time passed by? This he embraces by recollection. Is time present? This he uses. Is it still to come? This he anticipates. He makes his life long by combining all times into one.

XVI

But those who forget the past, neglect the present, and fear for the future have a life that is very brief and troubled; when they have reached the end of it, the poor wretches perceive too late that for such a long while they have been busied in doing nothing. Nor because they sometimes invoke death, have you any reason to think it any proof that they find life long. In their folly they are harassed by shifting emotions which rush them into the very things they dread; they often pray for death because they fear it. And, too, you have no reason to think that this is any proof that they are living a long time—the fact that the day often seems to them long, the fact that they complain that the hours pass slowly until the time set for dinner arrives; for, whenever their engrossments fail them, they are restless because they are left with nothing to do, and they do not know how to dispose of their leisure or to drag out the time. And so they strive for something else to occupy them, and all the intervening time is irksome; exactly as they do when a gladiatorial exhibition is been announced, or when they are waiting for the appointed time of some other show or amusement, they want to skip over the days that lie between. All postponement of something they hope for seems long to them. Yet the time which they enjoy is short and swift, and it is made much shorter by their own fault; for they flee from one pleasure to another and cannot remain fixed in one desire. Their days are not long to them, but hateful; yet, on the other hand, how scanty seem the nights which they spend in the arms of a harlot or in wine! It is this also that accounts for the madness of poets in fostering human frailties by the tales in which they represent that Jupiter under the enticement of the pleasures of a lover doubled the length of the night. For what is it but to inflame our vices to inscribe the name of the gods as their sponsors, and to present the excused indulgence of divinity as an example to our own weakness? Can the nights which they pay for so dearly fail to seem all too short to these men? They lose the day in expectation of the night, and the night in fear of the dawn.

XVII

The very pleasures of such men are uneasy and disquieted by alarms of various sorts, and at the very moment of rejoicing the anxious thought comes over them: How long will these things last?" This feeling has led kings to weep over the power they possessed, and they have not so much delighted in the greatness of their fortune, as they have viewed with terror the end to which it must some time come. When the King of Persia, in all the insolence of his pride, spread his army over the vast plains and could not grasp its number but simply its measure, he shed copious tears because inside of a hundred years not a man of such a mighty army would be alive. But he who wept was to bring upon them their fate, was to give some to their doom on the sea, some on the land, some in battle, some in flight, and within a short time was to destroy all those for whose hundredth year he had such fear. And why is it that even their joys are uneasy from fear? Because they do not rest on stable causes, but are perturbed as groundlessly as they are born. But of what sort do you think those times are which even by their own confession are wretched, since even the joys by which they are exalted and lifted above mankind are by no means pure? All the greatest blessings are a source of anxiety, and at no time is fortune less wisely trusted than when it is best; to maintain prosperity there is need of other prosperity, and in behalf of the prayers that have turned out well we must make still other prayers. For everything that comes to us from chance is unstable, and the higher it rises, the more liable it is to fall. Moreover, what is doomed to perish brings pleasure to no one; very wretched, therefore, and not merely short, must the life of those be who work hard to gain what they must work harder to keep. By great toil they attain what they wish, and with anxiety hold what they have attained; meanwhile they take no account of time that will never more return. New engrossments take the place of the old, hope leads to new hope, ambition to new ambition. They do not seek an end of their wretchedness, but change the cause. Have we been tormented by our own public honours? Those of others take more of our time. Have we ceased to labour as candidates? We begin to canvass for others. Have we got rid of the troubles of a prosecutor? We find those of a judge. Has a man ceased to be a judge? He becomes president of a court. Has he become infirm in managing the property of others at a salary? He is perplexed by caring for his own wealth. Have the barracks set Marius free? The consulship keeps him busy. Does Quintius hasten to get to the end of his dictatorship? He will be called back to it from the plough. Scipio will go against the Carthaginians before he is ripe for so great an undertaking; victorious over Hannibal, victorious over Antiochus, the glory of his own consulship, the surety for his brother's, did he not stand in his own way, he would be set beside Jove; but the discord of civilians will vex their preserver, and, when as a young man he had scorned honours that rivalled those of the gods, at length, when he is old, his ambition will take delight in stubborn exile. Reasons for anxiety will never be lacking, whether born of prosperity or of wretchedness; life pushes on in a succession of engrossments. We shall always pray for leisure, but never enjoy it.

XVIII

And so, my dearest Paulinus, tear yourself away from the crowd, and, too much storm-tossed for the time you have lived, at length withdraw into a peaceful harbour. Think of how many waves you have encountered, how many storms, on the one hand, you have sustained in private life, how many, on the other, you have brought upon yourself in public life; long enough has your virtue been displayed in laborious and unceasing proofs—try how it will behave in leisure. The greater part of your life, certainly the better part of it, has been given to the state; take now some part of your time for yourself as well. And I do not summon you to slothful or idle inaction, or to drown all your native energy in slumbers and the pleasures that are dear to the crowd. That is not to rest; you will find far greater works than all those you have hitherto performed so energetically, to occupy you in the midst of your release and retirement. You, I know, manage the accounts of the whole world as honestly as you would a stranger's, as carefully as you would your own, as conscientiously as you would the state's. You win love in an office in which it is difficult to avoid hatred; but nevertheless believe me, it is better to have knowledge of the ledger of one's own life than of the corn-market. Recall that keen mind of yours, which is most competent to cope with the greatest subjects, from a service that is indeed honourable but hardly adapted to the happy life, and reflect that in all your training in the liberal studies, extending from your earliest years, you were not aiming at this—that it might be safe to entrust many thousand pecks of corn to your charge; you gave hope of something greater and more lofty. There will be no lack of men of tested worth and painstaking industry. But plodding oxen are much more suited to carrying heavy loads than thoroughbred horses, and who ever hampers the fleetness of such high-born creatures with a heavy pack? Reflect, besides, how much worry you have in subjecting yourself to such a great burden; your dealings are with the belly of man. A hungry people neither listens to reason, nor is appeased by justice, nor is bent by any entreaty. Very recently within those few day's after Gaius Caesar died—still grieving most deeply (if the dead have any feeling) because he knew that the Roman people were alive and had enough food left for at any rate seven or eight days while he was building his bridges of boats and playing with the resources of the empire, we were threatened with the worst evil that can befall men even during a siege—the lack of provisions; his imitation of a mad and foreign and misproud king was very nearly at the cost of the city's destruction and famine and the general revolution that follows famine. What then must have been the feeling of those who had charge of the corn-market, and had to face stones, the sword, fire—and a Caligula? By the greatest subterfuge they concealed the great evil that lurked in the vitals of the state—with good reason, you may be sure. For certain maladies must be treated while the patient is kept in ignorance; knowledge of their disease has caused the death of many.

XIX

Do you retire to these quieter, safer, greater things! Think you that it is just the same whether you are concerned in having corn from oversea poured into the granaries, unhurt either by the dishonesty or the neglect of those who transport it, in seeing that it does not become heated and spoiled by collecting moisture and tallies in weight and measure, or whether you enter upon these sacred and lofty studies with the purpose of discovering what substance, what pleasure, what mode of life, what shape God has; what fate awaits your soul; where Nature lays us to rest When we are freed from the body; what the principle is that upholds all the heaviest matter in the centre of this world, suspends the light on high, carries fire to the topmost part, summons the stars to their proper changes—and ether matters, in turn, full of mighty wonders? You really must leave the ground and turn your mind's eye upon these things! Now while the blood is hot, we must enter with brisk step upon the better course. In this kind of life there awaits much that is good to know—the love and practice of the virtues, forgetfulness of the passions, knowledge of living and dying, and a life of deep repose.

The condition of all who are engrossed is wretched, but most wretched is the condition of those who labour at engrossments that are not even their own, who regulate their sleep by that of another, their walk by the pace of another, who are under orders in case of the freest things in the world—loving and hating. If these wish to know how short their life is, let them reflect how small a part of it is their own.

XX

And so when you see a man often wearing the robe of office, when you see one whose name is famous in the Forum, do not envy him; those things are bought at the price of life. They will waste all their years, in order that they may have one year reckoned by their name. Life has left some in the midst of their first struggles, before they could climb up to the height of their ambition; some, when they have crawled up through a thousand indignities to the crowning dignity, have been possessed by the unhappy thought that they have but toiled for an inscription on a tomb; some who have come to extreme old age, while they adjusted it to new hopes as if it were youth, have had it fail from sheer weakness in the midst of their great and shameless endeavours. Shameful is he whose breath leaves him in the midst of a trial when, advanced in years and still courting the applause of an ignorant circle, he is pleading for some litigant who is the veriest stranger; disgraceful is he who, exhausted more quickly by his mode of living than by his labour, collapses in the very midst of his duties; disgraceful is he who dies in the act of receiving payments on account, and draws a smile from his long delayed heir. I cannot pass over an instance which occurs to me. Sextus Turannius was an old man of long tested diligence, who, after his ninetieth year, having received release from the duties of his office by Gaius Caesar's own act, ordered himself to be laid out on his bed and to be mourned by the assembled household as if he were dead. The whole house bemoaned the leisure of its old master, and did not end its sorrow until his accustomed work was restored to him. Is it really such pleasure for a man to die in harness? Yet very many have the same feeling; their desire for their labour lasts longer than their ability; they fight against the weakness of the body, they judge old age to be a hardship on no other score than because it puts them aside. The law does not draft a soldier after his fiftieth year, it does not call a senator after his sixtieth; it is more difficult for men to obtain leisure from themselves than from the law. Meantime, while they rob and are being robbed, while they break up each other's repose, while they make each other wretched, their life is without profit, without pleasure, without any improvement of the mind. No one keeps death in view, no one refrains from far-reaching hopes; some men, indeed, even arrange for things that lie beyond life—huge masses of tombs and dedications of public works and gifts for their funeral-pyres and ostentatious funerals. But, in very truth, the funerals of such men ought to be conducted by the light of torches and wax tapers, as though they had lived but the tiniest span.

Of a Happy Life

Book I

All men, brother Gallio, wish to live happily, but are dull at perceiving exactly what it is that makes life happy: and so far is it from being easy to attain the happiness that the more eagerly a man struggles to reach it the further he departs from it, if he takes the wrong road; for, since this leads in the opposite direction, his very swiftness carries him all the further away. We must therefore first define clearly what it is at which we aim: next we must consider by what path we may most speedily reach it, for on our journey itself, provided it be made in the right direction, we shall learn how much progress we have made each day, and how much nearer we are to the goal towards which our natural desires urge us. But as long as we wander at random, not following any guide except the shouts and discordant clamours of those who invite us to proceed in different directions, our short life will be wasted in useless roamings, even if we labour both day and night to get a good understanding. Let us not therefore decide whither we must tend, and by what path, without the advice of some experienced person who has explored the region which we are about to enter, because this journey is not subject to the same conditions as others; for in them some distinctly understood track and inquiries made of the natives make it impossible for us to go wrong, but here the most beaten and frequented tracks are those which lead us most astray. Nothing, therefore, is more important than that we should not, like sheep, follow the flock that has gone before us, and thus proceed not whither we ought, but whither the rest are going. Now nothing gets us into greater troubles than our subservience to common rumour, and our habit of thinking that those things are best which are most generally received as such, of taking many counterfeits for truly good things, and of living not by reason but by imitation of others. This is the cause of those great heaps into which men rush till they are piled one upon another. In a great crush of people, when the crowd presses upon itself, no one can fall without drawing some one else down upon him, and those who go before cause the destruction of those who follow them. You may observe the same thing in human life: no one can merely go wrong by himself, but he must become both the cause and adviser of another's wrong doing. It is harmful to follow the march of those who go before us, and since every one had rather believe another than form his own opinion, we never pass a deliberate judgment upon life, but some traditional error always entangles us and brings us to ruin, and we perish because we follow other men's examples: we should be cured of this if we were to disengage ourselves from the herd; but as it is, the mob is ready to fight against reason in defence of its own mistake. Consequently the same thing happens as at elections, where, when the fickle breeze of popular favour has veered round, those who have been chosen consuls and praetors are viewed with admiration by the very men who made them so. That we should all approve and disapprove of the same things is the end of every decision which is given according to the voice of the majority.

Book II

When we are considering a happy life, you cannot answer me as though after a division of the House, "This view has most supporters;" because for that very reason it is the worse of the two: matters do not stand so well with mankind that the majority should prefer the better course: the more people do a thing the worse it is likely to be. Let us therefore inquire, not what is most commonly done, but what is best for us to do, and what will establish us in the possession of undying happiness, not what is approved of by the vulgar, the worst possible exponents of truth. By "the vulgar" I mean both those who wear woollen cloaks and those who wear crowns[1]; for I do not regard the colour of the clothes with which they are covered: I do not trust my eyes to tell me what a man is: I have a better and more trustworthy light by which I can distinguish what is true from what is false: let the mind find out what is good for the mind. If a man ever allows his mind some breathing space and has leisure for communing with himself, what truths he will confess to himself, after having been put to the torture by his own self! He will say, "Whatever I have hitherto done I wish were undone: when I think over what I have said, I envy dumb people: whatever I have longed for seems to have been what my enemies would pray might befall me: good heaven, how far more endurable what I have feared seems to be than what I have lusted after. I have been at enmity with many men, and have changed my dislike of them into friendship, if friendship can exist between bad men: yet I have not yet become reconciled to myself," I have striven with all my strength to raise myself above the common herd, and to make myself remarkable for some talent: what have I effected save to make myself a mark for the arrows of my enemies, and show those who hate me where to wound me? Do you see those who praise your eloquence, who covet your wealth, who court your favour, or who vaunt your power? All these either are, or, which comes to the same thing, may be your enemies: the number of those who envy you is as great as that of those who admire you; why do I not rather seek for some good thing which I can use and feel, not one which I can show? these good things which men gaze at in wonder, which they crowd to see, which one points out to another with speechless admiration, are outwardly brilliant, but within are miseries to those who possess them."

---

[1] Lipsius's conjecture, "those who are dressed in white as well as those who are dressed in coloured clothes," alluding to the white robes of candidates for office, seems reasonable.

Book III

Let us seek for some blessing, which does not merely look fine, but is sound and good throughout alike, and most beautiful in the parts which are least seen: let us unearth this. It is not far distant from us; it can be discovered: all that is necessary is to know whither to stretch out your hand: but, as it is, we behave as though we were in the dark, and reach out beyond what is nearest to us, striking as we do so against the very things that we want. However, that I may not draw you into digressions, I will pass over the opinions of other philosophers, because it would take a long time to state and confute them all: take ours. When, however, I say "ours," I do not bind myself to any one of the chiefs of the Stoic school, for I too have a right to form my own opinion. I shall, therefore, follow the authority of some of them, but shall ask some others to discriminate their meaning[2]: perhaps, when after having reported all their opinions, I am asked for my own, I shall impugn none of my predecessors' decisions, and shall say, "I will also add somewhat to them." Meanwhile I follow nature, which is a point upon which every one of the Stoic philosophers are agreed: true wisdom consists in not departing from nature and in moulding our conduct according to her laws and model. A happy life, therefore, is one which is in accordance with its own nature, and cannot be brought about unless in the first place the mind be sound and remain so without interruption, and next, be bold and vigorous, enduring all things with most admirable courage, suited to the times in which it lives, careful of the body and its appurtenances, yet not troublesomely careful. It must also set due value upon all the things which adorn our lives, without over-estimating any one of them, and must be able to enjoy the bounty of Fortune without becoming her slave. You understand without my mentioning it that an unbroken calm and freedom ensue, when we have driven away all those things which either excite us or alarm us: for in the place of sensual pleasures and and [sic] those slight perishable matters which are connected with the basest crimes, we thus gain an immense, unchangeable, equable joy, together with peace, calmness and greatness of mind, and kindliness: for all savageness is a sign of weakness.

---

[2] The Latin words are literally "to divide" their vote, that is, "to separate things of different kinds comprised in a single vote so that they might be voted for separately." — Andrews. Sénèque fait allusion ici à une coutume pratiquée dans les assemblés du Sénat; et il nous explique lui-même ailleurs d'un manière très claire: "Si quelqu'un dans le Sénat," dit-il, "ouvre un avis, dont une partie me convienne, je le somme de la détacher du reste, et j'y adhère." - Ep. 21 - La Grange. [Translated: Here Seneca refers to a custom practiced in the Senate assemblies; and he explains himself to us elsewhere very clearly: "If someone in the Senate," he says, "begins an opinion, of which part suits me, I order him to detach it from the rest, and I subscribe to it." Letter 21 - La Grange.]

Book IV

Our highest good may also be defined otherwise that is to say, the same idea may be expressed in different language. Just as the same army may at one time be extended more widely, at another contracted into a smaller compass, and may either be curved towards the wings by a depression in the line of the centre, or drawn up in a straight line, while, in whatever figure it be arrayed, its strength and loyalty remain unchanged; so also our definition of the highest good may in some cases be expressed diffusely and at great length, while in others it is put into a short and concise form. Thus, it will come to the same thing, if I say "The highest good is a mind which despises the accidents of fortune, and takes pleasure in virtue": or, "It is an unconquerable strength of mind, knowing the world well, gentle in its dealings, showing great courtesy and consideration for those with whom it is brought into contact." Or we may choose to define it by calling that man happy who knows good and bad only in the form of good or bad minds: who worships honour, and is satisfied with his own virtue, who is neither puffed up by good fortune nor cast down by evil fortune, who knows no other good than that which he is able to bestow upon himself, whose real[?] pleasure lies in despising pleasures. If you choose to pursue this digression further, you can put this same idea into many other forms, without impairing or weakening its meaning: for what prevents our saying that a happy life consists in a mind which is free, upright, undaunted, and steadfast, beyond the influence of fear or desire, which thinks nothing good except honour, and nothing bad except blame[?], and regards everything else as a mass of mean details which can neither add anything to nor take anything away from the happiness of life, but which come and go without either increasing or diminishing the highest good? A man of these principles, whether he will or no, must be accompanied by a continual cheerfulness, a high happiness, which comes indeed from on high because he delights in what he has, and desires no greater pleasures than those which his home affords. Is he not right in allowing these to turn the scale against petty, ridiculous and shortlived movements of his wretched body? on the day on which he becomes proof against pleasure he also becomes proof against pain. See, on the other hand, how evil and guilty a slavery the man is forced to serve who is dominated in turn by pleasures and pains, those most untrustworthy and passionate of masters. We must, therefore, escape from them into freedom. This nothing will bestow upon us save contempt of Fortune: but if we attain to this, then there will dawn upon us those invaluable blessings, the repose of a mind that is at rest in a safe haven, its lofty imaginings, its great and steady delight at casting out errors and learning to know the truth, its courtesy, and its cheerfulness, in all of which we shall take delight, not regarding them as good things, but as proceeding from the proper good of man.

Book V

Since I have begun to make my definitions without a too strict adherence to the letter, a man may be called "happy" who, thanks to reason, has ceased either to hope or to fear: but rocks also feel neither fear nor sadness, nor do cattle, yet no one would call those things happy which cannot comprehend what happiness is. With them you may class men whose dull nature and want of self-knowledge reduces them to the level of cattle, mere animals: there is no difference between the one and the other, because the latter have no reason, while the former have only a corrupted form of it, crooked and cunning to their own hurt. For no one can be styled happy who is beyond the influence of truth: and consequently a happy life is unchangeable, and is founded upon a true and trustworthy discernment; for the mind is uncontaminated and freed from all evils only when it is able to escape not merely from wounds but also from scratches, when it will always be able to maintain the position which it has taken up, and defend it even against the angry assaults of Fortune: for with regard to sensual pleasures, though they were to surround one on every side, and use every means of assault, trying to win over the mind by caresses and making trial of every conceivable stratagem to attract either our entire selves or our separate parts, yet what mortal that retains any traces of human origin would wish to be tickled day and night, and, neglecting his mind, to devote himself to bodily enjoyments?

Book VI

"But," says our adversary, "the mind also will have pleasures of its own." Let it have them, then, and let it sit in judgment over luxury and pleasures; let it indulge itself to the full in all those matters which give sensual delights: then let it look back upon what it enjoyed before, and with all those faded sensualities fresh in its memory let it rejoice and look eagerly forward to those other pleasures which it experienced long ago, and intends to experience again, and while the body lies in helpless repletion in the present, let it send its thoughts onward towards the future, and take stock of its hopes: all this will make it appear, in my opinion, yet more wretched, because it is insanity to choose evil instead of good: now no insane person can be happy, and no one can be sane if he regards what is injurious as the highest good and strives to obtain it. The happy man, therefore, is he who can make a right judgment in all things: he is happy who in his present circumstances, whatever they may be, is satisfied and on friendly terms with the conditions of his life. That man is happy, whose reason recommends to him the whole posture of his affairs.

Book VII

Even those very people who declare the highest good to be in the belly, see what a dishonourable position they have assigned to it: and therefore they say that pleasure cannot be parted from virtue, and that no one can either live honourably without living cheerfully, nor yet live cheerfully without living honourably. I do not see how these very different matters can have any connexion with one another. What is there, I pray you, to prevent virtue existing apart from pleasure? of course the reason is that all good things derive their origin from virtue, and therefore even those things which you cherish and seek for come originally from its roots. Yet, if they were entirely inseparable, we should not see some things to be pleasant, but not honourable, and others most honourable indeed, but hard and only to be attained by suffering. Add to this, that pleasure visits the basest lives, but virtue cannot co-exist with an evil life; yet some unhappy people are not without pleasure, nay, it is owing to pleasure itself that they are unhappy; and this could not take place if pleasure had any connexion with virtue, whereas virtue is often without pleasure, and never stands in need of it. Why do you put together two things which are unlike and even incompatible one with another? virtue is a lofty quality, sublime, royal, unconquerable, untiring: pleasure is low, slavish, weakly, perishable; its haunts and homes are the brothel and the tavern. You will meet virtue in the temple, the market-place, the senate house, manning the walls, covered with dust, sunburnt, horny-handed: you will find pleasure skulking out of sight, seeking for shady nooks at the public baths, hot chambers, and places which dread the visits of the aedile, soft, effeminate, reeking of wine and perfumes, pale or perhaps painted and made up with cosmetics. The highest good is immortal: it knows no ending, and does not admit of either satiety or regret: for a right-thinking mind never alters or becomes hateful to itself, nor do the best things ever undergo any change: but pleasure dies at the very moment when it charms us most: it has no great scope, and therefore it soon cloys and wearies us, and fades away as soon as its first impulse is over: indeed, we cannot depend upon anything whose nature is to change. Consequently it is not even possible that there should be any solid substance in that which comes and goes so swiftly, and which perishes by the very exercise of its own functions, for it arrives at a point at which it ceases to be, and even while it is beginning always keeps its end in view.

Book VIII

What answer are we to make to the reflexion that pleasure belongs to good and bad men alike, and that bad men take as much delight in their shame as good men in noble things? This was why the ancients bade us lead the highest, not the most pleasant life, in order that pleasure might not be the guide but the companion of a right-thinking and honourable mind; for it is Nature whom we ought to make our guide: let our reason watch her, and be advised by her. To live happily, then, is the same thing as to live according to Nature: what this may be, I will explain. If we guard the endowments of the body and the advantages of nature with care and fearlessness, as things soon to depart and given to us only for a day; if we do not fall under their dominion, nor allow ourselves to become the slaves of what is no part of our own being; if we assign to all bodily pleasures and external delights the same position which is held by auxiliaries and light-armed troops in a camp; if we make them our servants, not our masters—then and then only are they of value to our minds. A man should be unbiased and not to be conquered by external things: he ought to admire himself alone, to feel confidence in his own spirit, and so to order his life as to be ready alike for good or for bad fortune. Let not his confidence be without knowledge, nor his knowledge without steadfastness: let him always abide by what he has once determined, and let there be no erasure in his doctrines. It will be understood, even though I append it not, that such a man will be tranquil and composed in his demeanour, high-minded and courteous in his actions. Let reason be encouraged by the senses to seek for the truth, and draw its first principles from thence: indeed it has no other base of operations or place from which to start in pursuit of truth: it must fall back upon itself. Even the all-embracing universe and God who is its guide extends himself forth into outward things, and yet altogether returns from all sides back to himself. Let our mind do the same thing: when, following its bodily senses it has by means of them sent itself forth into the things of the outward world, let it remain still their master and its own. By this means we shall obtain a strength and an ability which are united and allied together, and shall derive from it that reason which never halts between two opinions, nor is dull in forming its perceptions, beliefs, or convictions. Such a mind, when it has ranged itself in order, made its various parts agree together, and, if I may so express myself, harmonized them, has attained to the highest good: for it has nothing evil or hazardous remaining, nothing to shake it or make it stumble: it will do everything under the guidance of its own will, and nothing unexpected will befall it, but whatever may be done by it will turn out well, and that, too, readily and easily, without the doer having recourse to any underhand devices: for slow and hesitating action are the signs of discord and want of settled purpose. You may, then, boldly declare that the highest good is singleness of mind: for where agreement and unity are, there must the virtues be: it is the vices that are at war one with another.

Book IX

"But," says our adversary, "you yourself only practise virtue because you hope to obtain some pleasure from it." In the first place, even though virtue may afford us pleasure, still we do not seek after her on that account: for she does not bestow this, but bestows this to boot, nor is this the end for which she labours, but her labour wins this also, although it be directed to another end. As in a tilled-field, when ploughed for corn, some flowers are found amongst it, and yet, though these posies may charm the eye, all this labour was not spent in order to produce them — the man who sowed the field had another object in view, he gained this over and above it — so pleasure is not the reward or the cause of virtue, but comes in addition to it; nor do we choose virtue because she gives us pleasure, but she gives us pleasure also if we choose her. The highest good lies in the act of choosing her, and in the attitude of the noblest minds, which when once it has fulfilled its function and established itself within its own limits has attained to the highest good, and needs nothing more: for there is nothing outside of the whole, any more than there is anything beyond the end. You are mistaken, therefore, when you ask me what it is on account of which I seek after virtue: for you are seeking for something above the highest. Do you ask what I seek from virtue? I answer, Herself: for she has nothing better; she is her own reward. Does this not appear great enough, when I tell you that the highest good is an unyielding strength of mind, wisdom, magnanimity, sound judgment, freedom, harmony, beauty? Do you still ask me for something greater, of which these may be regarded as the attributes? Why do you talk of pleasures to me? I am seeking to find what is good for man, not for his belly; why, cattle and whales have larger ones than he.

Book X

"You purposely misunderstand what I say," says he, "for I too say that no one can live pleasantly unless he lives honorably also, and this cannot be the case with dumb animals who measure the extent of their happiness by that of their food. I loudly and publicly proclaim that what I call a pleasant life cannot exist without the addition of virtue." Yet who does not know that the greatest fools drink the deepest of those pleasures of yours? or that vice is full of enjoyments, and that the mind itself suggests to itself many perverted, vicious forms of pleasure ? — in the first place arrogance, excessive self-esteem, swaggering precedence over other men, a shortsighted, nay, a blind devotion to his own interests, dissolute luxury, excessive delight springing from the most trifling and childish causes, and also talkativeness, pride that takes a pleasure in insulting others, sloth, and the decay of a dull mind which goes to sleep over itself. All these are dissipated by virtue, which plucks a man by the ear, and measures the value of pleasures before she permits them to be used; nor does she set much store by those which she allows to pass current, for she merely allows their use, and her cheerfulness is not due to her use of them, but to her moderation in using them. "Yet when moderation lessens pleasure, it impairs the highest good." You devote yourself to pleasures, I check them; you indulge in pleasure, I use it; you think that it is the highest good, I do not even think it to be good: for the sake of pleasure I do nothing, you do everything.

Book XI

When I say that I do nothing for the sake of pleasure, I allude to that wise man, whom alone you admit to be capable of pleasure: now I do not call a man wise who is overcome by anything, let alone by pleasure: yet, if engrossed by pleasure, how will he resist toil, danger, want, and all the ills which surround and threaten the life of man? How will he bear the sight of death or of pain? How will he endure the tumult of the world, and make head against so many most active foes, if he be conquered by so effeminate an antagonist? He will do whatever pleasure advises him: well, do you not see how many things it will advise him to do ? "It will not," says our adversary, "be able to give him any bad advice, because it is combined with virtue?" Again, do you not see what a poor kind of highest good that must be which requires a guardian to ensure its being good at all? and how is virtue to rule pleasure if she follows it, seeing that to follow is the duty of a subordinate, to rule that of a commander? do you put that which commands in the background? According to your school, virtue has the dignified office of preliminary tester of pleasures. We shall, however, see whether virtue still remains virtue among those who treat her with such contempt, for if she leaves her proper station she can no longer keep her proper name: in the meanwhile, to keep to the point, I will show you many men beset by pleasures, men upon whom Fortune has showered all her gifts, whom you must needs admit to be bad men. Look at Nomentanus and Apicius, who digest all the good things, as they call them, of the sea and land, and review upon their tables the whole animal kingdom. Look at them as they lie on beds of roses gloating over their banquet, delighting their ears with music, their eyes with exhibitions, their palates with flavours: their whole bodies are titillated with soft and soothing applications, and lest even their nostrils should be idle, the very place in which they solemnized[3] the rites of luxury is scented with various perfumes. You will say that these men live in the midst of pleasures. Yet they are ill at ease, because they take pleasure in what is not good.

---

[3] Parentatur seems to mean where an offering is made to luxury — where they sacrifice to luxury. Perfumes were used at funerals. Lipsius suggests that these feasts were like funerals because the guests were carried away from them dead drunk.

Book XII

"They are ill at ease," replies he, " because many things arise which distract their thoughts, and their minds are disquieted by conflicting opinions." I admit that this is true: still these very men, foolish, inconsistent, and certain to feel remorse as they are, do nevertheless receive great pleasure, and we must allow that in so doing they are as far from feeling any trouble as they are from forming a right judgment, and that, as is the case with many people, they are possessed by a merry madness, and laugh while they rave. The pleasures of wise men, on the other hand, are mild, decorous, verging on dullness, kept under restraint and scarcely noticeable, and are neither invited to come nor received with honour when they come of their own accord, nor are they welcomed with any delight by those whom they visit, who mix them up with their lives and fill up empty spaces with them, like an amusing farce in the intervals of serious business. Let them no longer, then, join incongruous matters together, or connect pleasure with virtue, a mistake whereby they court the worst of men. The reckless profligate, always in liquor and belching out the fumes of wine, believes that he lives with virtue, because he knows that he lives with pleasure, for he hears it said that pleasure cannot exist apart from virtue; consequently he dubs his vices with the title of wisdom and parades all that he ought to conceal. So, men are not encouraged by Epicurus to run riot, but the vicious hide their excesses in the lap of philosophy, and flock to the schools in which they hear the praises of pleasure. They do not consider how sober and temperate — for so, by Hercules, I believe it to be — that " pleasure " of Epicurus is, but they rush at his mere name, seeking to obtain some protection and cloak for their vices. They lose, therefore, the one virtue which their evil life possessed, that of being ashamed of doing wrong: for they praise what they used to blush at, and boast of their vices. Thus modesty can never reassert itself, when shameful idleness is dignified with an honourable name. The reason why that praise which your school lavishes upon pleasure is so hurtful, is because the honourable part of its teaching passes unnoticed, but the degrading part is seen by all.

Book XIII

I myself believe, though my Stoic comrades would be unwilling to hear me say so, that the teaching of Epicurus was upright and holy, and even, if you examine it narrowly, stern: for this much talked of pleasure is reduced to a very narrow compass, and he bids pleasure submit to the same law which we bid virtue do — I mean, to obey nature. Luxury, however, is not satisfied with what is enough for nature. What is the consequence? Whoever thinks that happiness consists in lazy sloth, and alternations of gluttony and profligacy, requires a good patron for a bad action, and when he has become an Epicurean, having been led to do so by the attractive name of that school, he follows, not the pleasure which he there hears spoken of, but that which he brought thither with him, and, having learned to think that his vices coincide with the maxims of that philosophy, he indulges in them no longer timidly and in dark corners, but boldly in the face of day. I will not, therefore, like most of our school, say that the sect of Epicurus is the teacher of crime, but what I say is: it is ill spoken of, it has a bad reputation, and yet it does not deserve it. "Who can know this without having been admitted to its inner mysteries?" Its very outside gives opportunity for scandal, and encourages men's baser desires: it is like a brave man dressed in a woman's gown: your chastity is assured, your manhood is safe, your body is submitted to nothing disgraceful, but your hand holds a drum (like a priest of Cybele). Choose, then, some honourable superscription for your school, some writing which shall in itself arouse the mind: that which at present stands over your door has been invented by the vices. He who ranges himself on the side of virtue gives thereby a proof of a noble disposition : he who follows pleasure appears to be weakly, worn out, degrading his manhood, likely to fall into infamous vices unless someone discriminates his pleasures for him, so that he may know which remain within the bounds of natural desire, which are frantic and boundless, and become all the more insatiable the more they are satisfied. But come! let virtue lead the way: then every step will be safe. Too much pleasure is hurtful. but with virtue we need fear no excess of any kind, because moderation is contained in virtue herself. That which is injured by its own extent cannot be a good thing: besides, what better guide can there be than reason for beings endowed with a reasoning nature? so if this combination pleases you, if you are willing to proceed to a happy life thus accompanied, let virtue lead the way, let pleasure follow and hang about the body like a shadow: it is the part of a mind incapable of great things to hand over virtue, the highest of all qualities, as a handmaid to pleasure.

Book XIV

Let virtue lead the way and bear the standard: we shall have pleasure for all that, but we shall be her masters and controllers; she may win some concessions from us, but will not force us to do anything. On the contrary, those who have permitted pleasure to lead the van, have neither one nor the other: for they lose virtue altogether, and yet they do not possess pleasure, but are possessed by it, and are either tortured by its absence or choked by its excess, being wretched if deserted by it, and yet more wretched if overwhelmed by it, like those who are caught in the shoals of the Syrtes and at one time are left on dry ground and at another tossed on the flowing waves. This arises from an exaggerated want of self-control, and a hidden love of evil: for it is dangerous for one who seeks after evil instead of good to attain his object. As we hunt wild beasts with toil and peril, and even when they are caught find them an anxious possession, for they often tear their keepers to pieces, even so are great pleasures: they turn out to be great evils and take their owners prisoner. The more numerous and the greater they are, the more inferior and the slave of more masters does that man become whom the vulgar call a happy man. I may even press this analogy further: as the man who tracks wild animals to their lairs, and who sets great store on — "Seeking with snares the wandering brutes to noose," and "Making their hounds the spacious glade surround," that he may follow their tracks, neglects far more desirable things, and leaves many duties unfulfilled, so he who pursues pleasure postpones everything to it, disregards that first essential, liberty, and sacrifices it to his belly; nor does he buy pleasure for himself, but sells himself to pleasure.

Book XV

"But what," asks our adversary, "is there to hinder virtue and pleasure being combined together, and a highest good being thus formed, so that honour and pleasure may be the same thing?" Because nothing except what is honourable can form a part of honour, and the highest good would lose its purity if it were to see within itself anything unlike its own better part. Even the joy which arises from virtue, although it be a good thing, yet is not a part of absolute good, any more than cheerfulness or peace of mind, which are indeed good things, but which merely follow the highest good, and do not contribute to its perfection, although they are generated by the noblest causes. Whoever on the other hand forms an alliance, and that, too, a one-sided one, between virtue and pleasure, clogs whatever strength the one may possess by the weakness of the other, and sends liberty under the yoke, for liberty can only remain unconquered as long as she knows nothing more valuable than herself: for he begins to need the help of Fortune, which is the most utter slavery: his life becomes anxious, full of suspicion, timorous, fearful of accidents, waiting in agony for critical moments of time. You do not afford virtue a solid immoveable base if you bid it stand on what is unsteady: and what can be so unsteady as dependence on mere chance, and the vicissitudes of the body and of those things which act on the body? How can such a man obey God and receive everything which comes to pass in a cheerful spirit, never complaining of fate, and putting a good construction upon everything that befalls him, if he be agitated by the petty pin-pricks of pleasures and pains? A man cannot be a good protector of his country, a good avenger of her wrongs, or a good defender of his friends, if he be inclined to pleasures. Let the highest good, then, rise to that height from whence no force can dislodge it, whither neither pain can ascend, nor hope, nor fear, nor anything else that can impair the authority of the " highest good." Thither virtue alone can make her way: by her aid that hill must be climbed: she will bravely stand her ground and endure whatever may befall her not only resignedly, but even willingly: she will know that all hard times come in obedience to natural laws, and like a good soldier she will bear wounds, count scars, and when transfixed and dying will yet adore the general for whom she falls: she will bear in mind the old maxim " Follow God." On the other hand, he who grumbles and complains and bemoans himself is nevertheless forcibly obliged to obey orders, and is dragged away, however much against his will, to carry them out: yet what madness is it to be dragged rather than to follow? as great, by Hercules, as it is folly and ignorance of one's true position to grieve because one has not got something or because something has caused us rough treatment, or to be surprised or indignant at those ills which befall good men as well as bad ones, I mean diseases, deaths, illnesses, and the other cross accidents of human life. Let us bear with magnanimity whatever the system of the universe makes it needful for us to bear: we are all bound by this oath: "To bear the ills of mortal life, and to submit with a good grace to what we cannot avoid." We have been born into a monarchy: our liberty is to obey God.

Book XVI

True happiness, therefore, consists in virtue: and what will this virtue bid you do? Not to think anything bad or good which is connected neither with virtue nor with wickedness: and in the next place, both to endure un moved the assaults of evil, and, as far as is right, to form a god out of what is good. What reward does she promise you for this campaign? an enormous one, and one that raises you to the level of the gods: you shall be subject to no restraint and to no want; you shall be free, safe, unhurt; you shall fail in nothing that you attempt; you shall be debarred from nothing; everything shall turn out according to your wish; no misfortune shall befall you; nothing shall happen to you except what you expect and hope for. "What! does virtue alone suffice to make you happy?" why, of course, consummate and god-like virtue such as this not only suffices, but more than suffices: for when a man is placed beyond the reach of any desire, what can he possibly lack? if all that he needs is concentred in himself, how can he require anything from without? He, however, who is only on the road to virtue, although he may have made great progress along it, nevertheless needs some favour from fortune while he is still struggling among mere human interests, while he is untying that knot, and all the bonds which bind him to mortality. What, then, is the difference between them? it is that some are tied more or less tightly by these bonds, and some have even tied themselves with them as well; whereas he who has made progress towards the upper regions and raised himself upwards drags a looser chain, and though not yet free, is yet as good as free.

Book XVII

If, therefore, any one of those dogs who yelp at philosophy were to say, as they are wont to do, "Why, then, do you talk so much more bravely than you live? why do you check your words in the presence of your superiors, and consider money to be a necessary implement:' why are you disturbed when you sustain losses, and weep on hearing of the death of your wife or your friend? Why do you pay regard to common rumour, and feel annoyed by calumnious gossip? why is your estate more elaborately kept than its natural use requires? why do you not dine according to your own maxims? why is your furniture smarter than it need be? why do you drink wine that is older than yourself? why are your grounds laid out? Why do you plant trees which afford nothing except shade? why does your wife wear in her ears the price of a rich man's house? why are your children at school dressed in costly clothes? why is it a science to wait upon you at table? why is your silver plate not set down anyhow or at random, but skillfully disposed in regular order, with a superintendent to preside over the carving of the viands?" Add to this, if you like, the questions "Why do you own property beyond the seas? why do you own more than you know of? it is a shame to you not to know your slaves by sight: for you must be very neglectful of them if you only own a few, or very extravagant if you have too many for your memory to retain." I will add some reproaches afterwards, and will bring more accusations against myself than you think of: for the present I will make you the following answer. "I am not a wise man, and I will not be one in order to feed your spite: so do not require me to be on a level with the best of men, but merely to be better than the worst: I am satisfied, if every day I take away something from my vices and correct my faults. I have not arrived at perfect soundness of mind, indeed, I never shall arrive at it: I compound palliatives rather than remedies for my gout, and am satisfied if it comes at rarer interval - and does not shoot so painfully. Compared with your feet, which are lame, I am a racer." I make this speech, not on my own behalf, for I am steeped in vices of every kind, but on behalf of one who has made some progress in virtue.

Book XVIII

"You talk one way," objects our adversary, "and live another." You most spiteful of creatures, you who always show the bitterest hatred to the best of men, this reproach was flung at Plato, at Epicurus, at Zeno: for all these declared how they ought to live, not how they did live. I speak of virtue, not of myself, and when I blame vices, I blame my own first of all: when I have the power, I shall live as I ought to do: spite, however deeply steeped in venom, shall not keep me back from what is best: that poison itself with which you bespatter others, with which you choke yourselves, shall not hinder me from continuing to praise that life which I do not, indeed, lead, but which I know I ought to lead, from loving virtue and from following after her, albeit a long way behind her and with halting gait. Am I to expect that evil speaking will respect anything, seeing that it respected neither Rutilius nor Cato? Will anyone care about being thought too rich by men for whom Diogenes the Cynic was not poor enough? That most energetic philosopher fought against all the desires of the body, and was poorer even than the other Cynics, in that besides having given up possessing anything he had also given up asking for anything: yet they reproached him for not being sufficiently in want: as though forsooth it were poverty, not virtue, of which he professed knowledge.

Book XIX

They say that Diodorus, the Epicurean philosopher, who within these last few days put an end to his life with his own hand, did not act according to the precepts of Epicurus, in cutting his throat: some choose to regard this act as the result of madness, others of recklessness; he, meanwhile, happy and filled with the consciousness of his own goodness, has borne testimony to himself by his manner of departing from life, has commended the repose of a life spent at anchor in a safe harbour, and has said what you do not like to hear, because you too ought to do it.

"I've lived, I've run the race which Fortune set me."

You argue about the life and death of another, and yelp at the name of men whom some peculiarly noble quality has rendered great, just as tiny curs do at the approach of strangers: for it is to your interest that no one should appear to be good, as if virtue in another were a reproach to all your crimes. You enviously compare the glories of others with your own dirty actions, and do not understand how greatly to your disadvantage it is to venture to do so: for if they who follow after virtue be greedy, lustful, and fond of power, what must you be, who hate the very name of virtue? You say that no one acts up to his professions, or lives according to the standard which he sets up in his discourses: what wonder, seeing that the words which they speak are brave, gigantic, and able to weather all the storms which wreck mankind, whereas they themselves are struggling to tear themselves away from crosses into which each one of you is driving his own nail. Yet men who are crucified hang from one single pole, but these who punish themselves are divided between as many crosses as they have lusts, but yet are given to evil speaking, and are so magnificent in their contempt of the vices of others that I should suppose that they had none of their own, were it not that some criminals when on the gibbet spit upon the spectators.

Book XX

"Philosophers do not carry into effect all that they teach." No; but they effect much good by their teaching, by the noble thoughts which they conceive in their minds: would, indeed, that they could act up to their talk: what could be happier than they would be? but in the meanwhile you have no right to despise good sayings and hearts full of good thoughts. Men deserve praise for engaging in profitable studies, even though they stop short of producing any results. Why need we wonder if those who begin to climb a steep path do not succeed in ascending it very high? yet, if you be a man, look with respect on those who attempt great things, even though they fall. It is the act of a generous spirit to proportion its efforts not to its own strength but to that of human nature, to entertain lofty aims, and to conceive plans which are too vast to be carried into execution even by those who are endowed with gigantic intellects, who appoint for themselves the following rules: "I will look upon death or upon a comedy with the same expression of countenance : I will submit to labours, however great they may be, supporting the strength of my body by that of my mind: I will despise riches when I have them as much as when I have them not; if they be elsewhere I will not be more gloomy, if they sparkle around me I will not be more lively than I should otherwise be: whether Fortune comes or goes I will take no notice of her: I will view all lands as though they belong to me, and my own as though they belonged to all mankind: I will so live as to remember that I was born for others, and will thank Nature on this account: for in what fashion could she have done better for me? she has given me alone to all, and all to me alone. Whatever I may possess, I will neither hoard it greedily nor squander it recklessly. I will think that I have no possessions so real as those which I have given away to deserving people: I will not reckon benefits by their magnitude or number, or by anything except the value set upon them by the receiver: I never will consider a gift to be a large one if it be bestowed upon a worthy object. I will do nothing because of public opinion, but everything because of conscience: whenever I do anything alone by myself I will believe that the eyes of the Roman people are upon me while I do it. In eating and drinking my object shall be to quench the desires of Nature, not to fill and empty my belly. I will be agreeable with my friends, gentle and mild to my foes: I will grant pardon before I am asked for it, and will meet the wishes of honourable men half way: I will bear in mind that the world is my native city, that its governors are the gods, and that they stand above and around me, criticizing whatever I do or say. Whenever either Nature demands my breath again, or reason bids me dismiss it, I will quit this life, calling all to witness that I have loved a good conscience, and good pursuits; that no one's freedom, my own least of all, has been impaired through me." He who sets up these as the rules of his life will soar aloft and strive to make his way to the gods: of a truth, even though he fails, yet he

"Fails in a high emprise."[4]

But you, who hate both virtue and those who practise it, do nothing at which we need be surprised, for sickly lights cannot bear the sun, nocturnal creatures avoid the brightness of day, and at its first dawning become bewildered and all betake themselves to their dens together: creatures that fear the light hide themselves in crevices. So croak away, and exercise your miserable tongues in reproaching good men : open wide your jaws, bite hard: you will break many teeth before you make any impression.

---

[4] The quotation is from the epitaph on Phaeton.—See Ovid, Met. II. 327.

Book XXI

"But how is it that this man studies philosophy and nevertheless lives the life of a rich man? Why does he say that wealth ought to be despised and yet possess it? that life should be despised, and yet live? that health should be despised, and yet guard it with the utmost care, and wish it to be as good as possible? Does he consider banishment to be an empty name, and say, "What evil is there in changing one country for another?" and yet, if permitted, does he not grow old in his native land? does he declare that there is no difference between a longer and a shorter time, and yet, if he be not prevented, lengthen out his life and flourish in a green old age?" His answer is, that these things ought to be despised, not that he should not possess them, but that he should not possess them with fear and trembling: he does not drive them away from him, but when they leave him he follows after them unconcernedly. Where, indeed, can fortune invest riches more securely than in a place from whence they can always be recovered without any squabble with their trustee? Marcus Cato, when he was praising Curius and Coruncanius and that century in which the possession of a few small silver coins were an offence which was punished by the Censor, himself owned four million sesterces; a less fortune, no doubt, than that of Crassus, but larger than of Cato the Censor. If the amounts be compared, he had outstripped his great-grandfather further than he himself was outdone by Crassus, and if still greater riches had fallen to his lot, he would not have spurned them: for the wise man does not think himself unworthy of any chance presents: he does not love riches, but he prefers to have them; he does not receive them into his spirit, but only into his house: nor does he cast away from him what he already possesses, but keeps them, and is willing that his virtue should receive a larger subject-matter for its exercise.

Book XXII

Who can doubt, however, that the wise man, if he is rich, has a wider field for the development of his powers than if he is poor, seeing that in the latter case the only virtue which he can display is that of neither being perverted nor crushed by his poverty, whereas if he has riches, he will have a wide field for the exhibition of temperance, generosity, laboriousness, methodical arrangement, and grandeur. The wise man will not despise himself, however short of stature he may be, but nevertheless he will wish to be tall: even though he be feeble and one-eyed he may be in good health, yet he would prefer to have bodily strength, and that too, while he knows all the while that he has something which is even more powerful: he will endure illness, and will hope for good health: for some things, though they may be trifles compared with the sum total, and though they may be taken away without destroying the chief good, yet add somewhat to that constant cheerfulness which arises from virtue. Riches encourage and brighten up such a man just as a sailor is delighted at a favourable wind that bears him on his way, or as people feel pleasure at a fine day or at a sunny spot in the cold weather. What wise man, I mean of our school, whose only good is virtue, can deny that even these matters which we call neither good nor bad have in themselves a certain value, and that some of them are preferable to others? to some of them we show a certain amount of respect, and to some a great deal. Do not, then, make any mistake: riches belong to the class of desirable things. "Why then," say you, "do you laugh at me, since you place them in the same position that I do?" Do you wish to know how different the position is in which we place them? If my riches leave me, they will carry away with them nothing except themselves: you will be bewildered and will seem to be left without yourself if they should pass away from you: with me riches occupy a certain place, but with you they occupy the highest place of all. In fine, my riches belong to me, you belong to your riches.

Book XXIII

Cease, then, forbidding philosophers to possess money: no one has condemned wisdom to poverty. The philosopher may own ample wealth, but will not own wealth that which has been torn from another, or which is stained with another's blood: his must be obtained without wronging any man, and without its being won by base means; it must be alike honourably come by and honourably spent, and must be such as spite alone could shake its head at. Raise it to whatever figure you please, it will still be an honourable possession, if, while it includes much which every man would like to call his own, there be nothing which any one can say is his own. Such a man will not forfeit his right to the favour of Fortune, and will neither boast of his inheritance nor blush for it if it was honourably acquired: yet he will have something to boast of, if he throw his house open, let all his countrymen come among his property, and say, "If any one recognizes here anything belonging to him, let him take it." What a great man, how excellently rich will he be, if after this speech he possesses as much as he had before! I say, then, that if he can safely and confidently submit his accounts to the scrutiny of the people, and no one can find in them any item upon which he can lay hands, such a man may boldly and unconcealedly enjoy his riches. The wise man will not allow a single ill-won penny to cross his threshold: yet he will not refuse or close his door against great riches, if they are the gift of fortune and the product of virtue: what reason has he for grudging them good quarters: let them come and be his guests: he will neither brag of them nor hide them away: the one is the part of a silly, the other of a cowardly and paltry spirit, which, as it were, muffles up a good thing in its lap. Neither will he, as I said before, turn them out of his house: for what will he say? will he say, " You are useless," or " I do not know how to use riches?" As he is capable of performing a journey upon his own feet, but yet would prefer to mount a carriage, just so he will be capable of being poor, yet will wish to be rich; he will own wealth, but will view it as an uncertain possession which will someday fly away from him. He will not allow it to be a burden either to himself or to any one else: he will give it — why do you prick up your ears? why do you open your pockets?—he will give it either to good men or to those whom it may make into good men. He will give it after having taken the utmost pains to choose those who are fittest to receive it, as becomes one who bears in mind that he ought to give an account of what he spends as well as of what he receives. He will give for good and commendable reasons, for a gift ill bestowed counts as a shameful loss: he will have an easily opened pocket, but not one with a hole in it, so that much may be taken out of it, yet nothing may fall out of it.

Book XXIV

He who believes giving to be an easy matter, is mistaken: it offers very great difficulties, if we bestow our bounty rationally, and do not scatter it impulsively and at random. I do this man a service, I requite a good turn done me by that one: I help this other, because I pity him: this man, again, I teach to be no fit object for poverty to hold down or degrade. I shall not give some men anything, although they are in want, because, even if I do give to them they will still be in want: I shall proffer my bounty to some, and shall forcibly thrust it upon others: I cannot be neglecting my own interests while I am doing this: at no time do I make more people in my debt than when I am giving things away. "What ?" say you, " do you give that you may receive again?" At any rate I do not give that I may throw my bounty away: what I give should be so placed that although I cannot ask for its return, yet it may be given back to me. A benefit should be invested in the same manner as a treasure buried deep in the earth, which you would not dig up unless actually obliged. Why, what opportunities of conferring benefits the mere house of a rich man affords? for who considers generous behaviour due only to those who wear the toga? Nature bids me do good to mankind—what difference does it make whether they be slaves or freemen, free-born or emancipated, whether their freedom be legally acquired or bestowed by arrangement among friends? Wherever there is a human being, there is an opportunity for a benefit: consequently, money may be distributed even within one's own threshold, and a field may be found there for the practice of freehandedness, which is not so called because it is our duty towards free men, but because it takes its rise in a free-born mind. In the case of the wise man, this never falls upon base and unworthy recipients, and never becomes so exhausted as not, whenever it finds a worthy object, to flow as if its store was undiminished. You have, therefore, no grounds for misunderstanding the honourable, brave, and spirited language which you hear from those who are studying wisdom : and first of all observe this, that a student of wisdom is not the same thing as a man who has made himself perfect in wisdom. The former will say to you, "In my talk I express the most admirable sentiments, yet I am still weltering amid countless ills. You must not force me to act up to my rules: at the present time I am forming myself, moulding my character, and striving to rise myself to the height of a great example. If I should ever succeed in carrying out all that I have set myself to accomplish, you may then demand that my words and deeds should correspond." But he who has reached the summit of human perfection will deal otherwise with you, and will say, " In the first place, you have no business to allow yourself to sit in judgment upon your betters:" I have already obtained one proof of my righteousness in having become an object of dislike to bad men: however, to make you a rational answer, which I grudge to no man, listen to what I declare, and at what price I value all things. Riches, I say, are not a good thing; for if they were, they would make men good: now since that which is found even among bad men cannot be termed good, I do not allow them to be called so: nevertheless I admit that they are desirable and useful and contribute great comforts to our lives.

Book XXV

Learn, then, since we both agree that they are desirable, what my reason is amongst counting them among good things, and in what respects I should behave differently to you if I possessed them. Place me as master in the house of a very rich man: place me where gold and silver plate is used for the commonest purposes; I shall not think more of myself because of things which even though they are in my house are yet no part of me. Take me away to the wooden bridge[5] and put me down there among the beggars: I shall not despise myself because I am sitting among those who hold out their hands for alms: for what can the lack of a piece of bread matter to one who does not lack the power of dying? Well, then? I prefer the magnificent house to the beggar's bridge. Place me among magnificent furniture and all the appliances of luxury: I shall not think myself any happier because my, cloak is soft, because my guests rest upon purple. Change the scene: I shall be no more miserable if my weary head rests upon a bundle of hay, if I lie upon a cushion from the circus, with all the stuffing on the point of coming out through its patches of threadbare cloth. Well, then? I prefer, as far as my feelings go, to show myself in public dressed in woollen and in robes of office, rather than with naked or half-covered shoulders: I should like every day's business to turn out just as I wish it to do, and new congratulations to be constantly following upon the former ones: yet I will not pride myself upon this: change all this good fortune for its opposite, let my spirit be distracted by losses, grief, various kinds of attacks: let no hour pass without some dispute: I shall not on this account, though beset by the greatest miseries, call myself the most miserable of beings, nor shall I curse any particular day, for I have taken care to have no unlucky days. What, then, is the upshot of all this? it is that I prefer to have to regulate joys than to stifle sorrows. The great Socrates would say the same thing to you. "Make me," he would say, "the conqueror of all nations: let the voluptuous car of Bacchus bear me in triumph to Thebes from the rising of the sun: let the kings of the Persians receive laws from me: yet I shall feel myself to be a man at the very moment when all around salute me as a God. Straightway connect this lofty height with a headlong fall into misfortune: let me be placed upon a foreign chariot that I may grace the triumph of a proud and savage conqueror: I will follow another's car with no more humility than I showed when I stood in my own. What then? In spite of all this, I had rather be a conqueror than a captive. I despise the whole dominion of Fortune, but still, if I were given my choice, I would choose its better parts. I shall make whatever befalls me become a good

---

[5] The " Pons Sublicius," or "pile bridge," was built over the Tiber by Aliens Martins, one of the early kings of Rome, and was always kept in repair out of a superstitious feeling.

thing, but I prefer that what befalls me should be comfortable and pleasant and unlikely to cause me annoyance: for you need not suppose that any virtue exists without labour, but some virtues need spurs, while others need the curb. As we have to check our body on a downward path, and to urge it to climb a steep one; so also the path of some virtues leads downhill, that of others uphill. Can we doubt that patience, courage, constancy, and all the other virtues which have to meet strong opposition, and to trample Fortune under their feet, are climbing, struggling, winning their way up a steep ascent? Why! is it not equally evident that generosity, moderation, and gentleness glide easily downhill? With the latter we must hold in our spirit, lest it run away with us: with the former we must urge and spur it on. We ought, therefore to apply these energetic, combative virtues to poverty, and to riches those other more thrifty ones which trip lightly along, and merely support their own weight. This being the distinction between them, I would rather have to deal with those which I could practise in comparative quiet, than those of which one can only make trial through blood and sweat. "Wherefore," says the sage, " I do not talk one way and live another: but you do not rightly understand what I say: the sound of my words alone reaches your ears, you do not try to find out their meaning."

Book XXVI

"What difference, then, is there between me, who am a fool, and you, who are a wise man?" "All the difference in the world: for riches are slaves in the house of a wise man, but masters in that of a fool. You accustom yourself to them and cling to them as if somebody had promised that they should be yours forever, but a wise man never thinks so much about poverty as when he is surrounded by riches. No general ever trusts so implicitly is the maintenance of peace as not to make himself ready for a war, which, though it may not actually be waged, has nevertheless been declared; you are rendered over-proud by a fine house, as though it could never be burned or fall down, and your heads are turned by riches as though they were beyond the reach of all dangers and were so great that Fortune has not sufficient strength to swallow them up. You sit idly playing with your wealth and do not foresee the perils in store for it, as savages generally do when besieged, for, not understanding the use of siege artillery, they look on idly at the labours of the besiegers and do not understand the object of the machines which they are putting together at a distance: and this is exactly what happens to you: you go to sleep over your property, and never reflect how many misfortunes loom menacingly around you on all sides, and soon will plunder you of costly spoils , but if one takes away riches from the wise man, one leaves him still in possession of all that is his: for he lives happy in the present, and without fear for the future. The great Socrates, or anyone else who had the same superiority to and power to withstand the things of this life, would say,' I have no more fixed principle than that of not altering the course of my life to suit your prejudices: you may pour your accustomed talk upon me from all sides: I shall not think that you are abusing me, but that you are merely wailing like poor little babies.'" This is what the man will say who possesses wisdom, whose mind, being free from, vices, bids him reproach others, not because he hates them, but in order to improve them: and to this he will add, "Your opinion of me affects me with pain, not for my own sake but for yours, because to hate perfection and to assail virtue is in itself a resignation of all hope of doing well. You do me no harm; neither do men harm the gods when they overthrow their altars: but it is clear that your intention is an evil one and that you will wish to do -harm even where you are not able. I bear with your prating in the same spirit in which Jupiter, best and greatest, bears with the idle tales of the poets, one of whom represents him with wings, another with horns, another as an adulterer staying out all night, another is dealing harshly with the gods, another as unjust to men, another as the seducer of noble youths whom he carries off by force, and those, too, his own relatives, another as a parricide and the conqueror of another's kingdom, and that his father's. The only result of such tales is that men feel less shame at

Of a Happy Life

committing sin if they believe the gods to be guilty of such actions. But although this conduct of yours does not hurt me, yet, for your own sakes, I advise you, respect virtue: believe those who having long followed her cry aloud that what they follow is a thing of might, and daily appears mightier. Reverence her as you would the gods, and reverence her followers as you would the priests of the gods: and whenever any mention of sacred writings is made, favete liyiguis, favour us with silence: this word is not derived, as most people imagine, from favour, but commands silence, that divine service may be performed without being interrupted by any words of evil omen. It is much more necessary that you should be ordered to do this, in order that whenever utterance is made by that oracle, you may listen to it with attention and in silence. Whenever anyone beats a sistrum[6], pretending to do so by divine command, any proficient in grazing his own skin covers his arms and shoulders with blood from light cuts, any one crawls on his knees howling along the street, or any old man clad in linen comes forth in daylight with a lamp and laurel branch and cries out that one of the gods is angry, you crowd round him and listen to his words, and each increases the other's wonderment by declaring him to be divinely inspired.

---

[6] Sistrum. A metallic rattle used by the Egyptians in celebrating the rites of Isis, Sec.—Andrews.

Book XXVII

Behold! from that prison of his, which by entering he cleansed from shame and rendered more honourable than any senate house, Socrates addresses you, saying: "What is this madness of yours? what is this disposition, at war alike with gods and men, which leads you to calumniate virtue and to outrage holiness with malicious accusations? Praise good men, if you are able: if not, pass them by in silence: if indeed you take pleasure in this offensive abusiveness, fall foul of one another: for when you rave against Heaven, I do not say that you commit sacrilege, but you waste your time. I once afforded Aristophanes with the subject of a jest: since then all the crew of comic poets have made me a mark for their envenomed wit: my virtue has been made to shine more brightly by the very blows which have been aimed at it, for it is to its advantage to be brought before the public and exposed to temptation, nor do any people understand its greatness more than those who by their assaults have made trial of its strength. The hardness of flint is known to none so well as to those who strike it. I offer myself to all attacks, like some lonely rock in a shallow sea, which the waves never cease to beat upon from whatever quarter they may come, but which they cannot thereby move from its place nor yet wear away, for however many years they may unceasingly dash against it. Bound upon me, rush upon me, I will overcome you by enduring your onset: whatever strikes against that which is firm and unconquerable merely injures itself by its own violence. Wherefore, seek some soft and yielding object to pierce with your darts. But have you leisure to peer into other men's evil deeds and to sit in judgment upon anybody? to ask how it is that this philosopher has so roomy a house, or that one so good a dinner? Do you look at other people's pimples while yon yourselves are covered with countless ulcers? This is as though one who was eaten up by the mange were to point with scorn at the moles and warts on the bodies of the handsomest men. Reproach Plato with having sought for money, reproach Aristotle with having obtained it, Democritus with having disregarded it, Epicurus with having spent it: cast Phaedrus and Alcibiades in my own teeth, you who reach the height of enjoyment whenever you get an opportunity of imitating our vices! Why do you not rather cast your eyes around yourselves at the ills which tear you to pieces on every side, some attacking you from without, some burning in your own bosoms? However little you know your own place, mankind has not yet come to such a pass that you can have leisure to wag your tongues to the reproach of your betters.

Book XXVIII

This you do not understand, and you bear a countenance which does not befit your condition, like many men who sit in the circus or the theatre without having learned that their home is already in mourning: but I, looking forward from a lofty standpoint, can see what storms are either threatening you, and will burst in torrents upon you somewhat later, or are close upon you and on the point of sweeping away all that you possess. Why, though you are hardly aware of it, is there not a whirling hurricane at this moment spinning round and confusing your minds, making them seek and avoid the very same things, now raising them aloft and now dashing them below?"

Of Providence

I

YOU have asked me, Lucilius, why, if the world be ruled by providence, so many evils befall good men? The answer to this would be more conveniently given in the course of this work, after we have proved that providence governs the universe, and that God is amongst us: but, since you wish me to deal with one point apart from the whole, and to answer one replication before the main action has been decided, I will do what is not difficult, and plead the cause of the gods. At the present time it is superfluous to point out that it is not without some guardian that so great a work maintains its position, that the assemblage and movements of the stars do not depend upon accidental impulses, or that objects whose motion is regulated by chance often fall into confusion and soon stumble, whereas this swift and safe movement goes on, governed by eternal law, bearing with it so many things both on sea and land, so many most brilliant lights shining in order in the skies; that this regularity does not belong to matter moving at random, and that particles brought together by chance could not arrange themselves with such art as to make the heaviest weight, that of the earth, remain unmoved, and behold the flight of the heavens as they hasten round it, to make the seas pour into the valleys and so temper the climate of the land, without any sensible increase from the rivers which flow into them, or to cause huge growths to proceed from minute seeds. Even those phenomena which appear to be confused and irregular, I mean showers of rain and clouds, the rush of lightning from the heavens, fire that pours from the riven peaks of mountains, quakings of the trembling earth, and everything else which is produced on earth by the unquiet element in the universe, do not come to pass without reason, though they do so suddenly: but they also have their causes, as also have those things which excite our wonder by the strangeness of their position, such as warm springs amidst the waves of the sea, and new islands that spring up in the wide ocean. Moreover, anyone who has watched how the shore is laid bare by the retreat of the sea into itself, and how within a short time it is again covered, will believe that it is in obedience to some hidden law of change that the waves are at one time contracted and driven inwards, at another burst forth and regain their bed with a strong current, since all the while they wax in regular proportion, and come up at their appointed day and hour greater or less, according as the moon, at whose pleasure the ocean flows, draws them. Let these matters be set aside for discussion at their own proper season, but I, since you do not doubt the existence of providence but complain of it, will on that account more readily reconcile you to gods who are most excellent to excellent men: for indeed the nature of things does not ever permit good to be injured, by good. Between good men and the gods there is a friendship which is brought about by virtue—friendship do I say? nay, rather relationship and likeness, since the good man differs from a god in time alone, being his pupil and rival and true offspring, whom his glorious parent trains more severely than other men, insisting sternly on virtuous conduct, just as strict fathers do. When therefore you see men who are good and acceptable to the gods toiling, sweating, painfully struggling upwards, while bad men run riot and are steeped in pleasures, reflect that modesty pleases us in our sons, and forwardness in our house-born slave-boys; that the former are held in check by a somewhat stern rule, whereas the boldness of the latter is encouraged. Be thou sure that God acts in like manner: He does not pet the good man: He tries him, hardens him, and fits him for Himself.

II

Why do many things turn out badly for good men? Why, no evil can befall a good man; contraries cannot combine. Just as so many rivers, so many showers of rain from the clouds, such a number of medicinal springs, do not alter the taste of the sea, indeed, do not so much as soften it, so the pressure of adversity does not affect the mind of a brave man; for the mind of a brave man maintains its balance and throws its own complexion over all that takes place, because it is more powerful than any external circumstances. I do not say that he does not feel them, but he conquers them, and on occasion calmly and tranquilly rises superior to their attacks, holding all misfortunes to be trials of his own firmness. Yet who is there who, provided he be a man and have honourable ambition, does not long for due employment, and is not eager to do his duty in spite of danger? Is there any hard-working man to whom idleness is not a punishment? We see athletes, who study only their bodily strength, engage in contests with the strongest of men, and insist that those who train them for the arena should put out their whole strength when practising with them: they endure blows and maltreatment, and, if they cannot find any single person who is their match, they engage with several at once: their strength and courage droop without an antagonist: they can only prove how great and how mighty it is by proving how much they can endure. You should know that good men ought to act in like manner, so as not to fear troubles and difficulties, nor to lament their hard fate, to take in good part whatever befalls them, and force it to become a blessing to them. It does not matter what you bear, but how you bear it. Do you not see how differently fathers and mothers indulge their children? How the former urge them to begin their tasks betimes, will not suffer them to be idle even on holidays, and exercise them till they perspire, and sometimes till they shed tears—while their mothers want to cuddle them in their laps, and keep them out of the sun, and never wish them to be vexed, or to cry, or to work. God bears a fatherly mind towards good men, and loves them in a manly spirit. "Let them," says He, "be exercised by labours, sufferings, and losses, that so they may gather true strength." Those who are surfeited with ease break down not only with labour, but with mere motion and by their own weight. Unbroken prosperity cannot bear a single blow; but he who has waged an unceasing strife with his misfortunes has gained a thicker skin by his sufferings, yields to no disaster, and even though he fall yet fights on his knee. Do you wonder that God, who so loves the good, who would have them attain the highest goodness and preeminence, should appoint fortune to be their adversary? I should not be surprised if the gods sometimes experience a wish to behold great men struggling with some misfortune. We sometimes are delighted when a youth of steady courage receives on his spear the wild beast that attacks him; or when he meets the charge of a lion without flinching; and the more eminent the man is who acts thus[1], the more attractive is the sight: yet these are not matters which can attract the attention of the gods, but are mere pastime and diversions of human frivolity. Behold a sight worthy to be viewed by a god interested in his own work, behold a pair[2] worthy of a god, a brave man matched with evil fortune, especially if he himself has given the challenge. I say, I do not know what nobler spectacle Jupiter could find on earth, should he turn his eyes thither, than that of Cato, after his party had more than once been defeated, still standing upright amid the ruins of the commonwealth. Quoth he, "What though all be fallen into one man's power, though the land be guarded by his legions, the sea by his fleets, though Caesar's soldiers beset the city gate? Cato has a way out of it: with one hand he will open a wide path to freedom; his sword, which he has borne unstained by disgrace and innocent of crime even in a civil war, will still perform good and noble deeds; it will give to Cato that freedom which it could not give to his country. Begin, my soul, the work which thou so long hast contemplated, snatch thyself away from the world of man. Already Petreius and Juba have met and fallen, each slain by the other's hand—a brave and noble compact with fate, yet not one befitting my greatness: it is as disgraceful for Cato to beg his death of any one as it would be for him to beg his life."

It is clear to me that the gods must have looked on with great joy, while that man, his own most ruthless avenger, took thought for the safety of others and arranged the escape of those who departed, while even on his last night he pursued his studies, while he drove the sword into his sacred breast, while he tore forth his vitals and laid his hand upon that most holy life which was unworthy to be defiled by steel. This, I am inclined to think, was the reason that his wound was not well-aimed and mortal: the gods were not satisfied with seeing Cato die once: his courage was kept in action and recalled to the stage, that it might display itself in a more difficult part: for it needs a greater mind to return a second time to death. How could they fail to view their pupil with interest when leaving his life by such a noble and memorable departure? Men are raised to the level of the gods by a death which is admired even by those who fear them.

---

[1] honestior is opposed to the gladiator—the loftier the station of the combatant. The Gracchus of Juvenal, Sat. ii. and viii., illustrates the passage.

[2] par, a technical term in the language of sport (worthy of such a spectator).

III

However, as my argument proceeds, I shall prove that what appear to be evils are not so; for the present I say this, that what you call hard measure, misfortunes, and things against which we ought to pray, are really to the advantage, firstly, of those to whom they happen, and secondly, of all mankind, for whom the gods care more than for individuals; and next, that these evils befall them with their own good will, and that men deserve to endure misfortunes, if they are unwilling to receive them. To this I shall add, that misfortunes proceed thus by destiny, and that they befall good men by the same law which makes them good. After this, I shall prevail upon you never to pity any good man; for though he may be called unhappy, he cannot be so.

Of all these propositions that which I have stated first appears the most difficult to prove, I mean, that the things which we dread and shudder at are to the advantage of those to whom they happen. "Is it," say you, "to their advantage to be driven into exile, to be brought to want, to carry out to burial their children and wife, to be publicly disgraced, to lose their health?" Yes! if you are surprised at these being to any man's advantage, you will also be surprised at any man being benefited by the knife and cautery, or by hunger and thirst as well. Yet if you consider that some men, in order to be cured, have their bones scraped, and pieces of them extracted, that their veins are pulled out, and that some have limbs cut off, which could not remain in their place without ruin to the whole body, you will allow me to prove to you this also, that some misfortunes are for the good of those to whom they happen, just as much, by Hercules, as some things which are praised and sought after are harmful to those who enjoy them, like indigestions and drunkenness and other matters which kill us through pleasure. Among many grand sayings of our Demetrius is this, which I have but just heard, and which still rings and thrills in my ears: "No one," said he, "seems to me more unhappy than the man whom no misfortune has ever befallen." He never has had an opportunity of testing himself; though everything has happened to him according to his wish, nay, even before he has formed a wish, yet the gods have judged him unfavourably; he has never been deemed worthy to conquer ill fortune, which avoids the greatest cowards, as though it said, "Why should I take that man for my antagonist? He will straightway lay down his arms: I shall not need all my strength against him: he will be put to flight by a mere menace: he dares not even face me; let me look around for some other with whom I may fight hand to hand: I blush to join battle with one who is prepared to be beaten." A gladiator deems it a disgrace to be matched with an inferior, and knows that to win without danger is to win without glory. Just so doth Fortune; she seeks out

Of Providence

the bravest to match herself with, passes over some with disdain, and makes for the most unyielding and upright of men, to exert her strength against them. She tried Mucius by fire, Fabricius by poverty, Rutilius by exile, Regulus by torture, Socrates by poison, Cato by death: it is ill fortune alone that discovers these glorious examples. Was Mucius unhappy, because he grasped the enemy's fire with his right hand, and of his own accord paid the penalty of his mistake? because he overcame the King with his hand when it was burned, though he could not when it held a sword? Would he have been happier, if he had warmed his hand in his mistress's bosom; Was Fabricius unhappy, because when the state could spare him, he dug his own land? because he waged war against riches as keenly as against Pyrrhus? because he supped beside his hearth off the very roots and herbs which he himself, though an old man, and one who had enjoyed a triumph, had grubbed up while clearing his field of weeds? What then? would he have been happier if he had gorged himself with fishes from distant shores, and birds caught in foreign lands? if he had roused the torpor of his queasy stomach with shellfish from the upper and the lower sea? if he had piled a great heap of fruits round game of the first head, which many huntsmen had been killed in capturing? Was Rutilius unhappy, because those who condemned him will have to plead their cause for all ages? because he endured the loss of his country more composedly than that of his banishment? because he was the only man who refused anything to Sulla the dictator, and when recalled from exile all but went further away and banished himself still more. "Let those," said he, "whom thy fortunate reign catches at Rome, see to the Forum drenched with blood,[3] and the heads of Senators above the Pool of Servilius—the place where the victims of Sulla's proscriptions were stripped—the bands of assassins roaming at large through the city, and many thousands of Roman citizens slaughtered in one place, after, nay, by means of a promise of quarter. Let those who are unable to go into exile behold these things." Well! is Lucius Sulla happy, because when he comes down into the Forum. room is made for him with sword-strokes, because he allows the heads of consulars to be shown to him, and counts out the price of blood through the quaestor and the state exchequer? And this, this was the man who passed the Lex Cornelia! Let us now come to Regulus: what injury did fortune do him when she made him an example of good faith, an example of endurance? They pierce his skin with nails: wherever he leans his weary body, it rests on a wound; his eyes are fixed for ever open; the greater his sufferings, the greater is his glory. Would you know how far he is from regretting that he valued his honour at such a price? Heal his wounds and send him again into the senate-house; he will give the same advice. So, then, you think Maecenas a happier man, who when troubled by love, and weeping at the daily repulses of his ill-natured wife,

---

[3] vidirint — Let them see to it: it is no matter of mine.

sought for sleep by listening to distant strains of music? Though he drug himself with wine, divert himself with the sound of falling waters, and distract his troubled thoughts with a thousand pleasures, yet Maecenas will no more sleep on his down cushions than Regulus on the rack. Yet it consoles the latter that he suffers for the sake of honour, and he looks away from his torments to their cause: whilst the other, jaded with pleasures and sick with over-enjoyment, is more hurt by the cause of his sufferings than by the sufferings themselves. Vice has not so utterly taken possession of the human race that, if men were allowed to choose their destiny, there can be any doubt but that more would choose to be Reguluses than to be Maecenases: or if there were any one who dared to say that he would prefer to be born Maecenas than Regulus, that man, whether he says so or not, would rather have been Terentia (than Cicero).

Do you consider Socrates to have been badly used, because he took that draught which the state assigned to him as though it were a charm to make him immortal, and argued about death until death itself? Was he ill treated, because his blood froze and the current of his veins gradually stopped as the chill of death crept over them? How much more is this man to be envied than he who is served on precious stones, whose drink a creature trained to every vice, a eunuch or much the same, cools with snow in a golden cup? Such men as these bring up again all that they drink, in misery and disgust at the taste of their own bile, while Socrates cheerfully and willingly drains his poison. As for Cato, enough has been said, and all men must agree that the highest happiness was reached by one who was chosen by Nature herself as worthy to contend with all her terrors: "The enmity," says she, "of the powerful is grievous, therefore let him be opposed at once by Pompeius, Caesar, and Crassus: it is grievous, when a candidate for public offices, to be defeated by one's inferiors; therefore let him be defeated by Vatinius: it is grievous to take part in civil wars, therefore let him fight in every part of the world for the good cause with equal obstinacy and ill-luck: it is grievous to lay hands upon one's self, therefore let him do so. What shall I gain by this? That all men may know that these things, which I have deemed Cato worthy to undergo, are not real evils."

IV

Prosperity comes to the mob, and to low-minded men as well as to great ones; but it is the privilege of great men alone to send under the yoke[4] the disasters and terrors of mortal life: whereas to be always prosperous, and to pass through life without a twinge of mental distress, is to remain ignorant of one half of nature. You are a great man; but how am I to know it, if fortune gives you no opportunity of showing your virtue? You have entered the arena of the Olympic games, but no one else has done so: you have the crown, but not the victory: I do not congratulate you as I would a brave man, but as one who has obtained a consulship or praetorship. You have gained dignity. I may say the same of a good man, if troublesome circumstances have never given him a single opportunity of displaying the strength of his mind. I think you unhappy because you never have been unhappy: you have passed through your life without meeting an antagonist: no one will know your powers, not even you yourself." For a man cannot know himself without a trial; no one ever learnt what he could do without putting himself to the test; for which reason many have of their own free will exposed themselves to misfortunes which no longer came in their way, and have sought for an opportunity of making their virtue, which otherwise would have been lost in darkness, shine before the world. Great men, I say, often rejoice at crosses of fortune just as brave soldiers do at wars. I remember to have heard Triumphus, who was a gladiator[5] in the reign of Tiberius Caesar, complaining about the scarcity of prizes. "What a glorious time," said he, "is past." Valour is greedy of danger, and thinks only of whither it strives to go, not of what it will suffer, since even what it will suffer is part of its glory. Soldiers pride themselves on their wounds, they joyously display their blood flowing over their breastplate.[6] Though those who return unwounded from battle may have done as bravely, yet he who returns wounded is more admired. God, I say, favours those whom He wishes to enjoy the greatest honours, whenever He affords them the means of performing some exploit with spirit and courage, something which is not easily to be

---

[4] That is, to triumph over. "Two spears were set upright.... and a third was fastened across them at the top; and through this gateway the vanquished army marched out, as a token that they had been conquered in war, and owed their lives to the enemy's mercy. It was no peculiar insult devised for this occasion, but a common usage, so far as appears, in similar cases; like the modern ceremony of piling arms when a garrison or army surrender themselves as prisoners of war."—Arnold's History of Rome, ch. Xxxi

[5] He was a "mirmillo," a kind of gladiator who was armed with a Gaulish helmet.

[6] e lorica.

accomplished: you can judge of a pilot in a storm, of a soldier in a battle. How can I know with how great a spirit you could endure poverty, if you overflow with riches? How can I tell with how great firmness you could bear up against disgrace, dishonour, and public hatred, if you grow old to the sound of applause, if popular favour cannot be alienated from you, and seems to flow to you by the natural bent of men's minds? How can I know how calmly you would endure to be childless, if you see all your children around you? I have heard what you said when you were consoling others: then I should have seen whether you could have consoled yourself, whether yon could have forbidden yourself to grieve. Do not, I beg you, dread those things which the immortal gods apply to our minds like spurs: misfortune is virtue's opportunity. Those men may justly be called unhappy who are stupified with excess of enjoyment, whom sluggish contentment keeps as it were becalmed in a quiet sea: whatever befalls them will come strange to them. Misfortunes press hardest on those who are unacquainted with them: the yoke feels heavy to the tender neck. The recruit turns pale at the thought of a wound: the veteran, who knows that he has often won the victory after losing blood, looks boldly at his own flowing gore. In like manner God hardens, reviews, and exercises those whom He tests and loves: those whom He seems to indulge and spare, He is keeping out of condition to meet their coming misfortunes: for you are mistaken if you suppose that any one is exempt from misfortune: he who has long prospered will have his share some day; those who seem to have been spared them have only had them put off. Why does God afflict the best of men with ill-health, or sorrow, or other troubles? Because in the army the most hazardous services are assigned to the bravest soldiers: a general sends his choicest troops to attack the enemy in a midnight ambuscade, to reconnoitre his line of march, or to drive the hostile garrisons from their strong places. No one of these men says as he begins his march, " The general has dealt hardly with me," but "He has judged well of me." Let those who are bidden to suffer what makes the weak and cowardly weep, say likewise, "God has thought us worthy subjects on whom to try how much suffering human nature can endure." Avoid luxury, avoid effeminate enjoyment, by which men's minds are softened, and in which, unless something occurs to remind them of the common lot of humanity, they lie unconscious, as though plunged in continual drunkenness. He whom glazed windows have always guarded from the wind, whose feet are warmed by constantly renewed fomentations, whose dining-room is heated by hot air beneath the floor and spread through the walls, cannot meet the gentlest breeze without danger. While all excesses are hurtful, excess of comfort is the most hurtful of all; it affects the brain; it leads men's minds into vain imaginings; it spreads a thick cloud over the boundaries of truth and falsehood. Is it not better, with virtue by one's side, to endure continual misfortune, than to burst with an endless surfeit of good things? It is the overloaded stomach that is rent asunder: death treats starvation more gently. The gods deal with good men according to the same rule as schoolmasters with their pupils, who exact most labour from those of whom they have the surest hopes. Do you imagine that the Lacedaemonians, who test the mettle of their children by public flogging, do not love them? Their own fathers call upon them to endure the strokes of the rod bravely, and when they are torn and half dead, ask them to offer their wounded skin to receive fresh wounds. Why then should we wonder if God tries noble spirits severely? There can be no easy proof of virtue. Fortune lashes and mangles us: well, let us endure it: it is not cruelty, it is a struggle, in which the oftener we engage the braver we shall become. The strongest part of the body is that which is exercised by the most frequent use: we must entrust ourselves to fortune to be hardened by her against herself: by degrees she will make us a match for herself. Familiarity with danger leads us to despise it. Thus the bodies of sailors are hardened by endurance of the sea, and the hands of farmers by work; the arms of soldiers are powerful to hurl darts, the legs of runners are active: that part of each man which he exercises is the strongest: so by endurance the mind becomes able to despise the power of misfortunes. You may see what endurance might effect in us if you observe what labour does among tribes that are naked and rendered stronger by want. Look at all the nations that dwell beyond the Roman Empire: I mean the Germans and all the nomad tribes that war against us along the Danube. They suffer from eternal winter, and a dismal climate, the barren soil grudges them sustenance, they keep off the rain with leaves or thatch, they bound across frozen marshes, and hunt wild beasts for food. Do you think them unhappy? There is no unhappiness in what use has made part of one's nature: by degrees men find pleasure in doing what they were first driven to do by necessity. They have no homes and no resting-places save those which weariness appoints them for the day; their food, though coarse, yet must be sought with their own hands; the harshness of the climate is terrible, and their bodies are unclothed. This, which you think a hardship, is the mode of life of all these races: how then can you wonder at good men being shaken, in order that they may be strengthened? No tree which the wind does not often blow against is firm and strong; for it is stiffened by the very act of being shaken, and plants its roots more securely: those which grow in a sheltered valley are brittle: and so it is to the advantage of good men, and causes them to be undismayed, that they should live much amidst alarms, and learn to bear with patience what is not evil save to him who endures it ill.

V

Add to this that it is to the advantage of every one that the best men should, so to speak, be on active service and perform labours: God has the same purpose as the wise man, that is, to prove that the things which the herd covets and dreads are neither good nor bad in themselves. If, however, He only bestows them upon good men, it will be evident that they are good things, and bad, if He only inflicts them upon bad men. Blindness would be execrable if no one lost his eyes except those who deserve to have them pulled out; therefore let Appius and Metellus be doomed to darkness. Riches are not a good thing: therefore let Elius the pander possess them, that men who have consecrated money in the temple, may see the same in the brothel: for by no means can God discredit objects of desire so effectually as by bestowing them upon the worst of men, and removing them from the best." But," you say, "it is unjust that a good man should be enfeebled, or transfixed, or chained, while bad men swagger at large with a whole skin." What! is it not unjust that brave men should bear arms, pass the night in camps, and stand on guard along the rampart with their wounds still bandaged, while within the city eunuchs and professional profligates live at their ease? what? is it not unjust that maidens of the highest birth should be roused at night to perform Divine service, while fallen women enjoy the soundest sleep? Labour calls for the best men: the senate often passes the whole day in debate, while at the same time every scoundrel either amuses his leisure in the Campus Martius, or lurks in a tavern, or passes his time in some pleasant society. The same thing happens in this great commonwealth (of the world): good men labour, spend and are spent, and that too of their own free will; they are not dragged along by fortune, but follow her and take equal steps with her; if they knew how, they would outstrip her. I remember, also, to have heard this spirited saying of that stoutest-hearted of men, Demetrius. "Ye immortal Gods," said he, "the only complaint which I have to make of you is that you did not make your will known to me earlier; for then I would sooner have gone into that state of life to which I now have been called. Do you wish to take my children? it was for you that I brought them up. Do you wish to take some part of my body? take it: it is no great thing that I am offering you, I shall soon have done with the whole of it. Do you wish for my life? why should I hesitate to return to you what you gave me? whatever you ask you shall receive with my good will: nay, I would rather give it than be forced to hand it over to you: what need had you to take away what you did? you might have received it from me: yet even as it is you cannot take anything from me, because you cannot rob a man unless he resists."

Of Providence

I am constrained to nothing, I suffer nothing against my will, nor am I God's slave, but his willing follower, and so much the more because I know that everything is ordained and proceeds according to a law that endures forever. The fates guide us, and the length of every man's days is decided at the first hour of his birth: every cause depends upon some earlier cause: one long chain of destiny decides all things, public or private. Wherefore, everything must be patiently endured, because events do not fall in our way, as we imagine, but come by a regular law. It has long ago been settled at what you should rejoice and at what you should weep, and although the lives of individual men appear to differ from one another in a great variety of particulars, yet the sum total comes to one and the same thing: we soon perish, and the gifts which we receive soon perish. Why, then, should we be angry? why should we lament? we are prepared for our fate: let nature deal as she will with her own bodies; let us be cheerful whatever befalls, and stoutly reflect that it is not anything of our own that perishes. What is the duty of a good man? To submit himself to fate: it is a great consolation .-to be swept away together with the entire universe: whatever law is laid upon us that thus we must live and thus we must die, is laid upon the gods also: one unchangeable stream bears along men and gods alike: the creator and ruler of the universe himself, though he has given laws to the fates, yet is guided by them: he always obeys, he only once commanded. "But why was God so unjust in His distribution of fate, as to assign poverty, wounds, and untimely deaths to good men?" The workman cannot alter his materials: this is their nature. Some qualities cannot be separated from some others: they cling together; are indivisible. Dull minds, tending to sleep or to a waking state exactly like sleep, are composed of sluggish elements: it requires stronger stuff to form a man meriting careful description. His course will not be straightforward; he must go upwards and downwards, be tossed about, and guide his vessel through troubled waters: he must make his way in spite of fortune: he will meet with much that is hard which he must soften, much that is rough that he must make smooth. Fire tries gold, misfortune tries brave men. See how high virtue has to climb: you may be sure that it has no safe path to tread.

> "Steep is the path at first: the steeds, though strong,
> Fresh from their rest, can hardly crawl along;
> The middle part lies through the topmost sky,
> Whence oft, as I the earth and sea descry,
> I shudder, terrors through my bosom thrill.
> The ending of the path is sheer down hill,
> And needs the careful guidance of the rein,
> For ever when I sink beneath the main,
> Old Tethys trembles in her depths below

Lest headlong down upon her I should go."[7]

When the spirited youth heard this, he said, "I have no fault to find with the road: I will mount it, it is worthwhile to go through these places, even though one fall." His father did not cease from trying to scare his brave spirit with terrors:—

"Then, too, that thou may'st hold thy course aright,
And neither turn aside to left nor right,
Straight through the Bull's fell horns thy path must go,
Through the fierce Lion, and the Archer's bow."
After this Phaethon says:—

"Harness the chariot which you yield to me,
I am encouraged by these things with which you think to scare me: I long to stand where the Sun himself trembles to stand." It is the part of grovellers and cowards to follow the, safe track; courage loves a lofty path.

---

[7] The lines occur in Ovid's Metamorphoses, ii. 63. Phoebus is telling Phaethon how to drive the chariot of the Sun.

VI

"Yet, why does God permit evil to happen to good men?" He does not permit it: he takes away from them all evils, such as crimes and scandalous wickedness, daring thoughts, grasping schemes, blind lusts, and avarice coveting its neighbour's goods. He protects and saves them. Does anyone besides this demand that God should look after the baggage of good men also? Why, they themselves leave the care of this to God: they scorn external accessories. Democritus forswore riches, holding them to be a burden to a virtuous mind: what wonder then, if God permits that to happen to a good man, which a good man sometimes chooses should happen to himself? Good men, you say, lose their children: why should they not, since sometimes they even put them to death? They are banished: why should they not be, since sometimes they leave their country of their own free will, never to return? They are slain: why not, since sometimes they choose to lay violent hands on themselves? Why do they suffer certain miseries? it is that they may teach others how to do so. They are born as patterns. Conceive, therefore, that God says:—
"You, who have chosen righteousness, what complaint can you make of me? I have encompassed other men with unreal good things, and have deceived their inane minds as it were by a long and misleading dream: I have bedecked them with gold, silver, and ivory, but within them there is no good thing. Those men whom you regard as fortunate, if you could see, not their outward show, but their hidden life, are really unhappy, mean, and base, ornamented on the outside like the walls of their houses: that good fortune of theirs is not sound and genuine: it is only a veneer, and that a thin one. As long, therefore, as they can stand upright and display themselves as they choose, they shine and impose upon one; when something occurs to shake and unmask them, we see how deep and real a rottenness was hidden by that factitious magnificence. To you I have given sure and lasting good things, which become greater and better the more one turns them over and views them on every side: I have granted to you to scorn danger, to disdain passion. You do not shine outwardly, all your good qualities are turned inwards; even so does the world neglect what lies without it, and rejoices in the contemplation of itself. I have placed every good thing within your own breasts: it is your good fortune not to need any good fortune. 'Yet many things befall you which are sad, dreadful, hard to be borne.' Well, as I have not been able to remove these from your path, I have given your minds strength to combat all: bear them bravely. In this you can surpass God himself; He is beyond suffering evil; you are above it. Despise poverty; no man lives as poor as he was born: despise pain; either it will cease or you will cease: despise death; it either ends you or takes you elsewhere: despise fortune; I have given her no weapon that can reach the mind. Above all, I have taken care that no

one should hold you captive against your will: the way of escape lies open before you: if you do not choose to fight, you may fly. For this reason, of all those matters which I have deemed essential for you, I have made nothing easier for you than to die. I have set man's life as it were on a mountain side: it soon slips down.[8] Do but watch, and you will see how short and how ready a path leads to freedom. I have not imposed such long delays upon those who quit the world as upon those who enter it: were it not so, fortune would hold a wide dominion over you, if a man died as slowly as he is born. Let all time, let every place teach you, how simple it is to renounce nature, and to fling back her gifts to her: before the altar itself and during the solemn rites of sacrifice, while life is being prayed for, learn how to die. Fat oxen fall dead with a tiny wound; a blow from a man's hand fells animals of great strength: the sutures of the neck are severed by a thin blade, and when the joint which connects the head and neck is cut, all that great mass falls. The breath of life is not deep seated, nor only to be let forth by steel — the vitals need not be searched throughout by plunging a sword among them to the hilt: death lies near the surface. I have not appointed any particular spot for these blows — the body may be pierced wherever you please. That very act which is called dying, by which the breath of life leaves the body, is too short for you to be able to estimate its quickness: whether a knot crushes the windpipe, or water stops your breathing: whether you fall headlong from a height and perish upon the hard ground below, or a mouthful of fire checks the drawing of your breath—whatever it is, it acts swiftly. Do you not blush to spend so long a time in dreading what takes so short a time to do?"

---

[8] The lines occur in Ovid's Metamorphoses, ii. 63. Phoebus is telling Phaethon how to drive the chariot of the Sun.

On the Firmness of the Wise Man

I

I MIGHT truly say, Serenus, that there is as wide a difference between the Stoics and the other sects of philosophers as there is between men and women, since each class contributes an equal share to human society, but the one is born to command, the other to obey. The other philosophers deal with us gently and coaxingly, just as our accustomed family physicians usually do with our bodies, treating them not by the best and shortest method, but by that which we allow them to employ; whereas the Stoics adopt a manly course, and do not care about its appearing attractive to those who are entering upon it, but that it should as quickly as possible take us out of the world, and lead us to that lofty eminence which is so far beyond the scope of any missile weapon that it is above the reach of Fortune herself. "But the way by which we are asked to climb is steep and uneven." What then? Can heights be reached by a level path? Yet they are not so sheer and precipitous as some think. It is only the first part that has rocks and cliffs and no apparent outlet, just as many hills seen from a long way off appear abruptly steep and joined together, because the distance deceives our sight, and then, as we draw nearer, those very hills which our mistaken eyes had made into one gradually unfold themselves, those parts which seemed precipitous from afar assume a gently sloping outline. When just now mention was made of Marcus Cato, you whose mind revolts at injustice were indignant at Cato's own age having so little understood him, at its having allotted a place below Vatinius to one who towered above both Caesar and Pompeius; it seemed shameful to you, that when he spoke against some law in the Forum his toga was torn from him, and that he was hustled through the hands of a mutinous mob from the Rostra as far as the arch of Fabius, enduring all the bad language, spitting, and other insults of the frantic rabble.

II

I then answered, that you had good cause to be anxious on behalf of the commonwealth, which Publius Clodius on the one side, Vatinius and all the greatest scoundrels on the other, were putting up for sale, and, carried away by their blind covetousness, did not understand that when they sold it they themselves were sold with it; I bade you have no fears on behalf of Cato himself, because the wise man can neither receive injury nor insult, and it is more certain that the immortal gods have given Cato as a pattern of a wise man to us, than that they gave Ulysses or Hercules to the earlier ages; for these our Stoics have declared were wise men, unconquered by labours, despisers of pleasure, and superior to all terrors. Cato did not slay wild beasts, whose pursuit belongs to huntsmen and countrymen, nor did he exterminate fabulous creatures with fire and sword, or live in times when it was possible to believe that the heavens could be supported on the shoulders of one man. In an age which had thrown off its belief in antiquated superstitions, and had carried material knowledge to its highest point, he had to struggle against that many-headed monster, ambition, against that boundless lust for power which the whole world divided among three men could not satisfy. He alone withstood the vices of a worn-out State, sinking into ruin through its own bulk; he upheld the falling commonwealth as far as it could be upheld by one man's hand, until at last his support was withdrawn, and he shared the crash which he had so long averted, and perished together with that from which it was impious to separate him — for Cato did not outlive freedom, nor did freedom outlive Cato. Think you that the people could do any wrong to such a man when they tore away his praetorship or his toga? when they bespattered his sacred head with the rinsings of their mouths? The wise man is safe, and no injury or insult can touch him.

III

I think I see your excited and boiling temper. You are preparing to exclaim: "These are the things which take away all weight from your maxims ; you promise great matters, such as I should not even wish for, let alone believe to be possible, and then, after all your brave words, though you say that the wise man is not poor, you admit that he often is in want of servants, shelter, and food. You say that the wise man is not mad, yet you admit that he sometimes loses his reason, talks nonsense, and is driven to the wildest actions by the stress of his disorder. When you say that the wise man cannot be a slave, you do not deny that he will be sold, carry out orders, and perform menial services at the bidding of his master; so, for all your proud looks, you come down to the level of everyone else, and merely call things by different names. Consequently, I suspect that something of this kind lurks behind this maxim, which at first sight appears so beautiful and noble, 'that the wise man can neither receive injury nor insult.' It makes a great deal of difference whether you declare that the wise man is beyond feeling resentment, or beyond receiving injury; for if you say that he will bear it calmly, he has no special privilege in that, for he has developed a very common quality, and one which is learned by long endurance of wrong itself, namely, patience. If you declare that he can never receive an injury, that is, that no one will attempt to do him one, then I will throw up all my occupations in life and become a Stoic."

It has not been my object to decorate the wise man with mere imaginary verbal honours, but to raise him to a position where no injury will be permitted to reach him. "What? will there be no one to tease him, to try to wrong him?" There is nothing on earth so sacred as not to be liable to sacrilege; yet holy things exist on high none the less because there are men who strike at a greatness which is far above themselves, though with no hope of reaching it. The invulnerable is not that which is never struck, but that which is never wounded. In this class I will show you the wise man. Can we doubt that the strength which is never overcome in fight is more to be relied on than that which is never challenged, seeing that untested power is untrustworthy, whereas that solidity which hurls back all attacks is deservedly regarded as the most trustworthy of all? In like manner you may know that the wise man, if no injury hurts him, is of a higher type than if none is offered to him, and I should call him a brave man whom war does not subdue and the violence of the enemy does not alarm, not him who enjoys luxurious ease amid a slothful people. I say, then, that such a wise man is invulnerable against all injury; it matters not, therefore, how many darts be hurled at him, since he can be pierced by none of them. Just as the hardness of some stones is impervious to steel, and adamant can neither be cut, broken, or ground, but blunts all instruments used upon it; just as some things cannot be destroyed by fire, but when encircled by flame still retain their hardness and shape; just as some tall projecting cliffs break the waves of the sea, and though lashed by them through many centuries, yet show no traces of their rage; even so the mind of the wise man is firm, and gathers so much strength, that it is as safe from injury as any of those things which I have mentioned.

IV

"What then? Will there be no one who will try to do an injury to the wise man?" Yes, someone will try, but the injury will not reach him; for he is separated from the contact of his inferiors by so wide a distance that no evil impulse can retain its power of harm until it reaches him. Even when powerful men, raised to positions of high authority, and strong in the obedience of their dependents, strive to injure him, all their darts fall as far short of his wisdom as those which are shot upwards by bowstrings or catapults, which, although they rise so high as to pass out of sight, yet fall back again without reaching the heavens. Why, do you suppose that when that stupid king[1] clouded the daylight with the multitude of his darts, that any arrow of them all went into the sun? or that when he flung his chains into the deep, that he was able to reach Neptune? Just as sacred things escape from the hands of men, and no injury is done to the godhead by those who destroy temples and melt down images, so whoever attempts to treat the wise man with impertinence, insolence, or scorn, does so in vain. "It would be better," say you, "if no one wished to do so." You are expressing a wish that the whole human race were inoffensive, which may hardly be; moreover, those who would gain by such wrongs not being done are those who would do them, not he who could not suffer from them even if they were done; nay, I know not whether wisdom is not best displayed by calmness in the midst of annoyances, just as the greatest proof of a general's strength in arms and men consists in his quietness and confidence in the midst of an enemy's country.

---

[1] Xerxes.

V

If you think fit, my Serenus, let us distinguish between injury and insult. The former is naturally the more grievous, the latter less important, and grievous only to the thin-skinned, since it angers men but does not wound them. Yet such is the weakness of men's minds, that many think that there is nothing more bitter than insult; thus you will find slaves who prefer to be flogged to being slapped, and who think stripes and death more endurable than insulting words. To such a pitch of absurdity have we come that we suffer not only from pain, but from the idea of pain, like children, who are terror-stricken by darkness, misshapen masks, and distorted faces, and whose tears flow at hearing names unpleasing to their ears, at the movement of our fingers, and other things which they ignorantly shrink from with a sort of mistaken spasm. The object which injury proposes to itself is to do evil to someone. Now wisdom leaves no room for evil; to it, the only evil is baseness, which cannot enter into the place already occupied by virtue and honour. If, therefore, there can be no injury without evil, and no evil without baseness, and baseness cannot find any place with a man who is already filled with honour, it follows that no injury can reach the wise man; for if injury be the endurance of some evil, and the wise man can endure no evil, it follows that no injury takes effect upon the wise man. All injury implies a making less of that which it affects, and no one can sustain an injury without some loss either of his dignity, or of some part of his body, or of some of the things external to ourselves; but the wise man can lose nothing. He has invested everything in himself, has entrusted nothing to fortune, has his property in safety, and is content with virtue, which does not need casual accessories, and therefore can neither be increased or diminished; for virtue, as having attained to the highest position, has no room for addition to herself, and fortune can take nothing away save what she gave. Now fortune does not give virtue; therefore she does not take it away. Virtue is free, inviolable, not to be moved, not to be shaken, and so hardened against misfortunes that she cannot be bent, let alone overcome by them. She looks unfalteringly on while tortures are being prepared for her; she makes no change of countenance, whether misery or pleasure be offered to her. The wise man therefore can lose nothing of whose loss he will be sensible, for he is the property of virtue alone, from whom he never can be taken away. He enjoys all other things at the good pleasure of fortune; but who is grieved at the loss of what is not his own? If, injury can hurt none of those things which are the peculiar property of the wise man, because while his virtue is safe they are safe, then it is impossible that an injury should be done to a wise man. Demetrius, who was surnamed Poliorcetes, took Megara, and the philosopher Stilbo, when asked by him whether he had lost anything, answered, "No, I carry all my property about me." Yet his inheritance had been given up to pillage, his daughters had been outraged by the enemy, his country had fallen under a foreign dominion, and it was the king, enthroned on high, surrounded by the spears of his victorious troops, who put this question to him; yet he struck the victory out of the king's hands, and proved that, though the city was taken, he himself was not only unconquered but unharmed, for he bore with him those true goods which no one can lay hands upon. What was being plundered and carried away hither and thither he did not consider to be his own, but to be merely things which come and go at the caprice of fortune; therefore he had not loved them as his own, for the possession of all things which come from without is slippery and insecure.

VI

Consider now, whether any thief, or false accuser, or headstrong neighbour, or rich man enjoying the power conferred by a childless old age, could do any injury to this man, from whom neither war nor an enemy whose profession was the noble art of battering city walls could take away anything. Amid the flash of swords on all sides, and the riot of the plundering soldiery, amid the flames and blood and ruin of the fallen city, amid the crash of temples falling upon their gods, one man was at peace. You need not therefore account that a reckless boast, for which I will give you a surety, if my words goes for nothing. Indeed, you would hardly believe so much constancy or such greatness of mind to belong to any man; but here a man comes forward to prove that you have no reason for doubting that one who is but of human birth can raise himself above human necessities, can tranquilly behold pains, losses, diseases, wounds, and great natural convulsions roaring around him, can bear adversity with calm and prosperity with moderation, neither yielding to the former nor trusting to the latter, that he can remain the same amid all varieties of fortune, and think nothing to be his own save himself, and himself too only as regards his better part. "Behold," says he, "I am here to prove to you that although, under the direction of that destroyer of so many cities, walls may be shaken by the stroke of the ram, lofty towers may be suddenly brought low by galleries and hidden mines, and mounds arise so high as to rival the highest citadel, yet that no siege engines can be discovered which can shake a well-established mind. I have just crept from amid the ruins of my house, and with conflagrations blazing all around I have escaped from the flames through blood. What fate has befallen my daughters, whether a worse one than that of their country, I know not. Alone and elderly, and seeing everything around me in the hands of the enemy, still I declare that my property is whole and untouched. I have, I hold whatever of mine I have ever had. There is no reason for you to suppose me conquered and yourself my conqueror. It is your fortune which has overcome mine. As for those fleeting possessions which change their owners, I know not where they are; what belongs to myself is with me, and ever will be. I see rich men who have lost their estates; lustful men who have lost their loves, the courtesans whom they cherished at the cost of much shame; ambitious men who have lost the senate, the law courts, the places set apart for the public display of men's vices; usurers who have lost their account-books, in which avarice vainly enjoyed an unreal wealth; but I possess everything whole and uninjured. Leave me, and go and ask those who are weeping and lamenting over the loss of their money, who are offering their bare breasts to drawn swords in its defence, or who are fleeing from the enemy with weighty pockets." See then, Serenus, that the perfect man, full of human and divine virtues, can lose nothing; his goods are surrounded by strong and impassable walls. You cannot compare with them the walls of Babylon, which Alexander entered, nor the fortifications of Carthage and Numantia, won by one and the same hand,[2] nor the Capitol and citadel of Rome, which are branded with the marks of the victors' insults; the ramparts which protect the wise man are safe from fire and hostile invasion; they afford no passage; they are lofty, impregnable, divine.

---

[2] Scipio.

VII

You have no cause for saying, as you are wont to do, that this wise man of ours[3] is nowhere to be found; we do not invent him as an unreal glory of the human race, or conceive a mighty shadow of an untruth, but we have displayed and will display him just as we sketch him, though he may perhaps be uncommon, and only one appears at long intervals; for what is great and transcends the common ordinary type is not often produced; but this very Marcus Cato himself, the mention of whom started this discussion, was a man who I fancy even surpassed our model. Moreover, that which hurts must be stronger than that which is hurt. Now wickedness is not stronger than virtue; therefore the wise man cannot be hurt. Only the bad attempt to injure the good. Good men are at peace among themselves; bad ones are equally mischievous to the good and to one another. If a man cannot be hurt by one weaker than himself, and a bad man be weaker than a good one, and the good have no injury to dread, except from one unlike themselves; then, no injury takes effect upon the wise man; for by this time I need not remind you that no one save the wise man is good.

"If," says our adversary, "Socrates was unjustly condemned, he received an injury." At this point it is needful for us to bear in mind that it is possible for someone to do an injury to me, and yet for me not to receive it, as if any one were to steal something from my country-house and leave it in my town-house, that man would commit a theft, yet I should lose nothing. A man may become mischievous, and yet do no actual mischief: if a man lies with his own wife as if she were a stranger, he will commit adultery, but his wife will not; if a man gives me poison and the poison lose its strength when mixed with food, that man, by administering the poison, has made himself a criminal, even though he has done no hurt. A man is no less a brigand because his sword becomes entangled in his victim's clothes and misses its mark. All crimes, as far as concerns their criminality, are completed before the actual deed is accomplished. Some crimes are of such a nature and bound by such conditions that the first part can take place without the second, though the second cannot take place without the first. I will endeavour to explain these words: I can move my feet and yet not run; but I cannot run without moving my feet. I can be in the water without swimming; but if I swim, I cannot help being in the water. The matter of which we are treating is of this character: if I have received an injury, it is necessary that someone must have done it to me; but if an injury has been done me, it is not necessary that I should have received one; for many

---

[3] **The Stoics.**

circumstances may intervene to avert the injury, as, for example, some chance may strike the hand that is aiming at us, and the dart, after it has been thrown, may swerve aside. So injuries of all kinds may by certain circumstances be thrown back and intercepted in mid-course, so that they may be done and yet not received.

VIII

Moreover, justice can suffer nothing unjust, because contraries cannot co-exist; but an injury can only be done unjustly, therefore an injury cannot be done to the wise man. Nor need you wonder at no one being able to do him an injury; for no one can do him any good service either. The wise man lacks nothing which he can accept by way of a present, and the bad man can bestow nothing that is worthy of the wise man's acceptance; for he must possess it before he can bestow it, and he possesses nothing which the wise man would rejoice to have handed over to him. Consequently, no one can do either harm or good to the wise man, because divine things neither want help nor are capable of being hurt; and the wise man is near, indeed very near to the gods, being like a god in every respect save that he is mortal. As he presses forward and makes his way towards the life that is sublime, well-ordered, without fear, proceeding in a regular and harmonious course, tranquil, beneficent, made for the good of mankind useful both to itself and to others, he will neither long nor weep for anything that is grovelling. He who, trusting to reason, passes through human affairs with godlike mind, has no quarter from which he can receive injury. Do you suppose that I mean merely from no man? He cannot receive an injury even from fortune, which, whenever she contends with virtue, always retires beaten. If we accept with an undisturbed and tranquil mind that greatest terror of all, beyond which the angry laws and the most cruel masters have nothing to threaten us with, in which fortune's dominion is contained—if we know that death is not an evil, and therefore is not an injury either, we shall much more easily endure the other things, such as losses, pains, disgraces, changes of abode, bereavements, and partings, which do not overwhelm the wise man even if they all befall him at once, much less does he grieve at them when they assail him separately. And if he bears the injuries of fortune calmly, how much more will he bear those of powerful men, whom he knows to be the hands of fortune.

IX

He therefore endures everything in the same spirit with which he endures the cold of winter and the severities of climate, fevers, diseases, and other chance accidents, nor does he entertain so high an opinion of any man as to suppose that he acts of set purpose, which belongs to the wise man alone. All other men have no plans, but only plots and deceits and irregular impulses of mind, which he reckons the same as pure accident; now, what depends upon pure accident cannot rage around us designedly. He reflects, also, that the largest sources of injury are to be found in those things by means of which danger is sought for against us, as, for example, by a suborned accuser, or a false charge, or by the stirring up against us of the anger of great men, and the other forms of the brigandage of civilized life. Another common type of injury is when a man loses some profit or prize for which he has long been angling, when an inheritance which he has spent great pains to render his own is left to someone else, or the favour of some noble house, through which he makes great gain, is taken from him. The wise man escapes all this, since he knows not what it is to live for hope or for fear. Add to this, that no one receives an injury unmoved, but is disturbed by the feeling of it. Now, the man free from mistakes has no disturbance; he is master of himself, enjoying a deep and tranquil repose of mind,; for if an injury reaches him it moves and rouses him. But the wise man is without anger, which is caused by the appearance of injury, and he could not be free from anger unless he were also free from injury, which he knows cannot be done to him; hence it is that he is so upright and cheerful, hence he is elate with constant joy. So far, however, is he from shrinking from the encounter either of circumstances or of men, that he makes use of injury itself to make trial of himself and test his own virtue. Let us, I beseech you, show favour to this thesis and listen with impartial ears and minds while the wise man is being made exempt from injury; for nothing is thereby taken away from your insolence, your greediest lusts, your blind rashness and pride; it is without prejudice to your vices that this freedom is sought for the wise man; we do not strive to prevent your doing an injury, but to enable him to sink all injuries beneath himself and protect himself from them by his own greatness of mind. So in the sacred games many have won the victory by patiently enduring the blows of their adversaries and so wearying them out. Think that the wise man belongs to this class, that of men who, by long and faithful practice, have acquired strength to endure and tire out all the violence of their enemies.

X

Since we have now discussed the first part of our subject, let us pass on to the second, in which we will prove by arguments, some of which are our own, but which for the most part are Stoic commonplaces, that the wise man cannot be insulted. There is a lesser form of injury, which we must complain of rather than avenge, which the laws also have considered not to deserve any special punishment. This passion is produced by a meanness of mind which shrinks at any act or deed which treats it with disrespect. "He did not admit me to his house today, although he admitted others; he either turned haughtily away or openly laughed when I spoke;" or, "he placed me at dinner, not on the middle couch (the place of honour), but on the lowest one;" and other matters of the same sort; which I can call nothing but the whinings of a queasy spirit. These matters chiefly affect the luxuriously-nurtured and prosperous; for those who are pressed by worse evils have no time to notice such things as these. Through excessive idleness, dispositions naturally weak and womanish and prone to indulge in fancies through want of real injuries are disturbed at these things, the greater part of which arise from misunderstanding. He therefore who is affected by insult shows that he possesses neither sense nor trustfulness; for he considers it certain that he is scorned, and this vexation affects him with a certain sense of degradation, as he effaces himself and takes a lower room; whereas the wise man is scorned by no one, for he knows his own greatness, gives himself to understand that he allows no one to have such power over him, and as for all of what I should not so much call distress as uneasiness of mind, he does not overcome it, but never so much as feels it. Some other things strike the wise man, though they may not shake his principles, such as bodily pain and weakness, the loss of friends and children, and the ruin of his country in war-time. I do not say that the wise man does not feel these, for we do not ascribe to him the hardness of stone or iron; there is no virtue but is conscious of its own endurance. What then does he? He receives some blows, but when he has received them he rises superior to them, heals them, and brings them to an end; these more trivial things he does not even feel, nor does he make use of his accustomed fortitude in the endurance of evil against them, but either takes no notice of them or considers them to deserve to be laughed at.

XI

Besides this, as most insults proceed from those who are haughty and arrogant and bear their prosperity ill, he has something wherewith to repel this haughty passion, namely, that noblest of all the virtues, magnanimity, which passes over everything of that kind as like unreal apparitions in dreams and visions of the night, which have nothing in them substantial or true. At the same time he reflects that all men are too low to venture to look down upon what is so far above them. The Latin word "contumelia" is derived from the word contempt, because no one does that injury to another unless he regards him with contempt; and no one can treat his elders and betters with contempt, even though he does what contemptuous persons are wont to do; for children strike their parents' faces, infants rumple and tear their mother's hair, and spit upon her and expose what should be covered before her, and do not shrink from using dirty language; yet we do not call any of these things contemptuous. And why? Because he who does it is not able to show contempt. For the same reason the scurrilous raillery of our slaves against their masters amuses us, as their boldness only gains licence to exercise itself at the expense of the guests if they begin with the master; and the more contemptible and the more an object of derision each one of them is, the greater licence he gives his tongue. Some buy forward slave-boys for this purpose, cultivate their scurrility and send them to school that they may vent premeditated libels, which we do not call insults, but smart sayings; yet what madness, at one time to be amused and at another to be affronted by the same thing, and to call a phrase an outrage when spoken by a friend, and an amusing piece of raillery when used by a slave-boy!

XII

In the same spirit in which we deal with boys, the wise man deals with all those whose childhood still endures after their youth is past and their hair is grey. What do men profit by age when their mind has all the faults of childhood and their defects are intensified by time? When they differ from children only in the size and appearance of their bodies, and are just as unsteady and capricious, eager for pleasure without discrimination, timorous and quiet through fear rather than through natural disposition? One cannot say that such men differ from children because the latter are greedy for knuckle-bones and nuts and coppers, while the former are greedy for gold and silver and cities; because the latter play amongst themselves at being magistrates, and imitate the purple-edged robe of state, the lictors' axes, and the judgment-seat, while the former play with the same things in earnest in the Campus Martius and the courts of justice; because the latter pile up the sand on the seashore into the likeness of houses, and the former, with an air of being engaged in important business, employ themselves in piling up stones and walls and roofs until they have turned what was intended for the protection of the body into a danger to it? Children and those more advanced in age both make the same mistake, but the latter deal with different and more important things; the wise man, therefore, is quite justified in treating the affronts which he receives from such men as jokes: and sometimes he corrects them, as he would children, by pain and punishment, not because he has received an injury, but because they have done one and in order that they may do so no more. Thus we break in animals with stripes, yet we are not angry with them when they refuse to carry their rider, but curb them in order that pain may overcome their obstinacy. Now, therefore, you know the answer to the question which was put to us, "Why, if the wise man receives neither injury nor insult, he punishes those who do these things?" He does not revenge himself, but corrects them.

XIII

What, then, is there to prevent your believing this strength of mind to belong to the wise man, when you can see the same thing existing in others, though not from the same cause? — for what physician is angry with a crazy patient? who takes to heart the curses of a fever-stricken one who is denied cold water? The wise man retains in his dealings with all men this same habit of mind which the physician adopts in dealing with his patients, whose parts of shame he does not scorn to handle should they need treatment, nor yet to look at their solid and liquid evacuations, nor to endure their reproaches when frenzied by disease. The wise man knows that all those who strut about in purple-edged togas,[4] healthy and embrowned, are brain-sick people, whom he regards as sick and full of follies. He is not, therefore, angry, should they in their sickness presume to bear themselves somewhat impertinently towards their physician, and in the same spirit as that in which he sets no value upon their titles of honour, he will set but little value upon their acts of disrespect to himself. He will not rise in his own esteem if a beggar pays his court to him, and he will not think it an affront if one of the dregs of the people does not return his greeting. So also he will not admire himself even if many rich men admire him; for he knows that they differ in no respect from beggars — nay, are even more wretched than they; for beggars want but a little, whereas rich men want a great deal. Again, he will not be moved if the King of the Medes, or Attalus, King of Asia, passes by him in silence with a scornful air when he offers his greeting; for he knows that such a man's position has nothing to render it more enviable than that of the man whose duty it is in some great household to keep the sick and mad servants in order. Shall I be put out if one of those who do business at the temple of Castor, buying and selling worthless slaves, does not return my salute, a man whose shops are crowded with throngs of the worst of bondmen? I trow not; for what good can there be in a man who owns none but bad men? As the wise man is indifferent to the courtesy or incivility of such a man, so is he to that of a king. "You own," says he, "the Parthians and Bactrians, but they are men whom you keep in order by fear, they are people whose possession forbids you to unstring the bow, they are fierce enemies, on sale, and eagerly looking out for a new master." He will not, then, be moved by an insult from any man for though all men differ one from

---

[4] Seneca here speaks of men wearing the toga as officials, contrasted with the mass of Roman citizens, among whom the wearing of the toga was already falling into disuse in the time of Augustus. See Macrob. "Sat.," vi. 5 extr., and Suetonius, "Life of Octavius," 40, where the author mentions that Augustus used sarcastically to apply the verse, Virg., 'AEn.,' i. 282, to the Romans of his day.

another, yet the wise man regards them all as alike on account of their equal folly; for should he once lower himself to the point of being affected by either injury or insult, he could never feel safe afterwards, and safety is the especial advantage of the wise man, and he will not be guilty of showing respect to the man who has done him an injury by admitting that he has received one, because it necessarily follows that he who is disquieted at any one's scorn would value that person's admiration.

XIV

Such madness possesses some men that they imagine it possible for an affront to be put upon them by a woman. What matters it who she may be, how many slaves bear her litter, how heavily her ears are laden, how soft her seat? she is always the same thoughtless creature, and unless she possesses acquired knowledge and much learning, she is fierce and passionate in her desires. Some are annoyed at being jostled by a heater of curling-tongs, and call the reluctance of a great man's porter to open the door, the pride of his nomenclator,[5] or the disdainfulness of his chamberlain, insults. O! what laughter is to be got out of such things, with what amusement the mind may be filled when it contrasts the frantic follies of others with its own peace! "How then? will the wise man not approach doors which are kept by a surly porter?" Nay, if any need calls him thither, he will make trial of him, how- ever fierce he may be, will tame him as one tames a dog by offering it food, and will not be enraged at having to expend entrance-money, reflecting that on certain bridges also one has to pay toll; in like fashion he will pay his fee to whoever farms this revenue of letting in visitors, for he knows that men are wont to buy whatever is offered for sale.[6] A man shows a poor spirit if he is pleased with himself for having answered the porter cavalierly, broken his staff, forced his way into his master's presence, and demanded a whipping for him. He who strives with a man makes himself that man's rival, and must be on equal terms with him before he can overcome him. But what will the wise man do when he receives a cuff? He will do as Cato did when he was struck in the face; he did not flare up and revenge the outrage, he did not even pardon it, but ignored it, showing more magnanimity in not acknowledging it than if he had forgiven it. We will not dwell long upon this point; for who is there who knows not that none of those things which are thought to be good or evil are looked upon by the wise man and by mankind in general in the same manner? He does not regard what all men think low or wretched; he does not follow the people's track, but as the stars move in a path opposite to that of the earth, so he proceeds contrary to the prejudices of all.

---

[5] See note, "De Beneficiis," vi. 33.

[6] Gertz reads "decet emere venalia", "there is no harm in buying what is for sale."

XV

    Cease then to say, "Will not the wise man, then, receive an injury if he be beaten, if his eye be knocked out? will he not receive an insult if he be hooted through the Forum by the foul voices of ruffians? if at a court banquet he be bidden to leave the table and eat with slaves appointed to degrading duties? if he be forced to endure anything else that can be thought of that would gall a high spirit?" However many or however severe these crosses may be, they will all be of the same kind; and if small ones do not affect him, neither will greater ones; if a few do not affect him, neither will more. It is from your own weakness that you form your idea of his colossal mind, and when you have thought how much you yourselves could endure to suffer, you place the limit of the wise man's endurance a little way beyond that. But his virtue has placed him in another region of the universe which has nothing in common with you. Seek out sufferings and all things hard to be borne, repulsive to be heard or seen; he will not be overwhelmed by their combination, and will bear all just as he bears each one of them. He who says that the wise man can bear this and cannot bear that, and restrains his magnanimity within certain limits, does wrong; for Fortune overcomes us unless she is entirely overcome. Think not that this is mere Stoic austerity. Epicurus, whom you adopt as the patron of your laziness, and who, you imagine, always taught what was soft and slothful and conducive to pleasure, said, "Fortune seldom stands in a wise man's way." How near he came to a manly sentiment! Do thou dare to speak more boldly, and clear her out of the way altogether! This is the house of the wise man — narrow, unadorned, without bustle and splendour, the threshold guarded by no porters who marshal the crowd of visitors with a haughtiness proportionate to their bribes — but Fortune cannot cross this open and unguarded threshold. She knows that there is no room for her where there is nothing of hers.

XVI

Now if even Epicurus, who made more concessions to the body than any one, takes a spirited tone with regard to injuries, what can appear beyond belief or beyond the scope of human nature amongst us Stoics? He says that injuries may be endured by the wise man, we say that they do not exist for him. Nor is there any reason why you should declare this to be repugnant to nature. We do not deny that it is an unpleasant thing to be beaten or struck, or to lose one of our limbs, but we say that none of these things are injuries. We do not take away from them the feeling of pain, but the name of "injury," which cannot be received while our virtue is unimpaired. We shall see which of the two is nearest the truth; each of them agree in despising injury. You ask what difference there is between them? All that there is between two very brave gladiators, one of whom conceals his wound and holds his ground, while the other turns round to the shouting populace, gives them to understand that his wound is nothing, and does not permit them to interfere on his behalf. You need not think that it is any great thing about which we differ; the whole gist of the matter, that which alone concerns you, is what both schools of philosophy urge you to do, namely, to despise injuries and insults, which I may call the shadows and outlines of injuries, to despise which does not need a wise man, but merely a sensible one, who can say to himself, "Do these things befall me deservedly or undeservedly? If deservedly, it is not an insult, but a judicial sentence; if undeservedly, then he who does injustice ought to blush, not I. And what is this which is called an insult? Someone has made a joke about the baldness of my head, the weakness of my eyes, the thinness of my legs, the shortness of my stature; what insult is there in telling me that which everyone sees? We laugh when tete-a-tete at the same thing at which we are indignant when it is said before a crowd, and we do not allow others the privilege of saying what we ourselves are wont to say about ourselves; we are amused at decorous jests, but are angry if they are carried too far."

XVII

Chrysippus says that a man was enraged because someone called him a sea-sheep; we have seen Fidus Cornelius, the son-in-law of Ovidius Naso, weeping in the Senate-house because Corbulo called him a plucked ostrich; his command of his countenance did not fail him at other abusive charges, which damaged his character and way of life; at this ridiculous saying he burst into tears. So deplorable is the weakness of men's minds when reason no longer guides them. What of our taking offence if any one imitates our talk, our walk, or apes any defect of our person or our pronunciation? as if they would become more notorious by another's imitation than by our doing them ourselves. Some are unwilling to hear about their age and grey hairs, and all the rest of what men pray to arrive at. The reproach of poverty agonizes some men, and whoever conceals it makes it a reproach to himself; and therefore if you of your own accord are the first to acknowledge it, you cut the ground from under the feet of those who would sneer and politely insult you; no one is laughed at who begins by laughing at himself. Tradition tells us that Vatinius, a man born both to be laughed at and hated, was a witty and clever jester. He made many jokes about his feet and his short neck, and thus escaped the sarcasms of Cicero above all, and of his other enemies, of whom he had more than he had diseases. If he, who through constant abuse had forgotten how to blush, could do this by sheer brazenness, why should not he who has made some progress in the education of a gentleman and the study of philosophy? Besides, it is a sort of revenge to spoil a man's enjoyment of the insult he has offered to us; such men say, "Dear me, I suppose he did not understand it." Thus the success of an insult lies in the sensitiveness and rage of the victim; hereafter the insulter will sometimes meet his match; someone will be found to revenge you also.

XVIII

Gaius Caesar, among the other vices with which he overflowed, was possessed by a strange insolent passion for marking every one with some note of ridicule, he himself being the most tempting subject for derision; so ugly was the paleness which proved him mad, so savage the glare of the eyes which lurked under his old woman's brow, so hideous his misshapen head, bald and dotted about with a few cherished hairs; besides the neck set thick with bristles, his thin legs, his monstrous feet. It would be endless were I to mention all the insults which he heaped upon his parents and ancestors, and people of every class of life. I will mention those which brought him to ruin. An especial friend of his was Asiaticus Valerius, a proud-spirited man and one hardly likely to put up with another's insults quietly. At a drinking bout, that is, a public assembly, Gaius, at the top of his voice, reproached this man with the way his wife behaved in bed. Good gods! that a man should hear that the emperor knew this, and that he, the emperor, should describe his adultery and his disappointment to the lady's husband, I do not say to a man of consular rank and his own friend. Chaerea, on the other hand, the military tribune, had a voice not befitting his prowess, feeble in sound, and somewhat suspicious unless you knew his achievements. When he asked for the watchword Gaius at one time gave him "Venus," and at another "Priapus," and by various means reproached the man-at-arms with effeminate vice; while he himself was dressed in transparent clothes, wearing sandals and jewellery. Thus he forced him to use his sword, that he might not have to ask for the watchword oftener; it was Chaerea who first of all the conspirators raised his hand, who cut through the middle of Caligula's neck with one blow. After that, many swords, belonging to men who had public or private injuries to avenge, were thrust into his body, but he first showed himself a man who seemed least like one. The same Gaius construed everything as an insult (since those who are most eager to offer affronts are least able to endure them). He was angry with Herennius Macer for having greeted him as Gaius—nor did the chief centurion of triarii get off scot-free for having saluted him as Caligula; having been born in the camp and brought up as the child of the legions, he had been wont to be called by this name, nor was there any by which he was better known to the troops, but by this time he held "Caligula" to be a reproach and a dishonour. Let wounded spirits, then, console themselves with this reflexion, that, even though our easy temper may have neglected to revenge itself, nevertheless that there will be someone who will punish the impertinent, proud, and insulting man, for these are vices which he never confines to one victim or one single offensive act. Let us look at the examples of those men whose endurance we admire, as, for instance, that of Socrates, who took in good part the published and acted jibes of the comedians upon himself, and laughed no less than he did when he was drenched with dirty water by his wife Xanthippe. Antisthenes was reproached with his mother being a barbarian and a Thracian; he answered that the mother of the gods, too, came from Mount Ida.

XIX

We ought not to engage in quarrels and wrangling; we ought to betake ourselves far away and to disregard everything of this kind which thoughtless people do (indeed thoughtless people alone do it), and to set equal value upon the honours and the reproaches of the mob; we ought not to be hurt by the one or to be pleased by the other. Otherwise we shall neglect many essential points, shall desert our duty both to the state and in private life through excessive fear of insults or weariness of them, and sometimes we shall even miss what would do us good, while tortured by this womanish pain at hearing something not to our mind. Sometimes, too, when enraged with powerful men we shall expose this failing by our reckless freedom of speech; yet it is not freedom to suffer nothing — we are mistaken — freedom consists in raising one's mind superior to injuries and becoming a person whose pleasures come from himself alone, in separating oneself from external circumstances that one may not have to lead a disturbed life in fear of the laughter and tongues of all men; for if any man can offer an insult, who is there who cannot? The wise man and the would-be wise man will apply different remedies to this; for it is only those whose philosophical education is incomplete, and who still guide themselves by public opinion, who would suppose that they ought to spend their lives in the midst of insults and injuries; yet all things happen in a more endurable fashion to men who are prepared for them. The nobler a man is by birth, by reputation, or by inheritance, the more bravely he should bear himself, remembering that the tallest men stand in the front rank in battle. As for insults, offensive language, marks of disgrace, and such-like disfigurements, he ought to bear them as he would bear the shouts of the enemy, and darts or stones flung from a distance, which rattle upon his helmet without causing a wound; while he should look upon injuries as wounds, some received on his armour and others on his body, which he endures without falling or even leaving his place in the ranks. Even though you be hard pressed and violently attacked by the enemy, still it is base to give way; hold the post assigned to you by nature. You ask, what this post is? it is that of being a man. The wise man has another help, of the opposite kind to this; you are hard at work, while he has already won the victory. Do not quarrel with your own good advantage, and, until you shall have made your way to the truth, keep alive this hope in your minds, be willing to receive the news of a better life, and encourage it by your admiration and your prayers; it is to the interest of the commonwealth of mankind that there should be someone who is unconquered, someone against whom fortune has no power.

Of Anger – Book I

I

YOU have demanded of me, Novatus, that I should write how anger may be soothed, and it appears to me that you are right in feeling especial fear of this passion, which is above all others hideous and wild: for the others have some alloy of peace and quiet, but this consists wholly in action and the impulse of grief, raging with an utterly inhuman lust for arms, blood and tortures, careless of itself provided it hurts another, rushing upon the very point of the sword, and greedy for revenge even when it drags the avenger to ruin with itself. Some of the wisest of men have in consequence of this called anger a short madness: for it is equally devoid of self control, regardless of decorum, forgetful of kinship, obstinately engrossed in whatever it begins to do, deaf to reason and advice, excited by trifling causes, awkward at perceiving what is true and just, and very like a falling rock which breaks itself to pieces upon the very thing which it crushes. That you may know that they whom anger possesses are not sane, look at their appearance; for as there are distinct symptoms which mark madmen, such as a bold and menacing air, a gloomy brow, a stern face, a hurried walk, restless hands, changed colour, quick and strongly-drawn breathing; the signs of angry men, too, are the same: their eyes blaze and sparkle, their whole face is a deep red with the blood which boils up from the bottom of their heart, their lips quiver, their teeth are set, their hair bristles and stands on end, their breath is laboured and hissing, their joints crack as they twist them about, they groan, bellow, and burst into scarcely intelligible talk, they often clap their hands together and stamp on the ground with their feet, and their whole body is highly-strung and plays those tricks which mark a distraught mind, so as to furnish an ugly and shocking picture of self-perversion and excitement. You cannot tell whether this vice is more execrable or more disgusting. Other vices can be concealed and cherished in secret; anger shows itself openly and appears in the countenance, and the greater it is, the more plainly it boils forth. Do you not see how in all animals certain signs appear before they proceed to mischief, and how their entire bodies put off their usual quiet appearance and stir up their ferocity? Boars foam at the mouth and sharpen their teeth by rubbing them against trees, bulls toss their horns in the air and scatter the sand with blows of their feet, lions growl, the necks of enraged snakes swell, mad dogs have a sullen look — there is no animal so hateful and venomous by nature that it does not, when seized by anger, show additional fierceness. I know well that the other passions, can hardly be concealed, and that lust, fear, and boldness give signs of their presence and may be discovered beforehand, for there is no one of the. stronger passions that does not affect the countenance: what then is the difference between them and anger? Why, that the other passions are visible, but that this is conspicuous.

II

Next, if you choose to view its results and the mischief that it does, no plague has cost the human race more dear: you will see slaughterings and poisonings, accusations and counter-accusations, sacking of cities, ruin of whole peoples, the persons of princes sold into slavery by auction, torches applied to roofs, and fires not merely confined within city-walls but making whole tracts of country glow with hostile flame. See the foundations of the most celebrated cities hardly now to be discerned; they were ruined by anger. See deserts extending for many miles without an inhabitant: they have been desolated by anger. See all the chiefs whom tradition mentions as instances of ill fate; anger stabbed one of them in his bed, struck down another, though he was protected by the sacred rights of hospitality, tore another to pieces in the very home of the laws and in sight of the crowded forum, bade one shed his own blood by the parricide hand of his son, another to have his royal throat cut by the hand of a slave, another to stretch out his limbs on the cross: and hitherto I am speaking merely of individual cases. What, if you were to pass from the consideration of those single men against whom anger has broken out to view whole assemblies cut down by the sword, the people butchered by the soldiery let loose upon it, and whole nations condemned to death in one common ruin . ..."[1] as though by men who either freed themselves from our charge or despised our authority? Why, wherefore is the people angry with gladiators, and so unjust as to think itself wronged if they do not die cheerfully? It thinks itself scorned, and by looks, gestures, and excitement turns itself from a mere spectator into an adversary. Everything of this sort is not anger, but the semblance of anger, like that of boys who want to beat the ground when they have fallen upon it, and who often do not even know why they are angry, but are merely angry without any reason or having received any injury, yet not without some semblance of injury received, or without some wish to exact a penalty for it. Thus they are deceived by the likeness of blows, and are appeased

---

[1] Here a leaf or more has been lost, including the fragment cited in Lactantius, De ira dei, 17 Ira est cupiditas, &c. The entire passage is: — "But the Stoics did not perceive that there is a difference between right and wrong; that there is just and unjust anger: and as they could find no remedy for it, they wished to extirpate it. The Peripatetics, on the other hand, declared that it ought not to be destroyed, but restrained. These I have sufficiently answered in the sixth book of my Institutiones. It is clear that the philosophers did not comprehend the reason of anger, from the definitions of it which Seneca has enumerated in the books 'On Anger' which he has written. 'Anger,' he says, 'is the desire of avenging an injury.' Others, as Posidonius says, call it 'a desire to punish one by whom you think that you have been unjustly injured.' Some have defined it thus, 'Anger is an impulse of the mind to injure him who either has injured you or has sought to injure you.' Aristotle's definition differs but little from our own. He says, 'that anger is a desire to repay suffering,'" etc.

by the pretended tears of those who deprecate their wrath, and thus an unreal grief is healed by an unreal revenge.

III

"We often are angry," says our adversary, "not with men who have hurt us, but with men who are going to hurt us: so you may be sure that anger is not born of injury." It is true that we are angry with those who are going to hurt us, but they do already hurt us in intention, and one who is going to do an injury is already doing it. "The weakest of men," argues he, " are often angry with the most powerful: so you may be sure that anger is not a desire to punish their antagonist — for men do not desire to punish him when they cannot hope to do so." In the first place, I spoke of a desire to inflict punishment, not a power to do so: now men desire even what they cannot obtain. In the next place, no one is so low in station as not to be able to hope to inflict punishment even upon the greatest of men: we all are powerful for mischief. Aristotle's definition differs little from mine: for he declares anger to be a desire to repay suffering. It would be a long task to examine the differences between his definition and mine: it may be urged against both of them that wild beasts become angry without being excited by injury, and without any idea of punishing others or requiting them with pain: for, even though they do these things, these are not what they aim at doing. We must admit, however, that neither wild beasts nor any other creature except man is subject to anger: for, whilst anger is the foe of reason, it nevertheless does not arise in any place where reason cannot dwell. Wild beasts have impulses, fury, cruelty, combativeness : they have not anger any more than they have luxury: yet they indulge in some pleasures with less self-control than human beings. Do not believe the poet who says:

"The boar his wrath forgets, the stag forgets the hounds,The bear forgets how 'midst the herd he leaped with frantic bounds."[2] When he speaks of beasts being angry he means that they are excited, roused up: for indeed they know no more how to be angry than they know how to pardon. Dumb creatures have not human feelings, but have certain impulses which resemble them: for if it were not so, if they could feel love and hate, they would likewise be capable of friendship and enmity, of disagreement and agreement. Some traces of these qualities exist even in them, though properly all of them, whether good or bad, belong to the human breast alone. To no creature besides man has been given wisdom, foresight, industry, and reflexion. To animals not only human virtues but even human vices are forbidden: their whole constitution, mental and bodily, is unlike that of human beings: in them the royal[3] and leading

---

[2] Ovid, "Met." vii. 545-6.

[3] τό ἡγεμονικόν of the Stoics.

principle is drawn from another source, as, for instance, they possess a voice, yet not a clear one, but indistinct and incapable of forming words: a tongue, but one which is fettered and not sufficiently nimble for complex movements: so, too, they possess intellect, the greatest attribute of all, but in a rough and inexact condition. It is, consequently, able to grasp those visions and semblances which rouse it to action, but only in a cloudy and indistinct fashion. It follows from this that their impulses and outbreaks are violent, and that they do not feel fear, anxieties, grief, or anger, but some semblances of these feelings: wherefore they quickly drop them and adopt the converse of them : they graze after showing the most vehement rage and terror, and after frantic bellowing and plunging they straightway sink into quiet sleep.

IV

What anger is has been sufficiently explained. The difference between it and irascibility is evident: it is the same as that between a drunken man and a drunkard; between a frightened man and a coward. It is possible for an angry man not to be irascible ; an irascible man may sometimes not be angry. I shall omit the other varieties of anger, which the Greeks distinguish by various names, because we have no distinctive words for them in our language, although we call men bitter and harsh, and also peevish, frantic, clamorous, surly and fierce: all of which are different forms of irascibility. Among these you may class sulkiness, a refined form of irascibility; for there are some sorts of anger which go no further than noise, while some are as lasting as they are common: some are fierce in deed, but inclined to be sparing of words: some expend themselves in bitter words and curses: some do not go beyond complaining and turning one's back: some are great, deep-seated, and brood within a man: there are a thousand other forms of a multiform evil.

V

We have now finished our enquiry as to what anger is, whether it exists in any other creature besides man, what the difference is between it and irascibility, and how many forms it possesses. Let us now enquire whether anger be in accordance with nature, and whether it be useful and worth entertaining in some measure.

Whether it be according to nature will become evident if we consider man's nature, than which what is more gentle while it is in its proper condition? Yet what is more cruel than anger? What is more affectionate to others than man? Yet what is more savage against them than anger? Mankind is born for mutual assistance, anger for mutual ruin: the former loves society, the latter estrangement. The one loves to do good, the other to do harm ; the one to help even strangers, the other to attack even its dearest friends. The one is ready even to sacrifice itself for the good of others, the other to plunge into peril provided it drags others with it. Who, then, can be more ignorant of nature than he who classes this cruel and hurtful vice as belonging to her best and most polished work? Anger, as we have said, is eager to punish; and that such a desire should exist in man's peaceful breast is least of all according to his nature; for human life is founded on brnefits and harmony and is bound together into an alliance for the common help of all, not by terror, but by love towards one another.

VI

"What, then? Is not correction sometimes necessary?" Of course it is; but with discretion, not with anger; for it does not injure, but heals under the guise of injury. We char crooked spearshafts to straighten them, and force them by driving in wedges, not in order to break them, but to take the bends out of them; and, in like manner, by applying pain to the body or mind we correct dispositions which have been rendered crooked by vice. So the physician at first, when dealing with slight disorders, tries not to make much change in his patient's daily habits, to regulate his food, drink, and exercise, and to improve his health merely by altering the order in which he takes them. The next step is to see whether an alteration in their amount will be of service. If neither alteration of the order or of the amount is of use, he cuts off some and reduces others. If even this does not answer, he forbids food, and disburdens the body by fasting. If milder remedies have proved useless he opens a vein; if the extremities are injuring the body and infecting it with disease he lays his hands upon the limbs; yet none of his treatment is considered harsh if its result is to give health. Similarly, it is the duty of the chief administrator of the laws, or the ruler of a state, to correct ill-disposed men, as long as he is able, with words, and even with gentle ones, that he may persuade them to do what they ought, inspire them with a love of honour and justice, and cause them to hate vice and set store upon virtue. He must then pass on to severer language, still confining himself to advising and reprimanding; last of all he must betake himself to punishments, yet still making them slight and temporary. He ought to assign extreme punishments only to extreme crimes, that no one may die unless it be even to the criminal's own advantage that he should die. He will differ from the physician in one point alone; for whereas physicians render it easy to die for those to whom they cannot grant the boon of life, he will drive the condemned out of life with ignominy and disgrace, not because he takes pleasure in any man's being punished, for the wise man is far from such inhuman ferocity, but that they may be a warning to all men, and that, since they would not be useful when alive, the state may at any rate profit by their death. Man's nature is not, therefore, desirous of inflicting punishment; neither, therefore, is anger in accordance with man's nature, because that is desirous of inflicting punishment. I will also adduce Plato's argument—for what harm is there in using other men's arguments, so far as they are on our side? "A good man," says he, "does not do any hurt: it is only punishment which hurts. Punishment, therefore, does not accord with a good man: wherefore anger does not do so either, because punishment and anger accord one with another. If a good man takes no pleasure in punishment, he will also take no pleasure in that state of mind to which punishment gives pleasure: consequently anger is not natural to man."

VII

May it not be that, although anger be not natural, it may be right to adopt it, because it often proves useful? It rouses the spirit and excites it; and courage does nothing grand in war without it, unless its flame be supplied from this source; this is the goad which stirs up bold men and sends them to encounter perils. Some therefore consider it to be best to control anger, not to banish it utterly, but to cut off its extravagances, and force it to keep within useful bounds, so as to retain that part of it without which action will become languid and all strength and activity of mind will die away.

In the first place, it is easier to banish dangerous passions than to rule them; it is easier not to admit them than to keep them in order when admitted; for when they have established themselves in possession of the mind they are more powerful than the lawful ruler, and will in no wise permit themselves to be weakened or abridged. In the next place, Reason herself, who holds the reins, is only strong while she remains apart from the passions; if she mixes and befouls herself with them she becomes no longer able to restrain those whom she might once have cleared out of her path; for the mind, when once excited and shaken up, goes whither the passions drive it. There are certain things whose beginnings lie in our own power, but which, when developed, drag us along by their own force and leave us no retreat. Those who have flung themselves over a precipice have no control over their movements, nor can they stop or slacken their pace when once started, for their own headlong and irremediable rashness has left no room for either reflexion or remorse, and they cannot help going to lengths which they might have avoided. So, also, the mind, when it has abandoned itself to anger, love, or any other passion, is unable to check itself: its own weight and the downward tendency of vices must needs carry the man off and hurl him into the lowest depth.

VIII

The best plan is to reject straightway the first incentives to anger, to resist its very beginnings, and to take care not to be betrayed into it: for if once it begins to carry us away, it is hard to get back again into a healthy condition, because reason goes for nothing when once passion has been admitted to the mind, and has by our own free will been given a certain authority, it will for the future do as much as it chooses, not only as much as you will allow it. The enemy, I repeat, must be met and driven back at the outermost frontier-line: for when he has once entered the city and passed its gates, he will not allow his prisoners to set bounds to his victory. The mind does not stand apart and view its passions from without, so as not to permit them to advance further than they ought, but it is itself changed into a passion, and is therefore unable to check what once was useful and wholesome strength, now that it has become degenerate and misapplied: for passion and reason, as I said before, have not distinct and separate provinces, but consist of the changes of the mind itself for better or for worse. How then can reason recover itself when it is conquered and held down by vices, when it has given way to anger? or how can it extricate itself from a confused mixture, the greater part of which consists of the lower qualities ? "But," argues our adversary, "some men when in anger control themselves." Do they so far control themselves that they do nothing which anger dictates, or somewhat? If they do nothing thereof, it becomes evident that anger is not essential to the conduct of affairs, although your sect advocated it as possessing greater strength than reason Finally, I ask, is anger stronger or weaker than reason? If stronger, how can reason impose any check upon it, since it is only the less powerful that obey: if weaker, then reason is competent to effect its ends without anger, and does not need the help of a less powerful quality. "But some angry men remain consistent and control themselves." When do they do so? It is when their anger is disappearing and leaving them of its own accord, not when it was red-hot, for then it was more powerful than they. "What then? do not men, even in the height of their anger, sometimes let their enemies go whole and unhurt, and refrain from injuring them?" They do: but when do they do so? It is when one passion overpowers another, and either fear or greed gets the upper hand for a while. On such occasions, it is not thanks to reason that anger is stilled, but owing to an untrustworthy and fleeting truce between the passions.

IX

In the next place, anger has nothing useful in itself, and does not rouse up the mind to warlike deeds: for a virtue, being self-sufficient, never needs the assistance of a vice: whenever it needs an impetuous effort, it does not become angry, but rises to the occasion, and excites or soothes itself as far as it deems requisite, just as the machines which hurl darts may be twisted to a greater or lesser degree of tension at the manager's pleasure. "Anger," says Aristotle, "is necessary, nor can any fight be won without it, unless it fills the mind, and kindles up the spirit. It must, however, be made use of, not as a general, but as a soldier." Now this is untrue; for if it listens to reason and follows whither reason leads, it is no longer anger, whose characteristic is obstinacy: if, again, it is disobedient and will not be quiet when ordered, but is carried away by its own willful and headstrong spirit, it is then as useless an aid to the mind as a soldier who disregards the sounding of the retreat would be to a general. If, therefore, anger allows limits to be imposed upon it, it must be called by some other name, and ceases to be anger, which I understand to be unbridled and unmanageable: and if it does not allow limits to be imposed upon it, it is harmful and not to be counted among aids: wherefore either anger is not anger, or it is useless: for if any man demands the infliction of punishment, not because he is eager for the punishment itself, but because it is right to inflict it, he ought not to be counted as an angry man: that will be the useful soldier, who knows how to obey orders: the passions cannot obey any more than they can command.

X

For this cause reason will never call to its aid blind and fierce impulses, over whom she herself possesses no authority, and which she never can restrain save by setting against them similar and equally powerful passions, as for example, fear against anger, anger against sloth, greed against timidity. May virtue never come to such a pass, that reason should fly for aid to vices! The mind can find no safe repose there, it must needs be shaken and tempest-tossed if it be safe only because of its own defects, if it cannot be brave without anger, diligent without greed, quiet without fear: such is the despotism under which a man must live if he becomes the slave of a passion. Are you not ashamed to put virtues under the patronage of vices? Then, too, reason ceases to have any power if she can do nothing without passion, and begins to be equal and like unto passion; for what difference is there between them if passion without reason be as rash as reason without passion is helpless? They are both on the same level, if one cannot exist without the other. Yet who could endure that passion should be made equal to reason? "Then," says our adversary, "passion is useful, provided it be moderate." Nay, only if it be useful by nature: but if it be disobedient to authority and reason, all that we gain by its moderation is that the less there is of it, the less harm it does: wherefore a moderate passion is nothing but a moderate evil.

XI

"But," argues he, "against our enemies anger is necessary." In no case is it less necessary; since our attacks ought not to be disorderly, but regulated and under control. What, indeed, is it except anger, so ruinous to itself, that overthrows barbarians, who have so much more bodily strength than we, and are so much better able to endure fatigue? Gladiators, too, protect themselves by skill, but expose themselves to wounds when they are angry. Moreover, of what use is anger, when the same end can be arrived at by reason? Do you suppose that a hunter is angry with the beasts he kills? Yet he meets them when they attack him, and follows them when they flee from him, all of which is managed by reason without anger. When so many thousands of Cimbri and Teutones poured over the Alps, what was it that caused them to perish so completely, that no messenger, only common rumour, carried the news of that great defeat to their homes, except that with them anger stood in the place of courage? and anger, although sometimes it overthrows and breaks to pieces whatever it meets, yet is more often its own destruction. Who can be braver than the Germans? who charge more boldly? who have more love of arms, among which they are born and bred, for which alone they care, to the neglect of everything else? Who can be more hardened to undergo every hardship, since a large part of them have no store of clothing for the body, no shelter from the continual rigour of the climate: yet Spaniards and Gauls, and even the unwarlike races of Asia and Syria cut them down before the main legion comes within sight, nothing but their own irascibility exposing them to death. Give but intelligence to those minds, and discipline to those bodies of theirs, which now are ignorant of vicious refinements, luxury, and wealth, — to say nothing more, we should certainly be obliged to go back to the ancient Roman habits of life. By what did Fabius restore the shattered forces of the state, except by knowing how to delay and spin out time, which angry men know not how to do? The empire, which then was at its last gasp, would have perished if Fabius had been as daring as anger urged him to be: but he took thought about the condition of affairs, and after counting his force, no part of which could be lost without everything being lost with it, he laid aside thoughts of grief and revenge, turning his sole attention to what was profitable and to making the most of his opportunities, and conquered his anger before he conquered Hannibal. What did Scipio do? Did he not leave behind Hannibal and the Carthaginian army, and all with whom he had a right to be angry, and carry over the war into Africa with such deliberation that he made his enemies think him luxurious and lazy? What did the second Scipio do? Did he not remain a long, long time before Numantia, and bear with calmness the reproach to himself and to his country that Numantia took longer to conquer than Carthage? By blockading and investing his enemies, he brought them to such straits that they perished by their own swords. Anger, therefore, is not useful even in wars or battles: for it is prone to rashness, and while trying to bring others into danger, does not guard itself against danger. The most trustworthy virtue is that which long and carefully considers itself, controls itself, and slowly and deliberately brings itself to the front.

XII

"What, then," asks our adversary, "is a good man not to be angry if he sees his father murdered or his mother outraged?" No, he will not be angry, but will avenge them, or protect them. Why do you fear that filial piety will not prove a sufficient spur to him even without anger? You may as well say — "What then? When a good man sees his father or his son being cut down, I suppose he will not weep or faint," as we see women do whenever any trifling rumour of danger reaches them. The good man will do his duty without disturbance or fear, and he will perform the duty of a good man, so as to do nothing unworthy of a man. My father will be murdered: then I will defend him: he has been slain, then I will avenge him, not because I am grieved, but because it is my duty. "Good men are made angry by injuries done to their friends." When you say this, Theophrastus, you seek to throw discredit upon more manly maxims; you leave the judge and appeal to the mob: because everyone is angry when such things befall his own friends, you suppose that men will decide that it is their duty to do what they do: for as a rule every man considers a passion which he recognises to be a righteous one. But he does the same thing if the hot water is not ready for his drink, if a glass be broken, or his shoe splashed with mud. It is not filial piety, but weakness of mind that produces this anger, as children weep when they lose their parents, just as they do when they lose their toys. To feel anger on behalf of one's friends does not show a loving, but a weak mind: it is admirable and worthy conduct to stand forth as the defender of one's parents, children, friends, and countrymen, at the call of duty itself, acting of one's own free will, forming a deliberate judgment, and looking forward to the future, not in an impulsive, frenzied fashion. No passion is more eager for revenge than anger, and for that very reason it is unapt to obtain it: being over hasty and frantic, like almost all desires, it hinders itself in the attainment of its own object, and therefore has never been useful either in peace or war: for it makes peace like war, and when in arms forgets that Mars belongs to neither side, and falls into the power of the enemy, because it is not in its own. In the next place, vices ought not to be received into common use because on some occasions they have effected somewhat: for so also fevers are good for certain kinds of ill-health, but nevertheless it is better to be altogether free from them: it is a hateful mode of cure to owe one's health to disease. Similarly, although anger, like poison, or falling headlong, or being shipwrecked, may have unexpectedly done good, yet it ought not on that account to be classed as wholesome, for poisons have often proved good for the health.

XIII

Moreover, qualities which we ought to possess become better and more desirable the more extensive they are: if justice is a good thing, no one will say that it would be better if any part were subtracted from it; if bravery is a good thing, no one would wish it to be in any way curtailed: consequently the greater anger is, the better it is, for whoever objected to a good thing being increased? But it is not expedient that anger should be increased: therefore it is not expedient that it should exist at all, for that which grows bad by increase cannot be a good thing. "Anger is useful," says our adversary, "because it makes men more ready to fight." According to that mode of reasoning, then, drunkenness also is a good thing, for it makes men insolent and daring, and many use their weapons better when the worse for liquor: nay, according to that reasoning, also, you may call frenzy and madness essential to strength, because madness often makes men stronger. Why, does not fear often by the rule of contraries make men bolder, and does not the terror of death rouse up even arrant cowards to join battle? Yet anger, drunkenness, fear, and the like, are base and temporary incitements to action, and can furnish no arms to virtue, which has no need of vices, although they may at times be of some little assistance to sluggish and cowardly minds. No man becomes braver through anger, except one who without anger would not have been brave at all: anger does not therefore come to assist courage, but to take its place. What are we to say to the argument that, if anger were a good thing it would attach itself to all the best men? Yet the most irascible of creatures are infants, old men, and sick people. Every weakling is naturally prone to complaint.

XIV

It is impossible, says Theophrastus, for a good man not to be angry with bad men. By this reasoning, the better a man is, the more irascible he will be: yet will he not rather be more tranquil, more free from passions, and hating no one: indeed, what reason has he for hating sinners, since it is error that leads them into such crimes? now it does not become a sensible man to hate the erring, since if so he will hate himself: let him think how many things he does contrary to good morals, how much of what he has done stands in need of pardon, and he will soon become angry with himself also, for no righteous judge pronounces a different judgment in his own case and in that of others. No one, I affirm, will be found who can acquit himself. Every one when he calls himself innocent looks rather to external witnesses than to his own conscience. How much more philanthropic it is to deal with the erring in a gentle and fatherly spirit, and to call them into the right course instead of hunting them down? When a man is wandering about our fields because he has lost his way, it is better to place him on the right path than to drive him away.

XV

The sinner ought, therefore, to be corrected both by warning and by force, both by gentle and harsh means, and may be made a better man both towards himself and others by chastisement, but not by anger: for who is angry with the patient whose wounds he is tending? "But they cannot be corrected, and there is nothing in them that is gentle or that admits of good hope." Then let them be removed from mortal society, if they are likely to deprave everyone with whom they come in contact, and let them cease to be bad men in the only way in which they can: yet let this be done without hatred: for what reason have I for hating the man to whom I am doing the greatest good, since I am rescuing him from himself? Does a man hate his own limbs when he cuts them off? That is not an act of anger, but a lamentable method of healing. We knock mad dogs on the head, we slaughter fierce and savage bulls, and we doom scabby sheep to the knife, lest they should infect our flocks: we destroy monstrous births, and we also drown our children if they are born weakly or unnaturally formed; to separate what is useless from what is sound is an act, not of anger, but of reason. Nothing becomes one who inflicts punishment less than anger, because the punishment has all the more power to work reformation if the sentence be pronounced with deliberate judgment. This is why Socrates said to the slave, "I would strike you, were I not angry." He put off the correction of the slave to a calmer season; at the moment, he corrected himself. Who can boast that he has his passions under control, when Socrates did not dare to trust himself to his anger?

XVI

We do not, therefore, need an angry chastiser to punish the erring and wicked: for since anger is a crime of the mind, it is not right that sins should be punished by sin. "What! am I not to be angry with a robber, or a poisoner?" No: for I am not angry with myself when I bleed myself. I apply all kinds of punishment as remedies. You are as yet only in the first stage of error, and do not go wrong seriously, although you do so often: then I will try to amend you by a reprimand given first in private and then in public.[4] You, again, have gone too far to be restored to virtue by words alone; you must be kept in order by disgrace. For the next, some stronger measure is required, something that he can feel must be branded upon him; you, sir, shall be sent into exile and to a desert place. The next man's thorough villainy needs harsher remedies: chains and public imprisonment must be applied to him. You, lastly, have an incurably vicious mind, and add crime to crime: you have come to such a pass, that you are not influenced by the arguments which are never wanting to recommend evil, but sin itself is to you a sufficient reason for sinning: you have so steeped your whole heart in wickedness, that wickedness cannot be taken from you without bringing your heart with it. Wretched man! you have long sought to die; we will do you good service, we will take away that madness from which you suffer, and to you who have so long lived a misery to yourself and to others, we will give the only good thing which remains, that is, death. Why should I be angry with a man just when I am doing him good: sometimes the truest form of compassion is to put a man to death. If I were a skilled and learned physician, and were to enter a hospital, or a rich[5] man's house, I should not have prescribed the same treatment for all the patients who were suffering from various diseases. I see different kinds of vice in the vast number of different minds, and am called in to heal the whole body of citizens: let us seek for the remedies proper for each disease. This man may be cured by his own sense of honour, that one by travel, that one by pain, that one by want, that one by the

---

[4] The gospel rule, Matt, xviii. 15.

[5] Divitis (where there might be an army of slaves).

sword. If, therefore, it becomes my duty as a magistrate to put on black[6] robes, and summon an assembly by the sound of a trumpet,[7] I shall walk to the seat of judgment not in a rage or in a hostile spirit, but with the countenance of a judge; I shall pronounce the formal sentence in a grave and gentle rather than a furious voice, and shall bid them proceed sternly, yet not angrily. Even when I command a criminal to be beheaded, when I sew a parricide up in a sack, when I send a man to be punished by military law, when I fling a traitor or public enemy down the Tarpeian Rock, I shall be free from anger, and shall look and feel just as though I were crushing snakes and other venomous creatures. "Anger is necessary to enable us to punish." What? Do you think that the law is angry with men whom it does not know, whom it has never seen, who it hopes will never exist? We ought, therefore, to adopt the law's frame of mind, which does not become angry, but merely defines offences: for, if it is right for a good man to be angry at wicked crimes, it will also be right for him to be moved with envy at the prosperity of wicked men: what, indeed, is more scandalous than that in some cases the very men, for whose deserts no fortune

---

[6] "Lorsque le Preteur devoit prononcer la sentence d'un coupable, il se depouilloit de la robe pretexte, et se revêtoit alors d'une simple tunique, ou d'une autre robe, presque usee, et d'un blanc sale (sordida) ou d'un gris très foncé tirant sur le noir (toga pulla), telle qu'en portoient à Rome le peuple et les pauvres (pullaque paupertas). Dans les jours solemnelles et marqués par un deuil public, les Senateurs quittoient le laticlave, et les Magistrats la pretexte. La pourpre, la hache, les faisceaux, aucun de ces signes extérieurs de leur dignité ne les distinguoient alors des autres citoyens: sine insignibus Magistratus. Mais ce n'étoit pas seulement pendant le temps ou la ville était plongée dans le deuil et dans l'affliction, que les magistrats s'habilloient comme le peuple (sordidam vestem induebant); ils en usoient de même lorsqu'ils devoient condamner à mort un citoyen. C'est dans ces tristes circonstances qu'ils quittoient la prétexte et prenoient la robe de deuil: perversam vestem. (No doubt "inside out."—J. E. B. M.) "On pourrait supposer avec assez de vraisemblance que par cette expression, Séneque a voulu faire allusion à ce changement...... Peut-être les Magistrats qui devoient juger à mort un citoyen, portoient ils aussi leur robe renversée, ou la jettoient ils de travers ou confusément sur leurs épaules, pour mieux peindre par ce desordre le trouble de leur esprit. Si cette conjecture est vraie, comme je serais assez porté à croire, l'expression perversa vestis, dont Séneque s'est servi ici, indiqueroit plus d'un simple changement d'habit," &c. (La Grange's translation of Seneca, edited by J. A. Naigeon. Paris, 1778,)

[7] "Ceci fait allusion à une coutume que Caius Gracchus prétend avoir été pratiquée de tout tems à Rome. 'Lorsqu'un citoyen,'" dit il, "avoit un procès criminel qui alloit à la mort, s'il refusoit d'obéir aux sommations qui lui étoient faites; le jour qu'on devoit le juger, en envoyoit des le matin à la porte de sa maison un Officier l'appeller au son de la trompette, et jamais avant que cette cérémonie eût été observée, les Juges ne donneroient leur voix contre lui: tant ces hommes sages,' ajoute ce hardi Tribun, 'avoient de retenue et de precaution dans leurs jugements, quand il s'agissoit de la vie d'un citoyen.'" "C'étoit de même au son de la trompette que l'on convoquoit le peuple, lorsqu'on devoit faire mourir un citoyen, afin qu'il fût témoin de ce triste spectacle, et que la supplice du coupable pût lui servir d'exemple. Tacite dit qu'un Astrologue, nommé P. Marcius, fût exécuté, selon l'ancien usage, hors de la porte Esquiline, en presence du peuple Romain que les Consuls firent convoquer au son de la trompette. (Tac. Ann. II. 32.) L. Grom.

could be found bad enough, should flourish and actually be the spoiled children of success? Yet he will see their affluence without envy, just as he sees their crimes without anger: a good judge condemns wrongful acts, but does not hate them. "What then? when the wise man is dealing with something of this kind, will his mind not be affected by it and become excited beyond its usual wont?" I admit that it will: he will experience a slight and trifling emotion; for, as Zeno says, "Even in the mind of the wise man, a scar remains after the wound is quite healed." He will, therefore, feel certain hints and semblances of passions; but he will be free from the passions themselves.

XVII

Aristotle says that "certain passions, if one makes a proper use of them, act as arms ": which would be true if, like weapons of war, they could be taken up or laid aside at the pleasure of their wielder. These arms, which Aristotle assigns to virtue, fight of their own accord, do not wait to be seized by the hand, and possess a man instead of being possessed by him. We have no need of external weapons, nature has equipped us sufficiently by giving us reason. She has bestowed this weapon upon us, which is strong, imperishable, and obedient to our will, not uncertain or capable of being turned against its master. Reason suffices by itself not merely to take thought for the future, but to manage our affairs:[8] what, then, can be more foolish than for reason to beg anger for protection, that is, for what is certain to beg of what is uncertain? what is trustworthy of what is faithless? what is whole of what is sick? What, indeed? since reason is far more powerful by itself even in performing those operations in which the help of anger seems especially needful: for when reason has decided that a particular thing should be done, she perseveres in doing it; not being able to find anything better than herself to exchange with. She, therefore, abides by her purpose when it has once been formed; whereas anger is often overcome by pity: for it possesses no firm strength, but merely swells like an empty bladder, and makes a violent beginning, just like the winds which rise from the earth and are caused by rivers and marshes, which blow furiously without any continuance: anger begins with a mighty rush, and then falls away, becoming fatigued too soon: that which but lately thought of nothing but cruelty and novel forms of torture, is become quite softened and gentle when the time comes for punishment to be inflicted. Passion soon cools, whereas reason is always consistent: yet even in cases where anger has continued to burn, it often happens that although there may be many who deserve to die, yet after the death of two or three it ceases to slay. Its first onset is fierce, just as the teeth of snakes when first roused from their lair are venomous, but become harmless after repeated bites have exhausted their poison. Consequently those who are equally guilty are not equally punished, and often he who has done less is punished more, because he fell in the way of anger when it was fresher. It is altogether irregular; at one time it runs into undue excess, at another it falls short of its duty: for it indulges its own feelings and gives sentence according to its caprices, will not listen to evidence, allows the defence no opportunity of being heard, clings to what it has wrongly assumed, and will not suffer its opinion to be wrested from it, even when it is a mistaken

---

[8] i.e., not only for counsel, but for action

one.

XVIII

Reason gives each side time to plead; moreover, she herself demands adjournment, that she may have sufficient scope for the discovery of the truth; whereas anger is in a hurry: reason wishes to give a just decision; anger wishes its decision to be thought just: reason looks no further than the matter in hand; anger is excited by empty matters hovering on the outskirts of the case: it is irritated by anything approaching to a confident demeanour, a loud voice, an unrestrained speech, dainty apparel, high-flown pleading, or popularity with the public. It often condemns a man because it dislikes his patron; it loves and maintains error even when truth is staring it in the face. It hates to be proved wrong, and thinks it more honourable to persevere in a mistaken line of conduct than to retract it. I remember Gnaeus Piso, a man who was free from many vices, yet of a perverse disposition, and one who mistook harshness for consistency. In his anger he ordered a soldier to be led off to execution because he had returned from furlough without his comrade, as though he must have murdered him if he could not show him. When the man asked for time for search, he would not grant it: the condemned man was brought outside the rampart, and was just offering his neck to the axe, when suddenly there appeared his comrade who was thought to be slain. Hereupon the centurion in charge of the execution bade the guardsman sheathe his sword, and led the condemned man back to Piso, to restore to him the innocence which Fortune had restored to the soldier. They were led into his presence by their fellow soldiers amid the great joy of the whole camp, embracing one another and accompanied by a vast crowd. Piso mounted the tribunal in a fury and ordered them both to be executed, both him who had not murdered and him who had not been slain. What could be more unworthy than this? Because one was proved to be innocent, two perished. Piso even added a third: for he actually ordered the centurion, who had brought back the condemned man, to be put to death. Three men were set up to die in the same place because one was innocent. O, how clever is anger at inventing reasons for its frenzy! "You," it says, "I order to be executed, because you have been condemned to death: you, because you have been the cause of your comrade's condemnation, and you, because when ordered to put him to death you disobeyed your general." He discovered the means of charging them with three crimes, because he could find no crime in them.

XIX

Irascibility, I say, has this fault—it is loath to be ruled: it is angry with the truth itself, if it comes to light against its will: it assails those whom it has marked for its victims with shouting and riotous noise and gesticulation of the entire body, together with reproaches and curses. Not thus does reason act: but if it must be so, she silently and quietly wipes out whole households, destroys entire families of the enemies of the state, together with their wives and children, throws down their very dwellings, levels them with the ground, and roots out the names of those who are the foes of liberty. This she does without grinding her teeth or shaking her head, or doing anything unbecoming to a judge, whose countenance ought to be especially calm and composed at the time when he is pronouncing an important sentence. "What need is there," asks Hieronymus, "for you to bite your own lips when you want to strike some one?" What would he have said, had he seen a proconsul leap down from the tribunal, snatch the fasces from the lictor, and tear his own clothes because those of others were not torn as fast as he wished. "Why need you upset the table, throw down the drinking cups, knock yourself against the columns, tear your hair, smite your thigh and your breast? How vehement do you suppose anger to be, if it thus turns back upon itself, because it cannot find vent on another as fast as it wishes? Such men, therefore, are held back by the bystanders and are begged to become reconciled with themselves. But he who while free from anger assigns to each man the penalty which he deserves, does none of these things. He often lets a man go after detecting his crime, if his penitence for what he has done gives good hope for the future, if he perceives that the man's wickedness is not deeply rooted in his mind, but is only, as the saying is, skindeep. He will grant impunity in cases where it will hurt neither the receiver nor the giver. In some cases he will punish great crimes more leniently than lesser ones, if the former were the result of momentary impulse, not of cruelty, while the latter were instinct with secret, under-hand, long-practised craftiness. The same fault, committed by two separate men, will not be visited by him with the same penalty, if the one was guilty of it through carelessness, the other with a premeditated intention of doing mischief. In all dealing with crime he will remember that the one form of punishment is meant to make bad men better, and the other to put them out of the way. In either case he will look to the future, not to the past: for, as Plato says, "no wise man punishes any one because he has sinned, but that he may sin no more: for what is past cannot be recalled, but what is to come may be checked." Those, too, whom he wishes to make examples of the ill success of wickedness, he executes publicly, not merely in order that they themselves may die, but that by dying they may deter others from doing likewise. You see how free from any mental disturbance a man ought to be who has to weigh and consider all this, when he deals with a matter which ought to be handled with the utmost care, I mean, the power of life and death. The sword of justice is ill-placed in the hands of an angry man.

XX

Neither ought it to be believed that anger contributes anything to magnanimity: what it gives is not magnanimity but vain glory. The increase which disease produces in bodies swollen with morbid humours is not healthy growth, but bloated corpulence. All those whose madness raises them above human considerations, believe themselves to be inspired with high and sublime ideas; but there is no solid ground beneath, and what is built without foundation is liable to collapse in ruin. Anger has no ground to stand upon, and does not rise from a firm and enduring foundation, but is a windy, empty quality, as far removed from true magnanimity as fool-hardiness from courage, boastfulness from confidence, gloom from austerity, cruelty from strictness. There is, I say, a great difference between a lofty and a proud mind: anger brings about nothing grand or beautiful. On the other hand, to be constantly irritated seems to me to be the part of a languid and unhappy mind, conscious of its own feebleness, like folk with diseased bodies covered with sores, who cry out at the lightest touch. Anger, therefore, is a vice which for the most part affects women and children. "Yet it affects men also." Because many men, too, have womanish or childish intellects. "But what are we to say? do not some words fall from angry men which appear to flow from a great mind?" Yes, to those who know not what true greatness is: as, for example, that foul and hateful saying, " Let them hate me, provided they fear me," which you may be sure was written in Sulla's time. I know not which was the worse of the two things he wished for, that he might be hated or that he might be feared. It occurs to his mind that someday people will curse him, plot against him, crush him: what prayer does he add to this? May all the gods curse him — for discovering a cure for hate so worthy of it. "Let them hate." How? "Provided they obey me?" No!" Provided they approve of me?" No! How then? "Provided they fear me!" I would not even be loved upon such terms. Do you imagine that this was a very spirited saying? You are wrong: this is not greatness, but monstrosity. You should not believe the words of angry men, whose speech is very loud and menacing, while their mind within them is as timid as possible: nor need you suppose that the most eloquent of men, Titus Livius, was right in describing somebody as being "of a great rather than a good disposition." The things cannot be separated: he must either be good or else he cannot be great, because I take greatness of mind to mean that it is unshaken, sound throughout, firm and uniform to its very foundation; such as cannot exist in evil dispositions. Such dispositions may be terrible, frantic, and destructive, but cannot possess greatness; because greatness rests upon goodness, and owes its strength to it. "Yet by speech, action, and all outward show they will make one think them great." True, they will say something which you may think shows a great spirit, like Gaius Caesar, who when angry with heaven because it interfered with his ballet-dancers, whom he imitated more carefully than he attended to them when they acted, and because it frightened his revels by its thunders, surely ill-directed,[9] challenged Jove to fight, and that to the death, shouting the Homeric verse :—

"Carry me off, or I will carry thee!How great was his madness! He must have believed either that he could not be hurt even by Jupiter himself, or that he could hurt even Jupiter itself. I imagine that this saying of his had no small weight in nerving the minds of the conspirators for their task: for it seemed to be the height of endurance to bear one who could not bear Jupiter.

---

[9] Prorsus parum certis [i.e., the thunderbolts missed their aim in not striking him dead)

XXI

There is therefore nothing great or noble in anger, even when it seems to be powerful and to contemn both gods and men alike. Anyone who thinks that anger produces greatness of mind, would think that luxury produces it: such a man wishes to rest on ivory, to be clothed with purple, and roofed with gold; to remove lands, embank seas, hasten the course of rivers, suspend woods in the air. He would think that avarice shows greatness of mind: for the avaricious man broods over heaps of gold and silver, treats whole provinces as merely fields on his estate, and has larger tracts of country under the charge of single bailiffs than those which consuls once drew lots to administer. He would think that lust shows greatness of mind: for the lustful man swims across straits, castrates troops of boys, and puts himself within reach of the swords of injured husbands with complete scorn of death. Ambition, too, he would think shows greatness of mind: for the ambitious man is not content with office once a year, but, if possible, would fill the calendar of dignities with his name alone, and cover the whole world with his titles. It matters nothing to what heights or lengths these passions may proceed: they are narrow, pitiable, grovelling. Virtue alone is lofty and sublime, nor is anything great which is not at the same time tranquil.

Of Anger – Book II

I

MY first book, Novatus, had a more abundant subject: for carriages roll easily down hill:[1] now we must proceed to drier matters. The question before us is whether anger arises from deliberate choice or from impulse, that is, whether it acts of its own accord or like the greater part of those passions which spring up within us without our knowledge. It is necessary for our debate to stoop to the consideration of these matters, in order that it may afterwards be able to rise to loftier themes; for likewise in our bodies the parts which are first set in order are the bones, sinews, and joints, which are by no means fair to see, albeit they are the foundation of our frame and essential to its life: next to them come the parts of which all beauty of face and appearance consists; and after these, colour, which above all else charms the eye, is applied last of all, when the rest of the body is complete. There is no doubt that anger is roused by the appearance of an injury being done: but the question before us is, whether anger straightway follows the appearance, and springs up without assistance from the mind, or whether it is roused with the sympathy of the mind. Our (the Stoics') opinion is, that anger can venture upon nothing by itself, without the approval of mind: for to conceive the idea of a wrong having been done, to long to avenge it, and to join the two propositions, that we ought not to have been injured and that it is our duty to avenge our injuries, cannot belong to a mere impulse which is excited without our consent. That impulse is a simple act; this is a complex one, and composed of several parts. The man understands something to have happened: he becomes indignant thereat: he condemns the deed; and he avenges it. All these things cannot be done without his mind agreeing to those matters which touched him.

---

[1] "Vehiculorum ridicule Koch," says Gertz, justly, "viliorum makes excellent sense."—J. E. B. M.

II

Whither, say you, does this inquiry tend? That we may know what anger is: for if it springs up against our will, it never will yield to reason: because all the motions which take place without our volition are beyond our control and unavoidable, such as shivering when cold water is poured over us, or shrinking when we are touched in certain places. Men's hair rises up at bad news, their faces blush at indecent words, and they are seized with dizziness when looking down a precipice; and as it is not in our power to prevent any of these things, no reasoning can prevent their taking place. But anger can be put to flight by wise maxims; for it is a voluntary defect of the mind, and not one of those things which are evolved by the conditions of human life, and which, therefore, may happen even to the wisest of us. Among these and in the first place must be ranked that thrill of the mind which seizes us at the thought of wrongdoing. We feel this even when witnessing the mimic scenes of the stage, or when reading about things that happened long ago. We often feel angry with Clodius for banishing Cicero, and with Antonius for murdering him. Who is not indignant with the wars of Marius, the proscriptions of Sulla? who is not enraged against Theodotus and Achillas and the boy king who dared to commit a more than boyish crime?[2] Sometimes songs excite us, and quickened rhythm and the martial noise of trumpets; so, too, shocking pictures and the dreadful sight of tortures, however well deserved, affect our minds. Hence it is that we smile when others are smiling, that a crowd of mourners makes us sad, and that we take a glowing interest in another's battles; all of which feelings are not anger, any more than that which clouds our brow at the sight of a stage shipwreck is sadness, or what we feel, when we read how Hannibal after Cannae beset the walls of Rome, can be called fear. All these are emotions of minds which are loath to be moved, and are not passions, but rudiments which may grow into passions. So, too, a soldier starts at the sound of a trumpet, although he may be dressed as a civilian and in the midst of a profound peace, and camp horses prick up their ears at the clash of arms. It is said that Alexander, when Xenophantus was singing, laid his hand upon his weapons.

---

[2] The murder of Pompeius, B.C. 48. Achillas and Theodotus acted under the nominal orders of Ptolemy XII., Cleopatra's brother, then about seventeen years of age.

III

None of these things which casually influence the mind deserve to be called passions: the mind, if I may so express it, rather suffers passions to act upon itself than forms them. A passion, therefore, consists not in being affected by the sights which are presented to us, but in giving way to our feelings and following up these chance promptings: for whoever imagines that paleness, bursting into tears, lustful feelings, deep sighs, sudden flashes of the eyes, and so forth, are signs of passion and betray the state of the mind, is mistaken, and does not understand that these are merely impulses of the body. Consequently, the bravest of men often turns pale while he is putting on his armour; when the signal for battle is given, the knees of the boldest soldier shake for a moment; the heart even of a great general leaps into his mouth just before the lines clash together, and the hands and feet even of the most eloquent orator grow stiff and cold while he is preparing to begin his speech. Anger must not merely move, but break out of bounds, being an impulse: now, no impulse can take place without the consent of the mind: for it cannot be that we should deal with revenge and punishment without the mind being cognisant of them. A man may think himself injured, may wish to avenge his wrongs, and then may be persuaded by some reason or other to give up his intention and calm down: I do not call that anger, it is an emotion of the mind which is under the control of reason. Anger is that which goes beyond reason and carries her away with it: wherefore the first confusion of a man's mind when struck by what seems an injury is no more anger than the apparent injury itself: it is the subsequent mad rush, which not only receives the impression of the apparent injury, but acts upon it as true, that is anger, being an exciting of the mind to revenge, which proceeds from choice and deliberate resolve. There never has been any doubt that fear produces flight, and anger a rush forward; consider, therefore, whether you suppose that anything can be either sought or avoided without the participation of the mind.

IV

Furthermore, that you may know in what manner passions begin and swell and gain spirit, learn that the first emotion is involuntary, and is, as it were, a preparation for a passion, and a threatening of one. The next is combined with a wish, though not an obstinate one, as, for example, "It is my duty to avenge myself, because I have been injured," or "It is right that this man should be punished, because he has committed a crime." The third emotion is already beyond our control, because it overrides reason, and wishes to avenge itself, not if it be its duty, but whether or no. We are not able by means of reason to escape from that first impression on the mind, any more than we can escape from those things which we have mentioned as occurring to the body: we cannot prevent other people's yawns temping us to yawn: we cannot help winking when fingers are suddenly darted at our eyes. Reason is unable to overcome these habits, which perhaps might be weakened by practice and constant watchfulness: they differ from an emotion which is brought into existence and brought to an end by a deliberate mental act.

V

We must also enquire whether those whose cruelty knows no bounds, and who delight in shedding human blood, are angry when they kill people from whom they have received no injury, and who they themselves do not think have done them any injury; such as were Apollodorus or Phalaris. This is not anger, it is ferocity: for it does not do hurt because it has received injury: but is even willing to receive injury, provided it may do hurt. It does not long to inflict stripes and mangle bodies to avenge its wrongs, but for its own pleasure. What then are we to say? This evil takes its rise from anger; for anger, after it has by long use and indulgence made a man forget mercy, and driven all feelings of human fellowship from his mind, passes finally into cruelty. Such men therefore laugh, rejoice, enjoy themselves greatly, and are as unlike as possible in countenance to angry men, since cruelty is their relaxation. It is said that when Hannibal saw a trench full of human blood, he exclaimed, "O, what a beauteous sight!" How much more beautiful would he have thought it, if it had filled a river or a lake? Why should we wonder that you should be charmed with this sight above all others, you who were born in bloodshed and brought up amid slaughter from a child? Fortune will follow you and favour your cruelty for twenty years, and will display to you everywhere the sight that you love. You will behold it both at Trasumene and at Cannae, and lastly at your own city of Carthage. Volesus, who not long ago, under the Emperor Augustus, was proconsul of Asia Minor, after he had one day beheaded three hundred persons, strutted out among the corpses with a haughty air, as though he had performed some grand and notable exploit, and exclaimed in Greek, "What a kingly action!" What would this man have done, had he been really a king? This was not anger, but a greater and an incurable disease.

VI

"Virtue," argues our adversary, "ought to be angry with what is base, just as she approves of what is honourable." What should we think if he said that virtue ought to be both mean and great; yet this is what he means, when he wants her to be raised and lowered, because joy at a good action is grand and glorious, while anger at another's sin is base and befits a narrow mind: and virtue will never be guilty of imitating vice while she is repressing it; she considers anger to deserve punishment for itself, since it often is even more criminal than the faults with which it is angry. To rejoice and be glad is the proper and natural function of virtue: it is as much beneath her dignity to be angry, as to mourn: now, sorrow is the companion of anger, and all anger ends in sorrow, either from remorse or from failure. Secondly, if it be the part of the wise man to be angry with sins, he will be more angry the greater they are, and will often be angry: from which it follows that the wise man will not only be angry but irascible. Yet if we do not believe that great and frequent anger can find any place in the wise man's mind, why should we not set him altogether free from this passion? for there can be no limit, if he ought to be angry in proportion to what every man does: because he will either be unjust if he is equally angry at unequal crimes, or he will be the most irascible of men, if he blazes into wrath as often as crimes deserve his anger.

VII

What, too, can be more unworthy of the wise man, than that his passions should depend upon the wickedness of others? If so, the great Socrates will no longer be able to return home with the same expression of countenance with which he set out. Moreover, if it be the duty of the wise man to be angry at base deeds, and to be excited and saddened at crimes, then is there nothing more unhappy than the wise man, for all his life will be spent in anger and grief. What moment will there be at which he will not see something deserving of blame? whenever he leaves his house, he will be obliged to walk among men who are criminals, misers, spendthrifts, profligates, and who are happy in being so: he can turn his eyes in no direction without their finding something to shock them. He will faint, if he demands anger from himself as often as reason calls for it. All these thousands who are hurrying to the law courts at break of day, how base are their causes, and how much baser their advocates? One impugns his father's will, when he would have done better to deserve it; another appears as the accuser of his mother; a third comes to inform against a man for committing the very crime of which he himself is yet more notoriously guilty. The judge, too, is chosen to condemn men for doing what he himself has done, and the audience takes the wrong side, led astray by the fine voice of the pleader.

VIII

Why need I dwell upon individual cases? Be assured, when you see the Forum crowded with a multitude, the Saepta[3] swarming with people, or the great Circus, in which the greater part of the people find room to show themselves at once, that among them there are as many vices as there are men. Among those whom you see in the garb of peace there is no peace: for a small profit any one of them will attempt the ruin of another: no one can gain anything save by another's loss. They hate the fortunate and despise the unfortunate: they grudgingly endure the great, and oppress the small: they are fired by diverse lusts: they would wreck everything for the sake of a little pleasure or plunder: they live as though they were in a school of gladiators, fighting with the same people with whom they live: it is like a society of wild beasts, save that beasts are tame with one another, and refrain from biting their own species, whereas men tear one another, and gorge themselves upon one another. They differ from dumb animals in this alone, that the latter are tame with those who feed them, whereas the rage of the former preys on those very persons by whom they were brought up.

---

[3] The voting-place in the Campus Martius.

IX

The wise man will never cease to be angry, if he once begins, so full is every place of vices and crimes. More evil is done than can be healed by punishment: men seem engaged in a vast race of wickedness. Every day there is greater eagerness to sin, less modesty. Throwing aside all reverence for what is better and more just, lust rushes whithersoever it thinks fit, and crimes are no longer committed by stealth, they take place before our eyes, and wickedness has become so general and gained such a footing in everyone's breast that innocence is no longer rare, but no longer exists. Do men break the law singly, or a few at a time? Nay, they rise in all quarters at once, as though obeying some universal signal, to wipe out the boundaries of right and wrong.

"Host is not safe from guest,
Father-in-law from son; but seldom love
Exists 'twixt brothers; wives long to destroy
Their husbands, husbands long to slay their wives,
Stepmothers deadly aconite prepare
And child-heirs wonder when their sires will die."

And how small a part of men's crimes are these! The poet[4] has not described one people divided into two hostile camps, parents and children enrolled on opposite sides, Rome set on fire by the hand of a Roman, troops of fierce horsemen scouring the country to track out the hiding- places of the proscribed, wells defiled with poison, plagues created by human .hands, trenches dug by children round their beleaguered parents, crowded prisons, conflagrations that consume whole cities, gloomy tyrannies, secret plots to establish despotisms and ruin peoples, and men glorying in those deeds which, as long as it was possible to repress them, were counted as crimes — I mean rape, debauchery, and lust ...... Add to these, public acts of national bad faith, broken treaties, everything that cannot defend itself carried off as plunder by the stronger, knaveries, thefts, frauds, and disownings of debt such as three of our present law-courts would not suffice to deal with. If you want the wise man to be as angry as the atrocity of men's crimes requires, he must not merely be angry, but must go mad with rage.

---

[4] Ovid, Metamorphoses, i., 144, sqq. The same lines are quoted in the essay on Benefits, v. 15.

X

You will rather think that we should not be angry with people's faults; for what shall we say of one who is angry with those who stumble in the dark, or with deaf people who cannot hear his orders, or with children, because they forget their duty and interest themselves in the games and silly jokes of their companions? What shall we say if you choose to be angry with weaklings for being sick, for growing old, or becoming fatigued? Among the other misfortunes of humanity is this, that men's intellects are confused, and they not only cannot help going wrong, but love to go wrong. To avoid being angry with individuals, you must pardon the whole mass, you must grant forgiveness to the entire human race. If you are angry with young and old men because they do wrong, you will be angry with infants also, for they soon will do wrong. Does anyone become angry with children, who are too young to comprehend distinctions? Yet, to be a human being is a greater and a better excuse than to be a child. Thus are we born, as creatures liable to as many disorders of the mind as of the body; not dull and slow-witted, but making a bad use of our keenness of wit, and leading one another into vice by our example. He who follows others who have started before him on the wrong road is surely excusable for having wandered on the highway.[5] A general's severity may be shown in the case of individual deserters; but where a whole army deserts, it must needs be pardoned. What is it that puts a stop to the wise man's anger? It is the number of sinners. He perceives how unjust and how dangerous it is to be angry with vices which all men share. Heraclitus, whenever he came out of doors and beheld around him such a number of men who were living wretchedly, nay, rather perishing wretchedly, used to weep: he pitied all those who met him joyous and happy. He was of a gentle but too weak disposition: and he himself was one of those for whom he ought to have wept. Democritus, on the other hand, is said never to have appeared in public without laughing; so little did men's serious occupations appear serious to him. What room is there for anger? Everything ought either to move us to tears or to laughter. The wise man will not be angry with sinners. Why not? Because he knows that no one is born wise, but becomes so: he knows that very few wise men are produced in any age, because he thoroughly understands the circumstances of human life. Now, no sane man is angry with nature: for what should we say if a man chose to be surprised that fruit did not hang on the thickets of a forest, or to wonder at bushes and thorns not being covered with some useful berry? No one is angry when nature excuses a defect. The wise man, therefore, being

---

[5] i.e., he can plead that he kept the beaten track.

tranquil, and dealing candidly with mistakes, not an enemy to but an improver of sinners, will go abroad every day in the following frame of mind: — "Many men will meet me who are drunkards, lustful, ungrateful, greedy, and excited by the frenzy of ambition." He will view all these as benignly as a physician does his patients. When a man's ship leaks freely through its opened seams, does he become angry with the sailors or the ship itself? No; instead of that, he tries to remedy it: he shuts out some water, bales out some other, closes all the holes that he can see, and by ceaseless labour counteracts those which are out of sight and which let water into the hold; nor does he relax his efforts because as much water as he pumps out runs in again. We need a long-breathed struggle against permanent and prolific evils; not, indeed, to quell them, but merely to prevent their overpowering us.

XI

"Anger," says our opponent, "is useful, because it avoids contempt, and because it frightens bad men." Now, in the first place, if anger is strong in proportion to its threats, it is hateful for the same reason that it is terrible: and it is more dangerous to be hated than to be despised. If, again, it is without strength, it is much more exposed to contempt, and cannot avoid ridicule: for what is more flat than anger when it breaks out into meaningless ravings? Moreover, because some things are somewhat terrible, they are not on that account desirable: nor does wisdom wish itto be said of the wise man, as it is of a wild beast, that the fear which he inspires is as a weapon to him. Why, do we not fear fever, gout, consuming ulcers? and is there, for that reason, any good in them? nay; on the other hand, they are all despised and thought to be foul and base, and are for this very reason feared. So, too, anger is in itself hideous and by no means to be feared; yet it is feared by many, just as a hideous mask is feared by children. How can we answer the fact that terror always works back to him who inspired it, and that no one is feared who is himself at peace? At this point it is well that you should remember that verse of Laberius, which, when pronounced in the theatre during the height of the civil war, caught the fancy of the whole people as though it expressed the national feeling: —

"He must fear many, whom so many fear."

Thus has nature ordained, that whatever becomes great by causing fear to others is not free from fear itself. How disturbed lions are at the faintest noises! How excited those fiercest of beasts become at strange shadows, voices, or smells! Whatever is a terror to others, fears for itself. There can be no reason, therefore, for any wise man to wish to be feared, and no one need think that anger is anything great because it strikes terror, since even the most despicable things are feared, as, for example, noxious vermin whose bite is venomous: and since a string set with feathers stops the largest herds of wild beasts and guides them into traps, it is no wonder that from its effect it should be named a "Scarer."[6] Foolish creatures are frightened by foolish things: the movement of chariots and the sight of their wheels turning round drives lions back into their cage: elephants are frightened at the cries of pigs: and so also we fear anger just as children fear the dark, or wild beasts fear red feathers: it has in itself nothing solid or valiant, but it affects feeble minds.

---

[6] De Clem. i. 12, 5

XII

"Wickedness," says our adversary," must be removed from the system of nature, if you wish to remove anger: neither of which things can be done." In the first place, it is possible for a man not to be cold, although according to the system of nature it may be winter-time, nor yet to suffer from heat, although it be summer according to the almanac. He may be protected against the inclement time of the year by dwelling in a favoured spot, or he may have so trained his body to endurance that it feels neither heat nor cold. Next, reverse this saying: — You must remove anger from your mind before you can take virtue into the same, because vices and virtues cannot combine, and none can at the same time be both an angry man and a good man, any more than he can be both sick and well. "It is not possible," says he, " to remove anger altogether from the mind, nor does human nature admit of it." Yet there is nothing so hard and difficult that the mind of man cannot overcome it, and with which unremitting study will not render him familiar, nor are there any passions so fierce and independent that they cannot be tamed by discipline. The mind can carry out whatever orders it gives itself: some have succeeded in never smiling: some have forbidden themselves wine, sexual intercourse, or even drink of all kinds. Some, who are satisfied with short hours of rest, have learned to watch for long periods without weariness. Men have learned to run upon the thinnest ropes even when slanting, to carry huge burdens, scarcely within the compass of human strength, or to dive to enormous depths and suffer themselves to remain under the sea without any chance of drawing breath. There are a thousand other instances in which application has conquered all obstacles, and proved that nothing which the mind has set itself to endure is difficult. The men whom I have just mentioned gain either no reward or one that is unworthy of their unwearied application; for what great thing does a man gain by applying his intellect to walking upon a tight rope? or to placing great burdens upon his shoulders? or to keeping sleep from his eyes? or to reaching the bottom of the sea? and yet their patient labour brings all these things to pass for a trifling reward. Shall not we then call in the aid of patience, we whom such a prize awaits, the unbroken calm of a happy life? How great a blessing is it to escape from anger, that chief of all evils, and therewith from frenzy, ferocity, cruelty, and madness, its attendants?

XIII

There is no reason why we should seek to defend such a passion as this or excuse its excesses by declaring it to be either useful or unavoidable. What vice, indeed, is without its defenders? yet this is no reason why you should declare anger to be ineradicable. The evils from which we suffer are curable, and since we were born with a natural bias towards good, nature herself will help us if we try to amend our lives. Nor is the path to virtue steep and rough, as some think it to be: it may be reached on level ground. This is no untrue tale which I come to tell you: the road to happiness is easy; do you only enter upon it with good luck and the good help of the gods themselves. It is much harder to do what you are doing. What is more restful than a mind at peace, and what more toilsome than anger? What is more at leisure than clemency, what fuller of business than cruelty? Modesty keeps holiday while vice is overwhelmed with work. In fine, the culture of any of the virtues is easy, while vices require a great expense. Anger ought to be removed from our minds: even those who say that it ought to be kept low admit this to some extent: let it be got rid of altogether; there is nothing to be gained by it. Without it we can more easily and more justly put an end to crime, punish bad men, and amend their lives. The wise man will do his duty in all things without the help of any evil passion, and will use no auxiliaries which require watching narrowly lest they get beyond his control.

XIV

Anger, then, must never become a habit with us, but we may sometimes affect to be angry when we wish to rouse up the dull minds of those whom we address, just as we rouse up horses who are slow at starting with goads and firebrands. We must sometimes apply fear to persons upon whom reason makes no impression: yet to be angry is of no more use than to grieve or to be afraid. "What? do not circumstances arise which provoke us to anger?" Yes: but at those times above all others we ought to choke down our wrath. Nor is it difficult to conquer our spirit, seeing that athletes, who devote their whole attention to the basest parts of themselves, nevertheless are able to endure blows and pain, in order to exhaust the strength of the striker, and do not strike when anger bids them, but when opportunity invites them. It is said that Pyrrhus, the most celebrated trainer for gymnastic contests, used habitually to impress upon his pupils not to lose their tempers: for anger spoils their science, and thinks only how it can hurt: so that often reason counsels patience while anger counsels revenge, and we, who might have survived our first misfortunes, are exposed to worse ones. Some have been driven into exile by their impatience of a single contemptuous word, have been plunged into the deepest miseries because they would not endure the most trifling wrong in silence, and have brought upon themselves the yoke of slavery because they were too proud to give up the least part of their entire liberty.

XV

"That you may be sure," says our opponent, "that anger has in it something noble, pray look at the free nations, such as the Germans and Scythians, who are especially prone to anger." The reason of this is that stout and daring intellects are liable to anger before they are tamed by discipline; for some passions engraft themselves upon the better class of dispositions only, just as good land, even when waste, grows strong brushwood, and the trees are tall which stand upon a fertile soil. In like manner, dispositions which are naturally bold produce irritability, and, being hot and fiery, have no mean or trivial qualities, but their energy is misdirected, as happens with all those who without training come to the front by their natural advantages alone, whose minds, unless they be brought under control, degenerate from a courageous temper into habits of rashness and reckless daring. "What? are not milder spirits linked with gentler vices, such as tenderness of heart, love, and bashfulness?" Yes, and therefore I can often point out to you a good disposition by its own faults: yet their being the proofs of a superior nature does not prevent their being vices. Moreover, all those nations which are free because they are wild, like lions or wolves, cannot command any more than they can obey: for the strength of their intellect is not civilized, but fierce and unmanageable: now, no one is able to rule unless he is also able to be ruled. Consequently, the empire of the world has almost always remained in the hands of those nations who enjoy a milder climate. Those who dwell near the frozen north have uncivilized temper

"Just on the model of their native skies,"
as the poet has it.

XVI

Those animals, urges our opponent, are held to be the most generous who have large capacity for anger. He is mistaken when he holds up creatures who act from impulse instead of reason as patterns for men to follow, because in man reason takes the place of impulse. Yet even with animals, all do not alike profit by the same thing. Anger is of use to lions, timidity to stags, boldness to hawks, flight to doves. What if I declare that it is not even true that the best animals are the most prone to anger? I may suppose that wild beasts, who gain their food by rapine, are better the angrier they are; but I should praise oxen and horses who obey the rein for their patience. What reason, however, have you for referring mankind to such wretched models, when you have the universe and God, whom he alone of animals imitates because he alone comprehends Him ?" The most irritable men," says he, "are thought to be the most straightforward of all." Yes, because they are compared with swindlers and sharpers, and appear to be simple because they are outspoken. I should not call such men simple, but heedless. We give this title of "simple" to all fools, gluttons, spendthrifts, and men whose vices lie on the surface.

XVII

"An orator," says our opponent, "sometimes speaks better when he is angry." Not so, but when he pretends to be angry: for so also actors bring down the house by their playing, not when they are really angry, but when they act the angry man well: and in like manner, in addressing a jury or a popular assembly, or in any other position in which the minds of others have to be influenced at our pleasure, we must ourselves pretend to feel anger, fear, or pity before we can make others feel them, and often the pretence of passion will do what the passion itself could not have done. "The mind which does not feel anger," says he, "is feeble." True, if it has nothing stronger than anger to support it. A man ought to be neither robber nor victim, neither tender-hearted nor cruel. The former belongs to an over-weak mind, the latter to an over-hard one. Let the wise man be moderate, and when things have to be done somewhat briskly, let him call force, not anger, to his aid.

XVIII

Now that we have discussed the questions propounded concerning anger, let us pass on to the consideration of its remedies. These, I imagine, are two-fold: the one class preventing our becoming angry, the other preventing our doing wrong when we are angry. As with the body we adopt a certain regimen to keep ourselves in health, and use different rules to bring back health when lost, so likewise we must repel anger in one fashion and quench it in another. That we may avoid it, certain general rules of conduct which apply to all men's lives must be impressed upon us. We may divide these into such as are of use during the education of the young and in after-life. Education ought to be carried on with the greatest and most salutary assiduity: for it is easy to mould minds while they are still tender, but it is difficult to uproot vices which have grown up with ourselves.

XIX

A hot mind is naturally the most prone to anger: for as there are four elements,[7] consisting of fire, air, earth, and water, so there are powers corresponding and equivalent to each of these, namely, hot, cold, dry, and moist. Now the mixture of the elements is the cause of the diversities of lands and of animals, of bodies and of character, and our dispositions incline to one or the other of these according as the strength of each element prevails in us. Hence it is that we call some regions wet or dry, warm or cold. The same distinctions apply likewise to animals and mankind; it makes a great difference how much moisture or heat a man contains; his character will partake of whichever element has the largest share in him. A warm temper of mind will make men prone to anger; for fire is full of movement and vigour; a mixture of coldness makes men cowards, for cold is sluggish and contracted. Because of this, some of our Stoics think that anger is excited in our breasts by the boiling of the blood round the heart: indeed, that place is assigned to anger for no other reason than because the breast is the warmest part of the whole body. Those who have more moisture in them become angry by slow degrees, because they have no heat ready at hand, but it has to be obtained by movement; wherefore the anger of women and children is sharp rather than strong, and arises on lighter provocation. At dry times of life anger is violent and powerful, yet without increase, and adding little to itself, because as heat dies away cold takes its place. Old men are testy and full of complaints, as also are sick people and convalescents, and all whose store of heat has been consumed by weariness or loss of blood. Those who are wasted by thirst or hunger are in the same condition, as also are those whose frame is naturally bloodless and faints from want of generous diet. Wine kindles anger, because it increases heat; according to each man's disposition, some fly into a passion when they are heavily drunk, some when they are slightly drunk: nor is there any other reason than this why yellow-haired, ruddy-complexioned people should be excessively passionate, seeing that they are naturally of the colour which others put on during anger; for their blood is hot and easily set in motion.

---

[7] 1 Compare Shakespeare, "Julius Caesar," Act v. Sc. 5: -
"His life was gentle, and the elements
So mixed in him, that nature might stand up
And say to all the world, this was a man!"
See Mr. Aldis Wright's note upon the passage.

XX

But just as nature makes some men prone to anger, so there are many other causes which have the same power as nature. Some are brought into this condition by disease or bodily injury, others by hard work, long watching, nights of anxiety, ardent longings, and love: and everything else which is hurtful to the body or the spirit inclines the distempered mind to find fault. All these, however, are but the beginning and causes of anger. Habit of mind has very great power, and, if it be harsh, increases the disorder. As for nature, it is difficult to alter it, nor may we change the mixture of the elements which was formed once for all at our birth: yet knowledge will be so far of service, that we should keep wine out of the reach of hot-tempered men, which Plato thinks ought also to be forbidden to boys, so that fire be not made fiercer. Neither should such men be over-fed: for if so, their bodies will swell, and their minds will swell with them. Such men ought to take exercise, stopping short, however, of fatigue, in order that their natural heat may be abated, but not exhausted, and their excess of fiery spirit may be worked off. Games also will be useful: for moderate pleasure relieves the mind and brings it to a proper balance. With those temperaments which incline to moisture, or dryness and stiffness, there is no danger of anger, but there is fear of greater vices, such as cowardice, moroseness, despair, and suspiciousness: such dispositions therefore ought to be softened, comforted, and restored to cheerfulness: and since we must make use of different remedies for anger and for sullenness, and these two vices require not only unlike, bnt absolutely opposite modes of treatment, let us always attack that one of them which is gaining the mastery.

XXI

It is, I assure you, of the greatest service to boys that they should be soundly brought up, yet to regulate their education is difficult, because it is our duty to be careful neither to cherish a habit of anger in them, nor to blunt the edge of their spirit. This needs careful watching, for both qualities, both those which are to be encouraged, and those which are to be checked, are fed by the same things; and even a careful watcher may be deceived by their likeness. A boy's spirit is increased by freedom and depressed by slavery: it rises when praised, and is led to conceive great expectations of itself: yet this same treatment produces arrogance and quickness of temper: we must therefore guide him between these two extremes, using the curb at one time and the spur at another. He must undergo no servile or degrading treatment; he never must beg abjectly for anything, nor must he gain anything by begging; let him rather receive it for his own sake, for his past good behaviour, or for his promises of future good conduct. In contests with his comrades we ought not to allow him to become sulky or fly into a passion: let us see that he be on friendly terms with those whom he contends with, so that in the struggle itself he may learn to wish not to hurt his antagonist but to conquer him: whenever he has gained the day or done something praiseworthy, we should allow him to enjoy his victory, but not to rush into transports of delight: for joy leads to exultation, and exultation leads to swaggering and excessive self-esteem. We ought to allow him some relaxation, yet not yield him up to laziness and sloth, and we ought to keep him far beyond the reach of luxury, for nothing makes children more prone to anger than a soft and fond bringing-up, so that the more only children are indulged, and the more liberty is given to orphans, the more they are corrupted. He to whom nothing is ever denied, will not be able to endure a rebuff, whose anxious mother always wipes away his tears, whose paedagogus[8] is made to pay for his shortcomings. Do you not observe how a man's anger becomes more violent as he rises in station? This shows itself especially in those who are rich and noble, or in great place, when the favouring gale has roused all the most empty and trivial passions of their minds. Prosperity fosters anger, when a man's proud ears are surrounded by a mob of flatterers, saying, "That man [?] answer you! you do not act according to your dignity, you lower yourself." And so forth, with all the language which can hardly be resisted even by healthy and originally well-principled minds. Flattery, then, must be kept well out of the way of children. Let a child hear the truth, and sometimes fear it: let him always reverence it. Let him rise in the presence of his elders. Let him

---

[8] Paedagogiis was a slave who accompanied a boy to school, &c, to keep him out of mischief; he did not teach him anything.

obtain nothing by flying into a passion: let him be given when he is quiet what was refused him when he cried for it: let him behold, but not make use of his father's wealth: let him be reproved for what he does wrong. It will be advantageous to furnish boys with even-tempered teachers and paedagogi: what is soft and unformed clings to what is near, and takes its shape: the habits of young men reproduce those of their nurses and paedagogi. Once, a boy who was brought up in Plato's house went home to his parents, and, on seeing his father shouting with passion, said, "I never saw anyone at Plato's house act like that." I doubt not that he learned to imitate his father sooner than he learned to imitate Plato. Above all, let his food be scanty, his dress not costly, and of the same fashion as that of his comrades: if you begin by putting him on a level with many others, he will not be angry when someone is compared with him.

XXII

These precepts, however, apply to our children: in ourselves the accident of birth and our education no longer admits of either mistakes or advice; we must deal with what follows. Now we ought to fight against the first causes of evil: the cause of anger is the belief that we are injured; this belief, therefore, should not be lightly entertained. We ought not to fly into a rage even when the injury appears to be open and distinct: for some false things bear the semblance of truth. We should always allow some time- to elapse, for time discloses the truth. Let not our ears be easily lent to calumnious talk: let us know and be on our guard against this fault of human nature, that we are willing to believe what we are unwilling to listen to, and that we become angry before we have formed our opinion. What shall I say? we are influenced not merely by calumnies but by suspicions, and at the very look and smile of others we may fly into a rage with innocent persons because we put the worst construction upon it. We ought, therefore, to plead the cause of the absent against ourselves, and to keep Our anger in abeyance: for a punishment which has been postponed may yet be inflicted, but when once inflicted cannot be recalled.

XXIII

Everyone knows the story of the tyrannicide who, being caught before he had accomplished his task, and being tortured by Hippias to make him betray his accomplices, named the friends of the tyrant who stood around, and everyone to whom he knew the tyrant's safety was especially dear. As the tyrant ordered each man to be slain as he was named, at last the man, being asked if anyone else remained, said, "You remain alone, for I have left no one else alive to whom you are dear." Anger had made the tyrant lend his assistance to the tyrant-slayer, and cut down his guards with his own sword. How far more spirited was Alexander, who after reading his mother's letter warning him to beware of poison from his physician, Philip, nevertheless drank undismayed the medicine which Philip gave him! He felt more confidence in his friend: he deserved that his friend should be innocent, and deserved that his conduct should make him innocent. I praise Alexander's doing this all the more because he was above all men prone to anger; but the rarer moderation is among kings, the more it deserves to be praised. The great Gaius Caesar, who proved such a merciful conqueror in the civil war, did the same thing; he burned a packet of letters addressed to Gnaeus Pompeius by persons who had been thought to be either neutrals or on the other side. Though he was never violent in his anger, yet he preferred to put it out of his power to be angry: he thought that the kindest way to pardon each of them was not to know what his offence had been.

XXIV

Readiness to believe what we hear causes very great mischief; we ought often not even to listen, because in some cases it is better to be deceived than to suspect deceit. We ought to free our minds of suspicion and mistrust, those most untrustworthy causes of anger. "This man's greeting was far from civil; that one would not receive my kiss; one cut short a story I had begun to tell; another did not ask me to dinner; another seemed to view me with aversion." Suspicion will never lack grounds: what we want is straightforwardness, and a kindly interpretation of things. Let us believe nothing unless it forces itself upon bur sight and is unmistakable, and let us reprove ourselves for being too ready to believe, as often as our suspicions prove to be groundless: for this discipline will render us habitually slow to believe what we hear.

XXV

Another consequence of this will be, that we shall not be exasperated by the slightest and most contemptible trifles. It is mere madness to be put out of temper because a slave is not quick, because the water we are going to drink is lukewarm or because our couch is disarranged or our table carelessly laid. A man must be in a miserably bad state of health if he shrinks from a gentle breath of wind ; his eyes must be diseased if they are distressed by the sight of white clothing; he must be broken down with debauchery if he feels pain at seeing another man work. It is said that there was one Mindyrides, a citizen of Sybaris, who one day seeing a man digging and vigorously brandishing a mattock, complained that the sight made him weary, and forbade the man to work where he could see him. The same man complained that he had suffered from the rose-leaves upon which he lay. being folded double. When pleasures have corrupted both the body and the mind, nothing seems endurable, not indeed because it is hard, but because he who has to bear it is soft: for why should we be driven to frenzy by any one's coughing and sneezing, or by a fly not being driven away with sufficient care, or by a dog's hanging about us, or a key dropping from a careless servant's hand? Will one whose ears are agonised by the noise of a bench being dragged along the floor be able to endure with unruffled mind the rude language of party strife, and the abuse which speakers in the forum or the senate house heap upon their opponents? Will he who is angry with his slave for icing his drink badly, be able to endure hunger, or the thirst of a long march in summer? Nothing, therefore, nourishes anger more than excessive and dissatisfied luxury: the mind ought to be hardened by rough treatment, so as not to feel any blow that is not severe.

XXVI

We are angry, either with those who can, or with those who cannot do us an injury. To the latter class belong some inanimate things, such as a book, which we often throw away when it is written in letters too small for us to read, or tear up when it is full of mistakes, or clothes which we destroy because we do not like them. How foolish to be angry with such things as these, which neither deserve nor feel our anger! "But of course it is their makers who really affront us." I answer that, in the first place, we often become angry before making this distinction clear in our minds, and secondly, perhaps even the makers might put forward some reasonable excuses: one of them, it may be, could not make them any better than he did, and it is not through any disrespect to you that he was unskilled in his trade: another may have done his work so without any intention of insulting you: and, finally, what can be more crazy than to discharge upon things the ill-feeling which one has accumulated against persons? Yet as it is the act of a madman to be angry with inanimate objects, so also is it to be angry with dumb animals, which can do us no wrong because they are not able to form a purpose; and we cannot call anything a wrong unless it be done intentionally. They are, therefore, able to hurt us, just as a sword or a stone may do so, but they are not able to do us a wrong. Yet some men think themselves insulted when the same horses which are docile with one rider are restive with another, as though it were through their deliberate choice, and not through habit and cleverness of handling that some horses are more easily managed by some men than by others. And as it is foolish to be angry with them, so it is to be angry with children, and with men who have little more sense than children: for all these sins, before a just judge, ignorance would be as effective an excuse as innocence.

XXVII

There are some things which are unable to hurt us, and whose power is exclusively beneficial and salutary, as, for example, the immortal gods, who neither wish nor are able to do harm: for their temperament is naturally gentle and tranquil, and no more likely to wrong others than to wrong themselves. Foolish people who know not the truth hold them answerable for storms at sea, excessive rain, and long winters, whereas all the while these phenomena by which we suffer or profit take place without any reference whatever to us: it is not for our sake that the universe causes summer and winter to succeed one another; these have a law of their own, according to which their divine functions are performed. We think too much of ourselves, when we imagine that we are worthy to have such prodigious revolutions effected for our sake: so, then, none of these things take place in order to do us an injury, nay, on the contrary, they all tend to our benefit. I have said that there are some things which cannot hurt us, and some which would not. To the latter class belong good men in authority, good parents, teachers, and judges, whose punishments ought to be submitted to by us in the same spirit in which we undergo the surgeon's knife, abstinence from food, and such like things which hurt us for our benefit. Suppose that we are being punished; let us think not only of what we suffer, but of what we have done: let us sit in judgement on our past life. Provided we are willing to tell ourselves the truth, we shall certainly decide that our crimes deserve a harder measure than they have received.

XXVIII

If we desire to be impartial judges of all that takes place, we must first convince ourselves of this, that no one of ns is faultless: for it is from this that most of our indignation proceeds. "I have not sinned, I have done no wrong." Say, rather, you do not admit that you have done any wrong. We are infuriated at being reproved, either by reprimand or actual chastisement, although we are sinning at that very time, by adding insolence and obstinacy to our wrong-doings. Who is there that can declare himself to have broken no laws? Even if there be such a man, what a stinted innocence it is, merely to be innocent by the letter of the law. How much further do the rules of duty extend than those of the law! how many things which are not to be found in the statute book, are demanded by filial feeling, kindness, generosity, equity, and honour? Yet we are not able to warrant ourselves even to come under that first narrowest definition of innocence: we have done what was wrong, thought what was wrong, wished for what was wrong, and encouraged what was wrong: in some cases we have only remained innocent because we did not succeed. When we think of this, let us deal more justly with sinners, and believe that those who scold us are right: in any case let us not be angry with ourselves (for with whom shall we not be angry, if we are angry even with our own selves?), and least of all with the gods: for whatever we suffer befalls us not by any ordinance of theirs but of the common law of all flesh. "But diseases and pains attack us." Well, people who live in a crazy dwelling must have some way of escape from it. Someone will be said to have spoken ill of you: think whether you did not first speak ill of him: think of how many persons you have yourself spoken ill. Let us not, I say, suppose that others are doing us a wrong, but are repaying one which we have done them, that some are acting with good intentions, some under compulsion, some in ignorance, and let us believe that even he who does so intentionally and knowingly did not wrong us merely for the sake of wronging us, but was led into doing so by the attraction of saying something witty, or did whatever he did, not out of any spite against us, but because he himself could not succeed unless he pushed us back. We are often offended by flattery even while it is being lavished upon us: yet whoever recalls to his mind how often he himself has been the victim of undeserved suspicion, how often fortune has given his true service an appearance of wrong-doing, how many persons he has begun by hating and ended by loving, will be able to keep himself from becoming angry straightway, especially if he silently says to himself when each offence is committed: "I have done this very thing myself." Where, however, will you find so impartial a judge? The same man who lusts after everyone's wife, and thinks that a woman's belonging to someone else is a sufficient reason for adoring her, will not allow anyone else to look at his own wife. No man expects such exact fidelity as a traitor: the perjurer himself takes vengeance of him who breaks his word : the pettifogging lawyer is most indignant at an action being brought against him: the man who is reckless of his own chastity cannot endure any attempt upon that of his slaves. We have other men's vices before our eyes, and our own behind our backs: hence it is that a father, who is worse than his son, blames the latter for giving extravagant feasts,[9] and disapproves of the least sign of luxury in another, although he was wont to set no bounds to it in his own case; hence it is that despots are angry with homicides, and thefts are punished by those who despoil temples. A great part of mankind is not angry with sins, but with sinners. Regard to our own selves[10] will make us more moderate, if we inquire of ourselves :—have we ever committed any crime of this sort? have we ever fallen into this kind of error? is it for our interest that we should condemn this conduct?

---

[9] Tempestiva, beginning before the usual hour.

[10] Fear of self-condemnation

XXIX

The greatest remedy for anger is delay: beg anger to grant you this at the first, not in order that it may pardon the offence, but that it may form a right judgment about it :- if it delays, it will come to an end. Do not attempt to quell it all at once, for its first impulses are fierce; by plucking away its parts we shall remove the whole. We are made angry by some things which we learn at second-hand, and hear or see. Now, we ought to be slow to believe what is told us. Many tell lies in order to deceive us, and many because they are themselves deceived. Some seek to win our favour by false accusations, and invent wrongs in order that they may appear angry at our having suffered them. One man lies out of spite, that he may set trusting friends at variance; some because they are suspicious,[11] and wish to see sport, and watch from a safe distance those whom they have set by the ears. If you were about to give sentence in court about ever so small a sum of money, you would take nothing as proved without a witness, and a witness would count for nothing except on his oath. You would allow both sides to be heard : you would allow them time: you would not despatch the matter at one sitting, because the oftener it is handled the more distinctly the truth appears. And do you condemn your friend offhand? Are you angry with him before you hear his story, before you have cross-examined him, before he can know either who is his accuser or with what he is charged. Why then, just now, in the case which you just tried, did you hear what was said on both sides? This very man who has informed against your friend, will say no more if he be obliged to prove what he says. "You need not," says he, "bring me forward as a witness; if I am brought forward I shall deny what I have said; unless you excuse me from appearing I shall never tell you anything." At the same time he spurs you on and withdraws himself from the strife and battle. The man who will tell you nothing save in secret hardly tells you anything at all. What can be more unjust than to believe in secret, and to be angry openly?

---

[11] Lipsius conjectures supprocax, mischievous

XXX

Some offences we ourselves witness: in these cases let us examine the disposition and purpose of the offender. Perhaps he is a child; let us pardon his youth, he knows not whether he is doing wrong: or he is a father; he has either rendered such great services, as to have won the right even to wrong ns—or perhaps this very act which offends ns is his chief merit: or a woman; well, she made a mistake. The man did it because he was ordered to do it. Who but an unjust person can be angry with what is done under compulsion? You had hurt him: well, there is no wrong in suffering the pain which you have been the first to inflict. Suppose that your opponent is a judge; then you ought to take his opinion rather than your own: or that he is a king; then, if he punishes the guilty, yield to him because he is just, and if he punishes the innocent, yield to him because he is powerful. Suppose that it is a dumb animal or as stupid as a dumb animal: then, if you are angry with it, you will make yourself like it. Suppose that it is a disease or a misfortune; it will take less effect upon you if you bear it quietly: or that it is a god; then you waste your time by being angry with him as much as if you prayed him to be angry with someone else. Is it a good man who has wronged you? do not believe it: is it a bad one? do not be surprised at this; he will pay to someone else the penalty which he owes to you—indeed, by his sin he has already punished himself.

XXXI

There are, as I have stated, two cases which produce anger: first, when we appear to have received an injury, about which enough has been said, and, secondly, when we appear to have been treated unjustly: this must now be discussed. Men think some things unjust because they ought not to suffer them, and some because they did not expect to suffer them: we think what is unexpected is beneath our deserts. Consequently, we are especially excited at what befalls us contrary to our hope and expectation: and this is why we are irritated at the smallest trifles in our own domestic affairs, and why we call our friends' carelessness deliberate injury. How is it, then, asks our opponent, that we are angered by the injuries inflicted by our enemies? It is because we did not expect those particular injuries, or, at any rate, not on so extensive a scale. This is caused by our excessive self-love: we think that we ought to remain uninjured even by our enemies: every man bears within his breast the mind of a despot, and is willing to commit excesses, but unwilling to submit to them. Thus it is either ignorance or arrogance that makes us angry: ignorance of common facts; for what is there to wonder at in bad men committing evil deeds? what novelty is there in your enemy hurting you, your friend quarrelling with you, your son going wrong, or your servant doing amiss? Fabius was wont to say that the most shameful excuse a general could make was "I did not think." I think it the most shameful excuse that a man can make. Think of everything, expect everything: even with men of good character something queer will crop up: human nature produces minds that are treacherous, ungrateful, greedy, and impious: when you are considering what any man's morals may be, think what those of mankind are. When you are especially enjoying yourself, be especially on your guard: when everything seems to you to be peaceful, be sure that mischief is not absent, but only asleep. Always believe that something will occur to offend you. A pilot never spreads all his canvas abroad so confidently as not to keep his tackle for shortening sail ready for use. Think, above all, how base and hateful is the power of doing mischief, and how unnatural in man, by whose kindness even fierce animals are rendered tame. See how bulls yield their necks to the yoke, how elephants[12] allow boys and women to dance on their backs unhurt, how snakes glide harmlessly over our bosoms and among our drinking-cups, how within their dens bears and lions submit to be handled with complacent mouths, and wild beasts fawn upon their master: let us blush to have exchanged habits with wild beasts. It is a crime to injure one's country: so it is, therefore, to injure any of our countrymen, for he is a part of our oountry;

---

[12] I have adopted the transposition of Haase and Koch

if the whole be sacred, the parts must be sacred too. Therefore it is also a crime to injure any man: for he is your fellow-citizen in a larger state. What, if the hands were to wish to hurt the feet? or the eyes to hurt the hands? As all the limbs act in unison, because it is the interest of the whole body to keep each one of them safe, so men should spare one another, because they are born for society. The bond of society, however, cannot exist unless it guards and loves all its members. We should not even destroy vipers and water-snakes and other creatures whose teeth and claws are dangerous, if we were able to tame them as we do other animals, or to prevent their befog a peril to us: neither ought we, therefore, to hurt a man because he has done wrong, but lest he should do wrong, and our punishment should always look to the future, and never to the past, because it is inflicted in a spirit of precaution, not of anger: for if everyone who has a crooked and vicious disposition were to be punished, no one would escape punishment.

XXXII

"But anger possesses a certain pleasure of its own, and it is sweet to pay back the pain you have suffered." Not at all; it is not honourable to requite injuries by injuries, in the same way as it is to repay benefits by benefits. In the latter case it is a shame to be conquered; in the former it is a shame to conquer. Revenge and retaliation are words which men use and even think to be righteous, yet they do not greatly differ from wrong-doing, except in the order in which they are done: he who renders pain for pain has more excuse for his sin; that is all. Someone who did not know Marcus Cato struck him in the public bath in his ignorance, for who would knowingly have done him an injury? Afterwards when he was apologizing, Cato replied, "I do not remember being struck." He thought it better to ignore the insult than to revenge it. You ask, "Did no harm befall that man for his insolence?" No, but rather much good; he made the acquaintance of Cato. It is the part of a great mind to despise wrongs done to it; the most contemptuous form of revenge is not to deem one's adversary worth taking vengeance upon. Many have taken small injuries much more seriously to heart than they need, by revenging them: that man is great and noble who like a large wild animal hears unmoved the tiny curs that bark at him.

XXXIII

"We are treated," says our opponent," with more respect if we revenge our injuries."If we make use of revenge merely as a remedy, let us use it without anger, and not regard revenge as pleasant, but as useful: yet often it is better to pretend not to have received an injury than to avenge it. The wrongs of the powerful must not only be borne, but borne with a cheerful countenance: they will repeat the wrong if they think they have inflicted it. This is the worst trait of minds rendered arrogant by prosperity, they hate those whom they have injured. Everyone knows the saying of the old courtier, who, when someone asked him how he had achieved the rare distinction of living at court till he reached old age, replied, "By receiving wrongs and returning thanks for them." It is often so far from expedient to avenge our wrongs, that it will not do even to admit them. Gaius Caesar, offended at the smart clothes and well-dressed hair of the son of Pastor, a distinguished Roman knight, sent him to prison. When the father begged that his son might suffer no harm, Gaius, as if reminded by this to put him to death, ordered him to be executed, yet, in order to mitigate his brutality to the father, invited him that very day to dinner. Pastor came with a countenance which betrayed no ill will. Caesar pledged him in a glass of wine, and set a man to watch him. The wretched creature went through his part, feeling as though he were drinking his son's blood: the emperor sent him some perfume and a garland, and gave orders to watch whether he used them: he did so. On the very day on which he had buried, nay, on which he had not even buried his son, he sat down as one of a hundred guests, and, old and gouty as he was, drank to an extent which would have been hardly decent on a child's birthday; he shed no tear the while; he did not permit his grief to betray itself by the slightest sign; he dined just as though his entreaties had gained his son's life. You ask me why he did so? he had another son. What did Priam do in the Iliad? Did he not conceal his wrath and embrace the knees of Achilles? did he not raise to his lips that death-dealing hand, stained with the blood of his son, and sup with his slayer? True! but there were no perfumes and garlands, and his fierce enemy encouraged him with many soothing words to eat, not to drain huge goblets with a guard standing over him to see that he did it. Had he only feared for himself, the father would have treated the tyrant with scorn: but love for his son quenched his anger: he deserved the emperor's permission to leave the banquet and gather up the bones of his son: but, meanwhile, that kindly and polite youth the emperor would not even permit him to do this, but tormented the old man with frequent invitations to drink, advising him thereby to lighten his sorrows. He, on the other hand, appeared to be in good spirits, and to have forgotten what had been done that day: he would have lost his second son had he proved an unacceptable guest to the murderer of his eldest.

XXXIV

We must, therefore, refrain from anger, whether he who provokes us be on a level with ourselves, or above us, or below us. A contest with one's equal is of uncertain issue, with one's superior is folly, and with one's inferior is contemptible. It is the part of a mean and wretched man to turn and bite one's biter: even mice and ants show their teeth if you put your hand to them, and all feeble creatures think that they are hurt if they are touched. It will make us milder tempered to call to mind any services which he with whom we are angry may have done us, and to let his deserts balance his offence. Let us also reflect, how much credit the tale of our forgiveness will confer upon us, how many men may be made into valuable friends by forgiveness. One of the lessons which Sulla's cruelty teaches us is not to be angry with the children of our enemies, whether they be public or private; for he drove the sons of the proscribed into exile. Nothing is more unjust than that any one should inherit the quarrels of his father. Whenever we are loath to pardon anyone, let us think whether it would be to our advantage that all men should be inexorable. He who refuses to pardon, how often has he begged it for himself? how often has he grovelled at the feet of those whom he spurns from his own? How can we gain more glory than by turning anger into friendship? what more faithful allies has the Roman people than those who have been its most unyielding enemies? where would the empire be to-day, had not a wise foresight united the conquered and the conquerors? If anyone is angry with you, meet his anger by returning benefits for it: a quarrel which is only taken up on one side falls to the ground: it takes two men to fight. But suppose that there is an angry struggle on both sides, even then, he is the better man who first gives way; the winner is the real loser. He struck you; well then, do you fall back: if you strike him in turn you will give him both an opportunity and an excuse for striking you again: you will not be able to withdraw yourself from the struggle when you please.

XXXV

Does anyone wish to strike his enemy so hard, as to leave his own hand in the wound, and not to be able, to recover his balance after the blow? yet such a weapon is anger: it is scarcely possible to draw it back. We are careful to choose for ourselves light weapons, handy and manageable swords: shall we not avoid these clumsy, unwieldy, and never-to-be-recalled impulses of the mind? The only swiftness of which men approve is that which, when bidden, checks itself and proceeds no further, and which can be guided, and reduced from a run to a walk: we know that the sinews are diseased when they move against our will. A man must be either aged or weakly who runs when he wants to walk: let us think that those are the most powerful and the soundest operations of our minds, which act under our own control, not at their own caprice. Nothing, however, will be of so much service as to consider, first, the hideousness, and, secondly, the danger of anger. No passion bears a more troubled aspect: it befouls the fairest face, makes fierce the expression which before was peaceful. From the angry "all grace has fled;" though their clothing may be fashionable, they will trail it on the ground and take no heed of their appearance; though their hair be smoothed down in a comely manner by nature or art, yet it will bristle up in sympathy with their mind. The veins become swollen, the breast will be shaken by quick breathing, the man's neck will be swelled as he roars forth his frantic talk: then, too, his limbs will tremble, his hands will be restless, his whole body will sway hither and thither. What, think you, must be the state of his mind within him, when its appearance without is so shocking? how far more dreadful a countenance he bears within his own breast, how far keener pride, how much more violent rage, which will burst him unless it finds some vent? Let us paint anger looking like those who are dripping with the blood of foemen or savage beasts, or those who are just about to slaughter them—like those monsters of the nether world fabled by the poet to be girt with serpents and breathing flame, when they sally forth from hell, most frightful to behold, in order that they may kindle wars, stir up strife between nations, and overthrow peace; let us paint her eyes glowing with fire, her voice hissing, roaring, grating, and making worse sounds if worse there be, while she brandishes weapons in both hands, for she cares not to protect herself, gloomy, stained with blood, covered with scars and livid with her own blows, reeling like a maniac, wrapped in a thick cloud, dashing hither and thither, spreading desolation and panic, loathed by everyone and by herself above all, willing, if otherwise she cannot hurt her foe, to overthrow alike-earth, sea, and heaven, harmful and hateful at the same time. Or, if we are to see her, let her be such as our poets have described her— "There with her blood-stained scourge Bellona fights, And Discord in her riven robe delights,"[13] or, if possible, let some even more dreadful aspect be invented for this dreadful passion.

---

[13] The lines are from Virgil, Æn. viii. 702, but are inaccurately quoted

XXXVI

Some angry people, as Sextius remarks, have been benefited by looking at the glass: they have been struck by so great an alteration in their own appearance: they have been, as it were, brought into their own presence and have not recognized themselves: yet how small a part of the real hideousness of anger did that reflected image in the mirror reproduce? Could the mind be displayed or made to appear through any substance, we should be confounded when we beheld how black and stained, how agitated, distorted, and swollen it looked: even at present if is very ugly when seen through all the screens of blood, bones, and so forth: what would it be, were it displayed uncovered? You say, that you do not believe that any one was ever scared out of anger by a mirror: and why not? because when he came to the mirror to change his mind, he had changed it already: to angry men no face looks fairer than one that is fierce and savage and such as they wish to look like. We ought rather to consider, how many men anger itself has injured. Some in their excessive heat have burst their veins; some by straining their voices beyond their strength have vomited blood, or have injured their sight by too violently injecting humours into their eyes, and have fallen sick when the fit passed off. No way loads more swiftly to madness: many have, consequently, remained always in the frenzy of anger, and, having once lost their reason, have never recovered it. Ajax was driven mad by anger, and driven to suicide by madness. Men, frantic with rage, call upon heaven to slay their children, to reduce themselves to poverty, and to ruin their houses, and yet declare that they are not either angry or insane. Enemies to their best friends, dangerous to their nearest find dearest, regardless of the laws save where they injure, swayed by the smallest trifles, unwilling to lend their ears to the advice or the services of their friends, they do everything by main force, and are ready either to fight with their swords or to throw themselves upon them, for the greatest of all evils, and one which surpasses all vices, has gained possession of them. Other passions gain a footing in the mind by slow degrees: anger's conquest is sudden and complete, and, moreover, it makes all other passions subservient to itself. It conquers the warmest love: men have thrust swords through the bodies of those whom they loved, and have slain those in whose arms they have lain. Avarice, that sternest and most rigid of passions, is trampled underfoot by anger, which forces it to squander its carefully collected wealth and set fire to its house and all its property in one heap. Why, has not even the ambitious man been known to fling away the most highly valued ensigns of rank, and to refuse high office when it was offered to him? There is no passion over which anger does not bear absolute rule.

Of Anger – Book III

I

WE will now, my Novatus, attempt to do that which you so especially long to do, that is, to drive out anger from our minds, or at all events to curb it and restrain its impulses. This may sometimes be done openly and without concealment, when we are only suffering from a slight attack of this mischief, and at other times it must be done secretly, when our anger is excessively hot, and when every obstacle thrown in its way increases it and makes it blaze higher. It is important to know how great and how fresh its strength may be, and whether it can be driven forcibly back and suppressed, or whether we must give way to it until its first storm blow over, lest it sweep away with it our remedies themselves. We must deal with each case according to each man's character: some yield to entreaties, others are rendered arrogant and masterful by submission: we may frighten some men out of their anger, while some may be turned from their purpose by reproaches, some by acknowledging oneself to be in the wrong, some by shame, and some by delay, a tardy remedy for a hasty disorder; which we ought only to use when all others have failed: for other passions admit of having their case put off, and may be healed at a later time; but the eager and self-destructive violence of anger does not grow up by slow degrees, but reaches its full height as soon as it begins. Nor does it, like other vices, merely disturb men's minds, but it takes them away, and torments them till they are incapable of restraining themselves and eager for the common ruin of all men, nor does it rage merely against its object, but against every obstacle which it encounters on its way. The other vices move our minds; anger hurls them headlong. If we are not able to withstand our passions, yet at any rate our passions ought to stand firm: but anger grows more and more powerful, like lightning flashes or hurricanes, or any other things which cannot stop themselves because they do not proceed along, but fall from above. Other vices affect our judgment, anger affects our sanity: others come in mild attacks and grow unnoticed, but men's minds plunge abruptly into anger. There is no passion that is more frantic, more destructive to its own self; it is arrogant if successful, and frantic if it fails. Even when defeated it does not grow weary, but if chance places its foe beyond its reach, it turns its teeth against itself. Its intensity is in no way regulated by its origin: for it rises to the greatest heights from the most trivial beginnings.

II

It passes over no time of life; no race of men is exempt from it: some nations have been saved from the knowledge of luxury by the blessing of poverty; some through their active and wandering habits have escaped from sloth; those whose manners are unpolished and whose life is rustic know not chicanery and fraud and all the evils to which the courts of law give birth: but there is no race which is not excited by anger, which is equally powerful with Greeks and barbarians, and is just as ruinous among law-abiding folk as among those whose only law is that of the stronger. Finally, the other passions seize upon individuals anger is the only one which sometimes possesses a whole state. No entire people ever fell madly in love with a woman, nor did any nation ever set its affections altogether upon gain and profit. Ambition attacks single individuals; ungovernable rage is the only passion that affects nations. People often fly into a passion by troops; men and women, old men and boys, princes and populace all act alike, and the whole multitude, after being excited by a very few words, outdoes even its exciter: men betake themselves straight-way to fire and sword, and proclaim a war against their neighbours or wage one against their countrymen. Whole houses are burned with the entire families which they contain, and he who but lately was honoured for his popular eloquence now finds that his speech moves people to rage. Legions aim their darts at their commander; the whole populace quarrels with the nobles; the senate, without waiting for troops to be levied or appointing a general, hastily chooses leaders, for its anger chases well-born men through the houses of Rome, and puts them to death with its own hand. Ambassadors are outraged, the law of nations violated, and an unnatural madness seizes the state. Without allowing time for the general excitement to subside, fleets are straightway launched and laden with a hastily enrolled soldiery. Without organization, without taking any auspices, the populace rushes into the field guided only by its own anger, snatches up whatever comes first to hand by way of arms, and then atones by a great defeat for the reckless audacity of its anger. This is usually the fate of savage nations when they plunge into war: as soon as their easily excited minds are roused by the appearance of wrong having been done them, they straightway hasten forth, and, guided only by their wounded feelings, fall like an avalanche upon our legions, without either discipline, fear, or precaution, and willfully seeking for danger. They delight in being struck, in pressing forward to meet the blow, writhing their bodies along the weapon, and perishing by a wound which they themselves make.

III

"No doubt," you say, "anger is very powerful and ruinous: point out, therefore, how it may be cured." Yet, as I stated in my former books, Aristotle stands forth in defence of anger, and forbids it to be uprooted, saying that it is the spur of virtue, and that when it is taken away, our minds become weaponless, and slow to attempt great exploits. It is therefore essential to prove its unseemliness and ferocity, and to place distinctly before our eyes how monstrous a thing it is that one man should rage against another, with what frantic violence he rushes to destroy alike himself and his foe, and overthrows those very things whose fall he himself must share. What, then? can anyone call this man sane, who, as though caught up by a hurricane, does not go but is driven, and is the slave of a senseless disorder? He does not commit to another the duty of revenging him, but himself exacts it, raging alike in thought and deed, butchering those who are dearest to him, and for whose loss he himself will ere long weep. Will any one give this passion as an assistant and companion to virtue, although it disturbs calm reason, without which virtue can do nothing? The strength which a sick man owes to a paroxysm of disease is neither lasting nor wholesome, and is strong only to its own destruction. You need not, therefore, imagine that I am wasting time over a useless task in defaming anger, as though men had not made up their minds about it, when there is someone, and he, too, an illustrious philosopher, who assigns it services to perform, and speaks of it as useful and supplying energy for battles, for the management of business, and indeed for everything which requires to be conducted with spirit. Lest it should delude any one into thinking that on certain occasions and in certain positions it may be useful, we must show its unbridled and frenzied madness, we must restore to it its attributes, the rack, the cord, the dungeon, and the cross, the fires lighted round men's buried bodies, the hook [1] that drags both living men and corpses, the different kinds of fetters, and of punishments, the mutilations of limbs, the branding of the forehead, the dens of savage beasts. Anger should be represented as standing among these her instruments, growling in an ominous and terrible fashion, herself more shocking than any of the means by which she gives vent to her fury.

---

[1] The hook alluded to was fastened to the neck of condemned criminals, and by it they were dragged to the Tiber. Also the bodies of dead gladiators were thus dragged out of the arena. The hook by which the dead bull is drawn away at a modern Spanish bull-fight is probably a survival of this custom.

IV

There may be some doubt about the others, but at any rate no passion has a worse look. We have described the angry man's appearance in our former books, how sharp and keen he looks, at one time pale as his blood is driven inwards and backwards, at another with all the heat and fire of his body directed to his face, making it reddish-coloured as if stained with blood, his eyes now restless and starting out of his head, now set motionless in one fixed gaze. Add to this his teeth, which gnash against one another, as though he wished to eat somebody, with exactly the sound of a wild boar sharpening his tusks: add also the cracking of his joints, the involuntary wringing of his hands, the frequent slaps he deals himself on the chest, his hurried breathing and deep-drawn sighs, his reeling body, his abrupt broken speech, and his trembling lips, which sometimes he draws tight as he hisses some curse through them. By Hercules, no wild beast, neither when tortured by hunger, or with a weapon struck through its vitals, not even when it gathers its last breath to bite its slayer, looks so shocking as a man raging with anger. Listen, if you have leisure, to his words and threats: how dreadful is the language of his agonized mind! Would not every man wish to lay aside anger when he sees that it begins by injuring himself? When men employ anger as the most powerful of agents, consider it to be a proof of power, and reckon a speedy revenge among the greatest blessings of great prosperity, would you not wish me to warn them that he who is the slave of his own anger is not powerful, nor even free? Would you not wish me to warn all the more industrious and circumspect of men, that while other evil passions assail the base, anger gradually obtains dominion over the minds even of learned and in other respects sensible men? So true is that, that some declare anger to be a proof of straight-forwardness, and it is commonly believed that the best-natured people are prone to it.

V

You ask me, whither does all this tend? To prove, I answer, that no one should imagine himself to be safe from anger, seeing that it rouses up even those who are naturally gentle and quiet to commit savage and violent acts. As strength of body and assiduous care of the health avail nothing against a pestilence, which attacks the strong and weak alike, so also steady and good-humoured people are just as liable to attacks of anger as those of unsettled character, and in the case of the former it is both more to be ashamed of and more to be feared, because it makes a greater alteration in their habits. Now as the first thing is not to be angry, the second to lay aside our anger, and the third to be able to heal the anger of others as well as our own, I will set forth first how we may avoid falling into anger; next, how we may set ourselves free from it, and, lastly, how we may restrain an angry man, appease his wrath, and bring him back to his right mind.

We shall succeed in avoiding anger, if from time to time we lay before our minds all the vices connected with anger, and estimate it at its real value: it must be prosecuted before us and convicted: its evils must be thoroughly investigated and exposed. That we may see what it is, let it be compared with the worst vices. Avarice scrapes together and amasses riches for some better man to use: anger spends money; few can indulge in it for nothing. How many slaves an angry master drives to run away or to commit suicide! how much more he loses by his anger than the value of what he originally became angry about! Anger brings grief to a father, divorce to a husband, hatred to a magistrate, failure to a candidate for office. It is worse than luxury, because luxury enjoys its own pleasure, while anger enjoys another's pain. It is worse than either spitefulness or envy; for they wish that someone may become unhappy, while anger wishes to make him so: they are pleased when evil befalls one by accident, but anger cannot wait upon Fortune; it desires to injure its victim personally, and is not satisfied merely with his being injured. Nothing is more dangerous than jealousy: it is produced by anger. Nothing is more ruinous than war: it is the outcome of powerful men's anger; and even the anger of humble private persons, though without arms or armies, is nevertheless war. Moreover, even if we pass over its immediate consequences, such as heavy losses, treacherous plots, and the constant anxiety produced by strife, anger pays a penalty at the same moment that it exacts one: it forswears human feelings. The latter urge us to love, anger urges us to hatred: the latter bid us do men good, anger bids us do them harm. Add to this that, although its rage arises from an excessive self-respect and appears to show high spirit, it really is contemptible and mean: for a man must be inferior to one by whom he thinks himself despised, whereas the truly great mind, which takes a true estimate of its own value, does not revenge an insult because it does not feel it. As weapons rebound from a hard surface, and solid substances hurt those who strike them, so also no insult can make a really great mind sensible of its presence, being weaker than that against which it is aimed. How far more glorious is it to throw back all wrongs and insults from oneself, like one wearing armour of proof against all weapons, for revenge is an admission that we have been hurt. That cannot be a great mind which is disturbed by injury. He who has hurt you must be either stronger or weaker than yourself. If he be weaker, spare him: if he be stronger, spare yourself.

VI

There is no greater proof of magnanimity than that nothing which befalls you should be able to move you to anger. The higher region of the universe, being more excellently ordered and near to the stars, is never gathered into clouds, driven about by storms, or whirled round by cyclones: it is free from all disturbance: the lightnings flash in the region below it. In like manner a lofty mind, always placid and dwelling in a serene atmosphere, restraining within itself all the impulses from which anger springs, is modest, commands respect, and remains calm and collected: none of which qualities will you find in an angry man: for who, when under the influence of grief and rage, does not first get rid of bashfulness? who, when excited and confused and about to attack someone, does not fling away any habits of shamefacedness he may have possessed? what angry man attends to the number or routine of his duties? who uses moderate language? Who keeps any part of his body quiet? who can guide himself when in full career? We shall find much profit in that sound maxim of Democritus which defines peace of mind to consist in not labouring much, or too much for our strength, either in public or private matters. A man's day, if he is engaged in many various occupations, never passes so happily that no man or no thing should give rise to some offence which makes the mind ripe for anger. Just as when one hurries through the crowded parts of the city one cannot help jostling many people, and one cannot help slipping at one place, being hindered at another, and splashed at another, so when one's life is spent in disconnected pursuits and wanderings, one must meet with many troubles and many accusations. One man deceives our hopes, another delays their fulfillment, another destroys them: our projects do not proceed according to our intention. No one is so favoured by Fortune as to find her always on his side if he tempts her often: and from this it follows that he who sees several enterprises turn out contrary to his wishes becomes dissatisfied with both men and things, and on the slightest provocation flies into a rage with people, with undertakings, with places, with fortune, or with himself. In order, therefore, that the mind may be at peace, it ought not to be hurried hither and thither, nor, as I said before, wearied by labour at great matters, or matters whose attainment is beyond its strength. It is easy to fit one's shoulder to a light burden, and to shift it from one side to the other without dropping it: but we have difficulty in bearing the burdens which others' hands lay upon us, and when overweighted by them we fling them off upon our neighbours. Even when we do stand upright under our load, we nevertheless reel beneath a weight which is beyond our strength.

VII

Be assured that the same rule applies both to public and private life: simple and manageable undertakings proceed according to the pleasure of the person in charge of them, but enormous ones, beyond his capacity to manage, are not easily undertaken. When he has got them to administer, they hinder him, and press hard upon him, and just as he thinks that success is within his grasp, they collapse, and carry him with them: thus it comes about that a man's wishes are often disappointed if he does not apply himself to easy tasks, yet wishes that the tasks which he undertakes may be easy. Whenever you would attempt anything, first form an estimate both of your own powers, of the extent of the matter which you are undertaking, and of the means by which you are to accomplish it: for if you have to abandon your work when it is half done, the disappointment will sour your temper. In such cases, it makes a difference whether one is of an ardent or of a cold and unenterprising temperament: for failure will rouse a generous spirit to anger, and will move a sluggish and dull one to sorrow. Let our undertakings, therefore, be neither petty nor yet presumptuous and reckless: let our hopes not range far from home: let us attempt nothing which if we succeed will make us astonished at our success.

VIII

Since we know not how to endure an injury, let us take care not to receive one: we should live with the quietest and easiest-tempered persons, not with anxious or with sullen ones: for our own habits are copied from those with whom we associate, and just as some bodily diseases are communicated by touch, so also the mind transfers its vices to its neighbours. A drunkard leads even those who reproach him to grow fond of wine: profligate society will, if permitted, impair the morals even of robust-minded men: avarice infects those nearest it with its poison. Virtues do the same thing in the opposite direction, and improve all those with whom they are brought in contact: it is as good for one of unsettled principles to associate with better men than himself as for an invalid to live in a warm country with a healthy climate. You will understand how much may be effected this way, if you observe how even wild beasts grow tame by dwelling among us, and how no animal, however ferocious, continues to be wild, if it has long been accustomed to human companionship: all its savageness becomes softened, and amid peaceful scenes is gradually forgotten. We must add to this, that the man who lives with quiet people is not only improved by their example, but also by the fact that he finds no reason for anger and does not practise his vice: it will, therefore, be his duty to avoid all those who he knows will excite his anger. You ask, who these are: many will bring about the same thing by various means; a proud man will offend you by his disdain, a talkative man by his abuse, an impudent man by his insults, a spiteful man by his malice, a quarrelsome man by his wrangling, a braggart and liar by his vain-gloriousness: you will not endure to be feared by a suspicious man, conquered by an obstinate one, or scorned by an ultra-refined one: Choose straightforward, good-natured, steady people, who will not provoke your wrath, and will bear with it. Those whose dispositions are yielding, polite and suave, will be of even greater service, provided they do not flatter, for excessive obsequiousness irritates bad-tempered men. One of my own friends was a good man indeed, but too prone to anger, and it was as dangerous to flatter him as to curse him. Caelius the orator, it is well known, was the worst-tempered man possible. It is said that once he was dining in his own chamber with an especially long-suffering client, but had great difficulty when thrown thus into a man's society to avoid quarrelling with him. The other thought it best to agree to whatever he said, and to play second fiddle, but Caelius could not bear his obsequious agreement, and exclaimed, "Do contradict me in something, that there may be two of us!" Yet even he, who was angry at not being angry, soon recovered his temper, because he had no one to fight with. If, then, we are conscious of an irascible disposition, let us especially choose for our friends those who will look and speak as we do: they will pamper us and lead us into a bad habit of listening to nothing that does not please us, but it will be good to give our anger respite and repose. Even those who are naturally crabbed and wild will yield to caresses: no creature continues either angry or frightened if you pat him. Whenever a controversy seems likely to be longer or more keenly disputed than usual, let us check its first beginnings, before it gathers strength. A dispute nourishes itself as it proceeds, and takes hold of those who plunge too deeply into it: it is easier to stand aloof than to extricate oneself from a struggle.

IX

Irascible men ought not to meddle with the more serious class of occupations, or, at any rate, ought to stop short of weariness in the pursuit of them; their mind ought not to be engaged upon hard subjects, but handed over to pleasing arts: let it be softened by reading poetry, and interested by legendary history: let it be treated with luxury and refinement. Pythagoras used to calm his troubled spirit by playing upon the lyre: and who does not know that trumpets and clarions are irritants, just as some airs are lullabies and soothe the mind? Green is good for wearied eyes, and some colours are grateful to weak sight, while the brightness of others is painful to it. In the same way cheerful pursuits soothe unhealthy minds. We must avoid law courts, pleadings, verdicts, and everything else that aggravates our fault, and we ought no less to avoid bodily weariness; for it exhausts all that is quiet and gentle in us, and rouses bitterness. For this reason those who cannot trust their digestion, when they are about to transact business of importance always allay their bile with food, for it is peculiarly irritated by fatigue, either because it draws the vital heat into the middle of the body, and injures the blood and stops its circulation by the clogging of the veins, or else because the worn-out and weakened body reacts upon the mind: this is certainly the reason why those who are broken by ill health or age are more irascible than other men. Hunger also and thirst should be avoided for the same reason; they exasperate and irritate men's minds: it is an old saying that "a weary man is quarrelsome ": and so also is a hungry or a thirsty man, or one who is suffering from any cause whatever: for just as sores pain one at the slightest touch, and afterwards even at the fear of being touched, so an unsound mind takes offence at the slightest things, so that even a greeting, a letter, a speech, or a question, provokes some men to anger.

X

That which is diseased can never bear to be handled without complaining: it is best, therefore, to apply remedies to oneself as soon as we feel that anything is wrong, to allow oneself as little licence as possible in speech, and to restrain one's impetuosity: now it is easy to detect the first growth of our passions: the symptoms precede the disorder. Just as the signs of storms and rain come before the storms themselves, so there are certain forerunners of anger, love, and all the storms which torment our minds. Those who suffer from epilepsy know that the fit is coming on if their extremities become cold, their sight fails, their sinews tremble, their memory deserts them, and their head swims: they accordingly check the growing disorder by applying the usual remedies: they try to prevent the loss of their senses by smelling or tasting some drug; they battle against cold and stiffness of limbs by hot fomentations; or, if all remedies fail, they retire apart, and faint where no one sees them fall. It is useful for a man to understand his disease, and to break its strength before it becomes developed. Let us see what it is that especially irritates us. Some men take offence at insulting words, others at deeds: one wishes his pedigree, another his person, to be treated with respect. This man wishes to be considered especially fashionable, that man to be thought especially learned: one cannot bear pride, another cannot bear obstinacy. One thinks it beneath him to be angry with his slaves, another is cruel at home, but gentle abroad. One imagines that he is proposed for office because he is unpopular, another thinks himself insulted because he is not proposed. People do not all take offence in the same way; you ought then to know what your own weak point is, that you may guard it with especial care.

XI

It is better not to see or to hear everything: many causes of offence may pass by us, most of which are disregarded by the man who ignores them. Would you not be irascible? then be not inquisitive. He who seeks to know what is said about him, who digs up spiteful tales even if they were told in secret, is himself the destroyer of his own peace of mind. Some stories may be so construed as to appear to be insults: wherefore it is best to put some aside, to laugh at others, and to pardon others. There are many ways in which anger may be checked; most things may be turned into jest. It is said that Socrates when he was given a box on the ear, merely said that it was a pity a man could not tell when he ought to wear his helmet out walking. It does not so much matter how an injury is done, as how it is borne; and I do not see how moderation can be hard to practise, when I know that even despots, though success and impunity combine to swell their pride, have sometimes restrained their natural ferocity. At any rate, tradition informs us that once, when a guest in his cups bitterly reproached Pisistratus, the despot of Athens, for his cruelty, many of those present offered to lay hands on the traitor, and one said one thing and one another to kindle his wrath, he bore it coolly, and replied to those who were egging him on, that he was no more angry with the man than he should be with one who ran against him blindfold.

XII

A large part of mankind manufacture their own grievances either by entertaining unfounded suspicions or by exaggerating trifles. Anger often comes to us, but we often go to it. It ought never to be sent for: even when it falls in our way it ought to be flung aside. No one says to himself, "I myself have done or might have done this very thing which I am angry with another for doing." No one considers the intention of the doer, but merely the thing done . yet we ought to think about him, and whether he did it intentionally or accidentally, under compulsion or under a mistake, whether he did it out of hatred for us, or to gain something for himself, whether he did it to please himself or to serve a friend. In some cases the age, in others the worldly fortunes of the culprit may render it humane or advantageous to bear with him and put up with what he has done. Let us put ourselves in the place of him with whom we are angry: at present an overweening conceit of our own importance makes us prone to anger, and we are quite willing to do to others what we cannot endure should be done to ourselves. No one will postpone his anger: yet delay is the best remedy for it, because it allows its first glow to subside, and gives time for the cloud which darkens the mind either to disperse or at any rate to become less dense. Of these wrongs which drive you frantic, some will grow lighter after an interval, not of a day, but even of an hour: some will vanish altogether. Even if you gain nothing by your adjournment, still what you do after it will appear to be the result of mature deliberation, not of anger. If you want to find out the truth about anything, commit the task to time: nothing can be accurately discerned at a time of disturbance. Plato, when angry with his slave, could not prevail upon himself to wait, but straightway ordered him to take off his shirt and present his shoulders to the blows which he meant to give him with his own hand: then, when he perceived that he was angry, he stopped the hand which he had raised in the air, and stood like one in act to strike. Being asked by a friend who happened to come in, what he was doing, he answered: "I am making an angry man expiate his crime." He retained the posture of one about to give way to passion, as if struck with astonishment at its being so degrading to a philosopher, forgetting the slave, because he had found another still more deserving of punishment. He therefore denied himself the exercise of authority over his own household, and once, being rather angry at some fault, said, "Speusippus, will you please to correct that slave with stripes; for I am in a rage." He would not strike him, for the very reason for which another man would have struck him. "I am in a rage," said he; "I should beat him more than I ought: I should take more pleasure than I ought in doing so: let not that slave fall into the power of one who is not in his own power." Can anyone wish to grant the power of revenge to an angry man, when Plato himself gave up his own right to exercise it? While you are angry, you ought not to be allowed to do anything. "Why?" do you ask? Because when you are angry there is nothing that you do not wish to be allowed to do.

XIII

Fight hard with yourself and if you cannot conquer anger, do not let it conquer you: you have begun to get the better of it if it does not show itself, if it is not given vent. Let us conceal its symptoms, and as far as possible keep it secret and hidden. It will give us great trouble to do this, for it is eager to burst forth, to kindle our eyes and to transform our face; but if we allow it to show itself in our outward appearance, it is our master. Let it rather be locked in the innermost recesses of our breast, and be borne by us, not bear us: nay, let us replace all its symptoms by their opposites; let us make our countenance more composed than usual, our voice milder, our step slower. Our inward thoughts gradually become influenced by our outward demeanour. With Socrates it was a sign of anger when he lowered his voice, and became sparing of speech; it was evident at such times that he was exercising restraint over himself. His friends, consequently, used to detect him acting thus, and convict him of being angry; nor was he displeased at being charged with concealment of anger; indeed, how could he help being glad that many men should perceive his anger, yet that none should feel it? they would however, have felt it had not he granted to his friends the same right of criticizing his own conduct which he himself assumed over theirs. How much more needful is it for us to do this? let us beg all our best friends to give us their opinion with the greatest freedom at the very time when we can bear it least, and never to be compliant with us when we are angry. While we are in our right senses, while we are under our own control, let us call for help against so powerful an evil, and one which we regard with such unjust favour. Those who cannot carry their wine discreetly, and fear to be betrayed into some rash and insolent act, give their slaves orders to take them away from the banquet when they are drunk; those who know by experience how unreasonable they are when sick give orders that no one is to obey them when they are in ill health. It is best to prepare obstacles beforehand for vices which are known, and above all things so to tranquilize our mind that it may bear the most sudden and violent shocks either without feeling anger, or, if anger be provoked by the extent of some unexpected wrong, that it may bury it deep, and not betray its wound. That it is possible to do this will be seen, if I quote a few of an abundance of examples, from which we may learn both how much evil there is in anger, when it exercises entire dominion over men in supreme power, and how completely it can control itself when over-awed by fear.

XIV

King Cambyses[2] was excessively addicted to wine. Præxaspes was the only one of his closest friends who advised him to drink more sparingly, pointing out how shameful a thing drunkenness was in a king, upon whom all eyes and ears were fixed. Cambyses answered, "That you may know that I never lose command of myself, I will presently prove to you that both my eyes and my hands are fit for service after I have been drinking." Hereupon he drank more freely than usual, using larger cups, and when heavy and besotted with wine ordered his reprover's son to go beyond the threshold and stand there with his left hand raised above his head; then he bent his bow and pierced the youth's heart, at which he had said that he aimed. He then had his. breast cut open, showed the arrow sticking exactly into the heart, and, looking at the boy's father, risked whether his hand was not steady enough. He replied, that Apollo himself could not have taken better aim. God confound such a man, a slave in mind, if not in station! He actually praised an act which he ought not to have endured to witness. He thought that the breast of his son being torn asunder, and his heart quivering with its wound, gave him an opportunity of making a complimentary speech. He ought to have raised a dispute with him about his success, and have called for another shot, that the king might be pleased to prove upon the person of the father that his hand was even steadier than when he shot the son. What a savage king! what a worthy mark for all his follower's arrows! Yet though we curse him for making his banquet end in cruelty and death, still it was worse to praise that arrow-shot than to shoot it. We shall see hereafter how a father ought to bear himself when standing over the corpse of his son, whose murder he had both caused and witnessed: the matter which we are now discussing, has been proved, I mean, that anger can be suppressed. He did not curse the king, he did not so much as let fall a single inauspicious word, though he felt his own heart as deeply wounded as that of his son. He may be said to have done well in choking down his words; for though he might have spoken as an angry man, yet he could not have expressed what he felt as a father. He may, I repeat, be thought to have behaved with greater wisdom on that occasion than when he tried to regulate the drink of one who was better employed in drinking wine than in drinking blood, and who granted men peace while his hands were busy with the winecup. He, therefore, added one more to the number of those who have shown to their bitter cost how little kings care for their friends' good advice.

---

[2] Heroditus, iii, 34, 35

XV

I have no doubt that Harpagus must have given some such advice to the king of the Persians and of himself, in anger at which the king placed Harpagus's own children before him on the dinner-table for him to eat, and asked him from time to time, whether he liked the seasoning. Then, when he saw that he was satiated with his own misery, he ordered their heads to be brought to him, and asked him how he liked his entertainment. The wretched man did not lose his readiness of speech; his face did not change. "Every kind of dinner," said he, "is pleasant at the king's table." What did he gain by this obsequiousness? He avoided being invited a second time to dinner, to eat what was left of them. I do not forbid a father to blame the act of his king, or to seek for some revenge worthy of so bloodthirsty a monster, but in the meanwhile I gather from the tale this fact, that even the anger which arises from unheard of outrages can be concealed, and forced into using language which is the very reverse of its meaning. This way of curbing anger is necessary, at least for those who have chosen this sort of life and who are admitted to dine at a king's table; this is how they must eat and drink, this is how they must answer, and how they must laugh at their own deaths. Whether life is worth having at such a price, we shall see hereafter; that is another question. Let us not console so sorry a crew, or encourage them to submit to the orders of their butchers; let us point out that however slavish a man's condition may be, there is always a path to liberty open to him, unless his mind be diseased. It is a man's own fault if he suffers, when by putting an end to himself he can put an end to his misery. To him whose king aimed arrows at the breasts of his friends, and to him whose master gorged fathers with the hearts of their children, I would say "Madman, why do you groan? for what are you waiting? for some enemy to avenge you by the destruction of your entire nation, or for some powerful king to arrive from a distant land? Wherever you turn your eyes you may see an end to your woes. Do you see that precipice? Down that lies the road to liberty; do you see that sea? that river? that well? Liberty sits at the bottom of them. Do you see that tree? stunted, blighted, dried up though it be, yet liberty hangs from its branches. Do you see your own throat, your own neck, your own heart? they are so many ways of escape from slavery. Are these modes which I point out too laborious, and needing much strength and courage? do you ask what path leads to liberty? I answer, any vein[3] in your body.

---

[3] Seneca's own death, by opening his veins, gives a melancholy interest to this passage

XVI

As long, however, as we find nothing in our life so unbearable as to drive us to suicide, let us, in whatever position we may be, set anger far from us: it is destructive to those who are its slaves. All its rage turns to its own misery, and authority becomes all the more irksome the more obstinately it is resisted. It is like a wild animal whose struggles only pull the noose by which it is caught tighter; or like birds who, while flurriedly trying to shake themselves free, smear birdlime onto all their feathers. No yoke is so grievous as not to hurt him who struggles against it more than him who yields to it: the only way to alleviate great evils is to endure them and to submit to do what they compel. This control of our passions, and especially of this mad and unbridled passion of anger, is useful to subjects, but still more useful to kings. All is lost when a man's position enables him to carry out whatever anger prompts him to do; nor can power long endure if it be exercised to the injury of many, for it becomes endangered as soon as common fear draws together those who bewail themselves separately. Many kings, therefore, have fallen victims, some to single individuals, others to entire peoples, who have been forced by general indignation to make one man the minister of their wrath. Yet many kings have indulged their anger as though it were a privilege of royalty, like Darius, who, after the dethronement of the Magian, was the first ruler of the Persians and of the greater part of the East: for when he declared war [4] against the Scythians who bordered on the empire of the East, Oeobazus, an aged noble, begged that one of his three sons might be left at home to comfort his father, and that the king might be satisfied with the services of two of them. Darius promised him more than he asked for, saying that he would allow all three to remain at home, and flung their dead bodies before their father's eyes. He would have been harsh, had he taken them all to the war with him. How much more good-natured was Xerxes,[5] who, when Pythias, the father of five sons, begged for one to be excused from service, permitted him to choose which he wished for. He then tore the son whom the father had chosen into two halves, placed one on each side of the road, and, as it were, purified his army by means of this propitiatory victim. He therefore had the end which he deserved, being defeated, and his army scattered far and wide in utter rout, while he in the midst of it walked among the corpses of his soldiers, seeing on all sides the signs of his own overthrow.

---

[4] Heroditus, iv, 84

[5] Heroditus, vii, 38, 39

XVII

So ferocious in their anger were those kings who had no learning, no tincture of polite literature: now I will show you King Alexander (the Great), fresh from the lap of Aristotle, who with his own hand while at table stabbed Clitus, his dearest friend, who had been brought up with him, because he did not flatter him enough, and was too slow in transforming himself from a free man and a Macedonian into a Persian slave. Indeed he shut up Lysimachus,[6] who was no less his friend than Clitus, in a cage with a lion; yet did this make Lysimachus, who escaped by some happy chance from the lion's teeth, any gentler when he became a king? Why, he mutilated his own friend, Telesphorus the Rhodian, cutting off his nose and ears, and kept him for a long while in a den, like some new and strange animal, after the hideousness of his hacked and disfigured face had made him no longer appear to be human, assisted by starvation and the squalid filth of a body loft to wallow in its own dung! Besides this, his hands and knees, which the narrowness of his abode forced him to use instead of his feet, became hard and callous, while his sides were covered with sores by rubbing against the walls, so that his appearance was no less shocking than frightful, and his punishment turned him into so monstrous a creature that he was not even pitied. Yet, however unlike a man he was who suffered this, even more unlike was he who inflicted it.

---

[6] Plut. Dem. 27

XVIII

Would to heaven that such savagery had contented itself with foreign examples, and that barbarity in anger and punishment had not been imported with other outlandish vices into our Roman manners! Marcus Marius, to whom the people erected a statue in every street, to whom they made offerings of incense and wine, had, by the command of Lucius Sulla, his legs broken, his eyes pulled out, his hands cut off, and his whole body gradually torn to pieces limb by limb, as if Sulla killed him as many times as he wounded him. Who was it who carried out Sulla's orders? who but Catiline, already practising his hands in every sort of wickedness? He tore him to pieces before the tomb of Quintus Catulus, an unwelcome burden to the ashes of that gentlest of men, above which one who was no doubt a criminal, yet nevertheless the idol of the people, and who was not undeserving of love, although men loved him beyond all reason, was forced to shed his blood drop by drop. Though Marius deserved such tortures, yet it was worthy of Sulla to order them, and of Catiline to execute them; but it was unworthy of the State to be stabbed by the swords of her enemy and her avenger alike. Why do I pry into ancient history? quite lately Gaius Caesar flogged and tortured Sextus Papinius, whose father was a consular, Betilienas Bassus, his own quaestor, and several others, both senators and knights, on the same day, not to carry out any judicial inquiry, but merely to amuse himself. Indeed, so impatient was he of any delay in receiving the pleasure which his monstrous cruelty never delayed in asking, that when walking with some ladies and senators in his mother's gardens, along the walk between the colonnade and the river, he struck off some of their heads by lamplight. What did he fear? what public or private danger could one night threaten him with? how very small a favour it would have been to wait until morning, and not to kill the Roman people's senators in his slippers?

XIX

It is to the purpose that we should know how haughtily his cruelty was exercised, although someone might suppose that we are wandering from the subject and embarking on a digression; but this digression is itself connected with unusual outbursts of anger. He beat senators with rods; he did it so often that he made men able to say, "It is the custom." He tortured them with all the most dismal engines in the world, with the cord, the boots, the rack, the fire, and the sight of his own face. Even to this we may answer, " To tear three senators to pieces with stripes and fire like criminal slaves was no such great crime for one who had thoughts of butchering the entire Senate, who was wont to wish that the Roman people had but one neck, that he might concentrate into one day and one blow all the wickedness which he divided among so many places and times. Was there ever anything so unheard-of as an execution in the night-time? Highway robbery seeks for the shelter of darkness, but the more public an execution is, the more power it has as an example and lesson. Here I shall be met by: "This, which you are so surprised at, was the daily habit of that monster; this was what he lived for, watched for, sat up at night for." Certainly one could find no one else who would have ordered all those whom he condemned to death to have their mouths closed by a sponge being fastened in them, that they might not have the power even of uttering a sound. What dying man was ever forbidden to groan? He feared that the last agony might find too free a voice, that he might hear what would displease him. He knew, moreover, that there were countless crimes, with which none but a dying man would dare to reproach him. When sponges were not forthcoming, he ordered the wretched men's clothes to be torn up, and the rags stuffed into their mouths. What savagery was this? Let a man draw his last breath: give room for his soul to escape through: let it not be forced to leave the body through a wound. It becomes tedious to add to this that in the same night he sent centurions to the houses of the executed men and made an end of their fathers also, that is to say, being a compassionate-minded man, he set them free from sorrow: for it is not my intention to describe the ferocity of Gaius, but the ferocity of anger, which does not merely vent its rage upon individuals, but rends in pieces whole nations, and even lashes cities, rivers, and things which have no sense of pain.

XX

Thus, the king of the Persians cut off the noses of a whole nation in Syria, wherefore the place is called Rhinocolura. Do you think that he was merciful, because he did not cut their heads off altogether? no, he was delighted at having invented a new kind of punishment. Something of the same kind would have befallen the Æthiopians,[7] who on account of their prodigiously long lives are called Macrobiotae; for, because they did not receive slavery with hands uplifted to heaven in thankfulness, and sent an embassy which used independent, or what kings call insulting language, Cambyses became wild with rage, and, without any store of provisions, or any knowledge of the roads, started with all his fighting men through an arid and trackless waste, where during the first day's march the necessaries of life failed, and the country itself furnished nothing, being barren and uncultivated, and untrodden by the foot of man. At first the tenderest parts of leaves and shoots of trees relieved their hunger, then hides softened by fire, and anything else that their extremity drove them to use as food. When as they proceeded neither roots nor herbs were to be found in the sand, and they found a wilderness destitute even of animal life, they chose each tenth man by lot and made of him a meal which was more cruel than hunger. Rage still drove the king madly forwards, until after he had lost one part of his army and eaten another he began to fear that he also might be called upon to draw the lot for his life; then at last he gave the order for retreat. Yet all the while his well-bred hawks were not sacrificed, and the means of feasting were carried for him on camels, while his soldiers were drawing lots for who should miserably perish, and who should yet more miserably live.

---

[7] Heroditus, iii, 17, sqq.

XXI

This man was angry with an unknown and inoffensive nation, which nevertheless was able to feel his wrath; but Cyrus[8] was angry with a river. When hurrying to besiege Babylon, since in making war it is above all things important to seize one's opportunity, he tried to ford the wide-spread river Gyndes, which it is hardly safe to attempt even when the river has been dried up by the summer heat and is at its lowest. Here one of the white horses which drew the royal chariot was washed away, and his loss moved the king to such violent rage, that he swore to reduce the river which had carried off his royal retinue to so low an ebb that even women should walk across it and trample upon it. He thereupon devoted all the resources of his army to this object, and remained working until by cutting one hundred and eighty channels across the bed of the river he divided it into three hundred and sixty brooks, and left the bed dry, the waters flowing through other channels. Thus he lost time, which is very important in great operations, and lost, also, the soldiers' courage, which was broken by useless labour, and the opportunity of falling upon his enemy unprepared, while he was waging against the river the war which he had declared against his foes. This frenzy, for what else can you call it, has befallen Romans also, for G. Caesar destroyed a most beautiful villa at Herculaneum because his mother was once imprisoned in it, and has thus made the place notorious by its misfortune; for while it stood, we used to sail past it without noticing it, but now people inquire why it is in ruins.

---

[8] Heroditus, I, 189, 190

XXII

These should be regarded as examples to be avoided, and what I am about to relate, on the contrary, to be followed, being examples of gentle and lenient conduct in men who both had reasons for anger and power to avenge themselves. What could have been easier than for Antigonus to order those two common soldiers to be executed who leaned against their king's tent while doing what all men especially love to do, and run the greatest danger by doing, I mean while they spoke evil of their king. Antigonus heard all they said, as was likely, since there was only a piece of cloth between the speakers and the listener, who gently raised it, .and said "Go a little further off, for fear the king should hear you." He also on one night, hearing some of his soldiers invoking everything that was evil upon their king for having brought them along that road and into that impassable mud, went to those who were in the greatest difficulties, and having extricated them without their knowing who was their helper, said, "Now curse Antigonus, by whose fault you have fallen into this trouble, but bless the man who has brought you out of this slough." This same Antigonus bore the abuse of his enemies as good-naturedly as that of his countrymen; thus when he was besieging some Greeks in a little fort, and they, despising their enemy through their confidence in the strength of their position, cut many jokes upon the ugliness of Antigonus, at one time mocking him for his shortness of stature, at another for his broken nose, he answered, "I rejoice, and expect some good fortune because I have a Silenus in my camp." After he had conquered these witty folk by hunger, his treatment of them was to form regiments of those who were fit for service, and sell the rest by public auction; nor would he, said he, have done this had it not been better that men who had such evil tongues should be under the control of a master.

XXIII

This man's grandson[9] was Alexander, who used to hurl his lance at his guests, who, of the two friends which I have mentioned above, exposed one to the rage of a wild beast, and the other to his own; yet of these two men, he who was exposed to the lion survived. He did not derive this vice from his grandfather, nor even from his father; for it was an especial virtue of Philip's to endure insults patiently, and was a great safeguard of his kingdom. Demochares, who was surnamed Parrhesiastes on account of his unbridled and impudent tongue, came on an embassy to him with other ambassadors from Athens. After graciously listening to what they had to say, Philip said to them, "Tell me, what can I do that will please the Athenians?" Demochares took him up, and answered, "Hang yourself." All the bystanders expressed their indignation at so brutal an answer, but Philip bade them be silent, and let this Thersites depart safe and sound. "But do you," said he, "you other ambassadors, tell the Athenians that those who say such things are much more arrogant than those who hear them without revenging themselves." The late Emperor Augustus also did and said many memorable things, which prove that he was not under the dominion of anger. Timagenes, the historical writer, made some remarks upon him, his wife, and his whole family: nor did his jests fall to the ground, for nothing spreads more widely or is more in people's mouths than reckless wit. Caesar often warned him to be less audacious in his talk, and as he continued to offend, forbade him his house. Timagenes after this passed the later years of his life as the guest of Asinius Pollio, and was the favourite of the whole city: the closing of Caesar's door did not close any other door against him. He read aloud the history which he wrote after this, but burned the books which contained the doings of Augustus Caesar. He was at enmity with Caesar, but yet no one feared to be his friend, no one shrank from him as though he were blasted by lightning: although he fell from so high a place, yet someone was found to catch him in his lap. Caesar, I say, bore this with patience, and was not even irritated by the historian's having laid violent hands upon his own glories and acts: he never complained of the man who afforded his enemy shelter, but merely said to Asinius Pollio "You are keeping a wild beast:" then, when the other would have excused his conduct, he stopped him, and said "Enjoy, my Pollio, enjoy his friendship." When Pollio said, "If you order me, Caesar, I will straightway forbid him my house," he answered, "Do you think that I am likely to do this, after having made you friends again?" for formerly Pollio had been angry with Timagenes, and ceased to be angry with him for no

---

[9] A mistake: Antigonus (Monophthalmus) was one of Alexander's generals

other reason than that Caesar began to be so.

XXIV

Let everyone, then, say to himself, whenever he is provoked, "Am I more powerful than Philip? yet he allowed a man to curse him with impunity. Have I more authority in my own house than the Emperor Augustus possessed throughout the world? yet he was satisfied with leaving the society of his maligner. Why should I make my slave atone by stripes and manacles for having answered me too loudly or having put on a stubborn look, or muttered something which I did not catch? Who am I, that it should be a crime to shock my ears? Many men have forgiven their enemies: shall I not forgive men for being lazy, careless, and gossipping?" We ought to plead age as an excuse for children, sex for women, freedom for a stranger, familiarity for a house-servant. Is this his first offence? think how long he has been acceptable. Has he often done wrong, and in many other cases? then let us continue to bear what we have borne so long. Is he a friend? then he did not intend to do it. Is he an enemy? then in doing it he did his duty. If he be a sensible man, let us believe his excuses; if a fool, let us grant him pardon; whatever he may be, let us say to ourselves on his behalf, that even the wisest of men are often in fault, that no one is so alert that his carefulness never betrays itself, that no one is of so ripe a judgment that his serious mind cannot be goaded by circumstances into some hotheaded action, that, in fine, no one, however much he may fear to give offence, can help doing so even while he tries to avoid it.

XXV

As it is a consolation to a humble man in trouble that the greatest are subject to reverses of fortune, and a man weeps more calmly over his dead son in the corner of his hovel if he sees a piteous[10] funeral proceed out of the palace as well; so one bears injury or insult more calmly if one remembers that no power is so great as to be above the reach of harm. Indeed, if even the wisest do wrong, who cannot plead a good excuse for his faults? Let us look back upon our own youth, and think how often we then were too slothful in our duty, too impudent in our speech, too intemperate in our cups. Is anyone angry then let us give him enough time to reflect upon what he has done, and he will correct his own self. But suppose he ought to pay the penalty of his deeds: well, that is no reason why we should act as he does. It cannot be doubted that he who regards his tormentor with contempt raises himself above the common herd and looks down upon them from a loftier position: it is the property of true magnanimity not to feel the blows which it may receive. So does a huge wild beast turn slowly and gaze at yelping curs: so does the wave dash in vain against a great cliff. The man who is not angry remains unshaken by injury: he who is angry has been moved by it. He, however, whom I have described as being placed too high for any mischief to reach him, holds as it were the highest good in his arms: he can reply, not only to any man, but to fortune herself: "Do what you will, you are too feeble to disturb my serenity: this is forbidden by reason, to whom I have entrusted the guidance of my life: to become angry would do me more harm than your violence can do me. 'More harm?' say you. Yes, certainly: I know how much injury you have done me, but I cannot tell to what excesses anger might not carry me."

---

[10] Acerbum = ἀωρου; the funeral of one who has been cut off in the flower of this youth

XXVI

You say, "I cannot endure it: injuries are hard to bear." You lie; for how can anyone not be able to bear injury, if he can bear to be angry? Besides, what you intend to do is to endure both injury and anger. Why do you bear with the delirium of a sick man, or the ravings of a madman, or the impudent blows of a child? Because, of course, they evidently do not know what they are doing: a man be not responsible for his actions, what does it matter by what malady he became so : the plea of ignorance holds equally good in every case. "What then?" say you, "shall he not be punished?" He will be, even supposing that you do not wish it: for the greatest punishment for having done harm is the sense of having done it, and no one is more severely punished than he who is given over to the punishment of remorse. In the next place, we ought to conder the whole state of mankind, in order to pass a just judgment on all the occurrences of life: for it is unjust to blame individuals for a vice which is common to all. The colour of an Æthiop is not remarkable among this own people, nor is any man in Germany ashamed of red hair rolled into a knot. You cannot call anything peculiar or disgraceful in a particular man if it is the general characteristic of his nation. Now, the cases which I have quoted are defended only by the usage of one out-of-the-way quarter of the world: see now, how far more deserving of pardon those crimes are which are spread abroad among all mankind. We all are hasty and careless, we all are untrustworthy, dissatisfied, and ambitious: nay, why do I try to hide our common wickedness by a too partial description? we all are bad. Every one of us therefore will find in his own breast the vice which he blames in another. Why do you remark how pale this man, or how lean that man is? there is a general pestilence. Let us therefore be more gentle one to another: we are bad men, living among bad men: there is only one thing which can afford us peace, and that is to agree to forgive one another. "This man has already injured me," say you, "and I have not yet injured him." No, but you have probably injured someone else, and you will injure him some day. Do not form your judgment by one hour, or one day: consider the whole tendency of your mind: even though you have done no evil, yet you are capable of doing it.

XXVII

How far better is it to heal an injury than to avenge it? Revenge takes up much time, and throws itself in the way of many injuries while it is smarting under one. We all retain our anger longer than we feel our hurt: how far better it were to take the opposite course and not meet one mischief by another. Would anyone think himself to be in his perfect mind if he were to return kicks to a mule or bites to a dog? "These creatures," you say, "know not that they are doing wrong." Then, in the first place, what an unjust judge you must be if a man has less chance of gaining your forgiveness than a beast! Secondly, if animals are protected from your anger by their want of reason, you ought to treat all foolish men in the like manner: for if a man has that mental darkness which excuses all the wrong-doings of dumb animals, what difference does it make if in other respects he be unlike a dumb animal? He has sinned. Well, is this the first time, or will this be the last time? Why, you should not believe him even if he said, "Never will I do so again." He will sin, and another will sin against him, and all his life he will wallow in wickedness. Savagery must be met by kindness: we ought to use, to a man in anger, the argument which is so effective with one in grief, that is, "Shall you leave off this at some time, or never? If you will do so at some time, how better is it that you should abandon anger than that anger should abandon you? Or, will this excitement never leave you? Do you see to what an unquiet life you condemn yourself? for what will be the life of one who is always swelling with rage?" Add to this, that after you have worked yourself up into a rage, and have from time to time renewed the cranes of your excitement, yet your anger will depart from you of its own accord, and time will sap its strength: how much better then is it that it should be overcome by you than by itself?

XXVIII

If you are angry, you will quarrel first with this man, and then with that: first with slaves, then with freedmen: first with parents, then with children: first with acquaintances, then with strangers: for there are grounds for anger in every case, unless your mind steps in and intercedes with you: your frenzy will drag you from one place to another, and from thence to elsewhere, your madness will constantly meet with newly-occurring irritants, and will never depart from you. Tell me, miserable man, what time you will have for loving? O, what good time you are wasting on an evil thing! How much better it would be to win friends, and disarm enemies: to serve the state, or to busy oneself with one's private affairs, rather than to cast about for what harm you can do to somebody, what wound you can inflict either upon his social position, his fortune, or his person, although you cannot succeed in doing so without a struggle and risk to yourself, even if your antagonist be inferior to you. Even supposing that he were handed over to you in chains, and that you were at liberty to torture him as much as you please, yet even then excessive violence in striking a blow often causes us to dislocate a joint, or entangles a sinew in the teeth which it has broken. Anger makes many men cripples, or invalids, even when it meets with an unresisting victim: and besides this, no creature is so weak that it can be destroyed without any danger to its destroyer: sometimes grief, sometimes chance, puts the weakest on a level with the strongest. What shall we say of the fact that the greater part of the things which enrage us are insults, not injuries? It makes a great difference whether a man thwarts my wishes or merely fails to carry them out, whether he robs me or does not give me anything: yet we count it all the same whether a man takes anything from us or refuses to give anything to us, whether he extinguishes our hope or defers it, whether his object be to hinder us or to help himself, whether he acts out of love for someone or out of hatred for us. Some men are bound to oppose us not only on the ground of justice, but of honour: one is defending his father, another his brother, another his country, another his friend: yet we do not forgive men for doing what we should blame them for not doing; nay, though one can hardly believe it, we often think well of an act, and ill of the man who did it. But, by Hercules, a great and just man looks with respect at the bravest of his enemies, and the most obstinate defender of his freedom and his country, and wishes that he had such a man for his own countryman and soldier.

XXIX

It is shameful to hate him whom you praise: but how much more shameful is it to hate a man for something for which he deserves to be pitied? If a prisoner of war, who has suddenly been reduced to the condition of a slave, still retains some remnants of liberty, and does not run nimbly to perform foul and toilsome tasks, if, having grown slothful by long rest, he cannot run fast enough to keep pace with his master's horse or carriage, if sleep overpowers him when weary with many days and nights of watching, if he refuses to undertake farm work, or does not do it heartily when brought away from the idleness of city service and put to hard labour, we ought to make a distinction between whether a man cannot or will not do it: we should pardon many slaves, if we began to judge them before we began to be angry with them: as it is, however, we obey our first impulse, and then, although we may prove to have been excited about mere trifles, yet we continue to be angry, lest we should seem to have begun to be angry without cause; and, most unjust of all, the injustice of our anger makes us persist in it all the more; for we nurse it and inflame it, as though to be violently angry proved our anger to be just.

XXX

How much better is it to observe how trifling, how inoffensive are the first beginnings of anger? You will see that men are subject to the same influences as dumb animals: we are put out by trumpery, futile matters. Bulls are excited by red colour, the asp raises its head at a shadow, bears or lions are irritated at the shaking of a rag, and all creatures who are naturally fierce and wild are alarmed at trifles. The same thing befalls men both of restless and of sluggish disposition; they are seized by suspicions, sometimes to such an extent that they call slight benefits injuries: and these form the most common and certainly the most bitter subject for anger: for we become angry with our dearest friends for having bestowed less upon us than we expected, and less than others have received from them: yet there is a remedy at hand for both these grievances. Has he favoured our rival more than ourselves? then let us enjoy what we have without making any comparisons. A man will never be well off to whom it is a torture to see any one better off than himself. Have I less than I hoped for? well, perhaps I hoped for more than I ought. This it is against which we ought to be especially on our guard: from hence arises the most destructive anger, sparing nothing, not even the holiest. The Emperor Julius was not stabbed by so many enemies as by friends whose insatiable hopes he had not satisfied. He was willing enough to do so, for no one ever made a more generous use of victory, of whose fruits he kept nothing for himself save the power of distributing them; but how could he glut such unconscionable appetites, when each man coveted as much as any one man could possess? This was why he saw his fellow-soldiers standing round his chair with drawn swords, Tillius Cimber, though he had a short time before been the keenest defender of his party, and others who only became Pompeians after Pompeius was dead. This it is which has turned the arms of kings against them, and made their trustiest followers meditate the death of him for whom and before whom[11] they once would have been glad to die.

---

[11] In point of time

XXXI

No man is satisfied with his own lot if he fixes his attention on that of another: and this leads to our being angry even with the gods, because somebody precedes us, though we forget of how many we take precedence, and that when a man envies few people, he must be followed in the background by a huge crowd of people who envy him. Yet so churlish is human nature, that, however much men may have received, they think themselves wronged if they are able to receive still more. "He gave me the praetorship. Yes, but I had hoped for the consulship. He bestowed the twelve axes upon me: true, but he did not make me a regular[12] consul. He allowed me to give my name to the year, but he did not help me to the priesthood. I have been elected a member of the college: but why only of one? He has bestowed upon me every honour that the state affords: yes, but he has added nothing to my private fortune. What he gave me he was obliged to give to somebody: he brought out nothing from his own pocket." Rather than speak thus, thank him for what you have received: wait for the rest, and be thankful that you are not yet too full to contain more: there is a pleasure in having something left to hope for. Are you preferred to everyone? then rejoice at holding the first place in the thoughts of your friend. Or are many others preferred before you? then think how many more are below you than there are above you. Do you ask, what is your greatest fault? It is, that you keep your accounts wrongly: you set a high value upon what you give, and a low one upon what you receive.

---

[12] Consul ordinarius, a regular consul, one who administered in office from the first of January, in opposition to consul suffectus, one chosen in the course of the year in the place of one who had died. The consul ordinarius gave his name to the year

XXXII

Let different qualities in different people keep us from quarrelling with them . let us fear to be angry with some, feel ashamed of being angry with others, and disdain to be angry with others. We do a fine thing, indeed, when we send a wretched slave to the workhouse! Why are we in such a hurry to flog him at once, to break his legs straightway? we shall not lose our boasted power if we defer its exercise. Let us wait for the time when we ourselves can give orders: at present we speak under constraint from anger. When it has passed away we shall see what amount of damage has been done; for this is what we are especially liable to make mistakes about: we use the sword, and capital punishment, and we appoint chains, imprisonment, and starvation to punish a crime which deserves only flogging with a light scourge. "In what way," say you, "do you bid us look at those things by which we think ourselves injured, that we may see how paltry, pitiful, and childish they are?" Of all things I would charge you to take to yourself a magnanimous spirit, and behold how low and sordid all these matters are about which we squabble and run to and fro till we are out of breath; to anyone who entertains any lofty and magnificent ideas, they are not worthy of a thought.

XXXIII

The greatest hullabaloo is about money: this it is which wearies out the law-courts, sows strife between father and son, concocts poisons, and gives swords to murderers just as to soldiers: it is stained with our blood: on account of it husbands and wives wrangle all night long, crowds press round the bench of magistrates, kings rage and plunder, and overthrow communities which it has taken the labour of centuries to build, that they may seek for gold and silver in the ashes of their cities. Do you like to look at your money-bags lying in the corner? it is for these that men shout till their eyes start from their heads, that the law-courts ring with the din of trials, and that jurymen brought from great distances sit to decide which man's covetousness is the more equitable. What shall we say if it be not even for a bag of money, but for a handful of coppers or a shilling scored up by a slave that some old man, soon to die without an heir, bursts with rage? what if it be an invalid money-lender whose feet are distorted by the gout, and who can no longer use his hands to count with, who calls for his interest of one thousandth a month,[13] and by his sureties demands his pence even during the paroxysms of his disease? If you were to bring to me all the money from all our mines, which we are at this moment sinking, if you were to bring to-night all that is concealed in hoards, where avarice returns money to the earth from whence it came, and pity that it ever was dug out—all that mass I should not think worthy to cause a wrinkle on the brow of a good man. What ridicule those things deserve which bring tears into our eyes!

---

[13] It seems inconceivable that so small an interest, 1-1/5 per cent. per an., can be meant

XXXIV

Come now, let us enumerate the other causes of anger: they are food, drink, and the showy apparatus connected with them, words, insults, disrespectful movements of the body, suspicions, obstinate cattle, lazy slaves, and spiteful construction put upon other men's words, so that even the gift of language to mankind becomes reckoned among the wrongs of nature. Believe me, the things which cause us such great heat are trifles, the sort of things that children fight and squabble over: there is nothing serious, nothing important in all that we do with such gloomy faces. It is, I repeat, the setting a great value on trifles that is the cause of your anger and madness. This man wanted to rob me of my inheritance, that one has brought a charge against me before persons[14] whom I had long courted with great expectations, that one has coveted my mistress. A wish for the same things, which ought to have been a bond of friendship, becomes a source of quarrels and hatred. A narrow path causes quarrels among those who pass up and down it; a wide and broadly spread road may be used by whole tribes without jostling. Those objects of desire of yours cause strife and disputes among those who covet the same things, because they are petty, and cannot be given to one man without being taken away from another.

---

[14] Captatis, Madvig. Adv. II. 394

XXXV

You are indignant at being answered back by your slave, your freedman, your wife, or your client: and then you complain of the state having lost the freedom which you have destroyed in your own house: then again if he is silent when you question him, you call it sullen obstinacy. Let him both speak and be silent, and laugh too. "In the presence of his master?" you ask. Nay, say rather "in the presence of the house-father." Why do you shout? why do you storm ? why do you in the middle of dinner call for a whip, because the slaves are talking, because a crowd as large as a public meeting is not as silent as the wilderness? You have ears, not merely that you may listen to musical sounds, softly and sweetly drawn out and harmonized: you ought to hear laughter and weeping, coaxing and quarrelling, joy and sorrow, the human voice and the roaring and barking of animals. Miserable one! why do you shudder at the noise of a slave, at the rattling of brass or the banging of a door? you cannot help hearing the thunder, however refined you may be. You may apply these remarks about your ears with equal truth to your eyes, which are just as dainty, if they have been badly schooled: they are shocked at stains and dirt, at silver plate which is not sufficiently bright, or at a pool whose water is not clear down to the bottom. Those same eyes which can only endure to see the most variegated marble, and that which has just been scoured bright, which will look at no table whose wood is not marked with a network of veining, and which at home are loath to tread upon anything that is not more precious than gold, will, when out of doors, gaze most calmly upon rough and miry paths, will see unmoved that the greater number of persons that meet them are shabbily dressed, and that the walls of the houses are rotten, full of cracks, and uneven. What, then, can be the reason that they are not distressed out of doors by sights which would shock them in their own home, unless it be that their temper is placid and long-suffering in one case, sulky and fault-finding in the other?

XXXVI

All our senses should be educated into strength: they are naturally able to endure much, provided that the spirit forbears to spoil them. The spirit ought to be brought up for examination daily. It was the custom of Sextius when the day was over, and he had betaken himself to rest, to inquire of his spirit: "What bad habit of yours have you cured to-day? what vice have you checked? in what respect are you better?" Anger will cease, and become more gentle, if it knows that every day it will have to appear before the judgment seat. What can be more admirable than this fashion of discussing the whole of the day's events? how sweet is the sleep which follows this self-examination? how calm, how sound, and careless is it when our spirit has either received praise or reprimand, and when our secret inquisitor and censor has made his report about our morals? I make use of this privilege, and daily plead my cause before myself: when the lamp is taken out of my sight, and my wife, who knows my habit, has ceased to talk, I pass the whole day in review before myself, and repeat all that I have said and done: I conceal nothing from myself, and omit nothing: for why should I be afraid of any of my shortcomings, when it is in my power to say, "I pardon you this time: see that you never do that anymore? In that dispute you spoke too contentiously: do not for the future argue with ignorant people: those who have never been taught are unwilling to learn. You reprimanded that man with more freedom than you ought, and consequently you have offended him instead of amending his ways: in dealing with other cases of the kind, you should look carefully, not only to the truth of what you say, but also whether the person to whom you speak can bear to be told the truth." A good man delights in receiving advice: all the worst men are the most impatient of guidance.

XXXVII

At the dinner-table some jokes and sayings intended to give you pain have been directed against you: avoid feasting with low people. Those who are not modest even when sober become much more recklessly impudent after drinking. You have seen your friend in a rage with the porter of some lawyer or rich man, because he has sent him back when about to enter, and you yourself on behalf of your friend have been in a rage with the meanest of slaves. Would you then be angry with a chained house-dog? Why, even he, after a long bout of barking, becomes gentle if you offer him food. So draw back and smile; for the moment your porter fancies himself to be somebody, because he guards a door which is beset by a crowd of litigants; for the moment he who sits within is prosperous and happy, and thinks that a street-door through which it is hard to gain entrance is the mark of a rich and powerful man; he knows not that the hardest door of all to open is that of the prison. Be prepared to submit to much. Is anyone surprised at being cold in winter? at being sick at sea? or at being jostled in the street? The mind is strong enough to bear those evils for which it is prepared. When you are not given a sufficiently distinguished place at table you have begun to be angry with your fellow-guests, with your host, and with him who is preferred above you. Idiot! What difference can it make what part of the couch you rest upon? Can a cushion give you honour or take it away? You have looked askance at somebody, because he has spoken slightingly of your talents; will you apply this rule to yourself? If so, Ennius, whose poetry you do not care for, would have hated you. Hortensius, if you had found fault with his speeches, would have quarreled with you, and Cicero, if you had laughed at his poetry, would have been your enemy. A candidate for office, will you resent men's votes?

XXXVIII

Someone has offered you an insult? Not a greater one, probably, than was offered to the Stoic philosopher Diogenes, in whose face an insolent young man spat just when he was lecturing upon anger. He bore it mildly and wisely. "I am not angry," said he, "but I am not sure that I ought not to be angry." Yet how much better did our Cato behave? When he was pleading, one Lentulus, whom our fathers remember as a demagogue and passionate man, spat all the phlegm he could muster upon his forehead. Cato wiped his face, and said, "Lentulus, I shall declare to all the world that men are mistaken when they say that you are wanting in cheek."

XXXIX

We have now succeeded, my Novatus, in properly regulating our own minds: they either do not feel anger or are above it: let us next see how we may soothe the wrath of others, for we do not only wish to be whole, but to heal. You should not attempt to allay the first burst of anger by words: it is deaf and frantic: we must give it scope; our remedies will only be effective when it slackens. We do not meddle with men's eyes when they are swollen, because we should only irritate their hard stiffness by touching them, nor do we try to cure other diseases when at their height: the best treatment in the first stage of illness is rest. "Of how very little value," say you, "is your remedy, if it appeases anger which is subsiding of its own accord?" In the first place, I answer, it makes it end quicker: in the next, it prevents a relapse. It can render harmless even the violent impulse which it dares not soothe: it will put out of the way all weapons which might be used for revenge: it will pretend to be angry, in order that its advice may have more weight as coming from an assistant and comrade in grief. It will invent delays, and postpone immediate punishment while a greater one is being sought for: it will use every artifice to give the man a respite from his frenzy. If his anger be unusually strong, it will inspire him with some irresistible feeling of shame or of fear: if weak, it will make use of conversation on amusing or novel subjects, and by playing upon his curiosity lead him to forget his passion. We are told that a physician, who was forced to cure the king's daughter, and could not without using the knife, conveyed a lancet to her swollen breast concealed under the sponge with which he was fomenting it. The same girl, who would have shrunk from the remedy if he had applied it openly, bore the pain because she did not expect it. Some diseases can only be cured by deceit.

XL

To one class of men you will say, "Beware, lest your anger give pleasure to your foes:" to the other, "Beware lest your greatness of mind and the reputation it bears among most people for strength become impaired. I myself, by Hercules, am scandalized at your treatment and am grieved beyond measure, but we must wait for a proper opportunity. He shall pay for what he has done; be well assured of that: when you are able you shall return it to him with interest." To reprove a man when he is angry is to add to his anger by being angry oneself. You should approach him in different ways and in a compliant fashion, unless perchance you be so great a personage that you can quash his anger, as the Emperor Augustus did when he was dining with Vedius Pollio.[15] One of the slaves had broken a crystal goblet of his: Vedius ordered him to be led away to die, and that too in no common fashion: he ordered him to be thrown to feed the muraenae, some of which fish, of great size, he kept in a tank. Who would not think that he did this out of luxury? but it was out of cruelty. The boy slipped through the hands of those who tried to seize him, and flung himself at Caesar's feet in order to beg for nothing more than that he might die in some different way, and not be eaten. Caesar was shocked at this novel form of cruelty, and ordered him to be let go, and, in his place, all the crystal ware which he saw before him to be broken, and the tank to be filled up. This was the proper way for Caesar to reprove his friend: he made a good use of his power. What are you, that when at dinner you order men to be put to death, and mangled by an unheard-of form of torture? Are a man's bowels to be torn asunder because your cup is broken? You must think a great deal of yourself, if even when the emperor is present you order men to be executed.

---

[15] See "On Clemency," i. 18, 2

XLI

If any one's power is so great that he can treat anger with the tone of a superior let him crush it out of existence, but only if it be of the kind of which I have just spoken, fierce, inhuman, bloodthirsty, and incurable save by fear of something more powerful than itself...let us give the mind that peace which is given by constant meditation upon wholesome maxims, by good actions, and by a mind directed to the pursuit of honour alone. Let us set our own conscience fully at rest, but make no efforts to gain credit for ourselves: so long as we deserve well, let us be satisfied, even if we should be ill spoken of. "But the common herd admires spirited actions, and bold men are held in honour, while quiet ones are thought to be indolent." True, at first sight they may appear to be so: but as soon as the even tenor of their life proves that this quietude arises not from dullness but from peace of mind, then that same populace respects and reverences them. There is, then, nothing useful in that hideous and destructive passion of anger, but on the contrary, every kind of evil, fire and sword. Anger tramples self-restraint under-foot, steeps its hands in slaughter, scatters abroad the limbs of its children: it leaves no place unsoiled by crime, it has no thoughts of glory, no fears of disgrace, and when once anger has hardened into hatred, no amendment is possible.

XLII

Let us be free from this evil, let us clear our minds of it, and extirpate root and branch a passion which grows again wherever the smallest particle of it finds a resting-place. Let us not moderate anger, but get rid of it altogether: what can moderation have to do with an evil habit? We shall succeed in doing this, if only we exert ourselves. Nothing will be of greater service than to bear in mind that we are mortal : let each man say to himself and to his neighbour, "Why should we, as though we were born to live forever, waste our tiny span of life in declaring anger against any one? why should days, which we might spend in honourable enjoyment, be misapplied in grieving and torturing others? Life is a matter which does not admit of waste, and we have no spare time to throw away. Why do we rush into the fray? why do we go out of our way to seek disputes? why do we, forgetful of the weakness of our nature, undertake mighty feuds, and, frail though we be, summon up all our strength to cut down other men? Ere long, fever or some other bodily ailment will make us unable to carry on this warfare of hatred which we so implacably wage: death will soon part the most vigorous pair of combatants. Why do we make disturbances and spend our lives in rioting? fate hangs over our heads, scores up to our account the days as they pass, and is ever drawing nearer and nearer. The time which you have marked for the death of another perhaps includes your own."

XLIII

Instead of acting thus, why do you not rather draw together what there is of your short life, and keep it peaceful for others and for yourself? why do you not rather make yourself beloved by everyone while you live, and regretted by everyone when you die? Why do you wish to tame that man's pride, because he takes too lofty a tone with you? why do you try with all your might to crush that other who snaps and snarls at you, a low and contemptible wretch, but spiteful and offensive to his betters? Master, why are you angry with your slave? Slave, why are you angry with your master? Client, why are you angry with your patron? Patron, why are you angry with your client? Wait but a little while. See, here comes death, who will make you all equals. We often see at a morning performance in the arena a battle between a bull and a bear, fastened together, in which the victor, after he has torn the other to pieces, is himself slain. We do just the same thing: we worry someone who is connected with us, although the end of both victor and vanquished is at hand, and that soon. Let us rather pass the little remnant of our lives in peace and quiet: may no one loathe us when we lie dead. A quarrel is often brought to an end by a cry of "Fire!" in the neighbourhood, and the appearance of a wild beast parts the highwayman from the traveller: men have no leisure to battle with minor evils when menaced by some overpowering terror. What have we to do with fighting and ambuscades? do you want anything more than death to befall him with whom you are angry? well, even though you sit quiet, he will be sure to die. You waste your pains: you want to do what is certain to be done. You say, "I do not wish necessarily to kill him, but to punish him by exile, or public disgrace, or loss of property." I can more easily pardon one who wishes to give his enemy a wound than one who wishes to give him a blister: for the latter is not only bad, but petty-minded. Whether you are thinking of extreme or slighter punishments, how very short is the time during which either your victim is tortured or you enjoy an evil pleasure in another's pain? This breath that we hold so dear will soon leave us: in the meantime, while we draw it, while we live among human beings, let us practise humanity: let us not be a terror or a danger to anyone. Let us keep our tempers in spite of losses, wrongs, abuse or sarcasm, and let us endure with magnanimity our shortlived troubles: while we are considering what is due to ourselves, as the saying is, and worrying ourselves, death will be upon us.

Of Leisure

I

.... why do they with great unanimity recommend vices to us? even though we attempt nothing else that would do us good, yet retirement in itself will be beneficial to us: we shall be better men when taken singly — and if so, what an advantage it will be to retire into the society of the best of men, and to choose some example by which we may guide our lives! This cannot be done without leisure: with leisure we can carry out that which we have once for all decided to be best, when there is no one to interfere with us and with the help of the mob pervert our as yet feeble judgment: with leisure only can life, which we distract by aiming at the most incompatible objects, flow on in a single gentle stream. Indeed, the worst of our various ills is that we change our very vices, and so we have not even the advantage of dealing with a well-known form of evil: we take pleasure first in one and then in another, and are, besides, troubled by the fact that our opinions are not only wrong, but lightly formed; we toss as it were on waves, and clutch at one thing after another: we let go what we just now sought for, and strive to recover what we have let go. We oscillate between desire and remorse, for we depend entirely upon the opinions of others, and it is that which many people praise and seek after, not that which deserves to be praised and sought after, which we consider to be best. Nor do we take any heed of whether our road be good or bad in itself, but we value it by the number of footprints upon it, among which there are none of any who have returned. You will say to me, "Seneca, what are you doing? do you desert your party? I am sure that our Stoic philosophers say we must be in motion up to the very end of our life, we will never cease to labour for the general good, to help individual people, and when stricken in years to afford assistance even to our enemies. We are the sect that gives no discharge for any number of years' service, and in the words of the most eloquent of poets: —

'We wear the helmet when our locks are grey.'[1]

We are they who are so far from indulging in any leisure until we die, that if circumstances permit it, we do not allow ourselves to be at leisure even when we are dying. Why do you preach the maxims of Epicurus in the very headquarters of Zeno? nay, if you are ashamed of your party, why do you not go openly altogether over to the enemy rather than betray your own side?" I

---

[1] Virg. " Æn." ix. 612. Compare Sir Walter Scott, "Lay of the Last Minstrel," canto iv.:—
"And still, in age, he spurned at rest,
And still his brows the helmet pressed,
Albeit the blanched locks below
Were white as Dinlay's spotless snow," &c.

will answer this question straightway: What more can you wish than that I should imitate my leaders? What then follows? I shall go whither they lead me, not whither they send me.

II

Now I will prove to you that I am not deserting the tenets of the Stoics: for they themselves have not deserted them: and yet I should be able to plead a very good excuse even if I did follow, not their precepts, but their examples. I shall divide what I am about to say into two parts: first, that a man may from the very beginning of his life give himself up entirely to the contemplation of truth; secondly, that a man when he has already completed his term of service, has the best of rights, that of his shattered health, to do this, and that he may then apply his mind to other studies after the manner of the Vestal virgins, who allot different duties to different years, first learn how to perform the sacred rites, and when they have learned them teach others.

III

I will show that this is approved of by the Stoics also, not that I have laid any commandment upon myself to do nothing contrary to the teaching of Zeno and Chrysippus, but because the matter itself allows me to follow the precepts of those men; for if one always follows the precepts of one man, one ceases to be a debater and becomes a partisan. Would that all things were already known, that truth were unveiled and recognized, and that none of our doctrines required modification! but as it is we have to seek for truth in the company of the very men who teach it. The two sects of Epicureans and Stoics differ widely in most respects, and on this point among the rest, nevertheless, each of them consigns us to leisure, although by a different road. Epicurus says, "The wise man will not take part in politics, except upon some special occasion ;" Zeno says, "The wise man will take part in politics, unless prevented by some special circumstance." The one makes it his aim in life to seek for leisure, the other seeks it only when he has reasons for so doing: but this word "reasons" has a wide signification. If the state is so rotten as to be past helping, if evil has entire dominion over it, the wise man will not labour in vain or waste his strength in unprofitable efforts. Should he be deficient in influence or bodily strength, if the state refuse to submit to his guidance, if his health stand in the way, then he will not attempt a journey for which he is unfit, just as he would not put to sea in a worn-out ship, or enlist in the army if he were an invalid. Consequently, one who has not yet suffered either in health or fortune has the right, before encountering any storms, to establish himself in safety, and thenceforth to devote himself to honourable industry and inviolate leisure, and the service of those virtues which can be practiced even by those who pass the quietest of lives. The duty of a man is to be useful to his fellow-men; if possible, to be useful to many of them; failing this, to be useful to a few; failing this, to be useful to his neighbours, and, failing them, to himself: for when he helps others, he advances the general interests of mankind. Just as he who makes himself a worse man does harm not only to himself but to all those to whom he might have done good if he had made himself a better one, so he who deserves well of himself does good to others by the very fact that he is preparing what will be of service to them.

IV

Let us grasp the fact that there are two republics, one vast and truly "public," which contains alike gods and men, in which we do not take account of this or that nook of land, but make the boundaries of our state reach as far as the rays of the sun: and another to which we have been assigned by the accident of birth. This may be that of the Athenians or Carthaginians, or of any other city which does not belong to all men but to some especial ones. Some men serve both of these states, the greater and the lesser, at the same time; some serve only the lesser, some only the greater. We can serve the greater commonwealth even when we are at leisure; indeed I am not sure that we cannot serve it better when we are at leisure to inquire into what virtue is, and whether it be one or many: whether it be nature or art that makes men good: whether that which contains the earth and sea and all that in them is be one, or whether God has placed therein many bodies of the same species: whether that out of which all things are made be continuous and solid, or containing interstices and alternate empty and full spaces: whether God idly looks on at His handiwork, or directs its course: whether He is without and around the world, or whether He pervades its entire surface: whether the world be immortal, or doomed to decay and belonging to the class of things which are born only for a time? What service does he who meditates upon these questions render to God? He prevents these His great works having no one to witness them.

V

We have a habit of saying that the highest good is to live according to nature: now nature has produced us for both purposes, for contemplation and for action. Let us now prove what we said before: nay, who will not think this proved if he bethinks himself how great a passion he has for discovering the unknown? how vehemently his curiosity is roused by every kind of romantic tale. Some men make long voyages and undergo the toils of journeying to distant lands for no reward except that of discovering something hidden and remote. This is what draws people to public shows, and causes them to pry into everything that is closed, to puzzle out everything that is secret, to clear up points of antiquity, and to listen to tales of the customs of savage nations. Nature has bestowed upon us an inquiring disposition, and being well aware of her own skill and beauty, has produced us to be spectators of her vast works, because she would lose all the fruits of her labour if she were to exhibit such vast and noble works of such complex construction, so bright and beautiful in so many ways, to solitude alone. That you may be sure that she wishes to be gazed upon, not merely looked at, see what a place she has assigned to us: she has placed us in the middle of herself and given us a prospect all around. She has not only set man erect upon his feet, but also with a view to making it easy for him to watch the heavens, she has raised his head on high and connected it with a pliant neck, in order that he might follow the course of the stars from their rising to their setting, and move his face round with the whole heaven. Moreover, by carrying six constellations across the sky by day, and six by night, she displays every part of herself in such a manner that by what she brings before man's eyes she renders him eager to see the rest also. For we have not beheld all things, nor yet the true extent of them, but our eyesight does but open to itself the right path for research, and lay the foundation, from which our speculations may pass from what is obvious to what is less known, and find out something more ancient than the world itself, from whence those stars came forth: inquire what was the condition of the universe before each of its elements were separated from the general mass: on what principle its confused and blended parts were divided: who assigned their places to things, whether it was by their own nature that what was heavy sunk downwards, and what was light flew upwards, or whether besides the stress and weight of bodies some higher power gave laws to each of them: whether that greatest proof that the spirit of man is divine be true, the theory, namely, that some parts and as it were sparks of the stars have fallen down upon earth and stuck there in a foreign substance. Our thought bursts through the battlements of heaven, and is not satisfied with knowing only what is shown to us: "I investigate," it says, "that which lies without the world, whether it be a bottomless abyss, or whether it also is confined within boundaries of its own: what the appearance of the things outside may be, whether they be shapeless and vague, extending equally in every direction, or whether they also are arranged in a certain kind of order: whether they are connected with this world of ours, or are widely separated from it and welter about in empty space: whether they consist of distinct atoms, of which everything that is and that is to be, is made, or whether their substance is uninterrupted and all of it capable of change: whether the elements are naturally opposed to one another, or whether they are not at variance, but work towards the same end by different means." Since man was born for such speculations as these, consider how short a time he has been given for them, even supposing that he makes good his claims to the whole of it, allows no part of it to be wrested from him through good nature, or to slip away from him through carelessness; though he watches over all his hours with most miserly care, though he live to the extreme confines of human existence, and though misfortune take nothing away from what Nature bestowed upon him, even then man is too mortal for the comprehension of immortality. I live according to Nature, therefore, if I give myself entirely up to her, and if I admire and reverence her. Nature, however, intended me to do both, to practise both contemplation and action: and I do both, because even contemplation is not devoid of action.

VI

"But," say you, "it makes a difference whether you adopt the contemplative life for the sake of your own pleasure, demanding nothing from it save unbroken contemplation without any result: for such a life is a sweet one and has attractions of its own." To this I answer you: It makes just as much difference in what spirit you lead the life of a public man, whether you are never at rest, and never set apart any time during which you may turn your eyes away from the things of earth to those of Heaven. It is by no means desirable that one should merely strive to accumulate property without any love of virtue, or do nothing but hard work without any cultivation of the intellect, for these things ought to be combined and blended together; and, similarly, virtue placed in leisure without action is but an incomplete and feeble good thing, because she never displays what she has learned. Who can deny that she ought to test her progress in actual work, and not merely think what ought to be done, but also sometimes use her hands as well as her head, and bring her conceptions into actual being? But if the wise man be quite willing to act thus, if it be the things to be done, not the man to do them that are wanting, will you not then allow him to live to himself? What is the wise man's purpose in devoting himself to leisure? He knows that in leisure as well as in action he will accomplish something by which he will be of service to posterity. Our school at any rate declares that Zeno and Chrysippus have done greater things than they would have done had they been in command of armies, or filled high offices, or passed laws: which latter indeed they did pass, though not for one single state, but for the whole human race. How then can it be unbecoming to a good man to enjoy a leisure such as this, by whose means he gives laws to ages to come, and addresses himself not to a few persons but to all men of all nations, both now and hereafter? To sum up the matter, I ask you whether Cleanthes, Chrysippus, and Zeno lived in accordance with their doctrine? I am sure that you will answer that they lived in the manner in which they taught that men ought to live: yet no one of them governed a state. "They had not," you reply, "the amount of property or social position which as a rule enables people to take part in public affairs." Yet for all that they did not live an idle life: they found the means of making their retirement more useful to mankind than the perspirings and runnings to and fro of other men: wherefore these persons are thought to have done great things, in spite of their having done nothing of a public character.

VII

Moreover, there are three kinds of life, and it is a stock question which of the three is the best: the first is devoted to pleasure, the second to contemplation, the third to action. First, let us lay aside all disputatiousness and bitterness of feeling, which, as we have stated, causes those whose paths in life are different to hate one another beyond all hope of reconciliation, and let us see whether all these three do not come to the same thing, although under different names: for neither he who decides for pleasure is without contemplation, nor is he who gives himself up to contemplation without pleasure: nor yet is he, whose life is devoted to action, without contemplation. "It makes," you say, "all the difference in the world, whether a thing is one's main object in life, or whether it be merely an appendage to some other object." I admit that the difference is considerable, nevertheless the one does not exist apart from the other: the one man cannot live in contemplation without action, nor can the other act without contemplation: and even the third, of whom we all agree in having a bad opinion, does not approve of passive pleasure, but of that which he establishes for himself by means of reason: even this pleasure-seeking sect itself, therefore, practises action also. Of course it does, since Epicurus himself says that at times he would abandon pleasure and actually seek for pain, if he became likely to be surfeited with pleasure, or if he thought that by enduring a slight pain he might avoid a greater one. With what purpose do I state this? To prove that all men are fond of contemplation. Some make it the object of their lives: to us it is an anchorage, but not a harbour.

VIII

Add to this that, according to the doctrine of Chrysippus, a man may live at leisure: I do not say that he ought to endure leisure, but that he ought to choose it. Our Stoics say that the wise man would not take part in the government of any state. What difference does it make by what path the wise man arrives at leisure, whether it be because the state is wanting to him, or he is wanting to the state? If the state is to be wanting to all wise men (and it always will be found wanting by refined thinkers), I ask you, to what state should the wise man betake himself; to that of the Athenians, in which Socrates is condemned to death, and from which Aristotle goes into exile lest he should be condemned to death? where virtues are borne down by jealousy? You will tell me that no wise man would join such a state. Shall then the wise man go to the commonwealth of the Carthaginians, where faction never ceases to rage, and liberty is the foe of all the best men, where justice and goodness are held of no account, where enemies are treated with inhuman cruelty and natives are treated like enemies: he will flee from this state also. If I were to discuss each one separately, I should not be able to find one which the wise man could endure, or which could endure the wise man. Now if such a state as we have dreamed of cannot be found on earth, it follows that leisure is necessary for everyone, because the one thing which might be preferred to leisure is nowhere to be found. If anyone says that to sail is the best of things, and then says that we ought not to sail in a sea in which shipwrecks were common occurrences, and where sudden storms often arise which drive the pilot back from his course, I should imagine that this man, while speaking in praise of sailing, was really forbidding me to unmoor my ship.

Of Peace of Mind

I [Serenus]

WHEN I examine myself, Seneca, some vices appear on the surface, and so that I can lay my hands upon them, while others are less distinct and harder to reach, and some are not always present, but recur at intervals: and these I should call the most troublesome, being like a roving enemy that assails one when he sees his opportunity, and who will neither let one stand on one's guard as in war, nor yet take one's rest without fear as in peace. The position in which I find myself more especially (for why should I not tell you the truth as I would to a physician), is that of neither being thoroughly set free from the vices which I fear and hate, nor yet quite in bondage to them: my state of mind, though not the worst possible, is a particularly discontented and sulky one: I am neither ill nor well. It is of no use for you to tell me that all virtues are weakly at the outset, and that they acquire strength and solidity by time, for I am well aware that even those which do but help our outward show, such as grandeur, a reputation for eloquence, and everything that appeals to others, gain power by time. Both those which afford us real strength and those which do but trick us out in a more attractive form, require long years before they gradually are adapted to us by time. But I fear that custom, which confirms most things, implants this vice more and more deeply in me. Long acquaintance with both good and bad people leads one to esteem them all alike. What this state of weakness really is, when the mind halts between two opinions without any strong inclination towards either good or evil, I shall be better able to show you piecemeal than all at once. I will tell you what befalls me, you must find out the name of the disease. I have to confess the greatest possible love of thrift: I do not care for a bed with gorgeous hangings, nor for clothes brought out of a chest, or pressed under weights and made glossy by frequent manglings, but for common and cheap ones, that require no care either to keep them or to put them on. For food I do not want what needs whole troops of servants to prepare it and admire it, nor what is ordered many days before and served up by many hands, but something handy and easily come at, with nothing far-fetched or costly about it, to be had in every part of the world, burdensome neither to one's fortune nor one's body, not likely to go out of the body by the same path by which it came in. I like[1] a rough and unpolished homebred servant, I like my servant born in my house: I like my country-bred father's heavy silver plate stamped with no maker's name: I do not want a table that is beauteous with dappled spots, or known to all the town by the number of fashionable people to whom it has successively belonged, but one which

---

[1] Cf Juv. ii. 150

Of Peace of Mind

stands merely for use, and which causes no guest's eye to dwell upon it with pleasure or to kindle at it with envy. While I am well satisfied with this, I am reminded of the clothes of a certain schoolboy, dressed with no ordinary care and splendour, of slaves bedecked with gold and a whole regiment of glittering attendants. I think of houses too, where one treads on precious stones, and where valuables lie about in every corner, where the very roof is brilliantly painted, and a whole nation attends and accompanies an inheritance on the road to ruin. What shall I say of waters, transparent to the very bottom, which flow round the guests, and banquets worthy of the theatre in which they take place? Coming as I do from a long course of dull thrift, I find myself surrounded by the most brilliant luxury, which echoes around me on every side: my sight becomes a little dazzled by it: I can lift up my heart against it more easily than my eyes. When I return from seeing it I am a sadder, though not a worse man, I cannot walk amid my own paltry possessions with so lofty a step as before, and silently there steals over me a feeling of vexation, and a doubt whether that way of life may not be better than mine. None of these things alter my principles, yet all of them disturb me. At one time I would obey the maxims of our school and plunge into public life, I would obtain office and become consul, not because the purple robe and lictor's axes attract me, but in order that I may be able to be of use to my friends, my relatives, to all my countrymen, and indeed to all mankind. Ready and determined, I follow the advice of Zeno, Cleanthes, and Chrysippus, all of whom bid one take part in public affairs, though none of them ever did so himself: and then, as soon as something disturbs my mind, which is not used to receiving shocks, as soon as something occurs which is either disgraceful, such as often occurs in all men's lives, or which does not proceed quite easily, or when subjects of very little importance require me to devote a great deal of time to them, I go back to my life of leisure, and, just as even tired cattle go faster when they are going home, I wish to retire and pass my life within the walls of my house. "No one," I say, "that will give me no compensation worth such a loss shall ever rob me of a day. Let my mind be contained within itself and improve itself: let it take no part with other men's affairs, and do nothing which depends on the approval of others: let me enjoy a tranquility undisturbed by either public or private troubles." But whenever my spirit is roused by reading some brave words, or some noble example spurs me into action, I want to rush into the law courts, to place my voice at one man's disposal, my services at another's, and to try to help him even though I may not succeed, or to quell the pride of some lawyer who is puffed up by ill-deserved success: but I think, by Hercules, that in philosophical speculation it is better to view things as they are, and to speak of them on their own account, and as for words, to trust to things for them, and to let one's speech, simply follow whither they lead. "Why do you want to construct a fabric that will endure for ages? Do you not wish to do this in order that posterity may talk of you: yet you were born to die, and a silent death is the least wretched. Write something therefore in a simple style, merely to pass the time, for your own use, and not for publication. Less labour is needed when one does not look beyond the present." Then again, when the mind is elevated by the greatness of its thoughts, it becomes ostentatious in its use of words, the loftier its aspirations, the more loftily it desires to express them, and its speech rises to the dignity of its subject. At such times I forget my mild and moderate determination and soar higher than is my wont, using a language that is not my own. Not to multiply examples, I am in all things attended by this weakness of a well-meaning mind, to whose level I fear that I shall be gradually brought down, or what is even more worrying, that I may always hang as though about to fall, and that there may be more the matter with me than I myself perceive: for we take a friendly view of our own private affairs, and partiality always obscures our judgment. I fancy that many men would have arrived at wisdom had they not believed themselves to have arrived there already, had they not purposely deceived themselves as to some parts of their character, and passed by others with their eyes shut: for you have no grounds for supposing that other people's flattery is more ruinous to us than our own. Who dares to tell himself the truth? Who is there, by however large a troop of caressing courtiers he may be surrounded, who in spite of them is not his own greatest flatterer? I beg you, therefore, if you have any remedy by which you could stop this vacillation of mine, to deem me worthy to owe my peace of mind to you. I am well aware that these oscillations of mind are not perilous and that they threaten me with no serious disorder: to express what I complain of by an exact simile, I am not suffering from a storm, but from sea-sickness. Take from me, then, this evil, whatever it may be, and help one who is in distress within sight of land.

II [Seneca]

I have long been silently asking myself, my friend Serenus, to what I should liken such a condition of mind, and I find that nothing more closely resembles it than the conduct of those who, after having recovered from a long and serious illness, occasionally experience slight touches and twinges, and, although they have passed through the final stages of the disease, yet have suspicions that it has not left them, and though in perfect health yet hold out their pulse to be felt by the physician, and whenever they feel warm suspect that the fever is returning. Such men, Serenus, are not unhealthy, but they are not accustomed to being healthy; just as even a quiet sea or lake nevertheless displays a certain amount of ripple when its waters are subsiding after a storm. What you need, therefore, is, not any of those harsher remedies to which allusion has been made, not that you should in some cases check yourself, in others be angry with yourself, in others sternly reproach yourself, but that you should adopt that which comes last in the list, have confidence in yourself, and believe that you are proceeding on the right path, without being led aside by the numerous divergent tracks of wanderers which cross it in every direction, some of them circling about the right path itself. What you desire, to be undisturbed, is a great thing, nay, the greatest thing of all, and one which raises a man almost to the level of a god. The Greeks call this calm steadiness of mind euthymia, and Democritus's treatise upon it is excellently written: I call it peace of mind: for there is no necessity for translating so exactly as to copy the words of the Greek idiom: the essential point is to mark the matter under discussion by a name which ought to have the same meaning as its Greek name, though perhaps not the same form. What we are seeking, then, is how the mind may always pursue a steady, unruffled course, may be pleased with itself, and look with pleasure upon its surroundings, and experience no interruption of this joy, but abide in a peaceful condition without being ever either elated or depressed: this will be "peace of mind." Let us now consider in a general way how it may be attained: then you may apply as much as you choose of the universal remedy to your own case. Meanwhile we must drag to light the entire disease, and then each one will recognize his own part of it: at the same time you will understand how much less you suffer by your self-depreciation than those who are bound by some showy declaration which they have made, and are oppressed by some grand title of honour, so that shame rather than their own free will forces them to keep up the pretence. The same thing applies both to those who suffer from fickleness and continual changes of purpose, who always are fondest of what they have given up, and those who merely yawn and dawdle: add to these those who, like bad sleepers, turn from side to side, and settle themselves first in one manner and then in another, until at last they find rest through sheer weariness: in forming the habits of their lives they often end by adopting some to which they are not kept by any dislike of change, but in the practice of which old age, which is slow to alter, has caught them living: add also those who are by no means fickle, yet who must thank their dullness, not their consistency for being so, and who go on living not in the way they wish, but in the way they have begun to live. There are other special forms of this disease without number, but it has but one effect, that of making people dissatisfied with themselves. This arises from a distemperature of mind and from desires which one is afraid to express or unable to fulfill, when men either dare not attempt as much as they wish to do, or fail in their efforts and depend entirely upon hope: such people are always fickle and changeable, which is a necessary consequence of living in a state of suspense: they take any way to arrive at their ends, and teach and force themselves to use both dishonourable and difficult means to do so, so that when their toil has been in vain they are made wretched by the disgrace of failure, and do not regret having longed for what was wrong, but having longed for it in vain. They then begin to feel sorry for what they have done, and afraid to begin again, and their mind falls by degrees into a state of endless vacillation, because they can neither command nor obey their passions, of hesitation, because their life cannot properly develop itself, and of decay, as the mind becomes stupefied by disappointments. All these symptoms become aggravated when their dislike of a laborious misery has driven them to idleness and to secret studies, which are unendurable to a mind eager to take part in public affairs, desirous of action and naturally restless, because, of course, it finds too few resources within itself: when therefore it loses the amusement which business itself affords to busy men, it cannot endure home, loneliness, or the walls of a room, and regards itself with dislike when left to itself. Hence arises that weariness and dissatisfaction with oneself, that tossing to and fro of a mind which can nowhere find rest, that unhappy and unwilling endurance of enforced leisure. In all cases where one feels ashamed to confess the real cause of one's suffering, and where modesty leads one to drive one's sufferings inward, the desires pent up in a little space without any vent choke one another. Hence comes melancholy and drooping of spirit, and a thousand waverings of the unsteadfast mind, which is held in suspense by unfulfilled hopes, and saddened by disappointed ones: hence comes the state of mind of those who loathe their idleness, complain that they have nothing to do, and view the progress of others with the bitterest jealousy: for an unhappy sloth favours the growth of envy, and men who cannot succeed themselves wish everyone else to be ruined. This dislike of other men's progress and despair of one's own produces a mind angered against fortune, addicted to complaining of the age in which it lives to retiring into corners and brooding over its misery, until it becomes sick and weary of itself: for the human mind is naturally nimble and apt at movement: it delights in every opportunity of excitement and forgetfulness of itself, and the worse a man's disposition the more he delights in this, because he likes to wear himself out with busy action, just as some sores long for the hands that injure them and delight in being touched, and the foul itch enjoys anything that scratches it. Similarly I assure you that these minds over which desires have spread like evil ulcers, take pleasure in toils and troubles, for there are some things which please our body while at the same time they give it a certain amount of pain, such as turning oneself over and changing one's side before it is wearied, or cooling oneself in one position after another. It is like Homer's Achilles lying first upon its face, then upon its back, placing itself in various attitudes, and, as sick people are wont, enduring none of them for long, and using changes as though they were remedies. Hence men undertake aimless wanderings, travel along distant shores, and at one time at sea, at another by land, try to soothe that fickleness of disposition which always is dissatisfied with the present. "Now let us make for Campania: now I am sick of rich cultivation: let us see wild regions, let us thread the passes of Bruttii and Lucania: yet amid this wilderness one wants some thing of beauty to relieve our pampered eyes after so long dwelling on savage wastes: let us seek Tarentum with its famous harbour, its mild winter climate, and its district, rich enough to support even the great hordes of ancient times. Let us now return to town: our ears have too long missed its shouts and noise: it would be pleasant also to enjoy the sight of human bloodshed." Thus one journey succeeds another, and one sight is changed for another. As Lucretius says:—

"Thus every mortal from himself doth flee;"

but what does he gain by so doing if he does not escape from himself? he follows himself and weighs himself down by his own most burdensome companionship. We must understand, therefore, that what we suffer from is not the fault of the places but of ourselves: we are weak when there is anything to be endured, and cannot support either labour or pleasure, either one's own business or anyone else's for long. This has driven some men to death, because by frequently altering their purpose they were always brought back to the same point, and had left themselves no room for anything new. They had become sick of life and of the world itself, and as all indulgences palled upon them they began to ask themselves the question, "How long are we to go on doing the same thing?"

III

You ask me what I think we had better make use of to help us to support this ennui. "The best thing," as Athenodorus says, "is to occupy oneself with business, with the management of affairs of state and the duties of a citizen: for as some pass the day in exercising themselves in the sun and in taking care of their bodily health, and athletes find it most useful to spend the greater part of their time in feeding up the muscles and strength to whose cultivation they have devoted their lives; so too for you who are training your mind to take part in the struggles of political life, it is far more honourable to be thus at work than to be idle. He whose object is to be of service to his countrymen and to all mortals, exercises himself and does good at the same time when he is engrossed in business and is working to the best of his ability both in the interests of the public and of private men. But," continues he, "because innocence is hardly safe among such furious ambitions and so many men who turn one aside from the right path, and it is always sure to meet with more hindrance than help, we ought to withdraw ourselves from the forum and from public life, and a great mind even in a private station can find room wherein to expand freely. Confinement in dens restrains the springs of lions and wild creatures, but this does not apply to human beings, who often effect the most important works in retirement. Let a man, however, withdraw himself only in such a fashion that wherever he spends his leisure his wish may still be to benefit individual men and mankind alike, both with his intellect, his voice, and his advice. The man that does good service to the state is not only he who brings forward candidates for public office, defends accused persons, and gives his vote on questions of peace and war, but he who encourages young men in well-doing, who supplies the present dearth of good teachers by instilling into their minds the principles of virtue, who seizes and holds back those who are rushing wildly in pursuit of riches and luxury, and, if he does nothing else, at least checks their course—such a man does service to the public though in a private station. Which does the most good, he who decides between foreigners and citizens (as praetor peregrinus), or, as praetor urbanus, pronounces sentence to the suitors in his court at his assistant's dictation, or he who shows them what is meant by justice, filial feeling, endurance, courage, contempt of death and knowledge of the gods, and how much a man is helped by a good conscience? If then you transfer to philosophy the time which you take away from the public service, you will not be a deserter or have refused to perform your proper task. A soldier is not merely one who stands in the ranks and defends the right or the left wing of the army, but he also who guards the gates—a service which, though less dangerous, is no sinecure—who keeps watch, and takes charge of the arsenal: though all these are bloodless duties, yet they count as military service. As soon as you have devoted yourself to philosophy, you will have overcome all disgust at life: you will not wish for darkness because you are weary of the light, nor will you be a trouble to yourself and useless to others: you will acquire many friends, and all the best men will be attracted towards you: for virtue, in however obscure a position, cannot be hidden, but gives signs of its presence: anyone who is worthy will trace it out by its footsteps: but if we give up all society, turn our backs upon the whole human race, and live communing with ourselves alone, this solitude without any interesting occupation will lead to a want of something to do: we shall begin to build up and to pull down, to dam out the sea, to cause waters to flow through natural obstacles, and generally to make a bad disposal of the time which Nature has given us to spend: some of us use it grudgingly, others wastefully; some of us spend it so that we can show a profit and loss account, others so that they have no assets remaining: than which nothing can be more shameful. Often a man who is very old in years has nothing beyond his age by which he can prove that he has lived a long time."

IV

To me, my dearest Serenus, Athenodorus seems to have yielded too completely to the times, to have fled too soon: I will not deny that sometimes one must retire, but one ought to retire slowly, at a foot's pace, without losing one's ensigns or one's honour as a soldier: those who make terms with arms in their hands are more respected by their enemies and more safe in their hands. This is what I think ought to be done by virtue and by one who practises virtue: if Fortune get the upper hand and deprive him of the power of action, let him not straightway turn his back to the enemy, throw away his arms, and run away seeking for a hiding-place, as if there were any place whither Fortune could not pursue him, but let him be more sparing in his acceptance of public office, and after due deliberation discover some means by which he can be of use to the state. He is not able to serve in the army: then let him become a candidate for civic honours: must he live in a private station? then let him be an advocate: is he condemned to keep silence? then let him help his countrymen with silent counsel. Is it dangerous for him even to enter the forum? then let him prove himself a good comrade, a faithful friend, a sober guest in people's houses, at public shows, and at wine-parties. Suppose that he has lost the status of a citizen; then let him exercise that of a man: our reason for magnanimously refusing to confine ourselves within the walls of one city, for having gone forth to enjoy intercourse with all lands and for professing ourselves to be citizens of the world is that we may thus obtain a wider theatre on which to display our virtue. Is the bench of judges closed to you, are you forbidden to address the people from the hustings, or to be a candidate at elections? then turn your eyes away from Rome, and see what a wide extent of territory, what a number of nations present themselves before you. Thus, it is never possible for so many outlets to be closed against your ambition that more will not remain open to it: but see whether the whole prohibition does not arise from your own fault. You do not choose to direct the affairs of the state except as consul or prytanis [2] or meddix[3] or sufes:[4] what should we say if you refused to serve in the army save as general or military tribune? Even though others may form the first line, and your lot may have placed you among the veterans of the third, do your duty there with your voice, encouragement, example, and spirit: even though a man's hands be cut off, he may find means to help his side in a battle, if he stands his

---

[2] The chief magistrate of the Greeks.

[3] The chief magistrate of the Uscans.

[4] The chief magistrate of the Carthaginians.

ground and cheers on his comrades. Do something of that sort yourself: if Fortune removes you from the front rank, stand your ground nevertheless and cheer on your comrades, and if somebody stops your mouth, stand nevertheless and help your side in silence. The services of a good citizen are never thrown away: he does good by being heard and seen, by his expression, his gestures, his silent determination, and his very walk. As some remedies benefit us by their smell as well as by their their taste and touch, so virtue even when concealed and at a distance sheds usefulness around. Whether she moves at her ease and enjoys her just rights, or can only appear abroad on sufferance and is forced to shorten sail to the tempest, whether it be unemployed, silent, and pent up in a narrow lodging, or openly displayed, in whatever guise she may appear, she always does good. What? do you think that the example of one who can rest nobly has no value? It is by far the best plan, therefore, to mingle leisure with business, whenever chance impediments or the state of public affairs forbid one's leading an active life: for one is never so cut off from all pursuits as to find no room left for honourable action.

V

Could you anywhere find a miserable city than that of Athens when it was being torn to pieces by the thirty tyrants? they slew thirteen hundred citizens, all the best men, and did not leave off because they had done so, but their cruelty became stimulated by exercise. In the city which possessed that most reverend tribunal, the Court of the Areopagus, which possessed a Senate, and a popular assembly which was like a Senate, there met daily a wretched crew of butchers, and the unhappy Senate House was crowded with tyrants. A state, in which there were so many tyrants that they would have been enough to form a bodyguard for one, might surely have rested from the struggle; it seemed impossible for men's minds even to conceive hopes of recovering their liberty, nor could they see any room for a remedy for such a mass of evil: for whence could the unhappy state obtain all the Harmodiuses it would need to slay so many tyrants? Yet Socrates was in the midst of the city, and consoled its mourning Fathers, encouraged those who despaired of the republic, by his reproaches brought rich men, who feared that their wealth would be their ruin, to a tardy repentance of their avarice, and moved about as a great example to those who wished to imitate him, because he walked a free man in the midst of thirty masters. However, Athens herself put him to death in prison, and Freedom herself could not endure the freedom of one who had treated a whole band of tyrants with scorn: you may know, therefore, that even in an oppressed state a wise man can find an opportunity for bringing himself to the front, and that in a prosperous and flourishing one wanton insolence, jealousy, and a thousand other cowardly vices bear sway. We ought therefore, to expand or contract ourselves according as the state presents itself to us, or as Fortune offers us opportunities: but in any case we ought to move and not to become frozen still by fear: nay, he is the best man who, though peril menaces him on every side and arms and chains beset his path, nevertheless neither impairs nor conceals his virtue: for to keep oneself safe does not mean to bury oneself. I think that Curius Dentatus spoke truly when he said that he would rather be dead than alive: the worst evil of all is to leave the ranks of the living before one dies; yet it is your duty, if you happen to live in an age when it is not easy to serve the state, to devote more time to leisure and to literature. Thus, just as though you were making a perilous voyage, you may from time to time put into harbour, and set yourself free from public business without waiting for it to do so.

VI

We ought, however, first to examine our own selves, next the business which we propose to transact, next those for whose sake or in whose company we transact it.

It is above all things necessary to form a true estimate of oneself, because as a rule we think that we can do more than we are able: one man is led too far through confidence in his eloquence, another demands more from his estate than it can produce, another burdens a weakly body with some toilsome duty. Some men are too shamefaced for the conduct of public affairs, which require an unblushing front: some men's obstinate pride renders them unfit for courts: some cannot control their anger, and break into unguarded language on the slightest provocation: some cannot rein in their wit or resist making risky jokes: for all these men leisure is better than employment: a bold, haughty and impatient nature ought to avoid anything that may lead it to use a freedom of speech which will bring it to ruin. Next we must form an estimate of the matter which we mean to deal with, and compare our strength with the deed we are about to attempt: for the bearer ought always to be more powerful than his load: indeed, loads which are too heavy for their bearer must of necessity crush him: some affairs also are not so important in themselves as they are prolific and lead to much more business, which employments, as they involve us in new and various forms of work, ought to be refused. Neither should you engage in anything from which you are not free to retreat: apply yourself to something which you can finish, or at any rate can hope to finish: you had better not meddle with those operations which grow in importance, while they are being transacted, and which will not stop where you intended them to stop.

VII

In all cases one should be careful in one's choice of men, and see whether they be worthy of our bestowing a part of our life upon them, or whether we shall waste our own time and theirs also: for some even consider us to be in their debt because of our services to them. Athenodorus said that "he would not so much as dine with a man who would not be grateful to him for doing so": meaning, I imagine, that much less would he go to dinner with those who recompense the services of their friends by their table, and regard courses of dishes as donatives, as if they overate themselves to do honour to others. Take away from these men their witnesses and spectators: they will take no pleasure in solitary gluttony. You must decide whether your disposition is better suited for vigorous action or for tranquil speculation and contemplation, and you must adopt whichever the bent of your genius inclines you for. Isocrates laid hands upon Ephorus and led him away from the forum, thinking that he would be more usefully employed in compiling chronicles; for no good is done by forcing one's mind to engage in uncongenial work: it is vain to struggle against Nature. Yet nothing delights the mind so much as faithful and pleasant friendship: what a blessing it is when there is one whose breast is ready to receive all your secrets with safety, whose knowledge of your actions you fear less than your own conscience, whose conversation removes your anxieties, whose advice assists your plans, whose cheerfulness dispels your gloom, whose very sight delights you! We should choose for our friends men who are, as far as possible, free from strong desires: for vices are contagious, and pass from a man to his neighbour, and injure those who touch them. As, therefore, in times of pestilence we have to be careful not to sit near people who are infected and in whom the disease is raging, because by so doing, we shall run into danger and catch the plague from their very breath; so, too, in choosing our friends' dispositions, we must take care to select those who are as far as may be unspotted by the world; for the way to breed disease is to mix what is sound with what is rotten. Yet I do not advise you to follow after or draw to yourself no one except a wise man: for where will you find him whom for so many centuries we have sought in vain? in the place of the best possible man take him who is least bad. You would hardly find any time that would have enabled you to make a happier choice than if you could have sought for a good man from among the Platos and Xenophons and the rest of the produce of the brood of Socrates, or if you had been permitted to choose one from the age of Cato: an age which bore many men worthy to be born in Cato's time (just as it also bore many men worse than were ever known before, planners of the blackest crimes: for it needed both classes in order to make Cato understood: it wanted both good men, that he might win their approbation, and bad men, against whom he could prove his strength): but at the present day, when there is such a dearth of good men, you must be less squeamish in your choice. Above all, however, avoid dismal men who grumble at whatever happens, and find something to complain of in everything. Though he may continue loyal and friendly towards you, still one's peace of mind is destroyed by a comrade whose mind is soured and who meets every incident with a groan.

VIII

Let us now pass on to the consideration of property, that most fertile source of human sorrows: for if you compare all the other ills from which we suffer—deaths, sicknesses, fears, regrets, endurance of pains and labours – with those miseries which our money inflicts upon us, the latter will far outweigh all the others. Reflect, then, how much less a grief it is never to have had any money than to have lost it: we shall thus understand that the less poverty has to lose, the less torment it has with which to afflict us: for you are mistaken if you suppose that the rich bear their losses with greater spirit than the poor: a wound causes the same amount of pain to the greatest and the smallest body. It was a neat saying of Bion's, "that it hurts bald men as much as hairy men to have their hairs pulled out": you may be assured that the same thing is true of rich and poor people, that their suffering is equal: for their money clings to both classes, and cannot be torn away without their feeling it: yet it is more endurable, as I have said, and easier not to gain property than to lose it, and therefore you will find that those upon whom Fortune has never smiled are more cheerful than those whom she has deserted. Diogenes, a man of infinite spirit, perceived this, and made it impossible that anything should be taken from him. Call this security from loss poverty, want, necessity, or any contemptuous name you please: I shall consider such a man to be happy, unless you find me another who can lose nothing. If I am not mistaken, it is a royal attribute among so many misers, sharpers, and robbers, to be the one man who cannot be injured. If any one doubts the happiness of Diogenes, he would doubt whether the position of the immortal gods was one of sufficient happiness, because they have no farms or gardens, no valuable estates let to strange tenants, and no large loans in the money market. Are you not ashamed of yourself, you who gaze upon riches with astonished admiration? Look upon the universe: you will see the gods quite bare of property, and possessing nothing though they give everything. Do you think that this man who has stripped himself of all fortuitous accessories is a pauper, or one like to the immortal gods? Do you call Demetrius, Pompeius's freedman, a happier man, he who was not ashamed to be richer than Pompiius, who was daily furnished with a list of the number of his slaves, as a general is with that of his army, though he had long deserved that all his riches should consist of a pair of underlings, and a roomier cell than the other slaves? But Diogenes's only slave ran away from him, and when he was pointed out to Diogenes, he did not think him worth fetching back. "It is a shame," he said, "that Manes should be able to live without Diogenes, and that Diogenes should not be able to live without Manes." He seems to me to have said, "Fortune, mind your own business: Diogenes has nothing left that belongs to you. Did my slave run away? nay, he went away from me as a free man." A household of slaves requires food and clothing: the bellies of so many hungry creatures have to be filled: we must buy raiment for them, we must watch their most thievish hands, and we must make use of the services of people who weep and execrate us. How far happier is he who is indebted to no man for anything except for what he can deprive himself of with the greatest ease! Since we, however, have not such strength of mind as this, we ought at any rate to diminish the extent of our property, in order to be less exposed to the assaults of fortune: those men whose bodies can be within the shelter of their armour, are more fitted for war than those whose huge size everywhere extends beyond it, and exposes them to wounds: the best amount of property to have is that which is enough to keep us from poverty, and which yet is not far removed from it.

IX

We shall be pleased with this measure of wealth if we have previously taken pleasure in thrift, without which no riches are sufficient, and with which none are insufficient, especially as the remedy is always at hand, and poverty itself by calling in the aid of thrift can convert itself into riches. Let us accustom ourselves to set aside mere outward show, and to measure things by their uses, not by their ornamental trappings: let our hunger be tamed by food, our thirst quenched by drinking, our lust confined within needful bounds; let us learn to use our limbs, and to arrange our dress and way of life according to what was approved of by our ancestors, not in imitation of new-fangled models: let us learn to increase our continence, to repress luxury, to set bounds to our pride, to assuage our anger, to look upon poverty without prejudice, to practise thrift, albeit many are ashamed to do so, to apply cheap remedies to the wants of nature, to keep all undisciplined hopes and aspirations as it were under lock and key, and to make it our business to get our riches from ourselves and not from Fortune. We never can so thoroughly defeat the vast diversity and malignity of misfortune with which we are threatened as not to feel the weight of many gusts if we offer a large spread of canvas to the wind: we must draw our affairs into a small compass, to make the darts of Fortune of no avail. For this reason, sometimes slight mishaps have turned into remedies, and more serious disorders have been healed by slighter ones. When the mind pays no attention to good advice, and cannot be brought to its senses by milder measures, why should we not think that its interests are being served by poverty, disgrace, or financial ruin being applied to it? one evil is balanced by another. Let us then teach ourselves to be able to dine without all Rome to look on, to be the slaves of fewer slaves, to get clothes which fulfill their original purpose, and to live in a smaller house. The inner curve is the one to take, not only in running races and in the contests of the circus, but also in the race of life; even literary pursuits, the most becoming thing for a gentleman to spend money upon, are only justifiable as long as they are kept within bounds. What is the use of possessing numberless books and libraries, whose titles their owner can hardly read through in a lifetime? A student is over-whelmed by such a mass, not instructed, and it is much better to devote yourself to a few writers than to skim through many. Forty thousand books were burned at Alexandria: some would have praised this library as a most noble memorial of royal wealth, like Titus Livius, who says that it was "a splendid result of the taste and attentive care of the kings."[5] It had nothing to do with taste or care, but was a piece of learned luxury, nay, not even learned, since they amassed it, not for the sake of learning, but to make a show, like many men who know less about letters than a slave is expected to know, and who uses his books not to help him in his studies but to ornament his dining-room. Let a man, then, obtain as many books as he wants, but none for show. "It is more respectable," say you, "to spend one's money on such books than on vases of Corinthian brass and paintings." Not so: everything that is carried to excess is wrong. What excuses can you find for a man who is eager to buy bookcases of ivory and citrus wood, to collect the works of unknown or discredited authors, and who sits yawning amid so many thousands of books, whose backs and titles please him more than any other part of them? Thus in the houses of the laziest of men you will see the works of all the orators and historians stacked upon bookshelves reaching right up to the ceiling. At the present day a library has become as necessary an appendage to a house as a hot and cold bath. I would excuse them straightway if they really were carried away by an excessive zeal for literature ; but as it is, these costly works of sacred genius, with all the illustrations that adorn them, are merely bought for display and to serve as wall-furniture.

---

[5] "Livy himself styled the Alexandrian library elegantiae regun. curaeque egregium opus: a liberal encomium, for which he is pertly criticised by the narrow stoicism of Seneca (Tranq., ch. ii.), whose wisdom, on this occasion, deviates into nonsense."—Gibbon, "Decline and Fall," ch. li., note.

X

Suppose, however, that your life has become full of trouble, and that without knowing what you were doing you have fallen into some snare which either public or private Fortune has set for you, and that you can neither untie it nor break it: then remember that fettered men suffer much at first from the burdens and clogs upon their legs: afterwards, when they have made up their minds not to fret themselves about them, but to endure them, necessity teaches them to bear them bravely, and habit to bear them easily. In every station of life you will find amusements, relaxations, and enjoyments; that is, provided you be willing to make light of evils rather than to hate them. Knowing to what sorrows we were born, there is nothing for which Nature more deserves our thanks than for having invented habit as an alleviation of misfortune, which soon accustoms us to the severest evils. No one could hold out against misfortune if it permanently exercised the same force as at its first onset. We are all chained to Fortune: some men's chain is loose and made of gold, that of others is tight and of meaner metal: but what difference does this make? we are all included in the same captivity, and even those who have bound us are bound themselves, unless you think that a chain on the left side is lighter to bear: one man may be bound by public office, another by wealth: some have to bear the weight of illustrious, some of humble birth: some are subject to the commands of others, some only to their own: some are kept in one place by being banished thither, others by being elected to the priesthood. All life is slavery: let each man therefore reconcile himself to his lot, complain of it as little as possible, and lay hold of whatever good lies within his reach. No condition can be so wretched that an impartial mind can find no compensations in it. Small sites, if ingeniously divided, may be made use of for many different purposes, and arrangement will render ever so narrow a room habitable. Call good sense to your aid against difficulties: it is possible to soften what is harsh, to widen what is too narrow, and to make heavy burdens press less severely upon one who bears them skillfully. Moreover, we ought not to allow our desires to wander far afield, but we must make them confine themselves to our immediate neighbourhood, since they will not endure to be altogether locked up. We must leave alone things which either cannot come to pass or can only be effected with difficulty, and follow after such things as are near at hand and within reach of our hopes, always remembering that all things are equally unimportant, and that though they have a different outward appearance, they are all alike empty within. Neither let us envy those who are in high places: the heights which look lofty to us are steep and rugged. Again, those whom unkind fate has placed in critical situations will be safer if they show as little pride in their proud position as may be, and do all they are able to bring down their fortunes to the level of other men's. There are many who must needs cling to their high pinnacle of power, because they cannot descend from it save by falling headlong: yet they assure us that their greatest burden is being obliged to be burdensome to others, and that they are nailed to their lofty post rather than raised to it: let them then, by dispensing justice, clemency, and kindness with an open and liberal hand, provide themselves with assistance to break their fall, and looking forward to this maintain their position more hopefully. Yet nothing sets as free from these alternations of hope and fear so well as always fixing some limit to our successes, and not allowing Fortune to choose when to stop our career, but to halt of our own accord long before we apparently need do so. By acting thus certain desires will rouse up our spirits, and yet being confined within bounds, will not lead us to embark on vast and vague enterprises.

XI

These remarks of mine apply only to imperfect, commonplace, and unsound natures, not to the wise man, who needs not to walk with timid and cautious gait: for he has such confidence in himself that he does not hesitate to go directly in the teeth of Fortune, and never will give way to her. Nor indeed has he any reason for fearing her, for he counts not only chattels, property, and high office, but even his body, his eyes, his hands, and everything whose use makes life dearer to us, nay, even his very self, to be things whose possession is uncertain; he lives as though he had borrowed them, and is ready to return them cheerfully whenever they are claimed. Yet he does not hold himself cheap, because he knows that he is not his own, but performs all his duties as carefully and prudently as a pious and scrupulous man would take care of property left in his charge as trustee. When he is bidden to give them up, he will not complain of Fortune, but will say, "I thank you for what I have had possession of: I have managed your property so as largely to increase it, but since you order me, I give it back to you and return it willingly and thankfully. If you still wish me to own anything of yours, I will keep it for you; if you have other views, I restore into your hands and make restitution of all my wrought and coined silver, my house and my household. Should Nature recall what she previously entrusted us with, let us say to her also: 'Take back my spirit, which is better than when you gave it me: I do not shuffle or hang back. Of my own free will I am ready to return what you gave me before I could think: take me away.'" What hardship can there be in returning to the place from whence one came? a man cannot live well if he knows not how to die well. We must, therefore, take away from this commodity its original value, and count the breath of life as a cheap matter. "We dislike gladiators," says Cicero, "if they are eager to save their lives by any means whatever: but we look favourably upon them if they are openly reckless of them." You may be sure that the same thing occurs with us: we often die because we are afraid of death. Fortune, which regards our lives as a show in the arena for her own enjoyment, says, "Why should I spare you, base and cowardly creature that you are? you will be pierced and hacked with all the more wounds because you know not how to offer your throat to the knife: whereas you, who receive the stroke without drawing away your neck or putting up your hands to stop it, shall both live longer and die more quickly." He who fears death will never act as becomes a living man: but he who knows that this fate was laid upon him as soon as he was conceived will live according to it, and by this strength of mind will gain this further advantage, that nothing can befall him unexpectedly: for by looking forward to everything which can happen as though it would happen to him, he takes the sting out of all evils, which can make no difference to those who expect it and are prepared to meet it: evil only comes hard upon those who have lived without giving it a thought and whose attention has been exclusively directed to happiness. Disease, captivity, disaster, conflagration, are none of them unexpected: I always knew with what disorderly company Nature had associated me. The dead have often been wailed for in my neighbourhood: the torch and taper have often been borne past my door before the bier of one who has died before his time: the crash of falling buildings has often resounded by my side: night has snatched away many of those with whom I have become intimate in the forum, the Senate-house, and in society, and has sundered the hands which were joined in friendship: ought I to be surprised if the dangers which have always been circling around me at last assail me? How large a part of mankind never think of storms when about to set sail? I shall never be ashamed to quote a good saying because it comes from a bad author. Publilius, who was a more powerful writer than any of our other playwrights, whether comic or tragic, whenever he chose to rise above farcical absurdities and speeches addressed to the gallery, among many other verses too noble even for tragedy, let alone for comedy, has this one :—

"What one hath suffered may befall us all."

If a man takes this into his inmost heart and looks upon all the misfortunes of other men, of which there is always a great plenty, in this spirit, remembering that there is nothing to prevent their coming upon him also, he will arm himself against them long before they attack him. It is too late to school the mind to endurance of peril after peril has done. "I did not think this would happen," and "Would you ever have believed that this would have happened?" say you. But why should it not? Where are the riches after which want, hunger, and beggary do not follow? what office is there whose purple robe, augur's staff, and patrician reins have not as their accompaniment rags and banishment, the brand of infamy, a thousand disgraces, and utter reprobation? what kingdom is there for which ruin, trampling under foot, a tyrant and a butcher are not ready at hand? nor are these matters divided by long periods of time, but there is but the space of an hour between sitting on the throne ourselves and clasping the knees of someone else as suppliants. Know then that every station of life is transitory, and that what has ever happened to anybody may happen to you also. You are wealthy: are you wealthier than Pompeius ? [6] Yet when Gaius,[7] his old relative and new host, opened Caesar's house to him in order that he might close his own, he lacked both bread and water: though he owned so many rivers which both rose and discharged themselves within his dominions, yet he had to beg for drops of

---

[6] Haase reads Ptolemaeus

[7] Caligula

water: he perished of hunger and thirst in the palace of his relative, while his heir was contracting for a public funeral for one who was in want of food. You have filled public offices: were they either as important, as unlooked for, or as all-embracing as those of Sejanus? Yet on the day on which the Senate disgraced him, the people tore him to pieces: the executioner [8] could find no part left large enough to drag to the Tiber, of one upon whom gods and men had showered all that could be given to man. You are a king: I will not bid you go to Croesus for an example, he who while yet alive saw his funeral pile both lighted and extinguished, being made to outlive not only his kingdom but even his own death, nor to Jugurtha, whom the people of Rome beheld as a captive within the year in which they had feared him. We have seen Ptolemaeus King of Africa, and Mithridates King of Armenia, under the charge of Gaius's [9] guards: the former was sent into exile, the latter chose it in order to make his exile more honourable. Among such continual topsy-turvy changes, unless you expect that whatever can happen will happen to you, you give adversity power against you, a power which can be destroyed by anyone who looks at it beforehand.

---

[8] It was the duty of the executioner to fasten a hook to the neck of condemned criminals, by which they were dragged to the Tiber

[9] Caligula

XII

The next point to these will be to take care that we do not labour for what is vain, or labour in vain: that is to say, neither to desire what we are not able to obtain, nor yet, having obtained our desire too late, and after much toil to discover the folly of our wishes: in other words, that our labour may not be without result, and that the result may not be unworthy of our labour: for as a rule sadness arises from one of these two things, either from want of success or from being ashamed of having succeeded. We must limit the running to and fro which most men practise, rambling about houses, theatres, and marketplaces. They mind other men's business, and always seem as though they themselves had something to do. If you ask one of them as he comes out of his own door, "Whither are you going?" he will answer, "By Hercules, I do not know: but I shall see some people and do something." They wander purposelessly seeking for something to do, and do, not what they have made up their minds to do, but what has casually fallen in their way. They move uselessly and without any plan, just like ants crawling over bushes, which creep up to the top and then down to the bottom again without gaining anything. Many men spend their lives in exactly the same fashion, which one may call a state of restless indolence. You would pity some of them when you see them running as if their house was on fire: they actually jostle all whom they meet, and hurry along themselves and others with them, though all the while they are going to salute someone who will not return their greeting, or to attend the funeral of someone whom they did not know: they are going to hear the verdict on one who often goes to law, or to see the wedding of one who often gets married : they will follow a man's litter, and in some places will even carry it: afterwards returning home weary with idleness, they swear that they themselves do not know why they went out, or where they have been, and on the following day they will wander through the same round again. Let all your work, therefore, have some purpose, and keep some object in view: these restless people are not made restless by labour, but are driven out of their minds by mistaken ideas: for even they do not put themselves in motion without any hope: they are excited by the outward appearance of something, and their crazy mind cannot see its futility. In the same way every one of those who walk out to swell the crowd in the streets, is led round the city by worthless and empty reasons; the dawn drives him forth, although he has nothing to do, and after he has pushed his way into many men's doors, and saluted their nomenclators one after the other, and been turned away from many others, he finds that the most difficult person of all to find at home is himself. From this evil habit comes that worst of all vices, tale-bearing and prying into public and private secrets, and the knowledge of many things which it is neither safe to tell nor safe to listen to.

XIII

It was, I imagine, following out this principle that Democritus taught that "he who would live at peace must not do much business either public or private," referring of course to unnecessary business: for if there be any necessity for it we ought to transact not only much but endless business, both public and private; in cases, however, where no solemn duty invites us to act, we had better keep ourselves quiet: for he who does many things often puts himself in Fortune's power, and it is safest not to tempt her often, but always to remember her existence, and never to promise oneself anything on her security. I will set sail unless anything happens to prevent me, I shall be praetor, if nothing hinders me, my financial operations will succeed, unless anything goes wrong with them. This is why we say that nothing befalls the wise man which he did not expect—we do not make him exempt from the chances of human life, but from its mistakes, nor does everything happen to him as he wished it would, but as he thought it would: now his first thought was that his purpose might meet with some resistance, and the pain of disappointed wishes must affect a man's mind less severely if he has not been at all events confident of success.

XIV

Moreover, we ought to cultivate an easy temper, and not become over fond of the lot which fate has assigned to us, but transfer ourselves to whatever other condition chance may lead us to, and fear no alteration, either in our purposes or our position in life, provided that we do not become subject to caprice, which of all vices is the most hostile to repose: for obstinacy, from which Fortune often wrings some concession, must needs be anxious and unhappy, but caprice, which can never restrain itself, must be more so. Both of these qualities, both that of altering nothing, and that of being dissatisfied with everything, are enemies to repose. The mind ought in all cases to be called away from the contemplation of external things to that of itself: let it confide in itself, rejoice in itself, admire its own works; avoid as far as may be those of others, and devote itself to itself; let it not feel losses, and put a good construction even upon misfortunes. Zeno, the chief of our school, when he heard the news of a shipwreck, in which all his property had been lost, remarked, "Fortune bids me follow philosophy in lighter marching order." A tyrant threatened Theodorus with death, and even with want of burial. "You are able to please yourself," he answered, "my half pint of blood is in your power: for, as for burial, what a fool you must be if you suppose that I care whether I rot above ground or under it." Julius Kanus, a man of peculiar greatness, whom even the fact of his having been born in this century does not prevent our admiring, had a long dispute with Gaius, and when as he was going away that Phalaris of a man said to him, "That you may not delude yourself with any foolish hopes, I have ordered you to be executed," he answered, "I thank you, most excellent prince." I am not sure what he meant: for many ways of explaining his conduct occur to me. Did he wish to be reproachful, and to show him how great his cruelty must be if death became a kindness? or did he upbraid him with his accustomed insanity? for even those whose children were put to. death, and whose goods were confiscated, used to thank him: or was it that he willingly received death, regarding it as freedom? Whatever he meant, it was a magnanimous answer. Someone may say, "After this Gaius might have let him live." Kanus had no fear of this: the good faith with which Gaius carried out such orders as these was well known. Will you believe that he passed the ten intervening days before his execution without the slightest despondency? it is marvellous how that man spoke and acted, and how peaceful he was. He was playing at draughts when the centurion in charge of a number of those who were going to be executed bade him, join them: on the summons he counted his men and said to his companion, "Mind you do not tell a lie after my death, and say that you won;" then, turning to the centurion, he said "You will bear me witness that I am one man ahead of him." Do you think that Kanus played upon that draught-board? nay, he played with it. His friends were sad at being about to lose so great a man: "Why," asked he, "are you sorrowful? you are enquiring whether our souls are immortal, but I shall presently know." Nor did he up to the very end cease his search after truth, and raised arguments upon the subject of his own death. His own teacher of philosophy accompanied him, and they were not far from the hill on which the daily sacrifice to Caesar our god was offered, when he said, "What are you thinking of now, Kanus? or what are your ideas?" "I have decided," answered Kanus, "at that most swiftly-passing moment of all to watch whether the spirit will be conscious of the act of leaving the body." He promised, too, that if he made any discoveries, he would come round to his friends and tell them what the condition of the souls of the departed might be. Here was peace in the very midst of the storm: here was a soul worthy of eternal life, which used its own fate as a proof of truth, which when at the last step of life experimented upon his fleeting breath, and did not merely continue to learn until he died, but learned something even from death itself. No man has carried the life of a philosopher further. I will not hastily leave the subject of a great man, and one who deserves to be spoken of with respect: I will hand thee down to all posterity, thou most noble heart, chief among the many victims of Gaius.

XV

Yet we gain nothing by getting rid of all personal causes of sadness, for sometimes we are possessed by hatred of the human race. When you reflect how rare simplicity is, how unknown innocence, how seldom faith is kept, unless it be to our advantage, when you remember such numbers of successful crimes, so many equally hateful losses and gains of lust, and ambition so impatient even of its own natural limits that it is willing to purchase distinction by baseness, the mind seems as it were cast into darkness, and shadows rise before it as though the virtues were all overthrown and we were no longer allowed to hope to possess them or benefited by their possession. We ought therefore to bring ourselves into such a state of mind that all the vices of the vulgar may not appear hateful to us, but merely ridiculous, and we should imitate Democritus rather than Heraclitus. The latter of these, whenever he appeared in public, used to weep, the former to laugh: the one thought all human doings to be follies, the other thought them to be miseries. We must take a higher view of all things, and bear with them more easily: it better becomes a man to scoff at life than to lament over it. Add to this that he who laughs at the human race deserves better of it than he who mourns for it, for the former leaves it some good hopes of improvement, while the latter stupidly weeps over what he has given up all hopes of mending. He who after surveying the universe cannot control his laughter shows, too, a greater mind than he who cannot restrain his tears, because his mind is only affected in the slightest possible degree, and he does not think that any part of all this apparatus is either important, or serious, or unhappy. As for the several causes which render us happy or sorrowful, let everyone describe them for himself, and learn the truth of Bion's saying, "That all the doings of men were very like what he began with, and that there is nothing in their lives which is more holy or decent than their conception." Yet it is better to accept public morals and human vices calmly without bursting into either laughter or tears; for to be hurt by the sufferings of others is to be forever miserable, while to enjoy the sufferings of others is an inhuman pleasure, just as it is a useless piece of humanity to weep and pull a long face because someone is burying his son. In one's own misfortunes, also, one ought so to conduct oneself as to bestow upon them just as much sorrow as reason, not as much as custom requires: for many shed tears in order to show them, and whenever no one is looking at them their eyes are dry, but they think it disgraceful not to weep when everyone does so. So deeply has this evil of being guided by the opinion of others taken root in us, that even grief, the simplest of all emotions, begins to be counterfeited.

XVI

There comes now a part of our subject which is wont with good cause to make one sad and anxious: I mean when good men come to bad ends; when Socrates is forced to die in prison, Rutilius to live in exile, Pompeius and Cicero to offer their necks to the swords of their own followers, when the great Cato, that living image of virtue, falls upon his sword and rips up both himself and the republic, one cannot help being grieved that Fortune should bestow her gifts so unjustly: what, too, can a good man hope to obtain when he sees the best of men meeting with the worst fates. Well, but see how each of them endured his fate, and if they endured it bravely, long in your heart for courage as great as theirs; if they died in a womanish and cowardly manner, nothing was lost: either they deserved that you should admire their courage, or else they did not deserve that you should wish to imitate their cowardice: for what can be more shameful than that the greatest men should die so bravely as to make people cowards. Let us praise one who deserves such constant praises, and say, "The braver you are the happier you are! You have escaped from all accidents, jealousies, diseases: you have escaped from prison: the gods have not thought you worthy of ill-fortune, but have thought that fortune no longer deserved to have any power over you": but when any one shrinks back in the hour of death and looks longingly at life, we must lay hands upon him. I will never weep for a man who dies cheerfully, nor for one who dies weeping: the former wipes away my tears, the latter by his tears makes himself unworthy that any should be shed for him. Shall I weep for Hercules because he was burned alive, or for Regulus because he was pierced by so many nails, or for Cato because he tore open his wounds a second time? All these men discovered how at the cost of a small portion of time they might obtain immortality, and by their deaths gained eternal life.

XVII

It also proves a fertile source of troubles if you take pains to conceal your feelings and never show yourself to any one undisguised, but, as many men do, live an artificial life, in order to impose upon others: for the constant watching of himself becomes a torment to a man, and he dreads being caught doing something at variance with his usual habits, and, indeed, we never can be at our ease if we imagine that everyone who looks at us is weighing our real value: for many things occur which strip people of their disguise, however reluctantly they may part with it, and even if all this trouble about oneself is successful, still life is neither happy nor safe when one always has to wear a mask. But what pleasure there is in that honest straight-forwardness which is its own ornament, and which conceals no part of its character? Yet even this life, which hides nothing from any one runs some risk of being despised; for there are people who disdain whatever they come close to: but there is no danger of virtue's becoming contemptible when she is brought near our eyes, and it is better to be scorned for one's simplicity than to bear the burden of unceasing hypocrisy. Still, we must observe moderation in this matter, for there is a great difference between living simply and living slovenly. Moreover, we ought to retire a great deal into ourselves: for association with persons unlike ourselves upsets all that we had arranged, rouses the passions which were at rest, and rubs into a sore any weak or imperfectly healed place in our minds. Nevertheless we ought to mix up these two things, and to pass our lives alternately in solitude and among throngs of people; for the former will make us long for the society of mankind, the latter for that of ourselves, and the one will counteract the other: solitude will cure us when we are sick of crowds, and crowds will cure us when we are sick of solitude. Neither ought we always to keep the mind strained to the same pitch, but it ought sometimes to be relaxed by amusement. Socrates did not blush to play with little boys, Cato used to refresh his mind with wine after he had wearied it with application to affairs of state, and Scipio would move his triumphal and soldierly limbs to the sound of music, not with a feeble and halting gait, as is the fashion now-a-days, when we sway in our very walk with more than womanly weakness, but dancing as men were wont in the days of old on sportive and festal occasions, with manly bounds, thinking it no harm to be seen so doing even by their enemies. Men's minds ought to have relaxation: they rise up better and more vigorous after rest. We must not force crops from rich fields, for an unbroken course of heavy crops will soon exhaust their fertility, and so also the liveliness of our minds will be destroyed by unceasing labour, but they will recover their strength after a short period of rest and relief: for continuous toil produces a sort of numbness and sluggishness. Men would not be so eager for this, if play and amusement did not possess natural attractions for them, although constant indulgence in them takes away all gravity and all strength from the mind: for sleep, also, is necessary for our refreshment, yet if you prolong it for days and nights together it will become death. There is a great difference between slackening your hold of a thing and letting it go. The founders of our laws appointed festivals, in order that men might be publicly encouraged to be cheerful, and they thought it necessary to vary our labours with amusements, and, as I said before, some great men have been wont to give themselves a certain number of holidays in every month, and some divided every day into play-time and work-time. Thus, I remember that great orator Asinius Pollio would not attend to any business after the tenth hour: he would not even read letters after that time for fear some new trouble should arise, but in those two hours [10] used to get rid of the weariness which he had contracted during the whole day. Some rest in the middle of the day, and reserve some light occupation for the afternoon. Our ancestors, too, forbade any new motion to be made in the Senate after the tenth hour. Soldiers divide their watches, and those who have just returned from active service are allowed to sleep the whole night undisturbed. We must humour our minds and grant them rest from time to time, which acts upon them like food, and restores their strength. It does good also to take walks out of doors, that our spirits may be raised and refreshed by the open air and fresh breeze: sometimes we gain strength by driving in a carriage, by travel, by change of air, or by social meals and a more generous allowance of wine: at times we ought to drink even to intoxication, not so as to drown, but merely to dip ourselves in wine: for wine washes away troubles and dislodges them from the depths of the mind, and acts as a remedy to sorrow as it does to some diseases. The inventor of wine is called Liber, not from the licence which he gives to our tongues, but because he liberates the mind from the bondage of cares, and emancipates it, animates it, and renders it more daring in all that it attempts. Yet moderation is wholesome both in freedom and in wine. It is believed that Solon and Arcesilaus used to drink deep. Cato is reproached with drunkenness: but whoever casts this in his teeth will find it easier to turn his reproach into a commendation than to prove that Cato did anything wrong: however, we ought not to do it often, for fear the mind should contract evil habits, though it ought sometimes to be forced into frolic and frankness, and to cast off dull sobriety for a while. If we believe the Greek poet, "it is sometimes pleasant to be mad "; again, Plato always knocked in vain at the door of poetry when he was sober; or, if we trust Aristotle, no great genius has ever been without a touch of insanity. The mind cannot use lofty language, above that of the common herd, unless it be excited. When it has spurned aside the commonplace environments of custom, and rises

---

[10] The Romans reckoned twelve hours from sunrise to sunset. These "two hours" were therefore the two last of the day

sublime, instinct with sacred fire, then alone can it chant a song too grand for mortal lips: as long as it continues to dwell within itself it cannot rise to any pitch of splendour: it must break away from the beaten track, and lash itself to frenzy, till it gnaws the curb and rushes away bearing up its rider to heights whither it would fear to climb when alone.

 I have now, my beloved Serenus, given you an account of what things can preserve peace of mind, what things can restore it to us, what can arrest the vices which secretly undermine it: yet be assured, that none of these is strong enough to enable us to retain so fleeting a blessing, unless we watch over our vacillating mind with intense and unremitting care.

Of Clemency – Book I

I

I HAVE determined to write a book upon clemency, Nero Caesar, in order that I may as it were serve as a mirror to you, and let you see yourself arriving at the greatest of all pleasures. For although the true enjoyment of good deeds consists in the performance of them, and virtues have no adequate reward beyond themselves, still it is worth your while to consider and investigate a good conscience from every point of view, and afterwards to cast your eyes upon this enormous mass of mankind — quarrelsome, factious, and passionate as they are; likely, if they could throw off the yoke of your government, to take pleasure alike in the ruin of themselves and of one another — and thus to commune with yourself: — "Have I of all mankind been chosen and thought fit to perform the office of a god upon earth? I am the arbiter of life and death to mankind: it rests with me to decide what lot and position in life each man possesses: fortune makes use of my mouth to announce what she bestows on each man: cities and nations are moved to joy by my words: no region anywhere can flourish without my favour and good will: all these thousands of swords now restrained by my authority, would be drawn at a sign from me: it rests with me to decide which tribes shall be utterly exterminated, which shall be moved into other lands, which shall receive and which shall be deprived of liberty, what kings shall be reduced to slavery and whose heads shall be crowned, what cities shall be destroyed and what new ones shall be founded. In this position of enormous power I am not tempted to punish men unjustly by anger, by youthful impulse, by the recklessness and insolence of men, which often overcomes the patience even of the best regulated minds, not even that terrible vanity, so common among great sovereigns, of displaying my power by inspiring terror. My sword is sheathed, nay, fixed in its sheath: I am sparing of the blood even of the lowest of my subjects: a man who has nothing else to recommend him, will nevertheless find favour in my eyes because he is a man. I keep harshness concealed, but I have clemency always at hand: I watch myself as carefully as though I had to give an account of my actions to those laws which I have brought out of darkness and neglect into the light of day. I have been moved to compassion by the youth of one culprit, and the age of another: I have spared one man because of his great place, another on account of his insignificance: when I could find no reason for showing mercy, I have had mercy upon myself. I am prepared this day, should the gods demand it, to render to them an account of the human race." You, Caesar, can boldly say that everything which has come into your charge has been kept safe, and that the state has neither openly nor secretly suffered any loss at your hands. You have coveted a glory which is most rare, and which has been obtained by no emperor before you, that of innocence. Your remarkable goodness is not thrown away, nor is it ungratefully or spitefully undervalued. Men feel gratitude towards you: no one person ever was so dear to another as you are to the people of Rome, whose great and enduring benefit you are. You have, however, taken upon yourself a mighty burden: no one any longer speaks of the good times of the late Emperor Augustus, or the first years of the reign of Tiberius, or proposes for your imitation any model outside yourself: yours is a pattern reign. This would have been difficult had your goodness of heart not been innate, but merely adopted for a time; for no one can wear a mask for long, and fictitious qualities soon give place to true ones. Those which are founded upon truth, and which, so to speak, grow out of a solid basis, only become greater and better as time goes on. The Roman people were in a state of great hazard as long as it was uncertain how your generous[1] disposition would turn out; now, however, the prayers of the community are sure of an answer, for there is no fear that you should suddenly forget your own character. Indeed, excess of happiness makes men greedy, and our desires are never so moderate as to be bounded by what they have obtained: great successes become the stepping-stones to greater ones, and those who have obtained more than they hoped, entertain even more extravagant hopes than before; yet by all your countrymen we hear it admitted that they are now happy, and moreover, that nothing can be added to the blessings that they enjoy, except that they should be eternal. Many circumstances force this admission from them, although it is the one which men are least willing to make: we enjoy a profound and prosperous peace, the power of the law has been openly asserted in the sight of all men, and raised beyond the reach of any violent interference: the form of our government is so happy, as to contain all the essentials of liberty except the power of destroying itself. It is nevertheless your clemency which is most especially admired by the high and low alike: every man enjoys or hopes to enjoy the other blessings of your rule according to the measure of his own personal good fortune, whereas from your clemency all hope alike: no one has so much confidence in his own innocence, as not to feel glad that in your presence stands a clemency which is ready to make allowance for human errors.

---

[1] Nobilis

II

I know, however, that there are some who imagine that clemency only saves the life of every villain, because clemency is useless except after conviction, and alone of all the virtues has no function among the innocent. But in the first place, although a physician is only useful to the sick, yet he is held in honour among the healthy also; and so clemency, though she be invoked by those who deserve punishment, is respected by innocent people as well. Next, she can exist also in the person of the innocent, because sometimes misfortune takes the place of crime; indeed, clemency not only succours the innocent, but often the virtuous, since in the course of time it happens that men are punished for actions which deserve praise. Besides this, there is a large part of mankind which might return to virtue if the hope of pardon were not denied them. Yet it is not right to pardon indiscriminately; for when no distinction is made between good and bad men, disorder follows, and all vices break forth; we must therefore take care to distinguish those characters which admit of reform from those which are hopelessly depraved. Neither ought we to show an indiscriminate and general, nor yet an exclusive clemency; for to pardon everyone is as great cruelty as to pardon none; we must take a middle course; but as it is difficult to find the true mean, let us be careful, if we depart from it, to do so upon the side of humanity.

III

But these matters will be treated of better in their own place. I will now divide this whole subject into three parts. The first will be of gentleness of temper:[2] the second will be that which explains the nature and disposition of clemency; for since there are certain vices which have the semblance of virtue, they cannot be separated unless you stamp upon them the marks which distinguish them from one another: in the third place we shall inquire how the mind may be led to practise this virtue, how it may strengthen it, and by habit make it its own.

That clemency, which is the most humane of virtues, is that which best befits a man, is necessarily an axiom, not only among our own sect, which regards man as a social animal, born for the good of the whole community, but even among those philosophers who give him up entirely to pleasure, and whose words and actions have no other aim than their own personal advantage. If man, as they argue, seeks for quiet and repose, what virtue is there which is more agreeable to his nature than clemency, which loves peace and restrains him from violence? Now clemency becomes no one more than a king or a prince; for great power is glorious and admirable only when it is beneficent; since to be powerful only for mischief is the power of a pestilence. That man's greatness alone rests upon a secure foundation, whom all men know to be as much on their side as he is above them, of whose watchful care for the safety of each and all of them they receive daily proofs, at whose approach they do not fly in terror, as though some evil and dangerous animal had sprung out from its den, but flock to him as they would to the bright and health- giving sunshine. They are perfectly ready to fling themselves upon the swords of conspirators in his defence, to offer their bodies if his only path to safety must be formed of corpses: they protect his sleep by nightly watches, they surround him and defend him on every side, and expose themselves to the dangers which menace him. It is not without good reason that nations and cities thus agree in sacrificing their lives and property for the defence and the love of their king whenever their leader's safety demands it; men do not hold themselves cheap, nor are they insane when so many thousands are put to the sword for the sake of one man, and when by so many deaths they save the life of one man alone, who not unfrequently is old and feeble. Just as the entire body is commanded by the mind, and although the body be so much larger and more beautiful while the mind is impalpable and hidden, and we are not certain as to where it is concealed, yet the hands, feet, and eyes work for it, the skin protects it; at its

---

[2] The text is corrupt. I have followed Gertz's conjectural emendation, mansuefactionis, but I believe that Lipsius is right in thinking that a great deal more than one word has been lost here.

bidding we either lie still or move restlessly about; when it gives the word, if it be an avaricious master, we scour the sea in search of gain, or if it be ambitious we straightway place our right hand in the flames like Mucius, or leap into the pit like Curtius, so likewise this enormous multitude which surrounds one man is directed by his will, is guided by his intellect, and would break and hurl itself into ruin by its own strength, if. it were not upheld by his wisdom.

IV

Men therefore love their own safety, when they draw up vast legions in battle on behalf of one man, when they rush to the front, and expose their breasts to wounds, for fear that their leader's standards should be driven back. He is the bond which fastens the commonwealth together, he is the breath of life to all those thousands, who by themselves would become merely an encumbrance and a source of plunder if that directing mind were withdrawn:—

Bees have but one mind, till their king doth die,
But when he dies, disorderly they fly.

Such a misfortune will be the end of the peace of Rome, it will wreck the prosperity of this great people; the nation will be free from this danger as long as it knows how to endure the reins: should it ever break them, or refuse to have them replaced if they were to fall off by accident, then this mighty whole, this complex fabric of government will fly asunder into many fragments, and the last day of Rome's empire will be that upon which it forgets how to obey. For this reason we need not wonder that princes, kings, and all other protectors of a state, whatever their titles may be, should be loved beyond the circle of their immediate relatives; for since right-thinking men prefer the interests of the state to their own, it follows that he who bears the burden of state affairs must be dearer to them than their own friends. Indeed, the emperor long ago identified himself so thoroughly with the state, that neither of them could be separated without injury to both, because the one requires power, while the other requires a head.

V

My argument seems to have wandered somewhat far from the subject, but, by Hercules, it really is very much to the point. For if, as we may infer from what has been said, you are the soul of the state, and the state is your body, you will perceive, I imagine, how necessary clemency is; for when you appear to spare another, you are really sparing yourself. You ought therefore to spare even blameworthy citizens, just as you spare weakly limbs; and when bloodletting becomes necessary, you must hold your hand, lest you should cut deeper than you need. Clemency therefore, as I said before, naturally befits all mankind, but more especially rulers, because in their case there is more for it to save, and it is displayed upon a greater scale. Cruelty in a private man can do but very little harm; but the ferocity of princes is war. Although there is a harmony between all the virtues, and no one is better or more honourable than another, yet some virtues befit some persons better than others. Magnanimity befits all mortal men, even the humblest of all; for what can be greater or braver than to resist ill fortune? Yet this virtue of magnanimity occupies a wider room in prosperity, and shows to greater advantage on the judgment seat than on the floor of the court. On the other hand, clemency renders every house into which it is admitted happy and peaceful ; but though it is more rare, it is on that account even more admirable in a palace. What can be more remarkable than that he whose anger might be indulged without fear of the consequences, whose decision, even though a harsh one, would be approved even by those who were to suffer by it, whom no one can interrupt, and of whom indeed, should he become violently enraged, no one would dare to beg for mercy, should apply a check to himself and use his power in a better and calmer spirit, reflecting: "Anyone may break the law to kill a man, no one but I can break it to save him "? A great position requires a great mind, for unless the mind raises itself to and even above the level of its station, it will degrade its station and draw it down to the earth; now it is the property of a great mind to be calm and tranquil and to look down upon outrages and insults with contempt. It is a womanish thing to rage with passion; it is the part of wild beasts, and that, too, not of the most noble ones, to bite and worry the fallen. Elephants and lions pass by those whom they have struck down; inveteracy is the quality of ignoble animals. Fierce and implacable rage does not befit a king, because he does not preserve his superiority over the man to whose level he descends by indulging in rage; but if he grants their lives and honours to those who are in jeopardy and who deserve to lose them, he does what can only be done by an absolute ruler; for life may be torn away even from those who are above us in station, but can never be granted save to those who are below us. To save men's lives is the privilege of the loftiest station, which never deserves admiration so much as when it is able to act like the gods, by whose kindness good and bad men alike are brought into the world. Thus a prince, imitating the mind of a god, ought to look with pleasure on some of his countrymen because they are useful and good men, while he ought to allow others to remain to fill up the roll; he ought to be pleased with the existence of the former, and to endure that of the latter.

VI

Look at this city of Rome, in which the widest streets become choked whenever anything stops the crowds which unceasingly pour through them like raging torrents, in which the people streaming to three theatres demand the roads at the same time, in which the produce of the entire world is consumed, and reflect what a desolate waste it would become if only those were left in it whom a strict judge would acquit. How few magistrates are there who ought not to be condemned by the very same laws which they administer? How few prosecutors are themselves faultless? I imagine, also, that few men are less willing to grant pardon, than those who have often had to beg it for themselves. We have all of us sinned, some more deeply than others, some of set purpose, some either by chance impulse or led away by the wickedness of others; some of us have not stood bravely enough by our good resolutions, and have lost our innocence, although unwillingly and after a struggle; nor have we only sinned, but to the very end of our lives we shall continue to sin. Even if there be any one who has so thoroughly cleansed his mind that nothing can hereafter throw him into disorder or deceive him, yet even he has reached this state of innocence through sin.

VII

Since I have made mention of the gods, I shall state the best model on which a prince may mould his life to be, that he deal with his countrymen as he would that the gods may deal with himself. Is it then desirable that the gods should show no mercy upon sins and mistakes, and that they should harshly pursue us to our ruin? In that case what king will be safe? Whose limbs will not be torn asunder and collected by the soothsayers? If, on the other hand, the gods are placable and kind, and do not at once avenge the crimes of the powerful with thunderbolts, is it not far more just that a man set in authority over other men should exercise his power in a spirit of clemency and should consider whether the condition of the -world is more beauteous and pleasant to the eyes on a fine calm day, or when everything is shaken with frequent thunder-claps and when lightning flashes on all sides! Yet the appearance of a peaceful and constitutional reign is the same as that of the calm and brilliant sky. A cruel reign is disordered and hidden in darkness, and while all shake with terror at the sudden explosions, not even he who caused all this disturbance escapes unharmed. It is easier to find excuses for private men who obstinately claim their rights; possibly they may have been injured, and their rage may spring from their wrongs; besides this, they fear to be despised, and not to return the injuries which they have received looks like weakness rather than clemency; but one who can easily avenge himself, if he neglects to do so, is certain to gain praise for goodness of heart. Those who are born in a humble station may with greater freedom exercise violence, go to law, engage in quarrels, and indulge their angry passions; even blows count for little between two equals; but in the case of a king, even loud clamour and unmeasured talk are unbecoming.

VIII

You think it a serious matter to take away from kings the right of free speech which the humblest enjoy. "This," you say, "is to be a subject, not a king." What, do you not find that we have the command, you the subjection? Your position is quite different to that of those who lie hid in the crowd which they never leave, whose very virtues cannot be manifested without a long struggle, and whose vices are shrouded in obscurity; rumour catches up your acts and sayings, and therefore no persons ought to be more careful of their reputation than those who are certain to have a great one, whatsoever one they may have deserved. How many things there are that you may not do which, thanks to you, we may do! I am able to walk alone without fear in any part of Rome whatever, although no companion accompanies me, though there is no guard at my house no sword by my side. You must live armed in the peace which you maintain.[3] You cannot stray away from your position; it besets you, and follows you with mighty pomp wherever you go. This slavery of not being able to sink one's rank belongs to the highest position of all; yet it is a burden which you share with the gods. They too are held fast in heaven, and it is no more possible for them to come down than it is safe[4] for you; you are chained to your lofty pinnacle. Of our movements few persons are aware; we can go forth and return home and change our dress without its being publicly known; but you are no more able to hide yourself than the sun. A strong light is all around you, the eyes of all are turned towards it. Do you think you are leaving your house? nay, you are dawning upon the world. You cannot speak without all nations everywhere hearing your voice; you cannot be angry, without making everything tremble, because you can strike no one without shaking all around him. Just as thunderbolts when they fall endanger few men but terrify all, so the chastisement inflicted by great potentates terrify more widely than they injure, and that for good reasons; for in the case of one whose power is absolute, men do not think of what he has done, so much as of what he may do. Add to this that private men endure wrongs more tamely, because they have already endured others; the safety of kings on the other hand is more surely founded on kindness, because frequent punishment may crush the hatred of a few, but excites that of all. A king ought to wish to pardon while he has still grounds for being severe; if he acts otherwise, just as lopped trees sprout forth again with numberless boughs, and many kinds of crops are cut down in order that they may grow more thickly, so a cruel king increases the number of his

---

[3] Pace

[4] Tutum

enemies by destroying them; for the parents and children of those who are put to death, and their relatives and friends, step into the place of each victim.

IX

I wish to prove the truth of this by an example drawn from your own family. The late Emperor Augustus was a mild prince, if in estimating his character one reckons from the era of his reign; yet he appealed to arms while the state was shared among the triumvirate. When he was just of your age, at the end of his twenty-second year, he had already hidden daggers under the clothes of his friends, he had already conspired to assassinate Marcus Antonius, the consul, he had already taken part in the proscription. But when he had passed his sixtieth[5] year, and was staying in Gaul, intelligence was brought to him that Lucius Cinna, a dull man, was plotting against him: the plot was betrayed by one of the conspirators, who told him where, when, and in what manner Cinna meant to attack him. Augustus determined to consult his own safety against this man, and ordered a council of his own friends to be summoned. He passed a disturbed night, reflecting that he would be obliged to condemn to death a youth of noble birth, who was guilty of no crime save this one, and who was the grandson of Gnaeus Pompeius. He, who had sat at dinner and heard M. Antonius[6] read aloud his edict for the proscription, could not now bear to put one single man to death. With groans he kept at intervals making various inconsistent exclamations: — "What! shall I allow my assassin to walk about at his ease while I am racked by fears? Shall the man not be punished who has plotted not merely to slay but actually to sacrifice at the altar" (for the conspirators intended to attack him when he was sacrificing), "now when there is peace by land and sea, that life which so many civil wars have sought in vain, which has passed unharmed through so many battles of fleets

---

[5] Gertz reads sexagesimum, his sixtieth year, which he calls "the not very audacious conjecture of Wesseling," and adds that he does so because of the words at the beginning of chap. xi. and the authority of Dion Cassius. The ordinary reading is quadragesimum, "his fortieth year," and this is the date to which Cinna's conspiracy is referred to by Merivale, "History of the Romans under the Empire," vol. iv. ch. 37. "A plot," he says, "was formed for his destruction, at the head of which was Cornelius Cinna, described as a son of Faustus Sulla by a daughter of the Great Pompeius." The story of Cinna's conspiracy is told by Seneca, de Clem. i. 9, and Dion iv. 14, foll. They agree in the main fact; but Seneca is our authority for the details of the interview between Augustus and his enemy, while Dion has doubtless invented his long conversation between the emperor and Livia. Seneca, however, calls the conspirator Lucius, and places the event in the fortieth year of Augustus (a.d. 731), the scene in Gaul: Dion, on the other, gives the names of Gnaeus, and supposes the circumstances to have occurred twenty-six years later, and at Rome. It may be observed that a son of Faustus Sulla must have been at least fifty at this latter date, nor do we know why he should bear the name of Cinna, though an adoption is not impossible.

[6] See Shakespeare's "Julius Caesar," Act IV. Sc. 1.

and armies?"

Then, after an interval of silence, he would say to himself in a far louder, angrier tone than he had used to Cinna, "Why do you live, if it be to so many men's advantage that you should die? Is there no end to these executions? to this bloodshed? I am a figure set up for nobly-born youths to sharpen their swords on. Is life worth having, if so many must perish to prevent my losing it?" At last his wife Livia interrupted him, saying: "Will you take a woman's advice? Do as the physicians do, who, when the usual remedies fail, try their opposites. Hitherto you have gained nothing by harsh measures: Salvidienus has been followed by Lepidus, Lepidus by Muraena, Muraena by Caepio, and Caepio by Egnatius, not to mention others of whom one feels ashamed of their having dared to attempt so great a deed. Now try what effect clemency will have: pardon Lucius Cinna. He has been detected, he cannot now do you any harm, and he can do your reputation much good." Delighted at finding someone to support his own view of the case, he thanked his wife, straightway ordered his friends, whose counsel he had asked for, to be told that he did not require their advice, and summoned Cinna alone. After ordering a second seat to be placed for Cinna, he sent everyone else out of the room, and said: — "The first request which I have to make of you is, that you will not interrupt me while I am speaking to you: that you will not cry out in the middle of my address to you: you shall be allowed time to speak freely in answer to me. Cinna, when I found you in the enemy's camp, you who had not become but were actually born my enemy, I saved your life, and restored to you the whole of your father's estate. You are now so prosperous and so rich, that many of the victorious party envy you, the vanquished one: when you were a candidate for the priesthood I passed over many others whose parents had served with me in the wars, and gave it to you: and now, after I have deserved so well of you, you have made up your mind to kill me." When at this word the man exclaimed that he was far from being so insane, Augustus replied, "You do not keep your promise, Cinna; it was agreed upon between us that you should not interrupt me. I repeat, you are preparing to kill me." He then proceeded to tell him of the place, the names of his accomplices, the day, the way in which they had arranged to do the deed, and which of them was to give the fatal stab. When he saw Cinna's eyes fixed upon the ground, and that he was silent, no longer because of the agreement, but from consciousness of his guilt, he said, "What is your intention in doing this? is it that you yourself may be emperor? The Roman people must indeed be in a bad way if nothing but my life prevents your ruling over them. You cannot even maintain the dignity of your own house: you have recently been defeated in a legal encounter by the superior influence of a freedman: and so you can find no easier task than to call your friends to rally round you against Ceesar. Come, now, if you think that I alone stand in the way of your ambition; will Paulus and Fabius Maximus, will the Cossi and the Servilii and all that band of nobles, whose names are no empty pretence, but whose ancestry really renders them illustrious — will they endure that you should rule over them?" Not to fill up the greater part of this book by repeating the whole of his speech — for he is known to have spoken for more than two hours, lengthening out this punishment, which was the only one which he intended to inflict — he said at last: "Cinna, I grant you your life for the second time: when I gave it you before you were an open enemy, you are now a secret plotter and parricide."[7] From this day forth let us be friends: let us try which of us is the more sincere, I in giving you your life, or you in owing your life to me." After this he of his own accord bestowed the consulship upon him, complaining of his not venturing to offer himself as a candidate for that office, and found him ever afterwards his most grateful and loyal adherent. Cinna made the emperor his sole heir, and no one ever again formed any plot against him.

---

[7] An allusion to the title of "Father of his country," bestowed by the Senate upon Augustus. See Merivale, ch, 33.

X

Your great-great-grandfather spared the vanquished: for whom could he have ruled over, had he not spared them? He recruited Sallustins, the Cocceii, the Deillii, and the whole inner circle of his court from the camp of his opponents. Soon afterwards his clemency gave him a Domitius, a Messala, an Asinius, a Cicero, and all the flower of the state. For what a long time he waited for Lepidus to die: for years he allowed him to retain all the insignia of royalty, and did not allow the office of pontifex maximus to be conferred upon himself until after Lepidus's death; for he wished it to be called a honourable office rather than a spoil stripped from a vanquished foe. It was this clemency which made him end his days in safety and security: this it was which rendered him popular and beloved, although he had laid his hands on the neck of the Romans when they were still unused to bearing the yoke: this gives him even at the present day a reputation such as hardly any prince has enjoyed during his own lifetime. "We believe him to be a god, and not merely because we are bidden to do so. We declare that Augustus was a good emperor, and that he was well worthy to bear his parent's name, for no other reason than because he did not even show cruelty in avenging personal insults, which most princes feel more keenly than actual injuries; because he smiled at scandalous jests against himself, because it was evident that he himself suffered when he punished others, because he was so far from putting to death even those whom he had convicted of intriguing with his daughter, that when they were banished he gave them passports to enable them to travel more safely. When you know that there will be many who will take your quarrel upon themselves, and will try to gain your favour by the murder of your enemies, you do indeed pardon them if you not only grant them their lives but ensure that they shall not lose them.

XI

Such was Augustus when an old man, or when growing old: in his youth he was hasty and passionate, and did many things upon which he looked back with regret. No one will venture to compare the rule of the blessed Augustus to the mildness of your own, even if your youth be compared with his more than ripe old age: he was gentle and placable, but it was after he had dyed the sea at Actinm with Roman blood; after he had wrecked both the enemy's fleet and his own at Sicily; after the holocaust of Perusia and the proscriptions. But I do not call it clemency to be wearied of cruelty; true clemency, Caesar, is that which you display, which has not begun from remorse at its past ferocity, on which there is no stain, which has never shed the blood of your countrymen: this, when combined with unlimited power, shows the truest self-control and all-embracing love of the human race as of one's self, not corrupted by any low desires, any extravagant ideas, or any of the bad examples of former emperors into trying, by actual experiment, how great a tyranny you would be allowed to exercise over his countrymen, but inclining rather to blunting your sword of empire. You, Caesar, have granted us the boon of keeping our state free from bloodshed, and that of which you boast, that you have not caused one single drop of blood to flow in any part of the world, is all the more magnanimous and marvellous because no one ever had the power of the sword placed in his hands at an earlier age. Clemency, then, makes princes safer as well as more respected, and is a glory to empires besides being their most trustworthy means of preservation. Why have legitimate sovereigns grown old on the throne, and bequeathed their power to their children and grandchildren, while the sway of despotic usurpers is both hateful and shortlived? What is the difference between the tyrant and the king—for their outward symbols of authority and their powers are the same — except it be that tyrants take delight in cruelty, whereas kings are only cruel for good reasons and because they cannot help it.[8]

---

[8] This whole comparison, which reads so meaninglessly both in Latin and in English, is borrowed from the eternal declamations of Plutarch and the Greek philosophers about βασιλετς and τύραυυοι. See Plutarch, Lives of Philopoemen and Aratus, Plato, Gorgias and Politicus; Arnold, "Appendix to Thucydides," vol. i., and "Dictionary of Antiquities," s.v.

XII

"What, then," say you, "do not kings also put men to death?" They do, but only when that measure is recommended by the public advantage: tyrants enjoy cruelty. A tyrant differs from a king in deeds, not in title: for the elder Dionysius deserves to be preferred before many kings, and what can prevent our styling Lucius Sulla a tyrant, since he only left off slaying because he had no more enemies to slay? Although he laid down his dictatorship and resumed the garb of a private citizen, yet what tyrant ever drank human blood as greedily as he, who ordered seven thousand Roman citizens to be butchered, and who, on hearing the shrieks of so many thousands being put to the sword as he sat in the temple of Bellona, said to the terror-stricken Senate, "Let us attend to our business, Conscript Fathers; it is only a few disturbers of the public peace who are being put to death by my orders." In saying this he did not lie: they really seemed few to Sulla. But we shall speak of Sulla presently, when we consider how we ought to feel anger against our enemies, at any rate when our own countrymen, members of the same community as ourselves, have been torn away from it and assumed the name of enemies: in the meanwhile, as I was saying, clemency is what makes the great distinction between kings and tyrants. Though each of them may be equally fenced around by armed soldiers, nevertheless the one uses his troops to safeguard the peace of his kingdom, the other uses them to quell great hatred by great terror: and yet he does not look with any confidence upon those to whose hands he entrusts himself. He is driven in opposite directions by conflicting passions: for since he is hated because he is feared, he wishes to be feared because he is hated: and he acts up to the spirit of that odious verse, which has cast so many headlong from their thrones —

"Why, let them hate me, if they fear me too!"—

not knowing how frantic men become when their hatred becomes excessive: for a moderate amount of fear restrains men, but a constant and keen apprehension of the worst tortures rouses up even the most grovelling spirits to deeds of reckless courage, and causes them to hesitate at nothing. Just so a string stuck full of feathers[9] will prevent wild beasts escaping: but should a horseman begin to shoot at them from another quarter, they will attempt to escape over the very thing that scared them, and will trample the cause of their alarm underfoot. No courage is so great as that which is born of utter desperation. In order to keep people down by terror, you must grant them a certain amount of security, and let them see that they have far more to hope

---

[9] De Ira, ii, II

for than to fear: for otherwise, if a man is in equal peril whether he sits still or takes action, he will feel actual pleasure in risking his life, and will fling it away as lightly as though it were not his own.

XIII

A calm and peaceful king trusts his guards, because he makes use of them to ensure the common safety of all his subjects, and his soldiers, who see that the security of the state depends upon their labours, cheerfully undergo the severest toil and glory in being the protectors of the father of their country: whereas your harsh and murderous tyrant must needs be disliked even by his own janissaries. No man can expect willing and loyal service from those whom he uses like the rack and the axe, as instruments of torture and death, to whom he casts men as he would cast them to wild beasts. No prisoner at the bar is so full of agony and anxiety as a tyrant; for while he dreads both gods and men because they have witnessed, and will avenge his crimes, he has at the same time so far committed himself to this course of action that he is not able to alter it. This is perhaps the very worst quality of cruelty: a man must go on exercising it, and it is impossible for him to retrace his steps and start in a better path; for crimes must be safeguarded by fresh crimes. Yet who can be more unhappy than he who is actually compelled to be a villain? How greatly he ought to be pitied: I mean, by himself, for it would be impious for others to pity a man who has made use of his power to murder and ravage, who has rendered himself mistrusted by everyone at home and abroad, who fears the very soldiers to whom he flees for safety, who dare not rely upon the loyalty of his friends or the affection of his children: who, whenever he considers what he has done, and what he is about to do, and calls to mind all the crimes and torturings with which his conscience is burdened, must often fear death, and yet must often wish for it, for he must be even more hateful to himself than he is to his subjects. On the other hand, he who takes an interest in the entire state, who watches over every department of it with more or less care, who attends to all the business of the state as well as if it were his own, who is naturally inclined to mild measures, and shows, even when it is to his advantage to punish, how unwilling he is to make use of harsh remedies; who has no angry or savage feelings, but wields his authority calmly and beneficially, being anxious that even his subordinate officers shall be popular with his countrymen, who thinks his happiness complete if he can make the nation share his prosperity, who is courteous in language, whose presence is easy of access, who looks obligingly upon his subjects, who is disposed to grant all their reasonable wishes, and does not treat their unreasonable wishes with harshness — such a prince is loved, protected, and worshipped by his whole empire. Men talk of such a one in private in the same words which they use in public: they are eager to bring up families under his reign, and they put an end to the childlessness which public misery had previously rendered general: everyone feels that he will indeed deserve that his children should be grateful to him for having brought them into so happy an age. Such a prince is rendered safe by his own beneficence; he has no need of guards their arms serve him merely as decorations.

XIV

What, then, is his duty? It is that of good parents, who sometimes scold their children good naturedly, sometimes threaten them, and sometimes even flog them. No man in his senses disinherits his son for his first offence he does not pass this extreme sentence upon him unless his patience has been worn out by many grievous wrongs, unless he fears that his son will do something worse than that which he punishes him for having done; before doing this he makes many attempts to lead his son's mind into the right way while it is still hesitating between good and evil and has only taken its first steps in depravity; it is only when its case is hopeless that he adopts this extreme measure. No one demands that people should be executed until after he has failed to reform them. This which is the duty of a parent, is also that of the prince whom with no unmeaning flattery we call "The Father of our Country." Other names are given as titles of honour: we have styled some men "The Great," "The Fortunate," or "The August" and have thus satisfied their passion for grandeur by bestowing upon them all the dignity that we could: but when we style a man "The Father of his Country " we give him to understand that we have entrusted him with a father's power over us, which is of the mildest character for a father takes thought for his children and subordinates his own interests to theirs. It is long before a father will cut off a member of his own body: even after he has cut it off he longs to replace it, and in cutting it off he laments and hesitates much and long: for he who condemns quickly is not far from being willing to condemn; and he who inflicts too great punishment comes very near to punishing unjustly.

XV

Within my own recollection the people stabbed in the forum with their writing-styles a Roman knight named Tricho, because he had flogged his son to death: even the authority of Augustus Caesar could hardly save him from the angry clutches of both fathers and sons: but everyone admired Tarius, who, on discovering that his son meditated parricide, tried him, convicted him, and was then satisfied with punishing him by exile, and that, too, to that pleasant place of exile, Marseilles, where he made him the same yearly allowance which he had done while he was innocent: the result of this generosity was that even in a city where every villain finds someone to defend him, no one doubted that he was justly condemned, since even the father who was unable to hate him, nevertheless had condemned him. In this very same instance I will give you an example of a good prince, which you may compare with a good father. Tarius, when about to sit in judgement on his son, invited Augustus Caesar to assist in trying him: Augustus came into his private house, sat beside the father, took part in another man's family council, and did not say, "Nay, let him rather come to my house," because if he had done so, the trial would have been conducted by Caesar and not by the father. When the cause had been heard, after all that the young man pleaded in his own defence and all that was alleged against him had been thoroughly discussed, the emperor begged that each man would write his sentence (instead of pronouncing it aloud), in order that they might not all follow Caesar in giving sentence: then, before the tablets were opened, he declared that if Tarius, who was a rich man, made him his heir, he would not accept the bequest. One might say "It showed a paltry mind in him to fear that people would think that he condemned the son in order to enable himself to inherit the estate." I am of a contrary opinion — any one of us ought to have sufficient trust in the consciousness of his own integrity to defend him against calumny, but princes must take great pains to avoid even the appearance of evil. He swore that he would not accept the property. On that day Tarius lost two heirs to his estate, but Caesar gained the liberty of forming an unbiased judgement: and when he had proved that his severity was disinterested, a point of which a prince should never lose sight, he gave sentence that the son should be banished to whatever place the father might choose. He did not sentence him to the sack and the snakes, or to prison, because he thought, not of who it was upon whom he was passing sentence, but of who it was with whom he was sitting in judgement: he said that a father ought to be satisfied with the mildest form of punishment for his stripling son, who had been seduced into a crime which he had attempted so fainteartedly as to be almost innocent of it, and that he ought to be removed from Rome and out of his father's sight.

XVI

How worthy was he to be invited by fathers to join their family councils: how worthy to be made co-heir with innocent children! This is the sort of clemency which befits a prince; wherever he goes, let him make every one more charitable. In the king's sight, no one ought to be so despicable that he should not notice whether he lives or dies: be his character what it may, he is a part of the empire. Let us take examples for great kingdoms from smaller ones. There are many forms of royalty: a prince reigns over his subjects, a father over his children, a teacher over his scholars, a tribune or centurion over his soldiers. Would not he, who constantly punished his children by beating them for the most trifling faults, be thought the worst of fathers? Which is worthier to impart a liberal education: he who flays his scholars alive if their memory be weak, or if their eyes do not run quickly along the lines as they read, or he who prefers to improve and instruct them by kindly warnings and moral influence? If a tribune or a centurion is harsh, he will make men deserters, and one cannot blame them for desertion. It is never right to rule a human being more harshly and cruelly than we rule dumb animals; yet a skilled horse-breaker will not scare a horse by frequent blows, because he will become timid and vicious if you do not soothe him with pats and caresses. So also a huntsman, both when he is teaching puppies to follow the tracks of wild animals, and when he uses dogs already trained to drive them from their lairs and hunt them, does not often threaten to beat them, for, if he does, he will break their spirit, and make them stupid and currish with fear; though, on the other hand, he will not allow them to roam and range about unrestrained. The same is the case with those who drive the slower draught cattle, which, though brutal treatment and wretchedness is their lot from their birth, still, by excessive cruelty may be made to refuse to draw.

XVII

No creature is more self-willed, requires more careful management, or ought to be treated with greater indulgence than man. What, indeed, can be more foolish than that we should blush to show anger against dogs or beasts of burden, and yet wish one man to be most abominably ill-treated by another? We are not angry with diseases, but apply remedies to them: but this also is a disease of the mind, and requires soothing medicine and a physician who is anything but angry with his patient. It is the part of a bad physician to despair of effecting a cure: he, to whom the care of all men's well-being is entrusted, ought to act like a good physician, and not be in a hurry to give up hope or to declare that the symptoms are mortal: he should wrestle with vices, withstand them, reproach some with their distemper, and deceive others by a soothing mode of treatment, because he will cure his patient more quickly and more thoroughly if the medicines which he administers escape his notice: a prince should take care not only of the recovery of his people, but also that their scars should be honourable. Cruel punishments do a king no honour: for who doubts that he is able to inflict them? but, on the other hand, it does him great honour to restrain his powers, to save many from the wrath of others, and sacrifice no one to his own.

XVIII

It is creditable to a man to keep within reasonable bounds in his treatment of his slaves. Even in the case of a human chattel one ought to consider, not how much one can torture him with impunity, but how far such treatment is permitted by natural goodness and justice, which prompts us to act kindly towards even prisoners of war and slaves bought for a price (how much more towards free-born, respectable gentlemen?), and not to treat them with scornful brutality as human chattels, but as persons somewhat below ourselves in station, who have been placed under our protection rather than assigned to us as servants. Slaves are allowed to run and take sanctuary at the statue of a god, though the laws allows a slave to be ill-treated to any extent, there are nevertheless some things which the common laws of life forbid us to do to a human being. Who does not hate Vedius Pollio[10] more even than his own slaves did, because he used to fatten his lampreys with human blood, and ordered those who had offended him in any way to be cast into his fish-pond, or rather snake-pond? That man deserved to die a thousand deaths, both for throwing his slaves to be devoured by the lampreys which he himself meant to eat, and for keeping lampreys that he might feed them in such a fashion. Cruel masters are pointed at with disgust in all parts of the city, and are hated and loathed; the wrong-doings of kings are enacted on a wider theatre: their shame and unpopularity endures for ages: yet how far better it would have been never to have been born than to be numbered among those who have been born to do their country harm!

---

[10] Vedius Pollio had a villa on the mountain now called Punta di Posilippo, which projects into the sea between Naples and Puteoli, which he left to Augustus, and which was afterwards possessed by the Emperor Trajan. He was a freedman by birth, and remarkable for nothing except his riches and his cruelty. Cf. Dion Cassius, LIV. 23; Pliny, H. N. IX. 23; and Seneca, "On Anger," III. 40. 2.

XIX

Nothing can be imagined which is more becoming to a sovereign than clemency, by whatever title and right he may be set over his fellow citizens. The greater his power, the more beautiful and admirable he will confess his clemency to be: for there is no reason why power should do any harm, if only it be wielded in accordance with the laws of nature. Nature herself has conceived the idea of a king, as you may learn from various animals, and especially from bees, among whom the king's cell is the roomiest, and is placed in the most central and safest part of the hive; moreover, he does no work, but employs himself in keeping the others up to their work. If the king be lost, the entire swarm disperses: they never endure to have more than one king at a time, and find out which is the better by making them fight with one another: moreover the king is distinguished by his statelier appearance, being both larger and more brilliantly coloured than the other bees. The most remarkable distinction, however, is the following: bees are very fierce, and for their size are the most pugnacious of creatures, and leave their stings in the wounds which they make, but the king himself has no sting: nature does not wish him to be savage or to seek revenge at so dear a rate, and so has deprived him of his weapon and disarmed his rage. She has offered him as a pattern to great sovereigns, for she is wont to practice herself in small matters, and to scatter abroad tiny models of the hugest structures. We ought to be ashamed of not learning a lesson in behaviour from these small creatures, for a man, who has so much more power of doing harm than they, ought to show a correspondingly greater amount of self-control. Would that human beings were subject to the same law, and that their anger destroyed itself together with its instrument, so that they could only inflict a wound once, and would not make use of the strength of others to carry out their hatreds: for their fury would soon grow faint if it carried its own punishment with it, and could only give rein to its violence at the risk of death. Even as it is, however, no one can exercise it with safety, for he must needs feel as much fear as he hopes to cause, he must watch every one's movements, and even when his enemies are not laying violent hands upon him he must bear in mind that they are plotting to do so, and he cannot have a single moment free from alarm. Would any one endure to live such a life as this, when he might enjoy the privileges of his high station to the general joy of all men, without injuring any one, and for that very reason have no one to fear? for it is a mistake to suppose that the king can be safe in a state where nothing is safe from the king: he can only purchase a life without anxiety for himself by guaranteeing the same for his subjects. He need not pile up lofty citadels, escarp steep hills, cut away the sides of mountains, and fence himself about with many lines of walls and towers: clemency will render a king safe even upon an open plain. The one fortification which cannot be stormed is the love of his countrymen. What can be more glorious than a life which every one spontaneously and without official pressure hopes may last long? to excite men's fears, not their hopes, if one's health gives way a little? to know that no one holds anything so dear that he would not be glad to give it in exchange for the health of his sovereign? "O, may no evil befall him!" they would cry: "he must live for his own sake, not only for ours: his constant proofs of goodness have made him belong to the state instead of the state belonging to him." Who would dare to plot any danger to such a king? Who would not rather, if he could, keep misfortune far from one under whom justice, peace, decency, security and merit flourish, under whom the state grows rich with an abundance of all good things, and looks upon its ruler in the same spirit of adoration and respect with which we should look upon the immortal gods, if they allowed us to behold them as we behold him? Why! does not that man come very close to the gods who acts in a god-like manner, and who is beneficent, open-handed, and powerful for good? Your aim and your pride ought to lie in being thought the best, as well as the greatest of mankind.

XX

A prince generally inflicts punishment for one of two reasons: he wishes either to assert his own rights or those of another. I will first discuss the case in which he is personally concerned, for it is more difficult for him to act with moderation when he acts under the impulse of actual pain than when he merely does so for the sake of the example. It is unnecessary in this place to remind him to be slow to believe what he hears, to ferret out the truth, to show favour to innocence, and to bear in mind that to prove it is as much the business of the judge as that of the prisoner; for these considerations are connected with justice, not with clemency: what we are now encouraging him to do is not to lose control over his feelings when he receives an unmistakeable injury, and to forego punishing it if he possibly can do so with safety, if not, to moderate the severity of the punishment, and to show himself far more unwilling to forgive wrongs done to others than those done to himself: for, just as the truly generous man is not he who gives away what belongs to others, but he who deprives himself of what he gives to another, so also I should not call a prince clement who looked good naturedly upon a wrong done to someone else, but one who is unmoved even by the sting of a personal injury, who understands how magnanimous it is for one whose power is unlimited to allow himself to be wronged, and that there is no more noble spectacle than that of a sovereign who has received an injury without avenging it.

XXI

Vengeance effects two purposes: it either affords compensation to the person to whom the wrong was done, or it ensures him against molestation for the future. A prince is too rich to need compensation, and his power is too evident for him to require to gain a reputation for power by causing anyone to suffer. I mean, when he is attacked and injured by his inferiors, for if he sees those who once were his equals in a position of inferiority to himself he is sufficiently avenged. A king may be killed by a slave, or a serpent, or an arrow: but no one can be saved except by someone who is greater than him whom he saves. He, therefore, who has the power of giving and of taking away life ought to use such a great gift of heaven in a spirited manner. Above all, if he once obtains this power over those who he knows were once on a level with himself, he has completed his revenge, and done all that he need to towards the punishment of his adversary: for he who owes his life to another must have lost it, and he who has been cast down from on high and lies at his enemy's feet with his kingdom and his life depending upon the pleasure of another, adds to the glory of his preserver if he be allowed to live, and increases his reputation much more by remaining unhurt than if he were put out of the way. In the former case he remains as an everlasting testimony to the valour of his conqueror; whereas if led in the procession of a triumph he would have soon passed out of sight.[11] If, however, his kingdom also may be safely left in his hands and he himself replaced upon the throne from which he has fallen, such a measure confers an immense increase of luster on him who scorned to take anything from a conquered king beyond the glory of having conquered him. To do this is to triumph even over one's own victory, and to declare that one has found nothing among the vanquished which it was worth the victor's while to take. As for his countrymen, strangers, and persons of mean condition, he ought to treat them with all the less severity because it costs so much less to overcome them. Some you would be glad to spare, against some you would disdain to assert your rights, and would forbear to touch them as you would to touch little insects which defile your hands when you crush them: but in the case of men upon whom all eyes are fixed, whether they be spared or condemned, you should seize the opportunity of making your clemency widely known.

---

[11] The conquered princes who were led through Rome in triumphs were as a rule put to death when the procession was over.

XXII

Let us now pass on to the consideration of wrongs done to others, in avenging which the law has aimed at three ends, which the prince will do well to aim at also: they are, either that it may correct him whom it punishes, or that his punishment may render other men better, or that, by bad men being put out of the way, the rest may live without fear. You will more easily correct the men themselves by a slight punishment, for he who has some part of his fortune remaining untouched will behave less recklessly; on the other hand, no one cares about respectability after he has lost it: it is a species of impunity to have nothing left for punishment to take away. It is conducive, however, to good morals in a state, that punishment should seldom be inflicted: for where there is a multitude of sinners men become familiar with sin, shame is less felt when shared with a number of fellow-criminals, and severe sentences, if frequently pronounced, lose the influence which constitutes their chief power as remedial measures. A good king establishes a good standard of morals for his kingdom and drives away vices if he is long-suffering with them, not that he should seem to encourage them, but to be very unwilling and to suffer much when he is forced to chastise them. Clemency in a sovereign even makes men ashamed to do wrong: for punishment seems far more grievous when inflicted by a merciful man.

XXIII

Besides this, you will find that sins which are frequently punished are frequently committed. Your father sewed up more parricides in sacks during five years, than we hear of in all previous centuries. As long as the greatest of crimes remained without any special law, children were much more timid about committing it. Our wise ancestors, deeply skilled in human nature, preferred to pass over this as being a wickedness too great for belief, and beyond the audacity of the worst criminal, rather than teach men that it might be done by appointing a penalty for doing it: parricides, consequently, were unknown until a law was made against them, and the penalty showed them the way to the crime. Filial affection soon perished, for since that time we have seen more men punished by the sack than by the cross. Where men are seldom punished innocence becomes the rule, and is encouraged as a public benefit. If a state thinks itself innocent, it will be innocent: it will be all the more angry with those who corrupt the general simplicity of manners if it sees that they are few in number. Believe me, it is a dangerous thing to show a state how great a majority of bad men it contains.

XXIV

A proposal was once made in the Senate to distinguish slaves from free men by their dress: it was then discovered how dangerous it would be for our slaves to be able to count our numbers. Be assured that the same thing would be the case if no one's offence is pardoned: it will quickly be discovered how far the number of bad men exceeds that of the good. Many executions are as disgraceful to a sovereign as many funerals are to a physician: one who governs less strictly is better obeyed. The human mind is naturally self-willed, kicks against the goad, and sets its face against authority; it will follow more readily than it can be led. As well-bred and high-spirited horses are best managed with a loose rein, so mercy gives men's minds a spontaneous bias towards innocence, and the public think that it is worth observing. Mercy, therefore, does more good than severity.

XXV

Cruelty is far from being a human vice, and is unworthy of man's gentle mind: it is mere bestial madness to take pleasure in blood and wounds, to cast off humanity and transform oneself into a wild beast of the forest. Pray, Alexander, what is the difference between your throwing Lysimachus into a lion's den and tearing his flesh with your own teeth? it is you that have the lion's maw, and the lion's fierceness. How pleased you would be if you had claws instead of nails, and jaws that were capable of devouring men! We do not expect of you that your hand, the sure murderer of your best friends, should restore health to any one; or that your proud spirit, that inexhaustible source of evil to all nations, should be satisfied with anything short of blood and slaughter: we rather call it mercy that your friend should have a human being chosen to be his butcher. The reason why cruelty is the most hateful of all vices is that it goes first beyond the ordinary limits, and then beyond those of humanity; that it devises new kinds of punishments, calls ingenuity to aid it in inventing devices for varying and lengthening men's torture, and takes delight in their sufferings: this accursed disease of the mind reaches its highest pitch of madness when cruelty itself turns into pleasure, and the act of killing a man becomes enjoyment. Such a ruler is soon cast down from his throne; his life is attempted by poison one day and by the sword the next; he is exposed to as many dangers as there are men to whom he is dangerous, and he is sometimes destroyed by the plots of individuals, and at others by a general insurrection. Whole communities are not roused to action by unimportant outrages on private persons; but cruelty which takes a wider range, and from which no one is safe, becomes a mark for all men's weapons Very small snakes escape our notice, and the whole country does not combine to destroy them; but when one of them exceeds the usual size and grows into a monster, when it poisons fountains with its spittle, scorches herbage with its breath, and spreads ruin wherever it crawls, we shoot at it with military engines. Trifling evils may cheat us and elude our observation, but we gird up our loins to attack great ones. One sick person does not so much as disquiet the house in which he lies; but when frequent deaths show that a plague is raging, there is a general outcry, men take to flight and shake their fists angrily at the very gods themselves. If a fire breaks out under one single roof, the family and the neighbours pour water upon it; but a wide conflagration which has consumed many houses must be smothered under the ruins of a whole quarter of a city.

XXVI

The cruelty even of private men has sometimes been revenged by their slaves in spite of the certainty that they will be crucified: whole kingdoms and nations when oppressed by tyrants or threatened by them, have attempted their destruction. Sometimes their own guards have risen in revolt, and have used against their master all the deceit, disloyalty, and ferocity which they have learned from him. What, indeed, can he expect from those whom he has taught to be wicked? A bad man will not long be obedient, and will not do only as much evil as he is ordered. But even if the tyrant may be cruel with safety, how miserable his kingdom must be: it must look like a city taken by storm, like some frightful scene of general panic. Everywhere sorrow, anxiety, disorder; men dread even their own pleasures; they cannot even dine with one another in safety when they have to keep watch over their tongues even when in their cups, nor can they safely attend the public shows when informers are ready to find grounds for their impeachment in their behaviour there. Although the spectacles be provided at an enormous expense, with royal magnificence and with world-famous artists, yet who cares for amusement when he is in prison? Ye gods! what a miserable life it is to slaughter and to rage, to delight in the clanking of chains, and to cut off one's countrymen's heads, to cause blood to flow freely wherever one goes, to terrify people, and make them flee away out of one's sight! It is what would happen if bears or lions were our masters, if serpents and all the most venomous creatures were given power over us. Even these animals, devoid of reason as they are, and accused by us of cruel ferocity, spare their own kind, and wild beasts themselves respect their own likeness: but the fury of tyrants does not even stop short at their own relations, and they treat friends and strangers alike, only becoming more violent the more they indulge their passions. By insensible degrees he proceeds from the slaughter of individuals to the ruin of nations, and thinks it a sign of power to set roofs on fire and to plough up the sites of ancient cities: he considers it unworthy of an emperor to order only one or two people to be put to death, and thinks that his cruelty is unduly restrained if whole troops of wretches are not sent to execution together. True happiness, on the other hand, consists in saving many men's lives, in calling them back from the very gates of death, and in being so merciful as to deserve a civic crown.[12] No decoration is more worthy or more becoming to a prince's rank than that crown "for saving the lives of fellow-citizens: not trophies torn from a vanquished enemy, not chariots wet with their

---

[12] The "civic" crown of oak-leaves was bestowed on him who had saved the life of a fellow-citizen in war. It was bestowed upon Augustus, and after him upon the other emperors, as preservers of the state.

savage owner's blood, not spoils captured in war. This power which saves men's lives by crowds and by nations, is godlike: the power of extensive and indiscriminate massacre is the power of downfall and conflagration.

Of Clemency – Book II

I

I HAVE been especially led to write about clemency, Nero Caesar, by a saying of yours, which I remember having heard with admiration and which I afterwards told to others: a noble saying, showing a great mind and great gentleness, which suddenly burst from you without premeditation, and was not meant to reach any ears but your own, and which displayed the conflict which was raging between your natural goodness and your imperial duties. Your prefect Burrus, an excellent man who was born to be the servant of such an emperor as you are, was about to order two brigands to be executed, and was pressing you to write their names and the grounds on which they were to be put to death: this had often been put off, and he was insisting that it should then be done. When he reluctantly produced the document and put it into your equally reluctant hands, you exclaimed: "Would that I had never learned my letters!" O what a speech, how worthy to be heard by all nations, both those who dwell within the Roman Empire, those who enjoy a debatable independence upon its borders, and those who either in will or in deed fight against it! It is a speech which ought to be spoken before a meeting of all mankind, whose words all kings and princes ought to swear to obey: a speech worthy of the days of human innocence, and worthy to bring back that golden age. Now in truth we ought all to agree to love righteousness and goodness; covetousness, which is the root of all evil, ought to be driven away, piety and virtue, good faith and modesty ought to resume their interrupted reign, and the vices which have so long and so shamefully ruled us ought at last to give way to an age of happiness and purity.

II

To a great extent, Caesar, we may hope and expect that this will come to pass. Let your own goodness of heart be gradually spread and diffused throughout the whole body of the empire, and all parts of it will mould themselves into your likeness. Good health proceeds from the head into all the members of the body: they are all either brisk and erect, or languid and drooping, according as their guiding spirit blooms or withers. Both Romans and allies will prove worthy of this goodness of yours, and good morals will return to all the world: your hands will everywhere find less to do. Allow me to dwell somewhat upon this saying of yours, not because it is a pleasant subject for your ears (indeed, this is not my way; I would rather offend by telling the truth than curry favour by flattery). What, then, is my reason? Besides wishing that you should be as familiar as possible with your own good deeds and good words, in order that what is now untutored impulse may grow into matured decision, I remember that many great but odious sayings have become part of human life and are familiar in men's mouths, such as that celebrated, "Let them hate me, provided that they fear me," which is like that Greek verse, ἐμοῦ θανουτος γαῖα μιχθητω πυρί, in which a man bids the earth perish in flame after he is dead, and others of the like sort. I know not how it is, but certainly human ingenuity seems to have found it easier to find emphatic and ardent expression for monstrous and cynical sentiments: I have never hitherto heard any spirited saying from a good and gentle person. What, then, is the upshot of all this? It is that, albeit seldom and against your will, and after much hesitation, you sometimes nevertheless must write that which made you hate your letters, but that you ought to do so with great hesitation and after many postponements, even as you now do.

III

But lest the plausible word "mercy" should sometimes deceive us and lead us into the opposite extreme, let us consider what mercy is, what its qualities are, and within what limits it is confined. Mercy is "a restraining of the mind from vengeance when it is in its power to avenge itself," or it is "gentleness shown by a powerful man in fixing the punishment of a weaker one." It is safer to have more than one definition, since one may not include the whole subject, and may, so to speak, lose its cause: mercy, therefore, may likewise be termed a tendency towards mildness in inflicting punishment. It is possible to discover certain inconsistencies in the definition which comes nearer the truth than all the rest, which is to call mercy "self-restraint, which remits some part of a fine which it deserves to receive and which is due to it." To this it will be objected that no virtue ever gives any man less than his due. However, all men understand mercy to consist in coming short of the penalty which might with justice be inflicted.

IV

The unlearned think that its opposite is strictness: but no virtue is the opposite of another virtue. What, then, is the opposite of mercy? Cruelty: which is nothing more than obstinacy in exacting punishments. "But," say you, "some men do not exact punishments, and nevertheless are cruel, such as those who kill the strangers whom they meet, not in order to rob them, but for killing's sake, and men who are not satisfied with killing, but kill with savage tortures, like the famous Busing,[1] and Procrustes, and pirates who flog their captives and burn them alive." This appears to be cruelty: but as it is not the result of vengeance (for it has received no wrong), and is not excited by any offence (for no crime has preceded it), it does not come within our definition, which was limited to "extravagance in exacting the penalties of wrongdoing." We may say that this is not cruelty, but ferocity, which finds pleasure in savagery: or we may call it madness; for madness is of various kinds, and there is no truer madness than that which takes to slaughtering and mutilating human beings. I shall, therefore, call those persons cruel who have a reason for punishing but who punish without moderation, like Phalaris, who is not said to have tortured innocent men, but to have tortured criminals with inhuman and incredible barbarity. We may avoid hairsplitting by defining cruelty to be "a tendency of the mind towards harsh measures." Mercy repels cruelty and bids it be far from her: with strictness she is on terms of amity.

At this point it is useful to inquire into what pity is; for many praise it as a virtue, and say that a good man is full of pity. This also is a disease of the mind. Both of these stand close to mercy and to strictness, and both ought to be avoided, lest under the name of strictness we be led into cruelty, and under the name of mercy into pity. It is less dangerous to make the latter mistake, but both lead us equally far away from the truth.

---

[1] A king of Egypt, who sacrificed strangers, and was himself slain by Hercules

V

Just as the gods are worshipped by religion, but are dishonoured by superstition, so all good men will show mercy and mildness, but will avoid pity, which is a vice incident to weak minds which cannot endure the sight of another's sufferings. It is, therefore, most commonly found in the worst people; there are old women and girls[2] who are affected by the tears of the greatest criminals, and who, if they could, would let them out of prison. Pity considers a man's misfortunes and does not consider to what they are due: mercy is combined with reason. I know that the doctrine of the Stoics is unpopular among the ignorant as being excessively severe and not at all likely to give kings and princes good advice; it is blamed because it declares that the wise man knows not how to feel pity or to grant pardon. These doctrines, if taken separately, are indeed odious, for they appear to give men no hope of repairing their mistakes but exact a penalty for every slip. If this were true, how can it be true wisdom to bid us put off human feeling, and to exclude us from mutual help, that surest haven of refuge against the attacks of Fortune? But no school of philosophy is more gentle and benignant, none is more full of love towards man or more anxious to promote the happiness of all, seeing that its maxims are, to be of service and assistance to others, and to consult the interests of each and all, not of itself ,alone. Pity is a disorder of the mind caused by the sight of other men's miseries, or it is a sadness caused by the evils with which it believes others to be undeservedly afflicted: but the wise man cannot be affected by any disorder: his mind is calm, and nothing can possibly happen to ruffle it. Moreover, nothing becomes a man more than magnanimity: but magnanimity cannot coexist with sorrow. Sorrow overwhelms men's minds, casts them down, contracts them: now this cannot happen to the wise man even in his greatest misfortunes, but he will beat back the rage of Fortune and triumph over it: he will always retain the same calm, undisturbed expression of countenance, which he never could do were he accessible to sorrow.

---

[2] "Three or four wenches where I stood, cried 'Alas, good soul!' and forgave him with all their hearts: but there's no heed to be taken of them; if Caesar had stabbed their mothers, they would have done no less."—"Julius Caesar," act i. sc. 2

VI

Add to this, that the wise man provides for the future and always has a distinct plan of action ready: yet nothing clear and true can flow from a disturbed source. Sorrow is awkward at reviewing the position of affairs, at devising useful expedients, avoiding dangerous courses, and weighing the merits of fair and just ones: therefore the wise man will not feel pity, because this cannot happen to a man unless his mind is disturbed. He will do willingly and highmindedly all that those who feel pity are wont to do; he will dry the tears of others, but will not mingle his own with them; he will stretch out his hand to the shipwrecked mariner, will offer hospitality to the exile, and alms to the needy—not in the offensive way in which most of those who wish to be thought tender-hearted fling their bounty to those whom they assist and shrink from their touch, but as one man would give another something out of the common stock—he will restore children to their weeping mothers, will loose the chains of the captive, release the gladiator from his bondage, and even bury the carcass of the criminal, but he will perform all this with a calm mind and unaltered expression of countenance. Thus the wise man will not pity men, but will help them and be of service to them, seeing that he is born to be a help to all men and a public benefit, of which he will bestow a share upon every one. He will even grant a proportional part of his bounty to those sufferers who deserve blame and correction; but he will much more willingly help those whose troubles and adversities are caused by misfortune. Whenever he is able he will interpose between Fortune and her victims: for what better employment can he find for his wealth or his strength than in setting up again what chance has overthrown? He will not show or feel any disgust at a man's having withered legs, or a flabby wrinkled skin, or supporting his aged body upon a staff; but he will do good to those who deserve it, and will, like a god, look benignantly upon all who are in trouble. Pity borders upon misery: it is partly composed of it and partly derived from it. You know that eyes must be weak, if they fill with rheum at the sight of another's blearedness, just as it is not real merriment but hysteria which makes people laugh because others laugh, and yawn whenever others open their jaws: pity is a defect in the mind of people who are extraordinarily affected by suffering, and he who requires a wise man to exhibit it is not far from requiring him to lament and groan when strangers are buried.

VII

But why should he not pardon?[3] Let us decide by exact definition this other slippery matter, the true nature of pardon, and we shall then perceive that the wise man ought not to grant it. Pardon is the remitting of a deserved punishment. The reasons why the wise man ought not to grant this remission are given at length by those of whom this question is specially asked: I will briefly say, as though it were no concern of mine to decide this point, "A man grants pardon to one whom he ought to punish: now the wise man does nothing which he ought not to do, and omits to no nothing which he ought to do: he does not, therefore, remit any punishment which he ought to exact. But the wise man will bestow upon you in a more honourable way that which you wish to obtain by pardon, for he will make allowances for you, will consult your interests, and will correct your bad habits: he will act just as though he were pardoning you, but nevertheless he will not pardon you, because he who pardons admits that in so doing he has neglected a part of his duty. He will only punish some people by reprimanding them, and will inflict no further penalty if he considers that they are of an age which admits of reformation: some people who are undeniably implicated in an odious charge he will acquit, because they were deceived into committing, or were not sober when they committed the offence with which they are charged: he will let his enemies depart unharmed, sometimes even with words of commendation, if they have taken up arms to defend their honour, their covenants with others, their freedom, or on any other honourable ground. All these doings come under the head of mercy, not of pardon. Mercy is free to come to what decision it pleases: she gives her decision, not under any statute, but according to equity and goodness: she may acquit the defendant, or impose what damages she pleases. She does not do any of these things as though she were doing less than justice requires, but as though the justest possible course were that which she adopts. On the other hand, to pardon is not to punish a man whom you have decided ought to be punished; pardon is the remission of a punishment which ought to be inflicted. The first advantage which mercy has over it is that she does not tell those whom she lets off that they ought to have suffered : she is more complete, more honourable than pardon."

In my opinion, this is a mere dispute about words, and we are agreed about the thing itself. The wise man will remit many penalties, and will save many who are wicked, but whose wickedness is not incurable. He will act like good husbandmen, who do not cultivate only straight and tall trees, but also

---

[3] See above [Of Clemency, Book I], ch. v

apply props to straighten those which have been rendered crooked by various causes; they trim some, lest the luxuriance of their boughs should hinder their upward growth, they nurse those which have been weakened by being planted in an unsuitable position, and they give air to those which are overshadowed by the foliage of others. The wise man will see the several treatments suitable to several dispositions, and how what is crooked may be straightened. . . .

On Benefits

Translator's Preface

Seneca, the favourite classic of the early fathers of the church and of the Middle Ages, whom Jerome, Tertullian, and Augustine speak of as "Seneca noster," who was believed to have corresponded with St. Paul, and upon whom[1] Calvin wrote a commentary, seems almost forgotten in modern times. Perhaps some of his popularity may have been due to his being supposed to be the author of those tragedies which the world has long ceased to read, but which delighted a period that preferred Euripides to Aeschylus: while casuists must have found congenial matter in an author whose fantastic cases of conscience are often worthy of Sanchez or Escobar. Yet Seneca's morality is always pure, and from him we gain, albeit at second hand, an insight into the doctrines of the Greek philosophers, Zeno, Epicurus, Chrysippus, &c., whose precepts and system of religious thought had in cultivated Roman society taken the place of the old worship of Jupiter and Quirinus.

Since Lodge's edition (fol. 1614), no complete translation of Seneca has been published in England, though Sir Roger L'Estrange wrote paraphrases of several Dialogues, which seem to have been enormously popular, running through more than sixteen editions. I think we may conjecture that Shakespeare had seen Lodge's translation, from several allusions to philosophy, to that impossible conception "the wise man," and especially from a passage in "All's Well that ends Well," which seems to breathe the very spirit of "De Beneficiis."

> "'Tis pity--
> That wishing well had not a body in it
> Which might be felt: that we, the poorer born,
> Whose baser stars do shut us up in wishes,
> Might with effects of them follow our friends
> And show what we alone must think; which never
> Returns us thanks."

All's Well that ends Well," Act i. sc. 1.

Though, if this will not fit the supposed date of that play, he may have taken the idea from "The Woorke of Lucius Annaeus Seneca concerning Benefyting, that is too say, the dooing, receyving, and requyting of good turnes, translated out of Latin by A. Golding. J. Day, London, 1578." And even during

---

[1] On the "De Clementia," an odd subject for the man who burned Servetus alive for differing with him.

the Restoration, Pepys's ideal of virtuous and lettered seclusion is a country house in whose garden he might sit on summer afternoons with his friend, Sir W. Coventry, "it maybe, to read a chapter of Seneca." In sharp contrast to this is Vahlen's preface to the minor Dialogues, which he edited after the death of his friend Koch, who had begun that work, in which he remarks that "he has read much of this writer, in order to perfect his knowledge of Latin, for otherwise he neither admires his artificial subtleties of thought, nor his childish mannerisms of style" (Vahlen, preface, p. v., ed. 1879, Jena).

Yet by the student of the history of Rome under the Caesars, Seneca is not to be neglected, because, whatever may be thought of the intrinsic merit of his speculations, he represents, more perhaps even than Tacitus, the intellectual characteristics of his age, and the tone of society in Rome--nor could we well spare the gossiping stories which we find imbedded in his graver dissertations. The following extract from Dean Merivale's "History of the Romans under the Empire" will show the estimate of him which has been formed by that accomplished writer:--

"At Rome, we, have no reason, to suppose that Christianity was only the refuge of the afflicted and miserable; rather, if we may lay any stress on the documents above referred to, it was first embraced by persons in a certain grade of comfort and respectability; by persons approaching to what we should call the MIDDLE CLASSES in their condition, their education, and their moral views. Of this class Seneca himself was the idol, the oracle; he was, so to speak, the favourite preacher of the more intelligent and humane disciples of nature and virtue. Now the writings of Seneca show, in their way, a real anxiety among this class to raise the moral tone of mankind around them; a spirit of reform, a zeal for the conversion of souls, which, though it never rose, indeed, under the teaching of the philosophers, to boiling heat, still simmered with genial warmth on the surface of society. Far different as was their social standing-point, far different as were the foundations and the presumed sanctions of their teaching respectively, Seneca and St. Paul were both moral reformers; both, be it said with reverence, were fellow-workers in the cause of humanity, though the Christian could look beyond the proximate aims of morality and prepare men for a final development on which the Stoic could not venture to gaze. Hence there is so much in their principles, so much even in their language, which agrees together, so that the one has been thought, though it must be allowed without adequate reason, to have borrowed directly from the other.[2]

But the philosopher, be it remembered, discoursed to a large and not inattentive audience, and surely the soil was not all unfruitful on which his seed was scattered when he proclaimed that God dwells not in temples of wood and stone, nor wants the ministrations of human hands;[3] that He has no delight in the blood of victims:[4] that He is near to all His creatures:[5] that His Spirit resides in men's hearts:[6] that all men are truly His offspring:[7] that we are members of one body, which is God or Nature;[8] that men must believe in God before they can approach Him:[9] that the true service of God is to be like unto Him:[10] that all men have sinned, and none performed all the works of the law:[11] that God is no respecter of nations, ranks, or conditions, but all, barbarian and Roman, bond and free, are alike under His all-seeing Providence.[12]

"St. Paul enjoined submission and obedience even to the tyranny of Nero, and Seneca fosters no ideas subversive of political subjection. Endurance

---

[2] It is hardly necessary to refer to the pretended letters between St. Paul and Seneca. Besides the evidence from style, some of the dates they contain are quite sufficient to condemn them as clumsy forgeries. They are mentioned, but with no expression of belief in their genuineness, by Jerome and Augustine. See Jones, "On the Canon," ii. 80.

[3] Sen., Ep. 95, and in Lactantius, Inst. vi.

[4] Ep. 116: "Colitur Deus non tauris sed pia et recta voluntate."

[5] Ep. 41, 73.

[6] Ep. 46: "Sacer intra nos spiritus sedet."

[7] Footnote: "De Prov," i.

[8] Ep. 93, 95: "Membra sumus magni corporis."

[9] Ep. 95: "Primus Deorum cultus est Deos credere."

[10] Ep. 95: "Satis coluit quisquis imitatus est."

[11] Sen. de Ira. i. 14; ii. 27: "Quis est iste qui se profitetur omnibus legibus innocentem?"

[12] "De Benef.," iii. 18: "Virtus omnes admittit, libertinos, servos, reges." These and many other passages are collected by Champagny, ii. 546, after Fabricius and others, and compared with well-known texts of Scripture. The version of the Vulgate shows a great deal of verbal correspondence. M. Troplong remarks, after De Maistre, that Seneca has written a fine book on Providence, for which there was not even a name at Rome in the time of Cicero.--"L'Influence du Christianisme," &c., i., ch. 4.

is the paramount virtue of the Stoic. To forms of government the wise man was wholly indifferent; they were among the external circumstances above which his spirit soared in serene self-contemplation. We trace in Seneca no yearning for a restoration of political freedom, nor does he even point to the senate, after the manner of the patriots of the day, as a legitimate check to the autocracy of the despot. The only mode, in his view, of tempering tyranny is to educate the tyrant himself in virtue. His was the self-denial of the Christians, but without their anticipated compensation. It seems impossible to doubt that in his highest flights of rhetoric--and no man ever recommended the unattainable with a finer grace--Seneca must have felt that he was labouring to build up a house without foundations; that his system, as Caius said of his style, was sand without lime. He was surely not unconscious of the inconsistency of his own position, as a public man and a minister, with the theories to which he had wedded himself; and of the impossibility of preserving in it the purity of his character as a philosopher or a man. He was aware that in the existing state of society at Rome, wealth was necessary to men high in station; wealth alone could retain influence, and a poor minister became at once contemptible. The distributor of the Imperial favours must have his banquets, his receptions, his slaves and freedmen; he must possess the means of attracting if not of bribing; he must not seem too virtuous, too austere, among an evil generation; in order to do good at all he must swim with the stream, however polluted it might be. All this inconsistency Seneca must have contemplated without blenching; and there is something touching in the serenity he preserved amidst the conflict that must have perpetually raged between his natural sense and his acquired principles. Both Cicero and Seneca were men of many weaknesses, and we remark them the more because both were pretenders to unusual strength of character; but while Cicero lapsed into political errors, Seneca cannot be absolved of actual crime. Nevertheless, if we may compare the greatest masters of Roman wisdom together, the Stoic will appear, I think, the more earnest of the two, the more anxious to do his duty for its own sake, the more sensible of the claims of mankind upon him for such precepts of virtuous living as he had to give. In an age of unbelief and compromise he taught that Truth was positive and Virtue objective. He conceived, what never entered Cicero's mind, the idea of improving his fellow-creatures; he had, what Cicero had not, a heart for conversion to Christianity."

To this eloquent account of Seneca's position and of the tendency of his writings I have nothing to add. The main particulars of his life, his Spanish extraction (like that of Lacan and Martial), his father's treatises on Rhetoric, his mother Helvia, his brothers, his wealth, his exile in Corsica, his outrageous flattery of Claudius and his satiric poem on his death--"The Vision of Judgment," Merivale calls it, after Lord Byron--his position as Nero's tutor, and his death, worthy at once of a Roman and a Stoic, by the orders of that tyrant, may be read of in "The History of the Romans under the Empire," or in the article "Seneca" in the "Dictionary of Classical Biography," and need not be reproduced here: but I cannot resist pointing out how entirely Grote's view of the "Sophists" as a sort of established clergy, and Seneca's account of the various sects of philosophers as representing the religious thought of the time, is illustrated by his anecdote of Julia Augusta, the mother of Tiberius, better known to English readers as Livia the wife of Augustus, who in her first agony of grief at the loss of her first husband applied to his Greek philosopher, Areus, as to a kind of domestic chaplain, for spiritual consolation.[13]

I take this opportunity of expressing my gratitude to the Rev. J. E. B. Mayor, Professor of Latin in the University of Cambridge, for his kindness in finding time among his many and important literary labours for reading and correcting the proofs of this work.

The text which I have followed for De Beneficiis is that of Gertz, Berlin (1876.).

AUBREY STEWART

London, March, 1887.

---

[13] "Ad Marciam de Consolatione," ch. iv.

On Benefits – Book I

I

Among the numerous faults of those who pass their lives recklessly and without due reflexion, my good friend Liberalis, I should say that there is hardly any one so hurtful to society as this, that we neither know how to bestow or how to receive a benefit. It follows from this that benefits are badly invested, and become bad debts: in these cases it is too late to complain of their not being returned, for they were thrown away when we bestowed them. Nor need we wonder that while the greatest vices are common, none is more common than ingratitude: for this I see is brought about by various causes. The first of these is, that we do not choose worthy persons upon whom to bestow our bounty, but although when we are about to lend money we first make a careful enquiry into the means and habits of life of our debtor, and avoid sowing seed in a worn-out or unfruitful soil, yet without any discrimination we scatter our benefits at random rather than bestow them. It is hard to say whether it is more dishonourable for the receiver to disown a benefit, or for the giver to demand a return of it: for a benefit is a loan, the repayment of which depends merely upon the good feeling of the debtor. To misuse a benefit like a spendthrift is most shameful, because we do not need our wealth but only our intention to set us free from the obligation of it; for a benefit is repaid by being acknowledged. Yet while they are to blame who do not even show so much gratitude as to acknowledge their debt, we ourselves are to blame no less. We find many men ungrateful, yet we make more men so, because at one time we harshly and reproachfully demand some return for our bounty, at another we are fickle and regret what we have given, at another we are peevish and apt to find fault with trifles. By acting thus we destroy all sense of gratitude, not only after we have given anything, but while we are in the act of giving it. Who has ever thought it enough to be asked for anything in an off-hand manner, or to be asked only once? Who, when he suspected that he was going to be asked for any thing, has not frowned, turned away his face, pretended to be busy, or purposely talked without ceasing, in order not to give his suitor a chance of preferring his request, and avoided by various tricks having to help his friend in his pressing need? and when driven into a corner, has not either put the matter off, that is, given a cowardly refusal, or promised his help ungraciously, with a wry face, and with unkind words, of which he seemed to grudge the utterance. Yet no one is glad to owe what he has not so much received from his benefactor, as wrung out of him. Who can be grateful for what has been disdainfully flung to him, or angrily cast at him, or been given him out of weariness, to avoid further trouble? No one need expect any return from those whom he has tired out with delays, or sickened with expectation. A benefit is received in the same temper in which it is given, and ought not, therefore, to be given carelessly, for a man thanks himself for that which he receives without the knowledge of the giver. Neither ought we to give after long delay, because in all good offices the will of the giver counts for much, and he who gives tardily must long have been unwilling to give at all. Nor, assuredly, ought we to give in offensive manner, because human nature is so constituted that insults sink deeper than kindnesses; the remembrance of the latter soon passes away, while that of the former is treasured in the memory; so what can a man expect who insults while he obliges? All the gratitude which he deserves is to be forgiven for helping us. On the other hand, the number of the ungrateful ought not to deter us from earning men's gratitude; for, in the first place, their number is increased by our own acts. Secondly, the sacrilege and indifference to religion of some men does not prevent even the immortal gods from continuing to shower their benefits upon us: for they act according to their divine nature and help all alike, among them even those who so ill appreciate their bounty. Let us take them for our guides as far as the weakness of our mortal nature permits; let us bestow benefits, not put them out at interest. The man who while he gives thinks of what he will get in return, deserves to be deceived. But what if the benefit turns out ill? Why, our wives and our children often disappoint our hopes, yet we marry--and bring up children, and are so obstinate in the face of experience that we fight after we have been beaten, and put to sea after we have been shipwrecked. How much more constancy ought we to show in bestowing benefits! If a man does not bestow benefits because he has not received any, he must have bestowed them in order to receive them in return, and he justifies ingratitude, whose disgrace lies in not returning benefits when able to do so. How many are there who are unworthy of the light of day? and nevertheless the sun rises. How many complain because they have been born? yet Nature is ever renewing our race, and even suffers men to live who wish that they had never lived. It is the property of a great and good mind to covet, not the fruit of good deeds, but good deeds themselves, and to seek for a good man even after having met with bad men. If there were no rogues, what glory would there be in doing good to many? As it is, virtue consists in bestowing benefits for which we are not certain of meeting with any return, but whose fruit is at once enjoyed by noble minds. So little influence ought this to have in restraining us from doing good actions, that even though I were denied the hope of meeting with a grateful man, yet the fear of not having my benefits returned would not prevent my bestowing them, because he who does not give, forestalls the vice of him who is ungrateful. I will explain what I mean. He who does not repay a benefit, sins more, but he who does not bestow one, sins earlier.

> "If thou at random dost thy bounties waste,
> Much must be lost, for one that's rightly placed."

II

In the former verse you may blame two things, for one should not cast them at random, and it is not right to waste anything, much less benefits; for unless they be given with judgement, they cease to be benefits, and, may be called by any other name you please. The meaning of the latter verse is admirable, that one benefit rightly bestowed makes amends for the loss of many that have been lost. See, I pray you, whether it be not truer and more worthy of the glory of the giver, that we should encourage him to give, even though none of his gifts should be worthily placed. "Much must be lost." Nothing is lost because he who loses had counted the cost before. The book-keeping of benefits is simple: it is all expenditure; if any one returns it, that is clear gain; if he does not return it, it is not lost, I gave it for the sake of giving. No one writes down his gifts in a ledger, or like a grasping creditor demands repayment to the day and hour. A good man never thinks of such matters, unless reminded of them by some one returning his gifts; otherwise they become like debts owing to him. It is a base usury to regard a benefit as an investment. Whatever may have been the result of your former benefits, persevere in bestowing others upon other men; they will be all the better placed in the hands of the ungrateful, whom shame, or a favourable opportunity, or imitation of others may some day cause to be grateful. Do not grow weary, perform your duty, and act as becomes a good man. Help one man with money, another with credit, another with your favour; this man with good advice, that one with sound maxims. Even wild beasts feel kindness, nor is there any animal so savage that good treatment will not tame it and win love from it. The mouths of lions are handled by their keepers with impunity; to obtain their food fierce elephants become as docile as slaves: so that constant unceasing kindness wins the hearts even of creatures who, by their nature, cannot comprehend or weigh the value of a benefit. Is a man ungrateful for one benefit? perhaps he will not be so after receiving a second. Has he forgotten two kindnesses? perhaps by a third he may be brought to remember the former ones also.

III

He who is quick to believe that he has thrown away his benefits, does really throw them away; but he who presses on and adds new benefits to his former ones, forces out gratitude even from a hard and forgetful breast. In the face of many kindnesses, your friend will not dare to raise his eyes; let him see you whithersoever he turns himself to escape from his remembrance of you; encircle him with your benefits. As for the power and property of these, I will explain it to you if first you will allow me to glance at a matter which does not belong to our subject, as to why the Graces are three in number, why they are sisters, why hand in hand, and why they are smiling and young, with a loose and transparent dress. Some writers think that there is one who bestows a benefit, one who receives it, and a third who returns it; others say that they represent the three sorts of benefactors, those who bestow, those who repay, and those who both receive and repay them. But take whichever you please to be true; what will this knowledge profit us? What is the meaning of this dance of sisters in a circle, hand in hand? It means that the course of a benefit is from hand to hand, back to the giver; that the beauty of the whole chain is lost if a single link fails, and that it is fairest when it proceeds in unbroken regular order. In the dance there is one. esteemed beyond the others, who represents the givers of benefits. Their faces are cheerful, as those of men who give or receive benefits are wont to be. They are young, because the memory of benefits ought not to grow old. They are virgins, because benefits are pure and untainted, and held holy by all; in benefits there should be no strict or binding conditions, therefore the Graces wear loose flowing tunics, which are transparent, because benefits love to be seen. People who are not under the influence of Greek literature may say that all this is a matter of course; but there can be no one who would think that the names which Hesiod has given them bear upon our subject. He named the eldest Aglaia, the middle one Euphrosyne, the third Thalia. Every one, according to his own ideas, twists the meaning of these names, trying to reconcile them with some system, though Hesiod merely gave his maidens their names from his own fancy. So Homer altered the name of one of them, naming her Pasithea, and betrothed her to a husband, in order that you may know that they are not vestal virgins.[1]

I could find another poet, in whose writings they are girded, and wear thick or embroidered Phrygian robes. Mercury stands with them for the same reason, not because argument or eloquence commends benefits, but because the painter chose to do so. Also Chrysippus, that man of piercing intellect who

---

[1] i.e. not vowed to chastity.

saw to the very bottom of truth, who speaks only to the point, and makes use of no more words than are necessary to express his meaning, fills his whole treatise with these puerilities, insomuch that he says but very little about the duties of giving, receiving, and returning a benefit, and has not so much inserted fables among these subjects, as he has inserted these subjects among a mass of fables. For, not to mention what Hecaton borrows from him, Chrysippus tells us that the three Graces are the daughters of Jupiter and Eurynome, that they are younger than the Hours, and rather more beautiful, and that on that account they are assigned as companions to Venus. He also thinks that the name of their mother bears upon the subject, and that she is named Eurynome because to distribute benefits requires a wide inheritance; as if the mother usually received her name after her daughters, or as if the names given by poets were true. In truth, just as with a 'nomenclator' audacity supplies the place of memory, and he invents a name for every one whose name he cannot recollect, so the poets think that it is of no importance to speak the truth, but are either forced by the exigencies of metre, or attracted by sweetness of sound, into calling every one by whatever name runs neatly into verse. Nor do they suffer for it if they introduce another name into the list, for the next poet makes them bear what name he pleases. That you may know that this is so, for instance Thalia, our present subject of discourse, is one of the Graces in Hesiod's poems, while in those of Homer she is one of the Muses.

IV

But lest I should do the very thing which I am blaming, I will pass over all these matters, which are so far from the subject that they are not even connected with it. Only do you protect me, if any one attacks me for putting down Chrysippus, who, by Hercules, was a great man, but yet a Greek, whose intellect, too sharply pointed, is often bent and turned back upon itself; even when it seems to be in earnest it only pricks, but does not pierce. Here, however, what occasion is there for subtlety? We are to speak of benefits, and to define a matter which is the chief bond of human society; we are to lay down a rule of life, such that neither careless openhandedness may commend itself to us under the guise of goodness of heart, and yet that our circumspection, while it moderates, may not quench our generosity, a quality in which we ought neither to exceed nor to fall short. Men must be taught to be willing to give, willing to receive, willing to return; and to place before themselves the high aim, not merely of equalling, but even of surpassing those to whom they are indebted, both in good offices and in good feeling; because the man whose duty it is to repay, can never do so unless he out-does his benefactor;[2] the one class must be taught to look for no return, the other to feel deeper gratitude. In this noblest of contests to outdo benefits by benefits, Chrysippus encourages us by bidding us beware lest, as the Graces are the daughters of Jupiter, to act ungratefully may not be a sin against them, and may not wrong those beauteous maidens. Do thou teach me how I may bestow more good things, and be more grateful to those who have earned my gratitude, and how the minds of both parties may vie with one another, the giver in forgetting, the receiver in remembering his debt. As for those other follies, let them be left to the poets, whose purpose is merely to charm the ear and to weave a pleasing story; but let those who wish to purify men's minds, to retain honour in their dealings, and to imprint on their minds gratitude for kindnesses, let them speak in sober earnest and act with all their strength; unless you imagine, perchance, that by such flippant and mythical talk, and such old wives' reasoning, it is possible for us to prevent that most ruinous consummation, the repudiation of benefits.

---

[2] That is, he never comes up to his benefactor unless he leaves him behind: he can only make a dead heat of it by getting a start.

V

However, while I pass over what is futile and irrelevant I must point out that the first thing which we have to learn is, what we owe in return for a benefit received. One man says that he owes the money which he has received, another that he owes a consulship, a priesthood, a province, and so on. These, however, are but the outward signs of kindnesses, not the kindnesses themselves. A benefit is not to be felt and handled, it is a thing which exists only in the mind. There is a great difference between the subject- matter of a benefit, and the benefit itself. Wherefore neither gold, nor silver, nor any of those things which are most highly esteemed, are benefits, but the benefit lies in the goodwill of him who gives them. The ignorant take notice only of that which comes before their eyes, and which can be owned and passed from hand to hand, while they disregard that which gives these things their value. The things which we hold in our hands, which we see with our eyes, and which our avarice hugs, are transitory, they may be taken from us by ill luck or by violence; but a kindness lasts even after the loss of that by means of which it was bestowed; for it is a good deed, which no violence can undo. For instance, suppose that I ransomed a friend from pirates, but another pirate has caught him and thrown him into prison. The pirate has not robbed him of my benefit, but has only robbed him of the enjoyment of it. Or suppose that I have saved a man's children from a shipwreck or a fire, and that afterwards disease or accident has carried them off; even when they are no more, the kindness which was done by means of them remains. All those things, therefore, which improperly assume the name of benefits, are means by which kindly feeling manifests itself. In other cases also, we find a distinction between the visible symbol and the matter itself, as when a general bestows collars of gold, or civic or mural crowns upon any one. What value has the crown in itself? or the purple-bordered robe? or the fasces? or the judgment-seat and car of triumph? None of these things is in itself an honour, but is an emblem of honour. In like manner, that which is seen is not a benefit--it is but the trace and mark of a benefit.

VI

What, then, is a benefit? It is the art of doing a kindness which both bestows pleasure and gains it by bestowing it, and which does its office by natural and spontaneous impulse. It is not, therefore, the thing which is done or given, but the spirit in which it is done or given, that must be considered, because a benefit exists, not in that which is done or given, but in the mind of the doer or giver. How great the distinction between them is, you may perceive from this, that while a benefit is necessarily good, yet that which is done or given is neither good nor bad. The spirit in which they are given can exalt small things, can glorify mean ones, and can discredit great and precious ones; the objects themselves which are sought after have a neutral nature, neither good nor bad; all depends upon the direction given them by the guiding spirit from which things receive their shape. That which is paid or handed over is not the benefit itself, just as the honour which we pay to the gods lies not in the victims themselves, although they be fat and glittering with gold,[3] but in the pure and holy feelings of the worshippers.

Thus good men are religious, though their offering be meal and their vessels of earthenware; whilst bad men will not escape from their impiety, though they pour the blood of many victims upon the altars.

---

[3] Alluding to the practice of gilding the horns of the victims.

VII

If benefits consisted of things, and not of the wish to benefit, then the more things we received the greater the benefit would be. But this is not true, for sometimes we feel more gratitude to one who gives us trifles nobly, who, like Virgil's poor old soldier, "holds himself as rich as kings," if he has given us ever so little with a good will a man who forgets his own need when he sees mine, who has not only a wish but a longing to help, who thinks that he receives a benefit when he bestows one, who gives as though he would receive no return, receives a repayment as though he had originally given nothing, and who watches for and seizes an opportunity of being useful. On the other hand, as I said before, those gifts which are hardly wrung from the giver, or which drop unheeded from his hands, claim no gratitude from us, however great they may appear and may be. We prize much more what comes from a willing hand, than what comes from a full one. This man has given me but little, yet more he could not afford, while what that one has given is much indeed, but he hesitated, he put it off, he grumbled when he gave it, he gave it haughtily, or he proclaimed it aloud, and did it to please others, not to please the person to whom he gave it; he offered it to his own pride, not to me.

VIII

As the pupils of Socrates, each in proportion to his means, gave him large presents, Aeschines, a poor pupil, said, "I can find nothing to give you which is worthy of you; I feel my poverty in this respect alone. Therefore I present you with the only thing I possess, myself. I pray that you may take this my present, such as it is, in good part, and may remember that the others, although they gave you much, yet left for themselves more than they gave." Socrates answered, "Surely you have bestowed a great present upon me, unless perchance you set a small value upon yourself. I will accordingly take pains to restore you to yourself a better man than when I received you." By this present Aeschines outdid Alcibiades, whose mind was as great as his Wealth, and all the splendour of the most wealthy youths of Athens.

IX

You see how the mind even in the straitest circumstances finds the means of generosity. Aeschines seems to me to have said, "Fortune, it is in vain that you have made me poor; in spite of this I will find a worthy present for this man. Since I can give him nothing of yours, I will give him something of my own." Nor need you suppose that he held himself cheap; he made himself his own price. By a stroke of genius this youth discovered a means of presenting Socrates to himself. We must not consider how great presents are, but in what spirit they are given.

A rich man is well spoken of if he is clever enough to render himself easy of access to men of immoderate ambition, and although he intends to do nothing to help them, yet encourages their unconscionable hopes; but he is thought the worse of if he be sharp of tongue, sour in appearance, and displays his wealth in an invidious fashion. For men respect and yet loathe a fortunate man, and hate him for doing what, if they had the chance, they would do themselves.

Men nowadays no longer secretly, but openly outrage the wives of others, and allow to others access to their own wives. A match is thought countrified, uncivilized, in bad style, and to be protested against by all matrons, if the husband should forbid his wife to appear in public in a litter, and to be carried about exposed to the gaze of all observers. If a man has not made himself notorious by a LIAISON with some mistress, if he does not pay an annuity to some one else's wife, married women speak of him as a poor-spirited creature, a man given to low vice, a lover of servant girls. Soon adultery becomes the most respectable form of marriage, and widowhood and celibacy are commonly practised. No one takes a wife unless he takes her away from some one else. Now men vie with one another in wasting what they have stolen, and in collecting together what they have wasted with the keenest avarice; they become utterly reckless, scorn poverty in others, fear personal injury more than anything else, break the peace by their riots, and by violence and terror domineer over those who are weaker than themselves. No wonder that they plunder provinces and offer the seat of judgment for sale, knocking it down after an auction to the highest bidder, since it is the law of nations that you may sell what you have bought.

X

However, my enthusiasm has carried me further than I intended, the subject being an inviting one. Let me, then, end by pointing out that the disgrace of these crimes does not belong especially to our own time. Our ancestors before us have lamented, and our children after us will lament, as we do, the ruin, of morality, the prevalence of vice, and the gradual deterioration of mankind; yet these things are really stationary, only moved slightly to and fro like the waves which at one time a rising tide washes further over the land, and at another an ebbing one restrains within a lower water mark. At one time the chief vice will be adultery, and licentiousness will exceed all bounds; at another time a rage for feasting will be in vogue, and men will waste their inheritance in the most shameful of all ways, by the kitchen; at another, excessive care for the body, and a devotion to personal beauty which implies ugliness of mind; at another time, injudiciously granted liberty will show itself in wanton recklessness and defiance of authority; sometimes there will be a reign of cruelty both in public and private, and the madness of the civil wars will come upon us, which destroy all that is holy and inviolable. Sometimes even drunkenness will be held in honour, and it will be a virtue to swallow most wine. Vices do not lie in wait for us in one place alone, but hover around us in changeful forms, sometimes even at variance one with another, so that in turn they win and lose the field; yet we shall always be obliged to pronounce the same verdict upon ourselves, that we are and always were evil, and, I unwillingly add, that we always shall be. There always will be homicides, tyrants, thieves, adulterers, ravishers, sacrilegious, traitors: worse than all these is the ungrateful man, except we consider that all these crimes flow from ingratitude, without which hardly any great wickedness has ever grown to full stature. Be sure that you guard against this as the greatest of crimes in yourself, but pardon it as the least of crimes in another. For all the injury which you suffer is this: you have lost the subject-matter of a benefit, not the benefit itself, for you possess unimpaired the best part of it, in that you have given it. Though we ought to be careful to bestow our benefits by preference upon those who are likely to show us gratitude for them, yet we must sometimes do what we have little hope will turn out well, and bestow benefits upon those who we not only think will prove ungrateful, but who we know have been so. For instance, if I should be able to save a man's children from a great danger with no risk to myself, I should not hesitate to do so. If a man be worthy I would defend him even with my blood, and would share his perils; if he be unworthy, and yet by merely crying for help I can rescue him from robbers, I would without reluctance raise the shout which would save a fellow- creature.

XI

The next point to be defined is, what kind of benefits are to be given, and in what manner. First let us give what is necessary, next what is useful, and then what is pleasant, provided that they be lasting. We must begin with what is necessary, for those things which support life affect the mind very differently from, those which adorn and improve it. A man may be nice, and hard to please, in things which he can easily do without, of which he can say, "Take them back; I do not want them, I am satisfied with what I have." Sometimes, we wish not only to, return what we have received, but even to throw it away. Of necessary things, the first class consists of things without which we cannot live; the second, of things without which we ought not to live; and the third, of things without which we should not care to live. The first class are, to be saved from the hands of the enemy, from the anger of tyrants, from proscription, and the various other perils which beset human life. By averting any one of these, we shall earn gratitude proportionate to the greatness of the danger, for when men think of the greatness of the misery from which they have been saved, the terror which they have gone through enhances the value of our services. Yet we ought not to delay rescuing any one longer than we are obliged, solely in order to make his fears add weight to our services. Next come those things without which we can indeed live, but in such a manner that it would be better to die, such as liberty, chastity, or a good conscience. After these are what we have come to hold dear by connexion and relationship and long use and custom, such as our wives and children, our household gods, and so on, to which the mind so firmly attaches itself that separation from them seems worse than death.

After these come useful things, which form a very wide and varied class; in which will be money, not in excess, but enough for living in a moderate style; public office, and, for the ambitious, due advancement to higher posts; for nothing can be more useful to a man than to be placed in a position in which he can benefit himself. All benefits beyond these are superfluous, and are likely to spoil those who receive them. In giving these we must be careful to make them acceptable by giving them at the appropriate time, or by giving things which are not common, but such as few people possess, or at any rate few possess in our times; or again, by giving things in such a manner, that though not naturally valuable, they become so by the time and place at which they are given. We must reflect what present will produce the most pleasure, what will most frequently come under the notice of the possessor of it, so that whenever he is with it he may be with us also; and in all cases we must be careful not to send useless presents, such as hunting weapons to a woman or old man, or books to a rustic, or nets to catch wild animals to a quiet literary man. On the other hand, we ought to be careful, while we wish to send what will please, that we do not send what will insultingly remind our friends of their failings, as, for example, if we send wine to a hard drinker or drugs to an invalid, for a present which contains an allusion to the shortcomings of the receiver, becomes an outrage.

XII

If we have a free choice as to what to give, we should above all choose lasting presents, in order that our gift may endure as long as possible; for few are so grateful as to think of what they have received, even when they do not see it. Even the ungrateful remember us by our gifts, when they are always in their sight and do not allow themselves to be forgotten, but constantly obtrude and stamp upon the mind the memory of the giver. As we never ought to remind men of what we have given them, we ought all the more to choose presents that will be permanent; for the things themselves will prevent the remembrance of the giver from fading away. I would more willingly give a present of plate than of coined money, and would more willingly give statues than clothes or other things which are soon worn out. Few remain grateful after the present is gone: many more remember their presents only while they make use of them. If possible, I should like my present not to be consumed; let it remain in existence, let it stick to my friend and share his life. No one is so foolish as to need to be told not to send gladiators or wild beasts to one who has just given a public show, or not to send summer clothing in winter time, or winter clothing in summer. Common sense must guide our benefits; we must consider the time and the place, and the character of the receiver, which are the weights in the scale, which cause our gifts to be well or ill received. How far more acceptable a present is, if we give a man what he has not, than if we give him what he has plenty of! if we give him what he has long been searching for in vain, rather than what he sees everywhere! Let us make presents of things which are rare and scarce rather than costly, things which even a rich man will be glad of, just as common fruits, such as we tire of after a few days, please us if they have ripened before the usual season. People will also esteem things which no one else has given to them, or which we have given to no one else.

XIII

When the conquest of the East had flattered Alexander of Macedon into believing himself to be more than man, the people of Corinth sent an embassy to congratulate him, and presented him with the franchise of their city. When Alexander smiled at this form of courtesy, one of the ambassadors said, "We have never enrolled any stranger among our citizens except Hercules and yourself." Alexander willingly accepted the proffered honour, invited the ambassadors to his table, and showed them other courtesies. He did not think of who offered the citizenship, but to whom they had granted it; and being altogether the slave of glory, though he knew neither its true nature or its limits, had followed in the footsteps of Hercules and Bacchus, and had not even stayed his march where they ceased; so that he glanced aside from the givers of this honour to him with whom he shared it, and fancied that the heaven to which his vanity aspired was indeed opening before him when he was made equal to Hercules. In what indeed did that frantic youth, whose only merit was his lucky audacity, resemble Hercules? Hercules conquered nothing for himself; he travelled throughout the world, not coveting for himself but liberating the countries which he conquered, an enemy to bad men, a defender of the good, a peacemaker both by sea and land; whereas the other was from his boyhood a brigand and desolator of nations, a pest to his friends and enemies alike, whose greatest joy was to be the terror of all mankind, forgetting that men fear not only the fiercest but also the most cowardly animals, because of their evil and venomous nature.

XIV

Let us now return to our subject. He who bestows a benefit without discrimination, gives what pleases no one; no one considers himself to be under any obligation to the landlord of a tavern, or to be the guest of any one with whom he dines in such company as to be able to say, "What civility has he shown to me? no more than he has shown to that man, whom he scarcely knows, or to that other, who is both his personal enemy and a man of infamous character. Do you suppose that he wished to do me any honour? not so, he merely wished to indulge his own vice of profusion." If you wish men to be grateful for anything, give it but seldom; no one can bear to receive what you give to all the world. Yet let no one gather from this that I wish to impose any bonds upon generosity; let her go to what lengths she will, so that she go a steady course, not at random. It is possible to bestow gifts in such a manner that each of those who receive them, although he shares them with many others, may yet feel himself to be distinguished from the common herd. Let each man have some peculiarity about his gift which may make him consider himself more highly favoured than the rest. He may say, "I received the same present that he did, but I never asked for it." "I received the same present, but mine was given me after a few days, whereas he had earned it by long service." "Others have the same present, but it was not given to them with the same courtesy and gracious words with which it was given to me." "That man got it because he asked for it; I did not ask." "That man received it as well as I, but then he could easily return it; one has great expectations from a rich man, old and childless, as he is; whereas in giving the same present to me he really gave more, because he gave it without the hope of receiving any return for it." Just as a courtesan divides her favours among many men, so that no one of her friends is without some proof of her affection, so let him who wishes his benefits to be prized consider how he may at the same time gratify many men, and nevertheless give each one of them some especial mark of favour to distinguish him from the rest.

XV

I am no advocate of slackness in giving benefits: the more and the greater they are, the more praise they will bring to the giver. Yet let them be given with discretion; for what is given carelessly and recklessly can please no one. Whoever, therefore, supposes that in giving this advice I wish to restrict benevolence and to confine it to narrower limits, entirely mistakes the object of my warning. What virtue do we admire more than benevolence? Which do we encourage more? Who ought to applaud it more than we Stoics, who preach the brotherhood of the human race? What then is it? Since no impulse of the human mind can be approved of, even though it springs from a right feeling, unless it be made into a virtue by discretion, I forbid generosity to degenerate into extravagance. It is, indeed, pleasant to receive a benefit with open arms, when reason bestows it upon the worthy, not when it is flung hither or thither thoughtlessly and at random; this alone we care to display and claim as our own. Can you call anything a benefit, if you feel ashamed to mention the person who gave it you? How far more grateful is a benefit, how far more deeply does it impress itself upon the mind, never to be forgotten, when we rejoice to think not so much of what it is, as from whom we have received it! Crispus Passienus was wont to say that some men's advice was to be preferred to their presents, some men's presents to their advice; and he added as an example, "I would rather have received advice from Augustus than a present; I would rather receive a present from Claudius than advice." I, however, think that one ought not to wish for a benefit from any man whose judgement is worthless. What then? Ought we not to receive what Claudius gives? We ought; but we ought to regard it as obtained from fortune, which may at any moment turn against us. Why do we separate this which naturally is connected? That is not a benefit, to which the best part of a benefit, that it be bestowed with judgment, is wanting: a really great sum of money, if it be given neither with discernment nor with good will, is no more a benefit than if it remained hoarded. There are, however, many things which we ought not to reject, yet for which we cannot feel indebted.

On Benefits – Book II

I

Let us consider, most excellent Liberalis, what still remains of the earlier part of the subject; in what way a benefit should be bestowed. I think that I can point out the shortest way to this; let us give in the way in which we ourselves should like to receive. Above all we should give willingly, quickly, and without any hesitation; a benefit commands no gratitude if it has hung for a long time in the hands of the giver, if he seems unwilling to part with it, and gives it as though he were being robbed of it. Even though some delay should intervene, let us by all means in our power strive not to seem to have been in two minds about giving it at all. To hesitate is the next thing to refusing to give, and destroys all claim to gratitude. For just as the sweetest part of a benefit is the kindly feeling of the giver, it follows that one who has by his very delay proved that he gives unwillingly, must be regarded not as having given anything, but as having been unable to keep it from an importunate suitor. Indeed, many men are made generous by want of firmness. The most acceptable benefits are those which are waiting for us to take them, which are easy to be received, and offer themselves to us, so that the only delay is caused by the modesty of the receiver. The best thing of all is to anticipate a person's wishes; the next, to follow them; the former is the better course, to be beforehand with our friends by giving them what they want before they ask us for it, for the value of a gift is much enhanced by sparing an honest man the misery of asking for it with confusion and blushes. He who gets what he asked for does not get it for nothing, for indeed, as our austere ancestors thought, nothing is so dear as that which is bought by prayers. Men would be much more modest in their petitions to heaven, if these had to be made publicly; so that even when addressing the gods, before whom we can with all honour bend our knees, we prefer to pray silently and within ourselves.

II

It is unpleasant, burdensome, and covers one with shame to have to say, "Give me." You should spare your friends, and those whom you wish to make your friends, from having to do this; however quick he may be, a man gives too late who gives what he has been asked for. We ought, therefore, to divine every man's wishes, and when we have discovered them, to set him free from the hard necessity of asking; you may be sure that a benefit which comes unasked will be delightful and will not be forgotten. If we do not succeed in anticipating our friends, let us at any rate cut them short when they ask us for anything, so that we may appear to be reminded of what we meant to do, rather than to have been asked to do it. Let us assent at once, and by our promptness make it appear that we meant to do so even before we were solicited. As in dealing with sick persons much depends upon when food is given, and plain water given at the right moment sometimes acts as a remedy, so a benefit, however slight and commonplace it may be, if it be promptly given without losing a moment of time, gains enormously in importance, and wins our gratitude more than a far more valuable present given after long waiting and deliberation. One who gives so readily must needs give with good will; he therefore gives cheerfully and shows his disposition in his countenance.

III

Many who bestow immense benefits spoil them by their silence or slowness of speech, which gives them an air of moroseness, as they say "yes" with a face which seems to say "no." How much better is it to join kind words to kind actions, and to enhance the value of our gifts by a civil and gracious commendation of them! To cure your friend of being slow to ask a favour of you, you may join to your gift the familiar rebuke, "I am angry with you for not having long ago let me know what you wanted, for having asked for it so formally, or for having made interest with a third party." "I congratulate myself that you have been pleased to make trial of me; hereafter, if you want anything, ask for it as your right; however, for this time I pardon your want of manners." By so doing you will cause him to value your friendship more highly than that, whatever it may have been, which he came to ask of you. The goodness and kindness of a benefactor never appears so great as when on leaving him one says, "I have to-day gained much; I am more pleased at finding him so kind than if I had obtained many times more of this, of which I was speaking, by some other means; I never can make any adequate return to this man for his goodness."

IV

Many, however, there are who, by harsh words and contemptuous manner, make their very kindnesses odious, for by speaking and acting disdainfully they make us sorry that they have granted our requests. Various delays also take place after we have obtained a promise; and nothing is more heartbreaking than to be forced to beg for the very thing which you already have been promised. Benefits ought to be bestowed at once, but from some persons it is easier to obtain the promise of them than to get them. One man has to be asked to remind our benefactor of his purpose; another, to bring it into effect; and thus a single present is worn away in passing through many hands, until hardly any gratitude is left for the original promiser, since whoever we are forced to solicit after the giving of the promise receives some of the gratitude which we owe to the giver. Take care, therefore, if you wish your gifts to be esteemed, that they reach those to whom they are promised entire, and, as the saying is, without any deduction. Let no one intercept them or delay them; for no one can take any share of the gratitude due for your gifts without robbing you of it.

V

Nothing is more bitter than long uncertainty; some can bear to have their hopes extinguished better than to have them deferred. Yet many men are led by an unworthy vanity into this fault of putting off the accomplishment of their promises, merely in order to swell the crowd of their suitors, like the ministers of royalty, who delight in prolonging the display of their own arrogance, hardly thinking themselves possessed of power unless they let each man see for a long time how powerful they are. They do nothing promptly, or at one sitting; they are indeed swift to do mischief, but slow to do good. Be sure that the comic poet speaks the most absolute truth in the verses:--

> "Know you not this? If you your gifts delay,
> You take thereby my gratitude away."

And the following lines, the expression of virtuous pain--a high-spirited man's misery,--

> "What thou doest, do quickly;"

and:--

> "Nothing in the world
> Is worth this trouble; I had rather you
> Refused it to me now."

When the mind begins through weariness to hate the promised benefit, or while it is wavering in expectation of it, how can it feel grateful for it? As the most refined cruelty is that which prolongs the torture, while to kill the victim at once is a kind of mercy, since the extremity of torture brings its own end with it-- the interval is the worst part of the execution--so the shorter time a benefit hangs in the balance, the more grateful it is to the receiver. It is possible to look forward with anxious disquietude even to good things, and, seeing that most benefits consist in a release from some form of misery, a man destroys the value of the benefit which he confers, if he has the power to relieve us, and yet allows us to suffer or to lack pleasure longer than we need. Kindness always eager to do good, and one who acts by love naturally acts at once; he who does us good, but does it tardily and with long delays, does not do so from the heart. Thus he loses two most important things: time, and the proof of his good will to us; for a lingering consent is but a form of denial.

VI

The manner in which things are said or done, my Liberalis, forms a very important part of every transaction. We gain much by quickness, and lose much by slowness. Just as in darts, the strength of the iron head remains the same, but there is an immeasureable difference between the blow of one hurled with the full swing of the arm and one which merely drops from the hand, and the same sword either grazes or pierces according as the blow is delivered; so, in like manner, that which is given is the same, but the manner in which it is given makes the difference. How sweet, how precious is a gift, when he who gives does not permit himself to be thanked, and when while he gives he forgets that he has given! To reproach a man at the very moment that you are doing him a service is sheer madness; it is to mix insult with your favours. We ought not to make our benefits burdensome, or to add any bitterness to them. Even if there be some subject upon which you wish to warn your friend, choose some other time for doing so.

VII

Fabius Verrucosus used to compare a benefit bestowed by a harsh man in an offensive manner to a gritty loaf of bread, which a hungry man is obliged to receive, but which is painful to eat. When Marius Nepos of the praetorian guard asked Tiberius Caesar for help to pay his debts, Tiberius asked him for a list of his creditors; this is calling a meeting of creditors, not paying debts. When the list was made out, Tiberius wrote to Nepos telling him that he had ordered the money to be paid, and adding some offensive reproaches. The result of this was that Nepos owed no debts, yet received no kindness; Tiberius, indeed, relieved him from his creditors, but laid him under no obligation. Tiberius, however, had some design in doing so; I imagine he did not wish more of his friends to come to him with the same request. His mode of proceeding was, perhaps, successful in restraining men's extravagant desires by shame, but he who wishes to confer benefits must follow quite a different path. In all ways you should make your benefit as acceptable as possible by presenting it in the most attractive form; but the method of Tiberius is not to confer benefits, but to reproach.

VIII

Moreover, if incidentally I should say what I think of this part of the subject, I do not consider that it is becoming even to an emperor to give merely in order to cover a man with shame. "And yet," we are told, "Tiberius did not even by this means attain his object; for after this a good many persons were found to make the same request. He ordered all of them to explain the reasons of their indebtedness before the senate, and when they did so, granted them certain definite sums of money." This is not an act of generosity, but a reprimand. You may call it a subsidy, or an imperial contribution; it is not a benefit, for the receiver cannot think of it without shame. I was summoned before a judge, and had to be tried at bar before I obtained what I asked for.

IX

Accordingly, all writers on ethical philosophy tell us that some benefits ought to be given in secret, others in public. Those things which it is glorious to receive, such as military decorations or public offices, and whatever else gains in value the more widely it is known, should be conferred in public; on the other hand, when they do not promote a man or add to his social standing, but help him when in weakness, in want, or in disgrace, they should be given silently, and so as to be known only to those who profit by them.

X

Sometimes even the person who is assisted must be deceived, in order that he may receive our bounty without knowing the source from whence it flows. It is said that Arcesilaus had a friend who was poor, but concealed his poverty; who was ill, yet tried to hide his disorder, and who had not money for the necessary expenses of existence. Without his knowledge, Arcesilaus placed a bag of money under his pillow, in order that this victim of false shame might rather seem to find what he wanted than to receive. "What," say you, "ought he not to know from whom he received it?" Yes; let him not know it at first, if it be essential to your kindness that he should not; afterwards I will do so much for him, and give him so much that he will perceive who was the giver of the former benefit; or, better still, let him not know that he has received any thing, provided I know that I have given it. "This," you say, "is to get too little return for one's goodness." True, if it be an investment of which you are thinking; but if a gift, it should be given in the way which will be of most service to the receiver. You should be satisfied with the approval of your own conscience; if not, you do not really delight in doing good, but in being seen to do good. "For all that," say you, "I wish him to know it." Is it a debtor that you seek for? "For all that, I wish him to know it." What! though it be more useful, more creditable, more pleasant for him not to know his benefactor, will you not consent to stand aside? "I wish him to know." So, then, you would not save a man's life in the dark? I do not deny that, whenever the matter admits of it, one ought to take into consideration the pleasure which we receive from the joy of the receiver of our kindness; but if he ought to have help and is ashamed to receive it--if what we bestow upon him pains him unless it be concealed--I forbear to make my benefits public. Why should I not refrain from hinting at my having given him anything, when the first and most essential rule is, never to reproach a man with what you have done for him, and not even to remind him of it. The rule for the giver and receiver of a benefit is, that the one should straightway forget that he has given, the other should never forget that he has received it.

XI

A constant reference to one's own services wounds our friend's feelings. Like the man who was saved from the proscription under the triumvirate by one of Caesar's friends, and afterwards found it impossible to endure his preserver's arrogance, they wish to cry, "Give me back to Caesar." How long will you go on saying, "I saved you, I snatched you from the jaws of death?" This is indeed life, if I remember it by my own will, but death if I remember it at yours; I owe you nothing, if you saved me merely in order to have some one to point at. How long do you mean to lead me about? how long do you mean to forbid me to forget my adventure? If I had been a defeated enemy, I should have been led in triumph but once. We ought not to speak of the benefits which we have conferred; to remind men of them is to ask them to return them. We should not obtrude them, or recall the memory of them; you should only remind a man of what you have given him by giving him something else. We ought not even to tell others of our good deeds. He who confers a benefit should be silent, it should be told by the receiver; for otherwise you may receive the retort which was made to one who was everywhere boasting of the benefit which he had conferred: "You will not deny," said his victim, "that you have received a return for it?" "When?" asked he. "Often," said the other, "and in many places, that is, wherever and whenever you have told the story." What need is there for you to speak, and to take the place which belongs to another? There is a man who can tell the story in a way much more to your credit, and thus you will gain glory for not telling it yourself. You would think me ungrateful if, through your own silence, no one is to know of your benefit. So far from doing this, even if any one tells the story in our presence, we ought to make answer, "He does indeed deserve much more than this, and I am aware that I have not hitherto done any great things for him, although I wish to do so." This should not be said jokingly, nor yet with that air by which some persons repel those whom they especially wish to attract. In addition to this, we ought to act with the greatest politeness towards such persons. If the farmer ceases his labours after he has put in the seed, he will lose what he has sown; it is only by great pains that seeds are brought to yield a crop; no plant will bear fruit unless it be tended with equal care from first to last, and the same rule is true of benefits. Can any benefits be greater than those which children receive from their parents? Yet these benefits are useless if they be deserted while young, if the pious care of the parents does not for a long time watch over the gift which they have bestowed. So it is with other benefits; unless you help them, you will lose them; to give is not enough, you must foster what you have given. If you wish those whom you lay under an obligation to be grateful to you, you must not merely confer benefits upon them, but you must also love them. Above all, as I said before, spare their ears; you will weary them if you remind them of your goodness, if you reproach them with it you will make them hate you. Pride ought above all things to be avoided when you confer a benefit. What need have you for disdainful airs, or swelling phrases? the act itself will exalt you. Let us shun vain boasting: let us be silent, and let our deeds speak for us. A benefit conferred with haughtiness not only wins no gratitude, but causes dislike.

XII

Gaius Caesar granted Pompeius Pennus his life, that is, if not to take away life be to grant it; then, when Pompeius was set free and returning thanks to him, he stretched out his left foot to be kissed. Those who excuse this action, and say that it was not done through arrogance, say that he wished to show him a gilded, nay a golden slipper studded with pearls. "Well," say they, "what disgrace can there be in a man of consular rank kissing gold and pearls, and what part of Caesar's whole body was it less pollution to kiss?" So, then, that man, the object of whose life was to change a free state into a Persian despotism, was not satisfied when a senator, an aged man, a man who had filled the highest offices in the state, prostrated himself before him in the presence of all the nobles, just as the vanquished prostrate themselves before their conqueror! He discovered a place below his knees down to which he might thrust liberty. What is this but trampling upon the commonwealth, and that, too, with the left foot, though you may say that this point does not signify? It was not a sufficiently foul and frantic outrage for the emperor to sit at the trial of a consular for his life wearing slippers, he must needs push his shoes into a senator's face.

XIII

O pride, the silliest fault of great good fortune! how pleasant it is to take nothing from thee! how dost thou turn all benefits into outrages! how dost thou delight in all excess! how ill all things become thee! The higher thou risest the lower thou art, and provest that the good things by which thou art so puffed up profit thee not; thou spoilest all that thou givest. It is worth while to inquire why it is that pride thus swaggers and changes the form and appearance of her countenance, so that she prefers a mask to her own face. It is pleasant to receive gifts when they are conferred in a kindly and gentle manner, when a superior in giving them does not exalt himself over me, but shows as much good feeling as possible, placing himself on a level with me, giving without parade, and choosing a time when I am glad of his help, rather than waiting till I am in the bitterest need. The only way by which you can prevail upon proud men not to spoil their gifts by their arrogance is by proving to them that benefits do not appear greater because they are bestowed with great pomp and circumstance; that no one will think them greater men for so doing, and that excessive pride is a mere delusion which leads men to hate even what they ought to love.

XIV

There are some things which injure those who receive them, things which it is not a benefit to give but to withhold; we should therefore consider the usefulness of our gift rather than the wish of the petitioner to receive it; for we often long for hurtful things, and are unable to discern how ruinous they are, because our judgment is biassed by our feelings; when, however, the longing is past, when that frenzied impulse which masters our good sense has passed away, we abhor those who have given us hurtful gifts. As we refuse cold water to the sick, or swords to the grief-stricken or remorseful, and take from the insane whatever they might in their delirium use to their own destruction, so must we persist in refusing to give anything whatever that is hurtful, although our friends earnestly and humbly, nay, sometimes even most piteously beg for it. We ought to look at the end of our benefits as well as the beginning, and not merely to give what men are glad to receive, but what they will hereafter be glad to have received. There are many who say, "I know that this will do him no good, but what am I to do? he begs for it, I cannot withstand his entreaties. Let him see to it; he will blame himself, not me." Not so: you he will blame, and deservedly; when he comes to his right mind, when the frenzy which now excites him has left him, how can he help hating the man who has assisted him to harm and to endanger himself? It is a cruel kindness to allow one's self to be won over into granting that which injures those who beg for it. Just as it is the noblest of acts to save men from harm against their will, so it is but hatred, under the mask of civility, to grant what is harmful to those who ask for it. Let us confer benefits of such a kind, that the more they are made use of the better they please, and which never can turn into injuries. I never will give money to a man if I know that he will pay it to an adulteress, nor will I be found in connexion with any wicked act or plan; if possible, I will restrain men from crime; if not, at least I will never assist them in it. Whether my friend be driven into doing wrong by anger, or seduced from the path of safety by the heat of ambition, he shall never gain the means of doing mischief except from himself, nor will I enable him one day to say, "He ruined me out of love for me." Our friends often give us what our enemies wish us to receive; we are driven by the unseasonable fondness of the former into the ruin which the latter hope will befall us. Yet, often as it is the case, what can be more shameful than that there should be no difference between a benefit and hatred?

XV

Let us never bestow gifts which may recoil upon us to our shame. As the sum total of friendship consists in making our friends equal to ourselves, we ought to consider the interests of both parties; I must give to him that wants, yet so that I do not want myself; I must help him who is perishing, yet so that I do not perish myself, unless by so doing I can save a great man or a great cause. I must give no benefit which it would disgrace me to ask for. I ought not to make a small benefit appear a great one, nor allow great benefits to be regarded as small; for although it destroys all feeling of gratitude to treat what you give like a creditor, yet you do not reproach a man, but merely set off your gift to the best advantage by letting him know what it is worth. Every man must consider what his resources and powers are, so that we may not give either more or less than we are able. We must also consider the character and position of the person to whom we give, for some men are too great to give small gifts, while others are too small to receive great ones. Compare, therefore, the character both of the giver and the receiver, and weigh that which you give between the two, taking care that what is given be neither too burdensome nor too trivial for the one to give, nor yet such as the receiver will either treat with disdain as too small, or think too great for him to deal with.

XVI

Alexander, who was of unsound mind, and always full of magnificent ideas, presented somebody with a city. When the man to whom he gave it had reflected upon the scope of his own powers, he wished to avoid the jealousy which so great a present would excite, saying that the gift did not suit a man of his position. "I do not ask," replied Alexander, "what is becoming for you to receive, but what is becoming for me to give." This seems a spirited and kingly speech, yet really it is a most foolish one. Nothing is by itself a becoming gift for any one: all depends upon who gives it, to whom he gives it, when, for what reason, where, and so forth, without which details it is impossible to argue about it. Inflated creature! if it did not become him to receive this gift, it could not become thee to give it. There should be a proportion between men's characters and the offices which they fill; and as virtue in all cases should be our measure, he who gives too much acts as wrongly as he who gives too little. Even granting that fortune has raised you so high, that, where other men give cups, you give cities (which it would show a greater mind in you not to take than to take and squander), still there must be some of your friends who are not strong enough to put a city in their pockets.

XVII

A certain cynic asked Antigonus for a talent. Antigonus answered that this was too much for a cynic to ask for. After this rebuff he asked for a penny. Antigonus answered that this was too little for a king to give. "This kind of hair-splitting" (you say) "is contemptible: he found the means of giving neither. In the matter of the penny he thought of the king, in that of the talent he thought of the cynic, whereas with respect to the cynic it would have been right to receive the penny, with respect to the king it would have been right to give the talent. Though there may be things which are too great for a cynic to receive, yet nothing is so small, that it does not become a gracious king to bestow it." If you ask me, I applaud Antigonus; for it is not to be endured that a man who despises money should ask for it. Your cynic has publicly proclaimed his hatred of money, and assumed the character of one who despises it: let him act up to his professions. It is most inconsistent for him to earn money by glorifying his poverty. I wish to use Chrysippus's simile of the game of ball, in which the ball must certainly fall by the fault either of the thrower or of the catcher; it only holds its course when it passes between the hands of two persons who each throw it and catch it suitably. It is necessary, however, for a good player to send the ball in one way to a comrade at a long distance, and in another to one at a short distance. So it is with a benefit: unless it be suitable both for the giver and the receiver, it will neither leave the one nor reach the other as it ought. If we have to do with a practised and skilled player, we shall throw the ball more recklessly, for however it may come, that quick and agile hand will send it back again; if we are playing with an unskilled novice, we shall not throw it so hard, but far more gently, guiding it straight into his very hands, and we shall run to meet it when it returns to us. This is just what we ought to do in conferring benefits; let us teach some men how to do so, and be satisfied if they attempt it, if they have the courage and the will to do so. For the most part, however, we make men ungrateful, and encourage them, to be so, as if our benefits were only great when we cannot receive any gratitude for them; just as some spiteful ball-players purposely put out their companion, of course to the ruin of the game, which cannot be carried on without entire agreement Many men are of so depraved a nature that they had rather lose the presents which they make than be thought to have received a return for them, because they are proud, and like to lay people under obligations: yet how much better and more kindly would it be if they tried to enable the others also to perform their parts, if they encouraged them in returning gratitude, put the best construction upon all their acts, received one who wished to thank them just as cordially as if he came to repay what he had received, and easily lent themselves to the belief that those whom they have laid under an obligation wish to repay it. We blame usurers equally when they press harshly for payment, and when they delay and make difficulties about taking back the money which they have lent; in the same way, it is just as right that a benefit should be returned, as it is wrong to ask any one to return it. The best man is he who gives readily, never asks for any return, and is delighted when the return is made, because, having really and truly forgotten what he gave, he receives it as though it were a present.

XVIII

Some men not only give, but even receive benefit haughtily, a mistake into which we ought not to fall: for now let us cross over to the other side of the subject, and consider how men should behave when they receive benefits. Every function which is performed by two persons makes equal demands upon both: after you have considered what a father ought to be, you will perceive that there remains an equal task, that of considering what a son ought to be: a husband has certain duties, but those of a wife are no less important. Each of these give and take equally, and each require a similar rule of life, which, as Hecaton observes, is hard to follow: indeed, it is difficult for us to attain to virtue, or even to anything that comes near virtue: for we ought not only to act virtuously but to do so upon principle. We ought to follow this guide throughout our lives, and to do everything great and small according to its dictates: according as virtue prompts us we ought both to give and to receive. Now she will declare at the outset that we ought not to receive benefits from every man. "From whom, then, ought we to receive them?" To answer you briefly, I should say, from those to whom we have given them. Let us consider whether we ought not to be even more careful in choosing to whom we should owe than to whom we should give. For even supposing that no unpleasantness should result (and very much always does), still it is a great misery to be indebted to a man to whom you do not wish to be under an obligation; whereas it is most delightful to receive a benefit from one whom you can love even after he has wronged you, and when the pleasure which you feel in his friendship is justified by the grounds on which it is based. Nothing is more wretched for a modest and honourable man than to feel it to be his duty to love one whom it does not please him to love. I must constantly remind you that I do not speak of wise men, who take pleasure in everything that is their duty, who have their feelings under command, and are able to lay down whatever law they please to themselves and keep it, but that I speak of imperfect beings struggling to follow the right path, who often have trouble in bending their passions to their will. I must therefore choose the man from whom I will accept a benefit; indeed, I ought to be more careful in the choice of my creditor for a benefit than for money; for I have only to pay the latter as much as I received of him, land when I have paid it I am free from all obligation; but to the other I must both repay more, and even when I have repaid his kindness we remain connected, for when I have paid my debt I ought again to renew it, while our friendship endures unbroken. Thus, as I ought not to make an unworthy man my friend, so I ought not to admit an unworthy man into that most holy bond of gratitude for benefits, from which friendship arises. You reply, "I cannot always say 'No': sometimes I must receive a benefit even against my will. Suppose I were given something by a cruel and easily offended tyrant, who would take it as an affront if his bounty were slighted? am I not to accept it? Suppose it were offered by a pirate, or a brigand, or a king of the temper of a pirate or brigand. What ought I to do? Such a man is not a worthy object for me to owe a benefit to." When I say that you ought to choose, I except vis major and fear, which destroy all power of choice. If you are free, if it lies with you to decide whether you will or not, then you will turn over in your own mind whether you will take a gift from a man or not; but if your position makes it impossible for you to choose, then be assured that you do not receive a gift, you merely obey orders. No one incurs any obligation by receiving what it was not in his power to refuse; if you want to know whether I wish to take it, arrange matters so that I have the power of saying 'No.' "Yet suppose he gave you your life." It does not matter what the gift was, unless it be given and received with good will: you are not my preserver because you have saved my life. Poison sometimes acts as a medicine, yet it is not on that account regarded as wholesome. Some things benefit us but put us under no obligation: for instance a man who intended to kill a tyrant, cut with his sword a tumour from which he suffered: yet the tyrant did not show him gratitude because by wounding him he had healed a disease which surgeons had feared to meddle with.

XIX

You see that the actual thing itself is not of much importance, because it is not regarded as a benefit at all, if you do good when you intended to do evil; in such a case the benefit is done by chance, the man did harm. I have seen a lion in the amphitheatre, who recognized one of the men who fought with wild beasts, who once had been his keeper, and protected him against the attacks of the other animals. Are we, then, to say that this assistance of the brute was a benefit? By no means, because it did not intend to do it, and did not do it with kindly intentions. You may class the lion and your tyrant together: each of them saved a man's life, yet neither conferred a benefit. Because it is not a benefit to be forced to receive one, neither is it a benefit to be under an obligation to a man to whom we do not wish to be indebted. You must first give me personal freedom of decision, and then your benefit.

XX

The question has been raised, whether Marcus Brutus ought to have received his life from the hands of Julius Caesar, who, he had decided, ought to be put to death.

As to the grounds upon which he put him to death, I shall discuss them elsewhere; for to my mind, though he was in other respects a great man, in this he seems to have been entirely wrong, and not to have followed the maxims of the Stoic philosophy. He must either have feared the name of "King," although a state thrives best under a good king, or he must have hoped that liberty could exist in a state where some had so much to gain by reigning, and others had so much to gain by becoming slaves. Or, again, he must have supposed that it would be possible to restore the ancient constitution after all the ancient manners had been lost, and that citizens could continue to possess equal rights, or laws remain inviolate, in a state in which he had seen so many thousands of men fighting to decide, not whether they should be slaves or free, but which master they should serve. How forgetful he seems to have been, both of human nature and of the history of his own country, in supposing that when one despot was destroyed another of the same temper would not take his place, though, after so many kings had perished by lightning and the sword, a Tarquin was found to reign! Yet Brutus did right in receiving his life from Caesar, though he was not bound thereby to regard Caesar as his father, since it was by a wrong that Caesar had come to be in a position to bestow this benefit. A man does not save your life who does not kill you; nor does he confer a benefit, but merely gives you your discharge. [The 'discharge' alluded to is that which was granted to the beaten one of a pair of gladiators, when their duel was not to the death.]

XXI

It seems to offer more opportunity for debate to consider what a captive ought to do, if a man of abominable vices offers him the price of his ransom? Shall I permit myself to be saved by a wretch? When safe, what recompense can I make to him? Am I to live with an infamous person? Yet, am I not to live with my preserver? I will tell you my opinion. I would accept money, even from such a person, if it were to save my life; yet I would only accept it as a loan, not as a benefit. I would repay him the money, and if I were ever able to preserve him from danger I would do so. As for friendship, which can only exist between equals, I would not condescend to be such a man's friend; nor would I regard him as my preserver, but merely as a money-lender, to whom I am only bound to repay what I borrowed from him.

A man may be a worthy person for me to receive a benefit from, but it will hurt him to give it. For this reason I will not receive it, because he is ready to help me to his own prejudice, or even danger. Suppose that he is willing to plead for me in court, but by so doing will make the king his enemy. I should be his enemy, if, when he is willing to risk himself for me, if I were not to risk myself without him, which moreover is easier for me to do.

As an instance of this, Hecaton calls the case of Arcesilaus silly, and not to the purpose. Arcesilaus, he says, refused to receive a large sum of money which was offered to him by a son, lest the son should offend his penurious father. What did he do deserving of praise, in not receiving stolen goods, in choosing not to receive them, instead of returning them? What proof of self-restraint is there in refusing to receive another man's property. If you want an instance of magnanimity, take the case of Julius Graecinus, whom Caius Caesar put to death merely on the ground that he was a better man than it suited a tyrant for anyone to be. This man, when he was receiving subscriptions from many of his friends to cover his expenses in exhibiting public games, would not receive a large sum which was sent him by Fabius Persicus; and when he was blamed for rejecting it by those who think more of what is given than of who gives it, he answered, "Am I to accept a present from a man when I would not accept his offer to drink a glass of wine with him?"

When a consular named Rebilius, a man of equally bad character, sent a yet larger sum to Graecinus, and pressed him to receive it. "I must beg," answered he, "that you will excuse me. I did not take money from Persicus either." Ought we to call this receiving presents, or rather taking one's pick of the senate?

XXII

When we have decided to accept, let us accept with cheerfulness, showing pleasure, and letting the giver see it, so that he may at once receive some return for his goodness: for as it is a good reason for rejoicing to see our friend happy, it is a better one to have made him so. Let us, therefore, show how acceptable a gift is by loudly expressing our gratitude for it; and let us do so, not only in the hearing of the giver, but everywhere. He who receives a benefit with gratitude, repays the first instalment of it.

XXIII

There are some, who only like to receive benefits privately: they dislike having any witnesses and confidants. Such men, we may believe, have no good intentions. As a giver is justified in dwelling upon those qualities of his gift which will please the receiver, so a man, when he receives, should do so publicly; you should not take from a man what you are ashamed to owe him. Some return thanks to one stealthily, in a corner, in a whisper. This is not modesty, but a kind of denying of the debt: it is the part of an ungrateful man not to express his gratitude before witnesses. Some object to any accounts being kept between them and their benefactors, and wish no brokers to be employed or witnesses to be called, but merely to give their own signature to a receipt. Those men do the like, who take care to let as few persons as possible know of the benefits which they have received. They fear to receive them in public, in order that their success may be attributed rather to their own talents than to the help of others: they are very seldom to be found in attendance upon those to whom they owe their lives and their fortunes, and thus, while avoiding the imputation of servility, they incur that of ingratitude.

XXIV

Some men speak in the most offensive terms of those to whom they owe most. There are men whom it is safer to affront than to serve, for their dislike leads them to assume the airs of persons who are not indebted to us: although nothing more is expected of them than that they should remember what they owe us, refreshing their memory from time to time, because no one can be grateful who forgets a kindness, and he who remembers it, by so doing proves his gratitude. We ought neither to receive benefits with a fastidious air, nor yet with a slavish humility: for if a man does not care for a benefit when it is freshly bestowed--a time at which all presents please us most--what will he do when its first charms have gone off? Others receive with an air of disdain, as much as to say. "I do not want it; but as you wish it so very much, I will allow you to give it to me." Others take benefits languidly, and leave the giver in doubt as to whether they know that they have received them; others barely open their lips in thanks, and would be less offensive if they said nothing. One ought to proportion one's thanks to the importance of the benefit received, and to use the phrases, "You have laid more of us than you think under an obligation," for everyone likes to find his good actions extend further than he expected. "You do not know what it is that you have done for me; but you ought to know how much more important it is than you imagine." It is in itself an expression of gratitude to speak of one's self as overwhelmed by kindness; or "I shall never be able to thank you sufficiently; but, at any rate, I will never cease to express everywhere my inability to thank you."

XXV

By nothing did Furnius gain greater credit with Augustus, and make it easy for him to obtain anything else for which he might ask, than by merely saying, when at his request Augustus pardoned his father for having taken Antonius's side, "One wrong alone I have received at your hands, Caesar; you have forced me to live and to die owing you a greater debt of gratitude than I can ever repay." What can prove gratitude so well as that a man should never be satisfied, should never even entertain the hope of making any adequate return for what he has received? By these and similar expressions we must try not to conceal our gratitude, but to display it as clearly as possible. No words need be used; if we only feel as we ought, our thankfulness will be shown in our countenances. He who intends to be grateful, let him think how he shall repay a kindness while he is receiving it. Chrysippus says that such a man must watch for his opportunity, and spring forward whenever it offers, like one who has been entered for a race, and who stands at the starting-point waiting for the barriers to be thrown open; and even then he must use great exertions and great swiftness to catch the other, who has a start of him.

XXVI

We must now consider what is the main cause of ingratitude. It is caused by excessive self-esteem, by that fault innate in all mortals, of taking a partial view of ourselves and our own acts, by greed, or by jealousy.

Let us begin with the first of these. Every one is prejudiced in his own favour, from which it follows that he believes himself to have earned all that he receives, regards it as payment for his services, and does not think that he has been appraised at a valuation sufficiently near his own. "He has given me this," says he, "but how late, after how much toil? how much more might I have earned if I had attached myself to So and so, or to So and so? I did not expect this; I have been treated like one of the herd; did he really think that I only deserved so little? why, it would have been less insulting to have passed me over altogether."

XXVII

The augur Cnaeus Lentulus, who, before his freedmen reduced him to poverty, was one of the richest of men, who saw himself in possession of a fortune of four hundred millions--I say advisedly, "saw," for he never did more than see it--was as barren and contemptible in intellect as he was in spirit. Though very avaricious, yet he was so poor a speaker that he found it easier to give men coins than words. This man, who owed all his prosperity to the late Emperor Augustus, to whom he had brought only poverty, encumbered with a noble name, when he had risen to be the chief man in Rome, both in wealth and influence, used sometimes to complain that Augustus had interrupted his legal studies, observing that he had not received anything like what he had lost by giving up the study of eloquence. Yet the truth was that Augustus, besides loading him with other gifts, had set him free from the necessity of making himself ridiculous by labouring at a profession in which he never could succeed.

Greed does not permit any one to be grateful; for what is given is never equal to its base desires, and the more we receive the more we covet, for avarice is much more eager when it has to deal with great accumulations of wealth, just as the power of a flame is enormously greater in proportion to the size of the conflagration from which it springs. Ambition in like manner suffers no man to rest satisfied with that measure of public honours, to gain which was once the limit of his wildest hope; no one is thankful for becoming tribune, but grumbles at not being at once promoted to the post of praetor; nor is he grateful for this if the consulship does not follow; and even this does not satisfy him if he be consul but once. His greed ever stretches itself out further, and he does not understand the greatness of his success because he always looks forward to the point at which he aims, and never back towards that from which he started.

XXVIII

A more violent and distressing vice than any of these is jealousy which disturbs us by suggesting comparisons. "He gave me this, but he gave more to that man, and he gave it to him before me;" after which he sympathises with no one, but pushes his own claims to the prejudice of every one else. How much more straightforward and modest is it to make the most of what we have received, knowing that no man is valued so highly by any one else as by his own, self! "I ought to have received more, but it was not easy for him to give more; he was obliged to distribute his liberality among many persons. This is only the beginning; let me be contented, and by my gratitude encourage him to show me more favour; he has not done as much as he ought, but he will do so the more frequently; he certainly preferred that man to me, but he has preferred me before many others; that man is not my equal either in virtue or in services, but he has some charm of his own: by complaining I shall not make myself deserve to receive more, but shall become unworthy of what I have received. More has been given to those most villainous men than has been given to me; well, what is that to the purpose? how seldom does Fortune show judgment in her choice? We complain every day of the success of bad men; very often the hail passes over the estates of the greatest villains and strikes down the crops of the best of men; every man has to take his chance, in friendship as well as in everything else." There is no benefit so great that spitefulness can pick no holes in it, none so paltry that it cannot be made more of by friendly interpretation. We shall never want a subject for complaint if we look at benefits on their wrong side.

XXIX

See how unjustly the gifts of heaven are valued even by some who profess themselves philosophers, who complain that we are not as big as elephants, as swift as stags, as light as birds, as strong as bulls; that the skins of seals are stronger, of hinds prettier, of bears thicker, of beavers softer than ours; that dogs excel us in delicacy of scent, eagles in keenness of sight, crows in length of days, and many beasts in ease of swimming. And although nature itself does not allow some qualities, as for example strength and swiftness, to be combined in the same person, yet they call it a monstrous thing that men are not compounded of different and inconsistent good qualities, and call the gods neglectful of us because we have not been given health which even our vices cannot destroy, or knowledge of the future. They scarcely refrain from rising to such a pitch of impudence as to hate nature because we are below the gods, and not on an equality with them. How much better is it to turn to the contemplation of so many great blessings, and to be thankful that the gods have been pleased to give us a place second only to themselves in this most beautiful abode, and that they have appointed us to be the lords of the earth! Can any one compare us with the animals over whom we rule? Nothing has been denied us except what could not have been granted. In like manner, thou that takest an unfair view of the lot of mankind, think what blessings our Father has bestowed upon us, how far more powerful animals than ourselves we have broken to harness, how we catch those which are far swifter, how nothing that has life is placed beyond the reach of our weapons! We have received so many excellencies, so many crafts, above all our mind, which can pierce at once whatever it is directed against, which is swifter than the stars in their courses, for it arrives before them at the place which they will reach after many ages; and besides this, so many fruits of the earth, so much treasure, such masses of various things piled one upon another. You may go through the whole order of nature, and since you find no entire creature which you would prefer to be, you may choose from each, the special qualities which you would like to be given to yourself; then, if you rightly appreciate the partiality of nature for you, you cannot but confess yourself to be her spoiled child. So it is; the immortal gods have unto this day always held us most dear, and have bestowed upon us the greatest possible honour, a place nearest to themselves. We have indeed received great things, yet not too great.

XXX

I have thought it necessary, my friend Liberalis, to state these facts, both because when speaking of small benefits one ought to make some mention of the greatest, and because also this shameless and hateful vice (of ingratitude), starting with these, transfers itself from them to all the rest. If a man scorn these, the greatest of all benefits, to whom will he feel gratitude, what gift will he regard as valuable or deserving to be returned: to whom will he be grateful for his safety or his life, if he denies that he has received from the gods that existence which he begs from them daily? He, therefore, who teaches men to be grateful, pleads the cause not only of men, but even of the gods, for though they, being placed above all desires, cannot be in want of anything, yet we can nevertheless offer them our gratitude.

No one is justified in seeking an excuse for ingratitude in his own weakness or poverty, or in saying, "What am I to do, and how? When can I repay my debt to my superiors the lords of heaven and earth?" Avaricious as you are, it is easy for you to give them thanks, without expense; lazy though you be, you can do it without labour. At the same instant at which you received your debt towards them, if you wish to repay it, you have done as much as any one can do, for he returns a benefit who receives it with good will.

XXXI

This paradox of the Stoic philosophy, that he returns a benefit who receives it with good will, is, in my opinion, either far from admirable, or else it is incredible. For if we look at everything merely from the point of view of our intentions, every man has done as much as he chose to do; and since filial piety, good faith, justice, and in short every virtue is complete within itself, a man may be grateful in intention even though he may not be able to lift a hand to prove his gratitude. Whenever a man obtains what he aimed at, he receives the fruit of his labour. When a man bestows a benefit, at what does he aim? clearly to be of service and afford pleasure to him upon whom he bestows it. If he does what he wishes, if his purpose reaches me and fills us each with joy, he has gained his object. He does not wish anything to be given to him in return, or else it becomes an exchange of commodities, not a bestowal of benefits. A man steers well who reaches the port for which he started: a dart hurled by a steady hand performs its duty if it hits the mark; one who bestows a benefit wishes it to be received with gratitude; he gets what he wanted if it be well received. "But," you say, "he hoped for some profit also." Then it was not a benefit, the property of which is to think nothing of any repayment. I receive what was given me in the same spirit in which it was given: then I have repaid it. If this be not true, then this best of deeds has this worst of conditions attached to it, that it depends entirely upon fortune whether I am grateful or not, for if my fortune is adverse I can make no repayment. The intention is enough. "What then? am I not to do whatever I may be able to repay it, and ought I not ever to be on the watch for an opportunity of filling the bosom[1] of him from whom I have received any kindness? True; but a benefit is in an evil plight if we cannot be grateful for it even when we are empty-handed.

---

[1] Sinus, the fold of the toga over the breast, used as a pocket by the Romans. The great French actor Talma, when dressed for the first time in correct classical costume, indignantly asked where he was to put his snuff-box.

XXXII

"A man," it is argued, "who has received a benefit, however gratefully he may have received it, has not yet accomplished all his duty, for there remains the part of repayment; just as in playing at ball it is something to catch the ball cleverly and carefully, but a man is not called a good player unless he can handily and quickly send back the ball which he has caught." This analogy is imperfect; and why? Because to do this creditably depends upon the movement and activity of the body, and not upon the mind: and an act of which we judge entirely by the eye, ought to be all clearly displayed. But if a man caught the ball as he ought to do, I should not call him a bad player for not returning it, if his delay in returning it was not caused by his own fault. "Yet," say you, "although the player is not wanting in skill, because he did one part of his duty, and was able to do the other part, yet in such a case the game is imperfect, for its perfection lies in sending the ball backwards and forwards." I am unwilling to expose this fallacy further; let us think that it is the game, not the player that is imperfect: so likewise in the subject which we are discussing, the thing which is given lacks something, because another equal thing ought to be returned for it, but the mind of the giver lacks nothing, because it has found another mind equal to itself, and as far as intentions go, has effected what it wished.

XXXIII

A man bestows a benefit upon me: I receive it just as he wished it to be received: then he gets at once what he wanted, and the only thing which he wanted, and therefore I have proved myself grateful. After this it remains for me to enjoy my own resources, with the addition of an advantage conferred upon me by one whom I have obliged; this advantage is not the remainder of an imperfect service, but an addition to a perfected service.[2] For example, Phidias makes a statue. Now the product of an art is one thing, and that of a trade is another. It is the business of the art to make the thing which he wished to make, and that of the trade to make it with a profit. Phidias has completed his work, even though he does not sell it. The product, therefore, of his work is threefold: there is the consciousness of having made it, which he receives when his work is completed; there is the fame which he receives; and thirdly, the advantage which he obtains by it, in influence, or by selling it, or otherwise. In like manner the first fruit of a benefit is the consciousness of it, which we feel when we have bestowed it upon the person whom we chose; secondly and thirdly there is the credit which we gain by doing so, and there are those things which we may receive in exchange for it. So when a benefit has been graciously received, the giver has already received gratitude, but has not yet received recompense for it: that which we owe in return is therefore something apart from the benefit itself, for we have paid for the benefit itself when we accept it in a grateful spirit.

---

[2] Nothing is wanted to make a benefit, conferred from good motives, perfect: if it is returned, the gratitude is to be counted as net profit.

XXXIV

"What," say you, "can a man repay a benefit, though he does nothing?" He has taken the first step, he has offered you a good thing with good feeling, and, which is the characteristic of friendship, has placed you both on the same footing. In the next place, a benefit is not repaid in the same manner as a loan: you have no reason for expecting me to offer you any payment; the account between us depends upon the feelings alone. What I say will not appear difficult, although it may not at first accord with your ideas, if you will do me the favour to remember that there are more things than there are words to express them. There is an enormous mass of things without names, which we do not speak of under distinctive names of their own, but by the names of other things transferred to them. We speak of our own foot, of the foot of a couch, of a sail, or of a poem; we apply the word 'dog' to a hound, a fish, and a star. Because we have not enough words to assign a separate name to each thing, we borrow a name whenever we want one. Bravery is the virtue which rightly despises danger, or the science of repelling, sustaining, or inviting dangers: yet we call a brave man a gladiator, and we use the same word for a good-for-nothing slave, who is led by rashness to defy death. Economy is the science of avoiding unnecessary expenditure, or the art of using one's income with moderation: yet we call a man of mean and narrow mind, most economical, although there is an immeasurable distance between moderation and meanness. These things are naturally distinct, yet the poverty of our language compels us to call both these men economical, just as he who views slight accidents with rational contempt, and he who without reason runs into danger are alike called brave. Thus a benefit is both a beneficent action, and also is that which is bestowed by that action, such as money, a house, an office in the state: there is but one name for them both, though their force and power are widely different.

XXXV

Wherefore, give me your attention, and you will soon perceive that I say nothing to which you can object. That benefit which consists of the action is repaid when we receive it graciously; that other, which consists of something material, we have not then repaid, but we hope to do so. The debt of goodwill has been discharged by a return of goodwill; the material debt demands a material return. Thus, although we may declare that he who has received a benefit with good-will has returned the favour, yet we counsel him to return to the giver something of the same kind as that which he has received. Some part of what we have said departs from the conventional line of thought, and then rejoins it by another path. We declare that a wise man cannot receive an injury; yet, if a man hits him with his fist, that man will be found guilty of doing him an injury. We declare that a fool can possess nothing; yet if a man stole anything from a fool, we should find that man guilty of theft. We declare that all men are mad, yet we do not dose all men with hellebore; but we put into the hands of these very persons, whom we call madmen, both the right of voting and of pronouncing judgment. Similarly, we say that a man who has received a benefit with good-will has returned the favour, yet we leave him in debt nevertheless--bound to repay it even though he has repaid it. This is not to disown benefits, but is an encouragement to us neither to fear to receive benefits, nor to faint under the too great burden of them. "Good things have been given to me; I have been preserved from starving; I have been saved from the misery of abject poverty; my life, and what is dearer than life, my liberty, has been preserved. How shall I be able to repay these favours? When will the day come upon which I can prove my gratitude to him?" When a man speaks thus, the day has already come. Receive a benefit, embrace it, rejoice, not that you have received it, but that you have to owe it and return it; then you will never be in peril of the great sin of being rendered ungrateful by mischance. I will not enumerate any difficulties to you, lest you should despair, and faint at the prospect of a long and laborious servitude. I do not refer you to the future; do it with what means you have at hand. You never will be grateful unless you are so straightway. What, then, will you do? You need not take up arms, yet perhaps you may have to do so; you need not cross the seas, yet it may be that you will pay your debt, even when the wind threatens to blow a gale. Do you wish to return the benefit? Then receive it graciously; you have then returned the favour--not, indeed, so that you can think yourself to have repaid it, but so that you can owe it with a quieter conscience.

On Benefits – Book III

I

Not to return gratitude for benefits, my AEbutius Liberalis, is both base in itself, and is thought base by all men; wherefore even ungrateful men complain of ingratitude, and yet what all condemn is at the same time rooted in all; and so far do men sometimes run into the other extreme that some of them become our bitterest enemies, not merely after receiving benefits from us, but because they have received them. I cannot deny that some do this out of sheer badness of nature; but more do so because lapse of time destroys their remembrance, for time gradually effaces what they felt vividly at the moment. I remember having had an argument with you about this class of persons, whom you wished to call forgetful rather than ungrateful, as if that which caused a man to be ungrateful was any excuse for his being so, or as if the fact of this happening to a man prevented his being ungrateful, when we know that it only happens to ungrateful men. There are many classes of the ungrateful, as there are of thieves or of homicides, who all have the same fault, though there is a great variety in its various forms. The man is ungrateful who denies that he has received a benefit; who pretends that he has not received it; who does not return it. The most ungrateful man of all is he who forgets it. The others, though they do not repay it, yet feel their debt, and possess some traces of worth, though obstructed by their bad conscience. They may by some means and at some time be brought to show their gratitude, if, for instance, they be pricked by shame, if they conceive some noble ambition such as occasionally rises even in the breasts of the wicked, if some easy opportunity of doing so offers; but the man from whom all recollection of the benefit has passed away can never become grateful. Which of the two do you call the worse--he who is ungrateful for kindness, or he who does not even remember it? The eyes which fear to look at the light are diseased, but those which cannot see it are blind. It is filial impiety not to love one's parents, but not to recognise them is madness.

II

Who is so ungrateful as he who has so completely laid aside and cast away that which ought to be in the forefront of his mind and ever before him, that he knows it not? It is clear that if forgetfulness of a benefit steals over a man, he cannot have often thought about repaying it.

In short, repayment requires gratitude, time, opportunity, and the help of fortune; whereas, he who remembers a benefit is grateful for it, and that too without expenditure. Since gratitude demands neither labour, wealth, nor good fortune, he who fails to render it has no excuse behind which to shelter himself; for he who places a benefit so far away that it is out of his sight, never could have meant to be grateful for it. Just as those tools which are kept in use, and are daily touched by the hand, are never in danger of growing rusty, while those which are not brought before our eyes, and lie as if superfluous, not being required for common use, collect dirt by the mere lapse of time, so likewise that which our thoughts frequently turn over and renew never passes from our memory, which only loses those things to which it seldom directs its eyes.

III

Besides this, there are other causes which at times erase the greatest services from our minds. The first and most powerful of these is that, being always intent upon new objects of desire, we think, not of what we have, but of what we are striving to obtain. Those whose mind is fixed entirely upon what they hope to gain, regard with contempt all that is their own already. It follows that since men's eagerness for something new makes them undervalue whatever they have received, they do not esteem those from whom they have received it. As long as we are satisfied with the position we have gained, we love our benefactor, we look up to him, and declare that we owe our position entirely to him; then we begin to entertain other aspirations, and hurry forward to attain them after the manner of human beings, who when they have gained much always covet more; straightway all that we used to regard as benefits slip from our memory, and we no longer consider the advantages which we enjoy over others, but only the insolent prosperity of those who have outstripped us. Now no one can at the same time be both jealous and grateful, because those who are jealous are querulous and sad, while the grateful are joyous. In the next place, since none of us think of any time but the present, and but few turn back their thoughts to the past, it results that we forget our teachers, and all the benefits which we have obtained from them, because we have altogether left our childhood behind us: thus, all that was done for us in our youth perishes unremembered, because our youth itself is never reviewed. What has been is regarded by every one, not only as past, but as gone; and for the same reason, our memory is weak for what is about to happen in the future.

IV

Here I must do Epicurus the justice to say that he constantly complains of our ingratitude for past benefits, because we cannot bring back again, or count among our present pleasures, those good things which we have received long ago, although no pleasures can be more undeniable than those which cannot be taken from us. Present good is not yet altogether complete, some mischance may interrupt it; the future is in suspense, and uncertain; but what is past is laid up in safety. How can any man feel gratitude for benefits, if he skips through his whole life entirely engrossed with the present and the future? It is remembrance that makes men grateful; and the more men hope, the less they remember.

V

In the same way, my Liberalis, as some things remain in our memory as soon as they are learned, while to know others it is not enough to have learned them, for our knowledge slips away from us unless it be kept up--I allude to geometry and astronomy, and such other sciences as are Hard to remember because of their intricacy-- so the greatness of some benefits prevents their being forgotten, while others, individually less, though many more in number, and bestowed at different times, pass from our minds, because, as I have stated above, we do not constantly think about them, and do not willingly recognize how much we owe to each of our benefactors. Listen to the words of those who ask for favours. There is not one of them who does not declare that his remembrance will be eternal, who does not vow himself your devoted servant and slave, or find, if he can, some even greater expression of humility with which to pledge himself. After a brief space of time these same men avoid their former expressions, thinking them abject, and scarcely befitting free-born men; afterwards they arrive at the same point to which, as I suppose, the worst and most ungrateful of men come-- that is, they forget. So little does forgetfulness excuse ingratitude, that even the remembrance of a benefit may leave us ungrateful.

VI

The question has been raised, whether this most odious vice ought to go unpunished; and whether the law commonly made use of in the schools, by which we can proceed against a man for ingratitude, ought to be adopted by the State also, since all men agree that it is just. "Why not?" you may say, "seeing that even cities cast in each other's teeth the services which they have performed to one another, and demand from the children some return for benefits conferred upon their fathers?" On the other hand, our ancestors, who were most admirable men, made demands upon their enemies alone, and both gave and lost their benefits with magnanimity. With the exception of Macedonia, no nation has ever established an action at law for ingratitude. And this is a strong argument against its being established, because all agree in blaming crime; and homicide, poisoning, parricide, and sacrilege are visited with different penalties in different countries, but everywhere with some penalty; whereas this most common vice is nowhere punished, though it is everywhere blamed. We do not acquit it; but as it would be most difficult to reckon accurately the penalty for so varying a matter, we condemn it only to be hated, and place it upon the list of those crimes which we refer for judgment to the gods.

VII

Many arguments occur to me which prove that this vice ought not to come under the action of the law. First of all, the best part of a benefit is lost if the benefit can be sued for at law, as in the case of a loan, or of letting and hiring. Indeed, the finest part of a benefit is that we have given it without considering whether we shall lose it or not, that we have left all this to the free choice of him who receives it: if I call him before a judge, it begins to be not a benefit, but a loan. Next, though it is a most honourable thing to show gratitude, it ceases to be honourable if it be forced, for in that case no one will praise a grateful man any more than he praises him who restores the money which was deposited in his keeping, or who pays what he borrowed without the intervention of a judge. We should therefore spoil the two finest things in human life,--a grateful man and a beneficent man; for what is there admirable in one who does not give but merely lends a benefit, or in one who repays it, not because he wishes, but because he is forced to do so? There is no credit in being grateful, unless it is safe to be ungrateful. Besides this, all the courts would hardly be enough for the action of this one law. Who would not plead under it? Who would not be pleaded against? for every one exalts his own merits, every one magnifies even the smallest matters which he has bestowed upon another. Besides this, those things which form the subject of a judicial inquiry can be distinctly defined, and cannot afford unlimited licence to the judge; wherefore a good cause is in a better position if it before a judge than before an arbitrator, because the words of the law tie down a judge and define certain limits beyond which he may not pass, whereas the conscience of an arbitrator is free and not fettered by any rules, so that he can either give or take away, and can arrange his decision, not according to the precepts of law and justice, but just as his own kindly feeling or compassion may prompt him. An action for ingratitude would not bind a judge, but would place him in the position of an autocrat. It cannot be known what or how great a benefit is; all that would be really important would be, how indulgently the judge might interpret it. No law defines an ungrateful person, often, indeed, one who repays what he has received is ungrateful, and one who has not returned it is grateful. Even an unpractised judge can give his vote upon some matters; for instance, when the thing to be determined is whether something has or has not been done, when a dispute is terminated by the parties giving written bonds, or when the casting up of accounts decides between the disputants. When, however, motives have to be guessed at, when matters upon which wisdom alone can decide, are brought into court, they cannot be tried by a judge taken at random from the list of "select judges,"[1] whom property and the inheritance of an equestrian fortune[2] has placed upon the roll.

---

[1] See Smith's "Dict. of Antiq.," s. v

[2] 400,000 sesterces

VIII

Ingratitude, therefore, is not only matter unfit to be brought into court, but no judge could be found fit to try it; and this you will not be surprised at, if you examine the difficulties of any one who should attempt to prosecute a man upon such a charge. One man may have given a large sum of money, but he is rich and would not feel it; another may have given it at the cost of his entire inheritance. The sum given is the same in each case, but the benefit conferred is not the same. Add another instance: suppose that to redeem a debtor from slavery one man paid money from his own private means, while another man paid the same sum, but had to borrow it or beg for it, and allow himself to be laid under a great obligation to some one; would you rank the man who so easily bestowed his benefit on an equality with him who was obliged to receive a benefit himself before he could bestow it? Some benefits are great, not because of their amount, but because of the time at which they are bestowed; it is a benefit to give an estate whose fertility can bring down the price of corn, and it is a benefit to give a loaf of bread in time of famine; it is a benefit to give provinces through which flow vast navigable rivers, and it is a benefit, when men are parched with thirst, and can scarcely draw breath through their dry throats, to show them a spring of water. Who will compare these cases with one another, or weigh one against the other? It is hard to give a decision when it is not the thing given, but its meaning, which has to be considered; though what is given is the same, yet if it be given under different circumstances it has a different value. A man may have bestowed a benefit upon me, but unwillingly; he may have complained of having given it; he may have looked at me with greater haughtiness than he was wont to do; he may have been so slow in giving it, that he would have done me a greater service if he had promptly refused it. How could a judge estimate the value of these things, when words, hesitation, or looks can destroy all their claim to gratitude?

IX

What, again, could he do, seeing that some things are called benefits because they are unduly coveted, whilst others are not benefits at all, according to this common valuation, yet are of even greater value, though not so showy? You call it a benefit to cause a man to be adopted as a member of a powerful city, to get him enrolled among the knights, or to defend one who is being tried for his life: what do you say of him who gives useful advice? of him who holds you back when you would rush into crime? of him who strikes the sword from the hands of the suicide? of him who by his power of consolation brings back to the duties of life one who was plunged in grief, and eager to follow those whom he had lost? of him who sits at the bedside of the sick man, and who, when health and recovery depend upon seizing the right moment, administers food in due season, stimulates the failing veins with wine, or calls in the physician to the dying man? Who can estimate the value of such services as these? who can bid us weigh dissimilar benefits one with another? "I gave you a house," says one. Yes, but I forewarned you that your own house would come down upon your head. "I gave you an estate," says he. True, but I gave a plank to you when shipwrecked. "I fought for you and received wounds for you," says another. But I saved your life by keeping silence. Since a benefit is both given and returned differently by different people, it is hard to make them balance.

X

Besides this, no day is appointed for repayment of a benefit, as there is for borrowed money; consequently he who has not yet repaid a benefit may do so hereafter: for tell me, pray, within what time a man is to be declared ungrateful? The greatest benefits cannot be proved by evidence; they often lurk in the silent consciousness of two men only; are we to introduce the rule of not bestowing benefits without witnesses? Next, what punishment are we to appoint for the ungrateful? is there to be one only for all, though the benefits which they have received are different? or should the punishment be varying, greater or less according to the benefit which each has received? Are our valuations to be restricted to pecuniary fines? what are we to do, seeing that in some cases the benefit conferred is life, and things dearer than life? What punishment is to be assigned to ingratitude for these? One less than the benefit? That would be unjust. One equal to it; death? What could be more inhuman than to cause benefits to result in cruelty?

XI

It may be argued, "Parents have certain privileges: these are regarded as exempt from the action of ordinary rules, and so also ought to be the case with other beneficent persons." Nay; mankind has assigned a peculiar sanctity to the position of parents, because it was advantageous that children should be reared, and people had to be tempted into undergoing the toil of doing so, because the issue of their experiment was doubtful. One cannot say to them, as one does to others who bestow benefits, "Choose the man to whom you give: you must only blame yourself if you are deceived; help the deserving." In rearing children nothing depends upon the judgment of those who rear them; it is a matter of hope: in order, therefore, that people may be more willing to embark upon this lottery, it was right that they should be given a certain authority; and since it is useful for youth to be governed, we have placed their parents in the position of domestic magistrates, under whose guardianship their lives may be ruled. Moreover, the position of parents differs from that of other benefactors, for their having given formerly to their children does not stand in the way of their giving now and hereafter; and also, there is no fear of their falsely asserting that they have given: with others one has to inquire not only whether they have received, but whether they have given; but the good deeds of parents are placed beyond doubt. In the next place, one benefit bestowed by parents is the same for all, and might be counted once for all; while the others which they bestow are of various kinds, unlike one to another, differing from one another by the widest possible intervals; they can therefore come under no regular rule, since it would be more just to leave them all unrewarded than to give the same reward to all.

XII

Some benefits cost much to the givers, some are of much value to the receivers but cost the givers nothing. Some are bestowed upon friends, others on strangers: now although that which is given be the same, yet it becomes more when it is given to one with whom you are beginning to be acquainted through the benefits which you have previously conferred upon him. One man may give us help, another distinctions, a third consolation. You may find one who thinks nothing pleasanter or more important than to have some one to save him from distress; you may again find one who would rather be helped to great place than to security; while some consider themselves more indebted to those who save their lives than to those who save their honour. Each of these services will be held more or less important, according as the disposition of our judge inclines to one or the other of them. Besides this, I choose my creditors for myself, whereas I often receive benefits from those from whom I would not, and sometimes I am laid under an obligation without my knowledge. What will you do in such a case? When a man has received a benefit unknown to himself, and which, had he known of it, he would have refused to receive, will you call him ungrateful if he does not repay it, however he may have received it? Suppose that some one has bestowed a benefit upon me, and that the same man has afterwards done me some wrong; am I to be bound by his one bounty to endure with patience any wrong that he may do me, or will it be the same as if I had repaid it, because he himself has by the subsequent wrong cancelled his own benefit? How, in that case, would you decide which was the greater; the present which the man has received, or the injury which has been done him? Time would fail me if I attempted to discuss all the difficulties which would arise.

XIII

It may be argued that "we render men less willing to confer benefits by not supporting the claim of those which have been bestowed to meet with gratitude, and by not punishing those who repudiate them." But you would find, on the other hand, that men would be far less willing to receive benefits, if by so doing they were likely to incur the danger of having to plead their cause in court, and having more difficulty in proving their integrity. This legislation would also render us less willing to give: for no one is willing to give to those who are unwilling to receive, but one who is urged to acts of kindness by his own good nature and by the beauty of charity, will give all the more freely to those who need make no return unless they choose. It impairs the credit of doing a service, if in doing it we are carefully protected from loss.

XIV

"Benefits, then, will be fewer, but more genuine: well, what harm is there in restricting people from giving recklessly?" Even those who would have no legislation upon the subject follow this rule, that we ought to be somewhat careful in giving, and in choosing those upon whom we bestow favours. Reflect over and over again to whom you are giving: you will have no remedy at law, no means of enforcing repayment. You are mistaken if you suppose that the judge will assist you: no law will make full restitution to you, you must look only to the honour of the receiver. Thus only can benefits retain their influence, and thus only are they admirable: you dishonour them if you make them the grounds of litigation, "Pay what you owe" is a most just proverb; and one which carries with it the sanction of all nations; but in dealing with benefits it is most shameful. "Pay!" How is a man to pay who owes his life, his position, his safety, or his reason to another? None of the greatest benefits can be repaid. "Yet," it is said, "you ought to give in return for them something of equal value." This is just what I have been saying, that the grandeur of the act is ruined if we make our benefits commercial transactions. We ought hot to encourage ourselves in avarice, in discontent, or in quarrels; the human mind is prone enough to these by nature. As far as we are able, let us check it, and cut off the opportunities for which it seeks.

XV

Would that we could indeed persuade men to receive back money which they have lent from those debtors only who are willing to pay! would that no agreement ever bound the buyer to the seller, and that their interests were not protected by sealed covenants and agreements, but rather by honour and a sense of justice! However, men prefer what is needful to what is truly best, and choose rather to force their creditors to keep faith with them than to trust that they will do so. Witnesses are called on both sides; the one, by calling in brokers, makes several names appear in his accounts as his debtors instead of one; the other is not content with the legal forms of question and answer unless he holds the other party by the hand. What a shameful admission of the dishonesty and wickedness of mankind! men trust more to our signet- rings than to our intentions. For what are these respectable men summoned? for what do they impress their seals? it is in order that the borrower may not deny that he has received what he has received. You regard these men, I suppose, as above bribes, as maintainers of the truth: well, these very men will not be entrusted with money except on the same terms. Would it not, then, be more honourable to be deceived by some than to suspect all men of dishonesty? To fill up the measure of avarice one thing only is lacking, that we should bestow no benefit without a surety. To help, to be of service, is the part of a generous and noble mind; he who gives acts like a god, he who demands repayment acts like a money-lender. Why then, by trying to protect the rights of the former class, should we reduce them to the level of the basest of mankind?

XVI

"More men," our opponent argues, "will be ungrateful, if no legal remedy exists against ingratitude." Nay, fewer, because then benefits will be bestowed with more discrimination, In the next place, it is not advisable that it should be publicly known how many ungrateful men there are: for the number of sinners will do away with the disgrace of the sin, and a reproach which applies to all men will cease to be dishonourable. Is any woman ashamed of being divorced, now that some noble ladies reckon the years of their lives, not by the number of the consuls, but by that of their husbands, now that they leave their homes in order to marry others, and marry only in order to be divorced? Divorce was only dreaded as long as it was unusual; now that no gazette appears without it, women learn to do what they hear so much about. Can any one feel ashamed of adultery, now that things have come to such a pass that no woman keeps a husband at all unless it be to pique her lover? Chastity merely implies ugliness. Where will you find any woman so abject, so repulsive, as to be satisfied with a single pair of lovers, without having a different one for each hour of the day; nor is the day long enough for all of them, unless she has taken her airing in the grounds of one, and passes the night with another. A woman is frumpish and old-fashioned if she does not know that "adultery with one paramour is nick-named marriage." Just as all shame at these vices has disappeared since the vice itself became so widely spread, so if you made the ungrateful begin to count their own numbers, you would both make them more numerous, and enable them to be ungrateful with greater impunity.

XVII

"What then? shall the ungrateful man go unpunished?" What then, I answer, shall we punish the undutiful, the malicious, the avaricious, the headstrong, and the cruel? Do you imagine that those things which are loathed are not punished, or do you suppose that any punishment is greater than the hate of all men? It is a punishment not to dare receive a benefit from anyone, not to dare to bestow one, to be, or to fancy that you are a mark for all men's eyes, and to lose all appreciation of so excellent and pleasant a matter. Do you call a man unhappy who has lost his sight, or whose hearing has been impaired by disease, and do you not call him wretched who has lost the power of feeling benefits? He fears the gods, the witnesses of all ingratitude; he is tortured by the thought of the benefit which he has misapplied, and, in fine, he is sufficiently punished by this great penalty, that, as I said before, he cannot enjoy the fruits of this most delightful act. On the other hand, he who takes pleasure in receiving a benefit, enjoys an unvarying and continuous happiness, which he derives from consideration, not of the thing given, but of the intention of the giver. A benefit gives perpetual joy to a grateful man, but pleases an ungrateful one only for a moment. Can the lives of such men be compared, seeing that the one is sad and gloomy--as it is natural that a denier of his debts and a defrauder should be, a man who does not give his parents, his nurses, or his teachers the honour which is their due--while the other is joyous, cheerful, on the watch for an opportunity of proving his gratitude, and gaining much pleasure from this frame of mind itself? Such a man has no wish to become bankrupt, but only to make the fullest and most copious return for benefits, and that not only to parents and friends, but also to more humble persons; for even if he receives a benefit from his own slave, he does not consider from whom he receives it, but what he receives.

XVIII

It has, however, been doubted by Hecaton and some other writers, whether a slave can bestow a benefit upon his master. Some distinguish between benefits, duties, and services, calling those things benefits which are bestowed by a stranger--that is, by one who could discontinue them without blame--while duties are performed by our children, our wives, and those whom relationship prompts and orders to afford us help; and, thirdly, services are performed by slaves, whose position is such that nothing which they do for their master can give them any claim upon him. . . .

Besides this, he who affirms that a slave does not sometimes confer a benefit upon his master is ignorant of the rights of man; for the question is, not what the station in life of the giver may be, but what his intentions are. The path of virtue is closed to no one, it lies open to all; it admits and invites all, whether they be free-born men, slaves or freed-men, kings or exiles; it requires no qualifications of family or of property, it is satisfied with a mere man. What, indeed, should we have to trust to for defence against sudden misfortunes, what could--a noble mind promise to itself to keep unshaken, if virtue could be lost together with prosperity? If a slave cannot confer a benefit upon his master, then no subject can confer a benefit upon his king, and no soldier upon his general; for so long as the man is subject to supreme authority, the form of authority can make no difference. If main force, or the fear of death and torture, can prevent a slave from gaining any title to his master's gratitude, they will also prevent the subjects of a king, or the soldiers of a general from doing so, for the same things may happen to either of these classes of men, though under different names.

Yet men do bestow benefits upon their kings and their generals; therefore slaves can bestow benefits upon their masters. A slave can be just, brave, magnanimous; he can therefore bestow a benefit, for this is also the part of a virtuous man. So true is it that slaves can bestow benefits upon their masters, that the masters have often owed their lives to them.

XIX

There is no doubt that a slave can bestow a benefit upon anyone; why, then, not upon his master? "Because," it is argued, "he cannot become his master's creditor if he gives him money. If this be not so, he daily lays his master under an obligation to him; he attends him when on a journey, he nurses him when sick, he works most laboriously at the cultivation of his estate; yet all these, which would be called benefits if done for us by anyone else, are merely called service when done by a slave. A benefit is that which some one bestows who has the option of withholding it:-- now a slave has no power to refuse, so that he does not afford us his help, but obeys our orders, and cannot boast of having done what he could not leave undone." Even under these conditions I shall win the day, and will place a slave in such positions, that for many purposes he will be free; in the meanwhile, tell me, if I give you an instance of a slave fighting for his master's safety without regard to himself, pierced through with wounds, yet spending the last drops of his blood, and gaining time for his master to escape by the sacrifice of his life, will you say that this man did not bestow a benefit upon his master because he was a slave? If I give an instance of one who could not be bribed to betray his master's secrets by any of the offers of a tyrant, who was not terrified by any threats, nor overpowered by any tortures, but who, as far as he was able, placed his questioners upon a wrong scent, and, paid for his loyalty with his life; will you say that this man did not confer a benefit upon his master because he was a slave? Consider, rather, whether an example of virtue in a slave be not all the greater because it is rarer than in free men, and whether it be not all the more gratifying that, although to be commanded is odious, and all submission to authority is irksome, yet in some particular cases love for a master has been more powerful than men's general dislike to servitude. A benefit does not, therefore, cease to be a benefit because it is bestowed by a slave, but is all the greater on that account, because not even slavery could restrain him from bestowing it.

XX

It is a mistake to imagine that slavery pervades a man's whole being; the better part of him is exempt from it: the body indeed is subjected and in the power of a master, but the mind is independent, and indeed is so free and wild, that it cannot be restrained even by this prison of the body, wherein it is confined, from following its own impulses, dealing with gigantic designs, and soaring into the infinite, accompanied by all the host of heaven. It is, therefore, only the body which misfortune hands over to a master, and which he buys and sells; this inward part cannot be transferred as a chattel. Whatever comes from this, is free; indeed, we are not allowed to order all things to be done, nor are slaves compelled to obey us in all things; they will not carry out treasonable orders, or lend their hands to an act of crime.

XXI

There are some things which the law neither enjoins nor forbids; it is in these that a slave finds the means of bestowing benefits. As long as we only receive what is generally demanded from a slave, that is mere service; when more is given than a slave need afford us, it is a benefit; as soon as what he does begins to partake of the affection of a friend, it can no longer be called service. There are certain things with which a master is bound to provide his slave, such as food and clothing; no one calls this a benefit; but supposing that he indulges his slave, educates him above his station, teaches him arts which free-born men learn, that is a benefit. The converse is true in the case of the slave; anything which goes beyond the rules of a slave's duty, which is done of his own free will, and not in obedience to orders, is a benefit, provided it be of sufficient importance to be called by such a name if bestowed by any other person.

XXII

It has pleased Chrysippus to define a slave as "a hireling for life." Just as a hireling bestows a benefit when he does more than he engaged himself to do, so when a slave's love for his master raises him above his condition and urges him to do something noble--something which would be a credit even to men more fortunate by birth--he surpasses the hopes of his master, and is a benefit found in the house. Do you think it is just that we should be angry with our slaves when they do less than their duty, and that we should not be grateful to them when they do more? Do you wish to know when their service is not a benefit? When the question can be asked, "What if he had refused to do it?" When he does that which he might have refused to do, we must praise his good will. Benefits and wrongs are opposites; a slave can bestow a benefit upon his master, if he can receive a wrong from his master. Now an official has been appointed to hear complaints of the wrongs done by masters to their slaves, whose duty it is to restrain cruelty and lust, or avarice in providing them with the necessaries of life. What follows, then? Is it the master who receives a benefit from his slave? nay, rather, it is one man who receives it from another. Lastly, he did all that lay in his power; he bestowed a benefit upon his master; it lies in your power to receive or not to receive it from a slave. Yet who is so exalted, that fortune may not make him need the aid even of the lowliest?

XXIII

I shall now quote a number of instances of benefits, not all alike, some even contradictory. Some slaves have given their master life, some death; have saved him when perishing, or, as if that were not enough, have saved him by their own death; others have helped their master to die, some have saved his life by stratagem. Claudius Quadrigarius tells us in the eighteenth book of his "Annals," that when Grumentum was being besieged, and had been reduced to the greatest straits, two slaves deserted to the enemy, and did valuable service. Afterwards, when the city was taken, and the victors were rushing wildly in every direction, they ran before every one else along the streets, which they well knew, to the house in which they had been slaves, and drove their mistress before them; when they were asked who she might be, they answered that she was their mistress, and a most cruel one, and that they were leading her away for punishment. They led her outside the walls, and concealed her with the greatest care until the fighting was over; then, as the soldiery, satisfied with the sack of the city, quickly resumed the manners of Romans, they also returned to their own countrymen, and themselves restored their mistress to them. She manumitted each of them on the spot, and was not ashamed to receive her life from men over whom she had held the power of life and death. She might, indeed, especially congratulate herself upon this; for had she been saved otherwise, she would merely have received a common and hackneyed piece of kindness, whereas, by being saved as she was, she became a glorious legend, and an example to two cities. In the confusion of the captured city, when every one was thinking only of his own safety, all deserted her except these deserters; but they, that they might prove what had been their intentions in effecting that desertion, deserted again from the victors to the captive, wearing the masks of unnatural murderers.

They thought--and this was the greatest part of the service which they rendered--they were content to seem to have murdered their mistress, if thereby their mistress might be saved from murder. Believe me, it is the mark of no slavish soul to purchase a noble deed by the semblance of crime.

When Vettius, the praetor of the Marsi, was being led into the presence of the Roman general, his slave snatched a sword from the soldier who was dragging him along, and first slew his master. Then he said, "It is now time for me to look to myself; I have already set my master free," and with these words transfixed himself with one blow. Can you tell me of anyone who saved his master more gloriously?

XXIV

When Caesar was besieging Corfinium, Domitius, who was shut up in the city, ordered a slave of his own, who was also a physician, to give him poison. Observing the man's hesitation, he said, "Why do you delay, as though the whole business was in your power? I ask for death with arms in my hands." Then the slave assented, and gave him a harmless drug to drink. When Domitius fell asleep after drinking this, the slave went to his son, and said, "Give orders for my being kept in custody until you learn from the result whether I have given your father poison or no." Domitius lived, and Caesar saved his life; but his slave had saved it before.

XXV

During the civil war, a slave hid his master, who had been proscribed, put on his rings and clothes, met the soldiers who were searching for him, and, after declaring that he would not stoop to entreat them not to carry out their orders, offered his neck to their swords. What a noble spirit it shows in a slave to have been willing to die for his master, at a time when few were faithful enough to wish their master to live! to be found kind when the state was cruel, faithful when it was treacherous! to be eager for the reward of fidelity, though it was death, at a time when such rich rewards were offered for treachery!

XXVI

I will not pass over the instances which our own age affords. In the reign of Tiberius Caesar, there was a common and almost universal frenzy for informing, which was more ruinous to the citizens of Rome than the whole civil war; the talk of drunkards, the frankness of jesters, was alike reported to the government; nothing was safe; every opportunity of ferocious punishment was seized, and men no longer waited to hear the fate of accused persons, since it was always the same. One Paulus, of the Praetorian guard, was at an entertainment, wearing a portrait of Tiberius Caesar engraved in relief upon a gem. It would be absurd for me to beat about the bush for some delicate way of explaining that he took up a chamber-pot, an action which was at once noticed by Maro, one of the most notorious informers of that time, and the slave of the man who was about to fall into the trap, who drew the ring from the finger of his drunken master. When Maro called the guests to witness that Paulus had dishonoured the portrait of the emperor, and was already drawing up an act of accusation, the slave showed the ring upon his own finger. Such a man no more deserves to be called a slave, than Maro deserved to be called a guest.

XXVII

In the reign of Augustus men's own words were not yet able to ruin them, yet they sometimes brought them into trouble. A senator named Rufus, while at dinner, expressed a hope that Caesar would not return safe from a journey for which he was preparing, and added that all bulls and calves wished the same thing. Some of those present carefully noted these words. At daybreak, the slave who had stood at his feet during the dinner, told him what he had said in his cups, and urged him to be the first to go to Caesar, and denounce himself. Rufus followed this advice, met Caesar as he was going down to the forum, and, swearing that he was out of his mind the day before, prayed that what he had said might fall upon his own head and that of his children; he then begged Caesar pardon him, and to take him back into favour. When Caesar said that he would do so, he added, "No one will believe that you have taken me back into favour unless you make me a present of something;" and he asked for and obtained a sum of money so large, that it would have been a gift not to be slighted even if bestowed by an unoffended prince. Caesar added: "In future I will take care never to quarrel with you, for my own sake." Caesar acted honourably in pardoning him, and in being liberal as well as forgiving; no one can hear this anecdote without praising Caesar, but he must praise the slave first. You need not wait for me to tell you that the slave who did his master this service was set free; yet his master did not do this for nothing, for Caesar had already paid him the price of the slave's liberty.

XXVIII

After so many instances, can we doubt that a master may sometimes receive a benefit from a slave? Why need the person of the giver detract from the thing which he gives? why should not the gift add rather to the glory of the giver. All men descend from the same original stock; no one is better born than another, except in so far as his disposition is nobler and better suited for the performance of good actions. Those who display portraits of their ancestors in their halls, and set up in the entrance to their houses the pedigree of their family drawn out at length, with many complicated collateral branches, are they not notorious rather than noble? The universe is the one parent of all, whether they trace their descent from this primary source through a glorious or a mean line of ancestors. Be not deceived when men who are reckoning up their genealogy, wherever an illustrious name is wanting, foist in that of a god in its place. You need despise no one, even though he bears a commonplace name, and owes little to fortune. Whether your immediate ancestors were freedmen, or slaves, or foreigners, pluck up your spirits boldly, and leap over any intervening disgraces of your pedigree; at its source, a noble origin awaits you. Why should our pride inflate us to such a degree that we think it beneath us to receive benefits from slaves, and think only of their position, forgetting their good deeds? You, the slave of lust, of gluttony, of a harlot, nay, who are owned as a joint chattel by harlots, can you call anyone else a slave? Call a man a slave? why, I pray you, whither are you being hurried by those bearers who carry your litter? whither are these men with their smart military-looking cloaks carrying you? is it not to the door of some door-keeper, or to the gardens of some one who has not even a subordinate office? and then you, who regard the salute of another man's slave as a benefit, declare that you cannot receive a benefit from your own slave. What inconsistency is this? At the same time you despise and fawn upon slaves, you are haughty and violent at home, while out of doors you are meek, and as much despised as you despise your slaves; for none abase themselves lower than those who unconscionably give themselves airs, nor are anymore prepared to trample upon others than those who have learned how to offer insults by having endured them.

XXIX

I felt it my duty to say this, in order to crush the arrogance of men who are themselves at the mercy of fortune, and to claim the right of bestowing a benefit for slaves, in order that I may claim it also for sons. The question arises, whether children can ever bestow upon their parents greater benefits than those which they have received from them.

It is granted that many sons become greater and more powerful than their parents, and also that they are better men. If this be true, they may give better gifts to their fathers than they have received from them, seeing that their fortune and their good nature are alike greater than that of their father. "Whatever a father receives from his son," our opponent will urge, "must in any case be less than what the son received from him, because the son owes to his father the very power of giving. Therefore the father can never be surpassed in the bestowal of benefits, because the benefit which surpasses his own is really his." I answer, that some things derive their first origin from others, yet are greater than those others; and a thing may be greater than that from which it took its rise, although without that thing to start from it never could have grown so great. All things greatly outgrow their beginnings. Seeds are the causes of all things, and yet are the smallest part of the things which they produce. Look at the Rhine, or the Euphrates, or any other famous rivers; how small they are, if you only view them at the place from whence they take their rise? they gain all that makes them terrible and renowned as they flow along. Look at the trees which are tallest if you consider their height, and the broadest if you look at their thickness and the spread of their branches; compared with all this, how small a part of them is contained in the slender fibres of the root? Yet take away their roots, and no more groves will arise, nor great mountains be clothed with trees. Temples and cities are supported by their foundations; yet what is built as the foundation of the entire building lies out of sight. So it is in other matters; the subsequent greatness of a thing ever eclipses its origin. I could never have obtained anything without having previously received the boon of existence from my parents; yet it does not follow from this that whatever I obtain is less than that without which I could not obtain it. If my nurse had not fed me when I was a child, I should not have been able to conduct any of those enterprises which I now carry on, both with my head and with my hand, nor should I ever have obtained the fame which is due to my labours both in peace and war; would you on that account argue that the services of a nurse were more valuable than the most important undertakings? Yet is not the nurse as important as the father, since without the benefits which I have received from each of them alike, I should have been alike unable to effect anything? If I owe all that I now can do to my original beginning, I cannot regard my father or my grandfather as being this original beginning; there always will be a spring further back, from which the spring next below is derived. Yet no one will argue that I owe more to unknown and forgotten ancestors than to my father; though really I do owe them more, if I owe it to my ancestors that my father begat me.

XXX

"Whatever I have bestowed upon my father," says my opponent, "however great it may be, yet is less valuable than what my father has bestowed upon me, because if he had not begotten me, it never could have existed at all." By this mode of reasoning, if a man has healed my father when ill, and at the point of death, I shall not be able to bestow anything upon him equivalent to what I have received from him; for had my father not been healed, he could not have begotten me. Yet think whether it be not nearer the truth to regard all that I can do, and all that I have done, as mine, due to my own powers and my own will? Consider what the fact of my birth is in itself; you will see that it is a small matter, the outcome of which is dubious, and that it may lead equally to good or to evil; no doubt it is the first step to everything, but because it is the first, it is not on that account more important than all the others. Suppose that I have saved my father's life, raised him to the highest honours, and made him the chief man in his city, that I have not merely made him illustrious by my own deeds, but have furnished him himself with an opportunity of performing great exploits, which is at once important, easy, and safe, as well as glorious; that I have loaded him with appointments, wealth, and all that attracts men's minds; still, even when I surpass all others, I am inferior to him. Now if you say, "You owe to your father the power of doing all this," I shall answer, "Quite true, if to do all this it is only necessary to be born; but if life is merely an unimportant factor in the art of living well, and if you have bestowed upon me only that which I have in common with wild beasts and the smallest, and some of the foulest of creatures, do not claim for yourself what did not come into being in consequence of the benefits which you bestowed, even though it could not have come into being without them."

XXXI

Suppose, father, that I have saved your life, in return for the life which I received from you: in this case also I have outdone your benefit, because I have given life to one who understands what I have done, and because I understood what I was doing, since I gave you your life not for the sake of, or by the means of my own pleasure; for just as it is less terrible to die before one has time to fear death, so it is a much greater boon to preserve one's life than to receive it. I have given life to one who will at once enjoy it, you gave it to one who knew not if he should ever live; I have given life to one who was in fear of death, your gift of life merely enables me to die; I have given you a life complete, perfect; you begat me without intelligence, a burden upon others. Do you wish to know how far from a benefit it was to give life under such conditions? You should have exposed me as a child, for you did me a wrong in begetting me. What do I gather from this? That the cohabitation of a father and mother is the very least of benefits to their child, unless in addition this beginning of kindnesses be followed up by others, and confirmed by other services. It is not a good thing to live, but to live well. "But," say you, "I do live well." True, but I might have lived ill; so that your part in me is merely this, that I live. If you claim merit to yourself for giving me mere life, bare and helpless, and boast of it as a great boon, reflect that this you claim merit for giving me is a boon which I possess in common with flies and worms. In the next place, if I say no more than that I have applied myself to honourable pursuits, and have guided the course of my life along the path of rectitude, then you have received more from your benefit than you gave; for you gave me to myself ignorant and unlearned, and I have returned to you a son such as you would wish to have begotten.

XXXII

My father supported me. If I repay this kindness, I give him more than I received, because he has the pleasure, not only of being supported, but of being supported by a son, and receives more delight from my filial devotion than from the food itself, whereas the food which he used to give me merely affected my body. What? if any man rises so high as to become famous among nations for his eloquence, his justice, or his military skill, if much of the splendour of his renown is shed upon his father also, and by its clear light dispels the obscurity of his birth, does not such a man confer an inestimable benefit upon his parents? Would anyone have heard of Aristo and Gryllus except through Xenophon and Plato, their sons? Socrates keeps alive the memory of Sophroniscus. It would take long to recount the other men whose names survive for no other reason than that the admirable qualities of their sons have handed them down to posterity. Did the father of Marcus Agrippa, of whom nothing was known, even after Agrippa became famous, confer the greater benefit upon his son, or was that greater which Agrippa conferred upon his father when he gained the glory, unique in the annals of war, of a naval crown, and when he raised so many vast buildings in Rome, which not only surpassed all former grandeur, but have been surpassed by none since? Did Octavius confer a greater benefit upon his son, or the Emperor Augustus upon his father, obscured as he was by the intervention of an adoptive father? What joy would he have experienced, if, after the putting down of the civil war, he had seen his son ruling the state in peace and security? He would not have recognized the good which he had himself bestowed, and would hardly have believed, when he looked back upon himself, that so great a man could have been born in his house. Why should I go on to speak of others who would now be forgotten, if the glory of their sons had not raised them from obscurity, and kept them in the light until this day? In the next place, as we are not considering what son may have given back to his father greater benefits than he received from him, but whether a son can give back greater benefits, even if the examples which I have quoted are not sufficient, and such benefits do not outweigh the benefits bestowed by the parents, if no age has produced an actual example, still it is not in the nature of things impossible. Though no solitary act can outweigh the deserts of a parent, yet many such acts combined by one son may do so.

XXXIII

Scipio, while under seventeen years of age, rode among the enemy in battle, and saved his father's life. Was it not enough, that in order to reach his father he despised so many dangers when they were pressing hardest upon the greatest generals, that he, a novice in his first battle, made his way through so many obstacles, over the bodies of so many veteran soldiers, and showed strength and courage beyond his years? Add to this, that he also defended his father in court, and saved him from a plot of his powerful enemies, that he heaped upon him a second and a third consulship and other posts which were coveted even by consulars, that when his father was poor he bestowed upon him the plunder which he took by military licence, and that he made him rich with the spoils of the enemy, which is the greatest honour of a soldier. If even this did not repay his debt, add to it that he caused him to be constantly employed in the government of provinces and in special commands, add, that after he had destroyed the greatest cities, and became without a rival either in the east or in the west, the acknowledged protector and second founder of the Roman Empire, he bestowed upon one who was already of noble birth the higher title of "the father of Scipio;" can we doubt that the commonplace benefit of his birth was outdone by his exemplary conduct, and by the valour which was at once the glory and the protection of his country? Next, if this be not enough, suppose that a son were to rescue his father from the torture, or to undergo it in his stead. You can suppose the benefits returned by the son as great as you please, whereas the gift he received from his father was of one sort only, was easily performed, and was a pleasure to the giver; that he must necessarily have given the same thing to many others, even to some to whom he knows not that he has given it, that he had a partner in doing so, and that he had in view the law, patriotism, the rewards bestowed upon fathers of families by the state, the maintenance of his house and family: everything rather than him to whom he was giving life. What? supposing that any one were to learn philosophy and teach it to his father, could it be any longer disputed that the son had given him something greater than he had received from him, having returned to his father a happy life, whereas he had received from him merely life?

XXXIV

"But," says our opponent, "whatever you do, whatever you are able to give to your father, is part of his benefit bestowed upon you." So it is the benefit of my teacher that I have become proficient in liberal studies; yet we pass on from those who taught them to us, at any rate from those who taught us the alphabet; and although no one can learn anything without them, yet it does not follow that whatsoever success one subsequently obtains, one is still inferior to those teachers. There is a great difference between the beginning of a thing and its final development; the beginning is not equal to the thing at its greatest, merely upon the ground that, without the beginning, it could never have become so great.

XXXV

It is now time for me to bring forth something, so to speak, from my own mint. So long as there is something better than the benefit which a man bestows, he may be outdone. A father gives life to his son; there is something better than life; therefore a father may be outdone, because there is something better than the benefit which he has bestowed. Still further, he who has given any one his life, if he be more than once saved from peril of death by him, has received a greater benefit than he bestowed. Now, a father has given life to his son: if, therefore, he be more than once saved from peril by his son, he can receive a greater benefit than he gave. A benefit becomes greater to the receiver in proportion to his need of it. Now he who is alive needs life more than he who has not been born, seeing that such a one can have no need at all; consequently a father, if his life is saved by his son, receives a greater benefit than his son received from him by being born. It is said, "The benefits conferred by fathers cannot be outdone by those returned by their sons." Why? "Because the son received life from his father, and had he not received it, he could not have returned any benefits at all." A father has this in common with all those who have given any men their lives; it is impossible that these men could repay the debt if they had not received their life. Then I suppose one cannot overpay one's debt to a physician, for a physician gives life as well as a father; or to a sailor who has saved us when shipwrecked? Yet the benefits bestowed by these and by all the others who give us life in whatever fashion, can be outdone: consequently those of our fathers can be outdone. If any one bestows upon me a benefit which requires the help of benefits from many other persons, whereas I give him what requires no one to help it out, I have given more than I have received; now a father gave to his son a life which, without many accessories to preserve it, would perish; whereas a son, if he gives life to his father, gives him a life which requires no assistance to make it lasting; therefore the father who receives life from his son, receives a greater benefit than he himself bestowed upon his son.

XXXVI

These considerations do not destroy the respect due to parents, or make their children behave worse to them, nay, better; for virtue is naturally ambitious, and wishes to outstrip those who are before it. Filial piety will be all the more eager, if, in returning a father's benefits, it can hope to outdo them; nor will this be against the will or the pleasure of the father, since in many contests it is to our advantage to be outdone. How does this contest become so desirable? How comes it to be such happiness to parents that they should confess themselves outdone by the benefits bestowed by their children? Unless we decide the matter thus, we give children an excuse, and make them less eager to repay their debt, whereas we ought to spur them on, saying, "Noble youths, give your attention to this! You are invited to contend in an honourable strife between parents and children, as to which party has received more than it has given. Your fathers have not necessarily won the day because they are first in the field: only take courage, as befits you, and do not give up the contest; you will conquer if you wish to do so. In this honourable warfare you will have no lack of leaders who will encourage you to perform deeds like their own, and bid you follow in their footsteps upon a path by which victory has often before now been won over parents.

XXXVII

AEneas conquered his father in well doing, for he himself had been but a light and a safe burden for him when he was a child, yet he bore his father, when heavy with age, through the midst of the. enemy's lines and the crash of the city which was falling around him, albeit the devout old man, who bore the sacred images and the household gods in his hands, pressed him with more than his own weight; nevertheless (what cannot filial piety accomplish!) AEneas bore him safe through the blazing city, and placed him in safety, to be worshipped as one of the founders of the Roman Empire. Those Sicilian youths outdid their parents whom they bore away safe, when Aetna, roused to unusual fury, poured fire over cities and fields throughout a great part of the island. It is believed that the fires parted, and that the flames retired on either side, so as to leave a passage for these youths to pass through, who certainly deserved to perform their daring task in safety. Antigonus outdid his father when, after having conquered the enemy in a great battle, he transferred the fruits of it to him, and handed over to him the empire of Cyprus. This is true kingship, to choose not to be a king when you might. Manlius conquered his father, imperious[3] though he was, when, in spite of his having previously been banished for a time by his father on, account of his dulness and stupidity as a boy, he came to an interview which he had demanded with the tribune of the people, who had filed an action against his father. The tribune had granted him the interview, hoping that he would betray his hated father, and believed that he had earned the gratitude of the youth, having, amongst other matters, reproached old Manlius with sending him into exile, treating it as a very serious accusation; but the youth, having caught him alone, drew a sword which he had hidden in his robe, and said, "Unless you swear to give up your suit against my father, I will run you through with this sword. It is in your power to decide how my father shall be freed from his prosecutor." The tribune swore, and kept his oath; he related the reason of his abandonment of his action to an assembly at the Rostra. No other man was ever permitted to put down a tribune with impunity.

---

[3] There is an allusion to the surname of both the father and the son, "Imperiosus" given them on account of their severity.

XXXVIII

There are instances without number of men who have saved their parents from danger, have raised them from the lowest to the highest station, and, taking them from the nameless mass of the lower classes, have given them a name glorious throughout all ages. By no force of words, by no power of genius, can one rightly express how desirable, how admirable, how never to be erased from human memory it is to be able to say, "I obeyed my parents, I gave way to them, I was submissive to their authority whether it was just, or unjust and harsh; the only point in which I resisted them was, not to be conquered by them in benefits." Continue this struggle, I beg of you, and even though weary, yet re-form your ranks. Happy are they who conquer, happy are they who are conquered. What can be more glorious than the youth who can say to himself--it would not be right to say it to another--"I have conquered my father with benefits"? What is more fortunate than that old man who declares everywhere to everyone that he has been conquered in benefits by his son? What, again, is more blissful than to be overcome in such a contest?"

On Benefits – Book IV

On Benefits – Book IV

I

Of all the matters which we have discussed, Aebutius Liberalis, there is none more essential, or which, as Sallust says, ought to be stated with more care than that which is now before us: whether the bestowal of benefits and the return of gratitude for them are desirable objects in themselves. Some men are found who act honourably from commercial motives, and who do not care for unrewarded virtue, though it can confer no glory if it brings any profit. What can be more base than for a man to consider what it costs him to be a good man, when virtue neither allures by gain nor deters by loss, and is so far from bribing any one with hopes and promises, that on the other hand she bids them spend money upon herself, and often consists in voluntary gifts? We must go to her, trampling what is merely useful under our feet: whithersoever she may call us or send us we must go, without any regard for our private fortunes, sometimes without sparing even our own blood, nor must we ever refuse to obey any of her commands. "What shall I gain," says my opponent, "if I do this bravely and gratefully?" You will gain the doing of it--the deed itself is your gain. Nothing beyond this is promised. If any advantage chances to accrue to you, count it as something extra. The reward of honourable dealings lies in themselves. If honour is to be sought after for itself, since a benefit is honourable, it follows that because both of these are of the same nature, their conditions must also be the same. Now it has frequently and satisfactorily been proved, that honour ought to be sought after for itself alone.

II

In this part of the subject we oppose the Epicureans, an effeminate and dreamy sect who philosophize in their own paradise, amongst whom virtue is the handmaid of pleasures, obeys them, is subject to them, and regards them as superior to itself. You say, "there is no pleasure without virtue." But wherefore is it superior to virtue? Do you imagine that the matter in dispute between them is merely one of precedence? Nay, it is virtue itself and its powers which are in question. It cannot be virtue if it can follow; the place of virtue is first, she ought to lead, to command, to stand in the highest rank; you bid her look for a cue to follow. "What," asks our opponent, "does that matter to you? I also declare that happiness is impossible without virtue. Without virtue I disapprove of and condemn the very pleasures which I pursue, and to which I have surrendered myself. The only matter in dispute is this, whether virtue be the cause of the highest good, or whether it be itself the highest good." Do you suppose, though this be the only point in question, that it is a mere matter of precedence? It is a confusion and obvious blindness to prefer the last to the first. I am not angry at virtue being placed below pleasure, but at her being mixed up at all with pleasure, which she despises, whose enemy she is, and from which she separates herself as far as possible, being more at home with labour and sorrow, which are manly troubles, than with your womanish good things.

III

It was necessary to insert this argument, my Liberalis, because it is the part of virtue to bestow those benefits which we are now discussing, and it is most disgraceful to bestow benefits for any other purpose than that they should be free gifts. If we give with the hope of receiving a return, we should give to the richest men, not to the most deserving: whereas we prefer a virtuous poor man to an unmannerly rich one. That is not a benefit, which takes into consideration the fortune of the receiver. Moreover, if our only motive for benefiting others was our own advantage, those who could most easily distribute benefits, such as rich and powerful men, or kings, and persons who do not stand in need of the help of others, ought never to do so at all; the gods would not bestow upon us the countless blessings which they pour upon us unceasingly by night and by day, for their own nature suffices them in all respects, and renders them complete, safe, and beyond the reach of harm; they will, therefore, never bestow a benefit upon any one, if self and self interest be the only cause for the bestowal of benefits. To take thought, not where your benefit will be best bestowed, but where it may be most profitably placed at interest, from whence you will most easily get it back, is not bestowal of benefits, but usury. Now the gods have nothing to do with usury; it follows, therefore, that they cannot be liberal; for if the only reason for giving is the advantage of the giver, since God cannot hope to receive any advantages from us, there is no cause why God should give anything.

IV

I know what answer may be made to this. "True; therefore God does not bestow benefits, but, free from care and unmindful of us, He turns away from our world and either does something else, or else does nothing, which Epicurus thought the greatest possible happiness, and He is not affected either by benefits or by injuries." The man who says this cannot surely hear the voices of worshippers, and of those who all around him are raising their hands to heaven and praying for the success both of their private affairs and those of the state; which certainly would not be the case, all men would not agree in this madness of appealing to deaf and helpless gods, unless we knew that their benefits are sometimes bestowed upon us unasked, sometimes in answer to our prayers, and that they give us both great and seasonable gifts, which shield us from the most terrible dangers. Who is there so poor, so uncared for, born to sorrow by so unkind a fate, as never to have felt the vast generosity of the Gods? Look even at those who complain and are discontented with their lot; you will find that they are not altogether without a share in the bounty of heaven, that there is no one upon whom something has not been shed from that most gracious fount. Is the gift which is bestowed upon all alike, at their birth, not enough? However unequally the blessings of after life may be dealt out to us, did nature give us too little when she gave us herself?

V

It is said, "God does not bestow benefits." Whence, then, comes all that you possess, that you give or refuse to give, that you hoard or steal? whence come these innumerable delights of our eyes, our ears, and our minds? whence the plenty which provides us even with luxury--for it is not our bare necessities alone against which provision is made; we are loved so much as actually to be pampered-- whence so many trees bearing various fruits, so many wholesome herbs, so many different sorts of food distributed throughout the year, so that even the slothful may find sustenance in the chance produce of the earth? Then, too, whence come the living creatures of all kinds, some inhabiting the dry land, others the waters, others alighting from the sky, that every part of nature may pay us some tribute; the rivers which encircle our meadows with most beauteous bends, the others which afford a passage to merchant fleets as they flow on, wide and navigable, some of which in summer time are subject to extraordinary overflowings in order that lands lying parched under a glowing sun may suddenly be watered by the rush of a midsummer torrent?

What of the fountains of medicinal waters? What of the bursting forth of warm waters upon the seashore itself? Shall I

> "Tell of the seas round Italy that flow,
> Which laves her shore above, and which below;
> Or of her lakes, unrivalled Larius, thee,
> Or thee, Benacus, roaring like a sea?"

VI

If any one gave you a few acres, you would say that you had received a benefit; can you deny that the boundless extent of the earth is a benefit? If any one gave you money, and filled your chest, since you think that so important, you would call that a benefit. God has buried countless mines in the earth, has poured out from the earth countless rivers, rolling sands of gold; He has concealed in every place huge masses of silver, copper and iron, and has bestowed upon you the means of discovering them, placing upon the surface of the earth signs of the treasures hidden below; and yet do you say that you have received no benefit? If a house were given you, bright with marble, its roof beautifully painted with colours and gilding, you would call it no small benefit. God has built for you a huge mansion that fears no fire or ruin, in which you see no flimsy veneers, thinner than the very saw with which they are cut, but vast blocks of most precious stone, all composed of those various and different substances whose paltriest fragments you admire so much; he has built a roof which glitters in one fashion by day, and in another by night; and yet do you say that you have received no benefit? When you so greatly prize what you possess, do you act the part of an ungrateful man, and think that there is no one to whom you are indebted for them? Whence comes the breath which you draw? the light by which you arrange and perform all the actions of your life? the blood by whose circulation your vital warmth is maintained? those meats which excite your palate by their delicate flavour after your hunger is appeased? those provocatives which rouse you when wearied with pleasure? that repose in which you are rotting and mouldering? Will you not, if you are grateful, say—

> "'Tis to a god that this repose I owe,
> For him I worship, as a god below.
> Oft on his altar shall my firstlings bleed,
> See, by his bounty here with rustic reed
> I play the airs I love the livelong day,
> The while my oxen round about me stray."

The true God is he who has placed, not a few oxen, but all the herds on their pastures throughout the world; who furnishes food to the flocks wherever they wander; who has ordained the alternation of summer and winter pasturage, and has taught us not merely to play upon a reed, and to reduce to some order a rustic and artless song, but who has invented so many arts and varieties of voice, so many notes to make music, some with our own breath, some with instruments. You cannot call our inventions our own any more than you call our growth our own, or the various bodily functions which correspond to each stage of our lives; at one time comes the loss of childhood's teeth, at another, when our age is advancing and growing into robuster manhood, puberty and the last wisdom-tooth marks the end of our youth. "We have implanted in us the seeds of all ages, of all arts, and God our master brings forth our intellects from obscurity.

VII

"Nature," says my opponent, "gives me all this." Do you not perceive when you say this that you merely speak of God under another name? for what is nature but God and divine reason, which pervades the universe and all its parts? You may address the author of our world by as many different titles as you please; you may rightly call him Jupiter, Best and Greatest, and the Thunderer, or the Stayer, so called, not because, as the historians tell us, he stayed the flight of the Roman army in answer to the prayer of Romulus, but because all things continue in their stay through his goodness. If you were to call this same personage Fate, you would not lie; for since fate is nothing more than a connected chain of causes, he is the first cause of all upon which all the rest depend. You will also be right in applying to him any names that you please which express supernatural strength and power: he may have as many titles as he has attributes.

VIII

Our school regards him as Father Liber, and Hercules, and Mercurius: he is Father Liber because he is the parent of all, who first discovered the power of seed, and our being led by pleasure to plant it; he is Hercules, because his might is unconquered, and when it is wearied after completing its labours, will retire into fire; he is Mercurius, because in him is reasoning, and numbers, and system, and knowledge. Whither-soever you turn yourself you will see him meeting you: nothing is void of him, he himself fills his own work. Therefore, most ungrateful of mortals, it is in vain that you declare yourself indebted, not to God, but to nature, because there can be no God without nature, nor any nature without God; they are both the same thing, differing only in their functions. If you were to say that you owe to Annaeus or to Lucius what you received from Seneca, you would not change your creditor, but only his name, because he remains the same man whether you use his first, second, or third name. So whether you speak of nature, fate, or fortune, these are all names of the same God, using his power in different ways. So likewise justice, honesty, discretion, courage, frugality, are all the good qualities of one and the same mind; if you are pleased with any one of these, you are pleased with that mind.

IX

However, not to drift aside into a distinct controversy, God bestows upon us very many and very great benefits without hope of receiving any return; since he does not require any offering from us, and we are not capable of bestowing anything upon him: wherefore, a benefit is desirable in itself. In it the advantage of the receiver is all that is taken into consideration: we study this without regarding our own interests. "Yet," argues our opponent, "you say that we ought to choose with care the persons upon whom we bestow benefits, because neither do husbandmen sow seed in the sand: now if this be true, we follow our own interest in bestowing benefits, just as much as in ploughing and sowing: for sowing is not desirable in itself. Besides this you inquire where and how you ought to bestow a benefit, which would not need to be done if the bestowal of a benefit was desirable in itself: because in whatever place and whatever manner it might be bestowed, it still would be a benefit." We seek to do honourable acts, solely because they are honourable; yet even though we need think of nothing else, we consider to whom we shall do them, and when, and how; for in these points the act has its being. In like manner, when I choose upon whom I shall bestow a benefit, and when I aim at making it a benefit; because if it were bestowed upon a base person, it could neither be a benefit nor an honourable action.

X

To restore what has been entrusted to one is desirable in itself; yet I shall not always restore it, nor shall I do so in any place or at any time you please. Sometimes it makes no difference whether I deny that I have received it, or return it openly. I shall consider the interests of the person to whom I am to return it, and shall deny that I have received a deposit, which would injure him if returned. I shall act in the same manner in bestowing a benefit: I shall consider when to give it, to whom, in what manner, and on what grounds. Nothing ought to be done without a reason: a benefit is not truly so, if it be bestowed without a reason, since reason accompanies all honorable action. How often do we hear men reproaching themselves for some thoughtless gift, and saying, "I had rather have thrown it away than have given it to him!" What is thoughtlessly given away is lost in the most discreditable manner, and it is much worse to have bestowed a benefit badly than to have received no return for it; that we receive no return is the fault of another; that we did not choose upon whom we should bestow it, is our own. In choosing a fit person, I shall not, as you expect, pay the least attention to whether I am likely to get any return from him, for I choose one who will be grateful, not one who will return my goodness, and it often happens that the man who makes no return is grateful, while he who returns a benefit is ungrateful for it. I value men by their hearts alone, and, therefore, I shall pass over a rich man if he be unworthy, and give to a good man though he be poor; for he will be grateful however destitute he may be, since whatever he may lose, his heart will still be left him.

XI

I do not fish for gain, for pleasure, or for credit, by bestowing benefits: satisfied in doing so with pleasing one man alone, I shall give in order to do my duty. Duty, however, leaves one some choice; do you ask me, how I am to choose? I shall choose an honest, plain, man, with a good memory, and grateful for kindness; one who keeps his hands off other men's goods, yet does not greedily hold to his own, and who is kind to others; when I have chosen such a man, I shall have acted to my mind, although fortune may have bestowed upon him no means of returning my kindness. If my own advantage and mean calculation made me liberal, if I did no one any service except in order that he might in turn do a service to me, I should never bestow a benefit upon one who was setting out for distant and foreign countries, never to return; I should not bestow a benefit upon one who was so ill as to be past hope of recovery, nor should I do so when I myself was failing, because I should not live long enough to receive any return. Yet, that you may know that to do good is desirable in itself, we afford help to strangers who put into our harbour only to leave it straightway; we give a ship and fit it out for a shipwrecked stranger to sail back in to his own country. He leaves us hardly knowing who it was who saved him, and, as he will never return to our presence, he hands over his debt of gratitude to the gods, and beseeches them to fulfil it for him: in the meanwhile we rejoice in the barren knowledge that we have done a good action. What? when we stand upon the extreme verge of life, and make our wills, do we not assign to others benefits from which we ourselves shall receive no advantage? How much time we waste, how long we consider in secret how much property we are to leave, and to whom! What then? does it make any difference to us to whom we leave our property, seeing that we cannot expect any return from any one? Yet we never give anything with more care, we never take such pains in deciding upon our verdict, as when, without any views of personal advantage, we think only of what is honourable, for we are bad judges of our duty as long as our view of it is distorted by hope and fear, and that most indolent of vices, pleasure: but when death has shut off all these, and brought us as incorrupt judges to pronounce sentence, we seek for the most worthy men to leave our property to, and we never take more scrupulous care than in deciding what is to be done with what does not concern us. Yet, by Hercules, then there steals over us a great satisfaction as we think, "I shall make this man richer, and by bestowing wealth upon that man I shall add lustre to his high position." Indeed, if we never give without expecting some return, we must all die without making our wills.

XII

It may be said, "You define a benefit as a loan which cannot be repaid: now a loan is not a desirable thing in itself." When we speak of a loan, we make use of a figure, or comparison, just as we speak of law as; the standard of right and wrong, although a standard is not a thing to be desired for its own sake. I have adopted this phrase in order to illustrate my subject: when I speak of a loan, I must be understood to mean something resembling a loan. Do you wish to know how it differs from one? I add the words "which cannot be repaid," whereas every loan both can and ought to be repaid. It is so far from being right to bestow a benefit for one's own advantage, that often, as I have explained, it is one's duty to bestow it when it involves one's own loss and risk: for instance, if I assist a man when beset by robbers, so that he gets away from them safely, or help some victim of power, and bring upon myself the party spite of a body of influential men, very, probably incurring myself the same disgrace from which I saved him, although I might have taken the other side, and looked on with safety at struggles with which I have nothing to do: if I were to give bail for one who has been condemned, and when my friend's goods were advertised for sale I were to give a bond to the effect that I would make restitution to the creditors, if, in order to save a proscribed person I myself run the risk of being proscribed. No one, when about to buy a villa at Tusculum or Tibur, for a summer retreat, because of the health of the locality, considers how many years' purchase he gives for it; this must be looked to by the man who makes a profit by it. The same is true with benefits; when you ask what return I get for them, I answer, the consciousness of a good action. "What return does one get for benefits?" Pray tell me what return one gets for righteousness, innocence, magnanimity, chastity, temperance? If you wish for anything beyond these virtues, you do not wish for the virtues themselves. For what does the order of the universe bring round the seasons? for what does the sun make the day now longer and now shorter? all these things are benefits, for they take place for our good. As it is the duty of the universe to maintain the round of the seasons, as it is the duty of the sun to vary the points of his rising and setting, and to do all these things by which we profit, without any reward, so is it the duty of man, amongst other things, to bestow benefits. Wherefore then does he give? He gives for fear that he should not give, lest he might lose an opportunity of doing a good action.

XIII

You Epicureans take pleasure in making a study of dull torpidity, in seeking for a repose which differs little from sound sleep, in lurking beneath the thickest shade, in amusing with the feeblest possible trains of thought that sluggish condition of your languid minds which you term tranquil contemplation, and in stuffing with food and drink, in the recesses of your gardens, your bodies which are pallid with want of exercise; we Stoics, on the other hand, take pleasure in bestowing benefits, even though they cost us labour, provided that they lighten the labours of others; though they lead us into danger, provided that they save others, though they straiten our means, if they alleviate the poverty and distresses of others. What difference does it make to me whether I receive benefits or not? even if I receive them, it is still my duty to bestow them. A benefit has in view the advantage of him upon whom we bestow it, not our own; otherwise we merely bestow it upon ourselves. Many things, therefore, which are of the greatest possible use to others lose all claim to gratitude by being paid for. Merchants are of use to cities, physicians to invalids, dealers to slaves; yet all these have no claim to the gratitude of those whom they benefit, because they seek their own advantage through that of others. That which is bestowed with a view to profit is not a benefit. "I will give this in order that I may get a return for it" is the language of a broker.

XIV

I should not call a woman modest, if she rebuffed her lover in order to increase his passion, or because she feared the law or her husband; as Ovid says:

"She that denies, because she does not dare
To yield, in spirit grants her lover's prayer."

Indeed, the woman who owes her chastity, not to her own virtue, but to fear, may rightly be classed as a sinner. In the same manner, he who merely gave in order that he might receive, cannot be said to have given. Pray, do we bestow benefits upon animals when we feed them for our use or for our table? do we bestow benefits upon trees when we tend them that they may not suffer from drought or from hardness of ground? No one is moved by righteousness and goodness of heart to cultivate an estate, or to do any act in which the reward is something apart from the act itself; but he is moved to bestow benefits, not by low and grasping motives, but by a kind and generous mind, which even after it has given is willing to give again, to renew its former bounties by fresh ones, which thinks only of how much good it can do the man to whom it gives; whereas to do any one a service because it is our interest to do so is a mean action, which deserves no praise, no credit. What grandeur is there in loving oneself, sparing oneself, gaining profit for oneself? The true love of giving calls us away from all this, forcibly leads us to put up with loss, and foregoes its own interest, deriving its greatest pleasure from the mere act of doing good.

XV

Can we doubt that the converse of a benefit is an injury? As the infliction of injuries is a thing to be avoided, so is the bestowal of benefits to be desired for its own sake. In the former, the disgrace of crime outweighs all the advantages which incite us to commit it; while we are urged to the latter course by the appearance of honour, in itself a powerful incentive to action, which attends it.

I should not lie if I were to affirm that every one takes pleasure in the benefits which he has bestowed, that everyone loves best to see the man whom he has most largely benefited. Who does not thinks that to have bestowed one benefit is a reason for bestowing a second? and would this be so, if the act of giving did not itself give us pleasure? How often you may hear a man say, "I cannot bear to desert one whose life I have preserved, whom I have saved from danger. True, he asks me to plead his cause against men of great influence. I do not wish to do so, yet what am I to do? I have already helped him once, nay twice." Do you not perceive how very powerful this instinct must be, if it leads us to bestow benefits first because it is right to do so, and afterwards because we have already bestowed somewhat? Though at the outset a man may have had no claim upon us, we yet continue to give to him because we have already given to him. So untrue is it that we are urged to bestow benefits by our own interest, that even when our benefits prove failures we continue to nurse them and encourage them out of sheer love of benefiting, which has a natural weakness even for what has been ill-bestowed, like that which we feel for our vicious children.

XVI

These same adversaries of ours admit that they are grateful, yet not because it is honourable, but because it is profitable to be so. This can be proved to be untrue all the more easily, because it can be established by the same arguments by which we have established that to bestow a benefit is desirable for its own sake. All our arguments start from this settled point, that honour is pursued for no reason except because it is honour. Now, who will venture to raise the question whether it be honourable to be grateful? who does not loathe the ungrateful man, useless as he is even to himself? How do you feel when any one is spoken of as being ungrateful for great benefits conferred upon him by a friend? Is it as though he had done something base, or had merely neglected to do something useful and likely to be profitable to himself? I imagine that you think him a bad man, and one who deserves punishment, not one who needs a guardian; and this would not be the case, unless gratitude were desirable in itself and honourable. Other qualities, it may be, manifest their importance less clearly, and require an explanation to prove whether they be honourable or no; this is openly proved to be so in the sight of all, and is too beautiful for anything to obscure or dim its glory. What is more praiseworthy, upon what are all men more universally agreed, than to return gratitude for good offices?

XVII

Pray tell me, what is it that urges us to do so? Is it profit? Why, unless a man despises profit, he is not grateful. Is it ambition? why, what is there to boast of in having paid what you owe? Is it fear? The ungrateful man feels none, for against this one crime we have provided no law, as though nature had taken sufficient precautions against it. Just as there is no law which bids parents love and indulge their children, seeing that it is superfluous to force us into the path which we naturally take, just as no one needs to be urged to love himself, since self-love begins to act upon him as soon as he is born, so there is no law bidding us to seek that which is honourable in itself; for such things please us by their very nature, and so attractive is virtue that the disposition even of bad men leads them to approve of good rather than of evil. Who is there who does not wish to appear beneficent, who does not even when steeped in crime and wrong-doing strive after the appearance of goodness, does not put some show of justice upon even his most intemperate acts, and endeavour to seem to have conferred a benefit even upon those whom he has injured? Consequently, men allow themselves to be thanked by those whom they have ruined, and pretend to be good and generous, because they cannot prove themselves so; and this they never would do were it not that a love of honour for its own sake forces them to seek a reputation quite at variance with their real character, and to conceal their baseness, a quality whose fruits we covet, though we regard it itself with dislike and shame. No one has ever so far rebelled against the laws of nature and put off human feeling as to act basely for mere amusement. Ask any of those who live by robbery whether he would not rather obtain what he steals and plunders by honest means; the man whose trade is highway robbery and the murder of travellers would rather find his booty than take it by force; you will find no one who would not prefer to enjoy the fruits of wickedness without acting wickedly. Nature bestows upon us all this immense advantage, that the light of virtue shines into the minds of all alike; even those who do not follow her, behold her.

XVIII

A proof that gratitude is desirable for itself lies in the fact that ingratitude is to be avoided for itself, because no vice more powerfully rends asunder and destroys the union of the human race. To what do we trust for safety, if not in mutual good offices one to another? It is by the interchange of benefits alone that we gain some measure of protection for our lives, and of safety against sudden disasters. Taken singly, what should we be? a prey and quarry for wild beasts, a luscious and easy banquet; for while all other animals have sufficient strength to protect themselves, and those which are born to a wandering solitary life are armed, man is covered by a soft skin, has no powerful teeth or claws with which to terrify other creatures, but weak and naked by himself is made strong by union.

God has bestowed upon him two gifts, reason and union, which raise him from weakness to the highest power; and so he, who if taken alone would be inferior to every other creature, possesses supreme dominion. Union has given him sovereignty over all animals; union has enabled a being born upon the earth to assume power over a foreign element, and bids him be lord of the sea also; it is union which has checked the inroads of disease, provided supports for our old age, and given us relief from pain; it is union which makes us strong, and to which we look for protection against the caprices of fortune. Take away union, and you will rend asunder the association by which the human race preserves its existence; yet you will take it away if you succeed in proving that ingratitude is not to be avoided for itself, but because something is to be feared for it; for how many are there who can with safety be ungrateful? In fine, I call every man ungrateful who is merely made grateful by fear.

XIX

No sane man fears the gods; for it is madness to fear what is beneficial, and no man loves those whom he fears. You, Epicurus, ended by making God unarmed; you stripped him of all weapons, of all power, and, lest anyone should fear him, you banished him out of the world. There is no reason why you should fear this being, cut off as he is, and separated from the sight and touch of mortals by a vast and impassable wall; he has no power either of rewarding or of injuring us; he dwells alone half-way between our heaven and that of another world, without the society either of animals, of men, or of matter, avoiding the crash of worlds as they fall in ruins above and around him, but neither hearing our prayers nor interested in us. Yet you wish to seem to worship this being just as a father, with a mind, I suppose, full of gratitude; or, if you do not wish to seem grateful, why should you worship him, since you have received no benefit from him, but have been put together entirely at random and by chance by those atoms and mites of yours? "I worship him," you answer, "because of his glorious majesty and his unique nature." Granting that you do this, you clearly do it without the attraction of any reward, or any hope; there is therefore something which is desirable for itself, whose own worth attracts you, that is, honour. Now what is more honourable than gratitude? the means of practising this virtue are as extensive as life itself.

XX

"Yet," argues he, "there is also a certain amount of profit inherent in this virtue." In what virtue is there not? But that which we speak of as desirable for itself is such, that although it may possess some attendant advantages, yet it would be desirable even if stripped of all these. It is profitable to be grateful; yet I will be grateful even though it harm me. What is the aim of the grateful man? is it that his gratitude may win for him more friends and more benefits? What then? If a man is likely to meet with affronts by showing his gratitude, if he knows that far from gaining anything by it, he must lose much even of what he has already acquired, will he not cheerfully act to his own disadvantage? That man is ungrateful who, in returning a kindness, looks forward to a second gift--who hopes while he repays. I call him ungrateful who sits at the bedside of a sick man because he is about to make a will, when he is at leisure to think of inheritances and legacies. Though he may do everything which a good and dutiful friend ought to do, yet, if any hope of gain be floating in his mind, he is a mere legacy-hunter, and is angling for an inheritance. Like the birds which feed upon carcases, which come close to animals weakened by disease, and watch till they fall, so these men are attracted by death and hover around a corpse.

XXI

A grateful mind is attracted only by a sense of the beauty of its purpose. Do you wish to know this to be so, and that it is not bribed by ideas of profit? There are two classes of grateful men: a man is called grateful who has made some return for what he received; this man may very possibly display himself in this character, he has something to boast of, to refer to. We also call a man grateful who receives a benefit with goodwill, and owes it to his benefactor with goodwill; yet this man's gratitude lies concealed within his own mind. What profit can accrue to him from this latent feeling? yet this man, even though he is not able to do anything more than this, is grateful; he loves his benefactor, he feels his debt to him, he longs to repay his kindness; whatever else you may find wanting, there is nothing wanting in the man. He is like a workman who has not the tools necessary for the practice of his craft, or like a trained singer whose voice cannot be heard through the noise of those who interrupt him. I wish to repay a kindness: after this there still remains something for me to do, not in order that I may become grateful, but that I may discharge my debt; for, in many cases, he who returns a kindness is ungrateful for it, and he who does not return it is grateful. Like all other virtues, the whole value of gratitude lies in the spirit in which it is done; so, if this man's purpose be loyal, any shortcomings on his part are due not to himself, but to fortune. A man who is silent may, nevertheless, be eloquent; his hands may be folded or even bound, and he may yet be strong; just as a pilot is a pilot even when upon dry land, because his knowledge is complete, and there is nothing wanting to it, though there may be obstacles which prevent his making use of it. In the same way, a man is grateful who only wishes to be so, and who has no one but himself who can bear witness to his frame of mind. I will go even further than this: a man sometimes is grateful when he appears to be ungrateful, when ill-judging report has declared him to be so. Such a man can look to nothing but his own conscience, which can please him even when overwhelmed by calumny, which contradicts the mob and common rumour, relies only upon itself, and though it beholds a vast crowd of the other way of thinking opposed to it, does not count heads, but wins by its own vote alone. Should it see its own good faith meet with the punishment due to treachery, it will not descend from its pedestal, and will remain superior to its punishment. "I have," it says, "what I wished, what I strove for. I do not regret it, nor shall I do so; nor shall fortune, however unjust she may be, ever hear me say, 'What did I want? What now is the use of having meant well?'" A good conscience is of value on the rack, or in the fire; though fire be applied to each of our limbs, gradually encircle our living bodies, and burst our heart, yet if our heart be filled with a good conscience, it will rejoice in the fire which will make its good faith shine before the world.

XXII

Now let that question also which has been already stated be again brought forward; Why is it that we should wish to be grateful when we are dying, that we should carefully weigh the various services rendered us by different individuals, and carefully review our whole life, that we may not seem to have forgotten any kindness? Nothing then remains for us to hope for; yet when on the very threshold, we wish to depart from human life as full of gratitude as possible. There is in truth an immense reward for this thing merely in doing it, and what is honourable has great power to attract men's minds, which are overwhelmed by its beauty and carried off their balance, enchanted by its brilliancy and splendour. "Yet," argues our adversary, "from it many advantages take their rise, and good men obtain a safer life and love, and the good opinion of the better class, while their days are spent in greater security when accompanied by innocence and gratitude."

Indeed, nature would have been most unjust had she rendered this great blessing miserable, uncertain, and fruitless. But consider this point, whether you would make your way to that virtue, to which it is generally safe and easy to attain, even though the path lay over rocks and precipices, and were beset with fierce beasts and venomous serpents. A virtue is none the less to be desired for its own sake, because it has some adventitious profit connected with it: indeed, in most cases the noblest virtues are accompanied by many extraneous advantages, but it is the virtues that lead the way, and these merely follow in their train.

XXIII

Can we doubt that the climate of this abode of the human race is regulated by the motion of the sun and moon in their orbits? that our bodies are sustained, the hard earth loosened, excessive moisture reduced, and the surly bonds of winter broken by the heat of the one, and that crops are brought to ripeness by the effectual all-pervading warmth of the other? that the fertility of the human race corresponds to the courses of the moon? that the sun by its revolution marks out the year, and that the moon, moving in a smaller orbit, marks out the months? Yet, setting aside all this, would not the sun be a sight worthy to be contemplated and worshipped, if he did no more than rise and set? would not the moon be worth looking at, even if it passed uselessly through the heavens? Whose attention is not arrested by the universe itself, when by night it pours forth its fires and glitters with innumerable stars? Who, while he admires them, thinks of their being of use to him? Look at that great company gliding over our heads, how they conceal their swift motion under the semblance of a fixed and immovable work. How much takes place in that night which you make use of merely to mark and count your days! What a mass of events is being prepared in that silence! What a chain of destiny their unerring path is forming! Those which you imagine to be merely strewn about for ornament are really one and all at work. Nor is there any ground for your belief that only seven stars revolve, and that the rest remain still: we understand the orbits of a few, but countless divinities, further removed from our sight, come and go; while the greater part of those whom our sight reaches move in a mysterious manner and by an unknown path.

XXIV

What then? would you not be captivated by the sight of such a stupendous work, even though it did not cover you, protect you, cherish you, bring you into existence and penetrate you with its spirit? Though these heavenly bodies are of the very first importance to us, and are, indeed, essential to our life, yet we can think of nothing but their glorious majesty, and similarly all virtue, especially that of gratitude, though it confers great advantages upon us, does not wish to be loved for that reason; it has something more in it than this, and he who merely reckons it among useful things does not perfectly comprehend it. A man, you say, is grateful because it is to his advantage to be so. If this be the case, then his advantage will be the measure of his gratitude. Virtue will not admit a covetous lover; men must approach her with open purse. The ungrateful man thinks, "I did wish to be grateful, but I fear the expense and danger and insults to which I should expose myself: I will rather consult my own interest." Men cannot be rendered grateful and ungrateful by the same line of reasoning: their actions are as distinct as their purposes. The one is ungrateful, although it is wrong, because it is his interest; the other is grateful, although it is not his interest, because it is right.

XXV

It is our aim to live in harmony with the scheme of the universe, and to follow the example of the gods. Yet in all their acts the gods have no object in view other than the act itself, unless you suppose that they obtain a reward for their work in the smoke of burnt sacrifices and the scent of incense. See what great things they do every day, how much they divide amongst us, with how great crops they fill the earth, how they move the seas with convenient winds to carry us to all shores, how by the fall of sudden showers they soften the ground, renew the dried-up springs of fountains, and call them into new life by unseen supplies of water. All this they do without reward, without any advantage accruing to themselves. Let our line of conduct, if it would not depart from its model, preserve this direction, and let us not act honourably because we are hired to do so. We ought to feel ashamed that any benefit should have a price: we pay nothing for the gods.

XXVI

"If," our adversary may say, "you wish to imitate the gods, then bestow benefits upon the ungrateful as well as the grateful; for the sun rises upon the wicked as well as the good, the seas are open even to pirates." By this question he really asks whether a good man would bestow a benefit upon an ungrateful person, knowing him to be ungrateful. Allow me here to introduce a short explanation, that we may not be taken in by a deceitful question. Understand that according to the system of the Stoics there are two classes of ungrateful persons. One man is ungrateful because he is a fool; a fool is a bad man; a man who is bad possesses every vice: therefore he is ungrateful. In the same way we speak of all bad men as dissolute, avaricious, luxurious, and spiteful, not because each man has all these vices in any great or remarkable degree, but because he might have them; they are in him, even though they be not seen. The second form of ungrateful person is he who is commonly meant by the term, one who is inclined by nature to this vice. In the case of him who has the vice of ingratitude just as he has every other, a wise man will bestow a benefit, because if he sets aside all such men there will be no one left for him to bestow it on. As for the ungrateful man who habitually misapplies benefits and acts so by choice, he will no more bestow a benefit upon him than he would lend money to a spendthrift, or place a deposit in the hands of one who had already often refused to many persons to give up the property with which they had entrusted him.

XXVII

We call some men timid because they are fools: in this they are like the bad men who are steeped in all vices without distinction. Strictly speaking, we call those persons timid who are alarmed even at unmeaning noises. A fool possesses all vices, but he is not equally inclined by nature to all; one is prone to avarice, another to luxury, and another to insolence. Those persons, therefore, are mistaken, who ask the Stoics, "What do you say, then? is Achilles timid? Aristides, who received a name for justice, is he unjust? Fabius, who 'by delays retrieved the day,' is he rash? Does Decius fear death? Is Mucius a traitor? Camillus a betrayer?" We do not mean that all vices are inherent in all men in the same way in which some especial ones are noticeable in certain men, but we declare that the bad man and the fool possess all vices; we do not even acquit them of fear when they are rash, or of avarice when they are extravagant. Just as a man has all his senses, yet all men have not on that account as keen a sight as Lynceus, so a man that is a fool has not all vices in so active and vigorous a form as some persons have spine of them, yet he has them all. All vices exist in all of them, yet all are not prominent in each individual. One man is naturally prone to avarice, another is the slave of wine, a third of lust; or, if not yet enslaved by these passions, he is so fashioned by nature that this is the direction in which his character would probably lead him. Therefore, to return to my original proposition, every bad man is ungrateful, because he has the seeds of every villainy in him; but he alone is rightly so called who is naturally inclined to this vice. Upon such a person as this, therefore, I shall not bestow a benefit. One who betrothed his daughter to an ill-tempered man from whom many women had sought a divorce, would be held to have neglected her interests; a man would be thought a bad father if he entrusted the care of his patrimony to one who had lost his own family estate, and it would be the act of a madman to make a will naming as the guardian of one's son a man who had already defrauded other wards. So will that man be said to bestow benefits as badly as possible, who chooses ungrateful persons, in whose hands they will perish.

XXVIII

"The gods," it may be said, "bestow much, even upon the ungrateful." But what they bestow they had prepared for the good, and the bad have their share as well, because they cannot be separated. It is better to benefit the bad as well, for the sake of benefiting the good, than to stint the good for fear of benefiting the bad. Therefore the gods have created all that you speak of, the day, the sun, the alternations of winter and summer, the transitions through spring and autumn from one extreme to the other, showers, drinking fountains, and regularly blowing winds for the use of all alike; they could not except individuals from the enjoyment of them. A king bestows honours upon those who deserve them, but he gives largesse to the undeserving as well. The thief, the bearer of false witness, and the adulterer, alike receive the public grant of corn, and all are placed on the register without any examination as to character; good and bad men share alike in all the other privileges which a man receives, because he is a citizen, not because he is a good man. God likewise has bestowed certain gifts upon the entire human race, from which no one is shut out. Indeed, it could not be arranged that the wind which was fair for good men should be foul for bad ones, while it is for the good of all men that the seas should be open for traffic and the kingdom of mankind be enlarged; nor could any law be appointed for the showers, so that they should not fall upon the fields of wicked and evil men. Some things are given to all alike: cities are founded for good and bad men alike; works of genius reach, by publication, even unworthy men; medicine points out the means of health even to the wicked; no one has checked the making up of wholesome remedies for fear that the undeserving should be healed. You must seek for examination and preference of individuals in such things as are bestowed separately upon those who are thought to deserve them; not in these, which admit the mob to share them without distinction. There is a great difference between not shutting a man out and choosing him. Even a thief receives justice; even murderers enjoy the blessings of peace; even those who have plundered others can recover their own property; assassins and private bravoes are defended against the common enemy by the city wall; the laws protect even those who have sinned most deeply against them. There are some things which no man could obtain unless they were given to all; you need not, therefore, cavil about those matters in which all mankind is invited to share. As for things which men receive or not at my discretion, I shall not bestow them upon one whom I know to be ungrateful.

XXIX

"Shall we, then," argues he, "not give our advice to an ungrateful man when he is at a loss, or refuse him a drink of water when he is thirsty, or not show him the path when he has lost his way? or would you do him these services and yet not give him anything?" Here I will draw a distinction, or at any rate endeavour to do so. A benefit is a useful service, yet all useful service is not a benefit; for some are so trifling as not to claim the title of benefits. To produce a benefit two conditions must concur. First, the importance of the thing given; for some things fall short of the dignity of a benefit. Who ever called a hunch of bread a benefit, or a farthing dole tossed to a beggar, or the means of lighting a fire? yet sometimes these are of more value than the most costly benefits; still their cheapness detracts from their value even when, by the exigency of time, they are rendered essential. The next condition, which is the most important of all, must necessarily be present, namely, that I should confer the benefit for the sake of him whom I wish to receive it, that I should judge him worthy of it, bestow it of my own free will, and receive pleasure from my own gift, none of which conditions are present in the cases of which we have just now spoken; for we do not bestow such things as those upon these who are worthy of them, but we give them carelessly, as trifles, and do not give them so much to a man as to humanity.

XXX

I shall not deny that sometimes I would give even to the unworthy, out of respect for others; as, for instance, in competition for public offices, some of the basest of men are preferred on account of their noble birth, to industrious men of no family, and that for good reasons; for the memory of great virtues is sacred, and more men will take pleasure in being good, if the respect felt for good men does not cease with their lives. What made Cicero's son a consul, except his father? What lately brought Cinna[1] out of the camp of the enemy and raised him to the consulate? What made Sextus Pompeius and the other Pompeii consuls, unless it was the greatness of one man, who once was raised so high that, by his very fall, he sufficiently exalted all his relatives. What lately made Fabius Persicus a member of more than one college of priests, though even profligates avoided his kiss? Was it not Verrucosus, and Allobrogicus, and the three hundred who to serve their country blocked the invader's path with the force of a single family? It is our duty to respect the virtuous, not only when present with us, but also when removed from our sight: as they have made it their study not to bestow their benefits upon one age alone, but to leave them existing after they themselves have passed away, so let us not confine our gratitude to a single age. If a man has begotten great men, he deserves to receive benefits, whatever he himself may be: he has given us worthy men. If a man descends from glorious ancestors, whatever he himself may be, let him find refuge under the shadow of his ancestry. As mean places are lighted up by the rays of the sun, so let the degenerate shine in the light of their forefathers.

---

[1] See Seneca on "Clemency," book i., ch. ix.

XXXI

In this place, my Liberalis, I wish to speak in defence of the gods. We sometimes say, "What could Providence mean by placing an Arrhidaeus upon the throne?" Do you suppose that the crown was given to Arrhidaeus? nay, it was given to his father and his brother. Why did Heaven bestow the empire of the world upon Caius Caesar, the most bloodthirsty of mankind, who was wont to order blood to be shed in his presence as freely as if he wished to drink of it? Why, do you suppose that it was given to him? It was given to his father, Germanicus, to his grandfather, his great grandfather, and to others before them, no less illustrious men, though they lived as private citizens on a footing of equality with others. Why, when you yourself were making Mamercus Scaurus consul, were you ignorant of his vices? did he himself conceal them? did he wish to appear decent?

Did you admit a man who was so openly filthy to the fasces and the tribunal? Yes, it was because you were thinking of the great old Scaurus, the chief of the Senate, and were unwilling that his descendant should be despised.

XXXII

It is probable that the gods act in the same manner, that they show greater indulgence to some for the sake of their parents and their ancestry, and to others for the sake of their children and grandchildren, and a long line of descendants beyond them; for they know the whole course of their works, and have constant access to the knowledge of all that shall hereafter pass through their hands. These things come upon us from the unknown future, and the gods have foreseen and are familiar with the events by which we are startled. "Let these men," says Providence, "be kings, because their ancestors were good kings, because they regarded righteousness and temperance as the highest rule of life, because they did not devote the state to themselves, but devoted themselves to the state. Let these others reign, because some one of their ancestors before them was a good man, who bore a soul superior to fortune, who preferred to be conquered rather than to conquer in civil strife, because it was more to the advantage of the state.[2] It was not possible to make a sufficient return to him for this during so long a time; let this other, therefore, out of regard for him, be chief of the people, not because he knows how, or is capable, but because the other has earned it for him. This man is misshapen, loathsome to look upon, and will disgrace the insignia of his office. Men will presently blame me, calling me blind and reckless, not knowing upon whom I am conferring what ought to be given to the greatest and noblest of men; but I know that, in giving this dignity to one man, I am paying an old debt to another. How should the men of to-day know that ancient hero, who so resolutely avoided the glory which pressed upon him, who went into danger with the same look which other men wear when they have escaped from danger, who never regarded his own interest as apart from that of the commonwealth?" "Where," you ask, "or who is he? whence does he come?" "You know him not; it lies with me to balance the debit and credit account in such cases as these; I know how much I owe to each man; I repay some after a long interval, others beforehand, according as my opportunities and the exigencies of my social system permit." I shall, therefore, sometimes bestow somewhat upon an ungrateful man, though not for his own sake.

---

[2] Gertz, "Stud. Crit," p. 159, note.

XXXIII

"What," argues he, "if you do not know whether your man be ungrateful or grateful--will you wait until you know, or will you not lose the opportunity of bestowing a benefit? To wait is a long business--for, as Plato says, it is hard to form an opinion about the human mind,--not to wait, is rash." To this objector we shall answer, that we never should wait for absolute knowledge of the whole case, since the discovery of truth is an arduous task, but should proceed in the direction in which truth appeared to direct us. All our actions proceed in this direction: it is thus that we sow seed, that we sail upon the sea, that we serve in the army, marry, and bring up children. The result of all these actions is uncertain, so we take that course from which we believe that good results may be hoped for. Who can guarantee a harvest to the sower, a harbour to the sailor, victory to the soldier, a modest wife to the husband, dutiful children to the father? We proceed in the way in which reason, not absolute truth, directs us. Wait, do nothing that will not turn out well, form no opinion until you have searched but the truth, and your life will pass in absolute in action. Since it is only the appearance of truth, not truth itself, which leads me hither or thither, I shall confer benefits upon the man who apparently will be grateful.

XXXIV

"Many circumstances," argues he, "may arise which may enable a bad man to steal into the place of a good one, or may cause a good man to be disliked as though he were a bad one; for appearances, to which we trust, are deceptive." Who denies it? Yet I can find nothing else by which to guide my opinion. I must follow these tracks in my search after truth, for I have none more trustworthy than these; I will take pains to weigh the value of these with all possible care, and will not hastily give my assent to them. For instance, in a battle, it may happen that my hand may be deceived by some mistake into turning my weapon against my comrade, and sparing my enemy as though he were on my side; but this will not often take place, and will not take place through any fault of mine, for my object is to strike the enemy, and defend my countryman. If I know a man to be ungrateful, I shall not bestow a benefit upon him. But the man has passed himself off as a good man by some trick, and has imposed upon me. Well, this is not at all the fault of the giver, who gave under the impression that his friend was grateful. "Suppose," asks he, "that you were to promise to bestow a benefit, and afterwards were to learn that your man was ungrateful, would you bestow it or not? If you do, you do wrong knowingly, for you give to one to whom you ought not; if you refuse, you do wrong likewise, for you do not give to him to whom you promised to give. This case upsets your consistency, and that proud assurance of yours that the wise man never regrets his actions, or amends what he has done, or alters his plans." The wise man never changes his plans while the conditions under which he formed them remain the same; therefore, he never feels regret, because at the time nothing better than what he did could have been done, nor could any better decision have been arrived at than that which was made; yet he begins everything with the saving clause, "If nothing shall occur to the contrary." This is the reason why we say that all goes well with him, and that nothing happens contrary to his expectation, because he bears in mind the possibility of something happening to prevent the realization of his projects. It is an imprudent confidence to trust that fortune will be on our side. The wise man considers both sides: he knows how great is the power of errors, how uncertain human affairs are, how many obstacles there are to the success of plans. Without committing himself, he awaits the doubtful and capricious issue of events, and weighs certainty of purpose against uncertainty of result. Here also, however, he is protected by that saving clause, without which he decides upon nothing, and begins nothing.

XXXV

When I promise to bestow a benefit, I promise it, unless something occurs which makes it my duty not to do so. What if, for example, my country orders me to give to her what I had promised to my friend? or if a law be passed forbidding any one to do what I had promised to do for him? Suppose that I have promised you my daughter in marriage, that then you turn out to be a foreigner, and that I have no right of intermarriage with foreigners; in this case, the law, by which I am forbidden to fulfil my promise, forms my defence. I shall be treacherous, and hear myself blamed for inconsistency, only if I do not fulfil, my promise when all conditions remain the same as when I made it; otherwise, any change makes me free to reconsider the entire case, and absolves me from my promise. I may have promised to plead a cause; afterwards it appears that this cause is designed to form a precedent for an attack upon my father. I may have promised to leave my country, and travel abroad; then news comes that the road is beset with robbers. I was going to an appointment at some particular place; but my son's illness, or my wife's confinement, prevented me. All conditions must be the same as they were when I made the promise, if you mean to hold me bound in honour to fulfil it. Now what greater change can take place than that I should discover you to be a bad and ungrateful man? I shall refuse to an unworthy man that which I had intended to give him supposing him to be worthy, and I shall also have reason to be angry with him for the trick which he has put upon me.

XXXVI

I shall nevertheless look into the matter, and consider what the value of the thing promised may be. If it be trifling, I shall give it, not because you are worthy of it, but because I promised it, and I shall not give it as a present, but merely in order to make good my words and give myself a twitch of the ear. I will punish my own rashness in promising by the loss of what I gave. "See how grieved you are; mind you take more care what you say in future." As the saying is, I will take tongue money from you. If the matter be important, I will not, as Maecenas said, let ten million sesterces reproach me. I will weigh the two sides of the question one against the other: there is something in abiding by what you have promised; on the other hand, there is a great deal in not bestowing a benefit upon one who is unworthy of it. Now, how great is this benefit? If it is a trifling one, let us wink and let it pass; but if it will cause me much loss or much shame to give it, I had rather excuse myself once for refusing it than have to do so ever after for giving it. The whole point, I repeat, depends upon how much the thing given is worth: let the terms of my promise be appraised. Not only shall I refuse to give what I may have promised rashly, but I shall also demand back again what I may have wrongly bestowed: a man must be mad who keeps a promise made under a mistake.

XXXVII

Philip, king of the Macedonians, had a hardy soldier whose services he had found useful in many campaigns. From time to time he made this man presents of part of the plunder as the reward of his valour, and used to excite his greedy spirit by his frequent gifts. This man was cast by shipwreck upon the estate of a certain Macedonian, who as soon as he heard the news hastened to him, restored his breath, removed him to his own farmhouse, gave up his own bed to him, nursed him out of his weakened and half-dead condition, took care of him at his own expense for thirty days, restored him to health and gave him a sum of money for his journey, as the man kept constantly saying, "If only I can see my chief, I will repay your kindness." He told Philip of his shipwreck, said nothing about the help which he had received, and at once demanded that a certain man's estate should be given to him. The man was a friend of his: it was that very man by whom he had been rescued and restored to health. Sometimes, especially in time of war, kings bestow many gifts with their eyes shut. One just man cannot deal with such a mass of armed selfishness. It is not possible for any one to be at the same time a good man and a good general. How are so many thousands of insatiable men to be satiated? What would they have, if every man had his own? Thus Philip reasoned with himself while he ordered the man to be put in possession of the property which he asked for. However, the other, when driven out of his estate, did not, like a peasant, endure his wrongs in silence, thankful that he himself was not given away also, but sent a sharp and outspoken letter to Philip, who, on reading it, was so much enraged that he straightway ordered Pausanias to restore the property to its former owner, and to brand that wickedest of soldiers, that most ungrateful of guests, that greediest of shipwrecked men, with letters bearing witness to his ingratitude. He, indeed, deserved to have the letters not merely branded but carved in his flesh, for having reduced his host to the condition in which he himself had been when he lay naked and shipwrecked upon the beach; still, let us see within what limits one ought to keep in punishing him. Of course what he had so villainously seized ought to be taken from him. But who would be affected by the spectacle of his punishment? The crime which he had committed would prevent his being pitied even by any humane person.

XXXVIII

Will Philip then give you a thing because he has promised to give it, even though he ought not to do so, even though he will commit a wrong by doing so, nay, a crime, even though by this one act he will make it impossible for shipwrecked men to reach the shore? There is no inconsistency in giving up an intention which we have discovered to be wrong and have condemned as wrong; we ought candidly to admit, "I thought that it was something different; I have been deceived." It is mere pride and folly to persist, "what I once have said, be it what it may, shall remain unaltered and settled." There is no disgrace in altering one's plans according to circumstances. Now, if Philip had left this man in possession of that seashore which he obtained by his shipwreck, would he not have practically pronounced sentence of banishment against all unfortunates for the future? "Rather," says Philip, "do thou carry upon thy forehead of brass those letters, that they may be impressed upon the eyes of all throughout my kingdom. Go, let men see how sacred a thing is the table of hospitality; show them your face, that upon it they may read the decree which prevents its being a capital crime to give refuge to the unfortunate under one's roof. The order will be more certainly respected by this means than if I had inscribed it upon tablets of brass."

XXXIX

"Why then," argues our adversary, "did your Stoic philosopher Zeno, when he had promised a loan of five hundred denarii to some person, whom he afterwards discovered to be of doubtful character, persist in lending it, because of his promise, though his friends dissuaded him from doing so?" In the first place a loan is on a different footing to a benefit. Even when we have lent money to an undesirable person we can recall it; I can demand payment upon a certain day, and if he becomes bankrupt, I can obtain my share of his property; but a benefit is lost utterly and instantly. Besides, the one is the act of a bad man, the other that of a bad father of a family. In the next place, if the sum had been a larger one, not even Zeno would have persisted in lending it. It was five hundred denarii; the sort of sum of which one says, "May he spend it in sickness," and it was worth paying so much to avoid breaking his promise. I shall go out to supper, even though the weather be cold, because I have promised to go; but I shall not if snow be falling. I shall leave my bed to go to a betrothal feast, although I may be suffering from indigestion; but I shall not do so if I am feverish. I will become bail for you, because I promised; but not if you wish me to become bail in some transaction of uncertain issue, if you expose me to forfeiting my money to the state. There runs through all these cases, I argue, an implied exception; if I am able, provided it is right for me to do so, if these things be so and so. Make the position the same when you ask me to fulfil my promise, as it was when I gave it, and it will be mere fickleness to disappoint you; but if something new has taken place in the meanwhile, why should you wonder at my intentions being changed when the conditions under which I gave the promise are changed? Put everything back as it was, and I shall be the same as I was. We enter into recognizances to appear, yet if we fail to do so an action will not in all cases lie against us, for we are excused for making default if forced to do so by a power which we cannot resist.

XL

You may take the same answer to the question as to whether we ought in all cases to show gratitude for kindness, and whether a benefit ought in all cases to be repaid. It is my duty to show a grateful mind, but in some cases my own poverty, in others the prosperity of the friend to whom I owe some return, will not permit me to give it. What, for instance, am I, a poor man, to give to a king or a rich man in return for his kindness, especially as some men regard it as a wrong to have their benefits repaid, and are wont to pile one benefit upon another? In dealing with such persons, what more can I do than wish to repay them? Yet I ought not to refuse to receive a new benefit, because I have not repaid the former one. I shall take it as freely as it is given, and will offer myself to my friend as a wide field for the exercise of his good nature: he who is unwilling to receive new benefits must be dissatisfied with what he has already received. Do you say, "I shall not be able to return them?" What is that to the purpose? I am willing enough to do so if opportunity or means were given me. He gave it to me, of course, having both opportunity and means: is he a good man or a bad one? if he is a good man, I have a good case against him, and I will not plead if he be a bad one. Neither do I think it right to insist on making repayment, even though it be against the will of those whom we repay, and to press it upon them however reluctant they may be; it is not repayment to force an unwilling man to resume what you were once willing to take. Some people, if any trifling present be sent to them, afterwards send back something else for no particular reason, and then declare that they are under no obligation; to send something back at once, and balance one present by another, is the next thing to refusing to receive it. On some occasions I shall not return a benefit, even though I be able to do so. When? When by so doing I shall myself lose more than he will gain, or if he would not notice any advantage to himself in receiving that which it would be a great loss to me to return. The man who is always eager to repay under all circumstances, has not the feeling of a grateful man, but of a debtor; and, to put it shortly, he who is too eager to repay, is unwilling to be in his friend's debt; he who is unwilling, and yet is in his friend's debt, is ungrateful.

On Benefits – Book V

I

In the preceding books I seem to have accomplished the object which I proposed to myself, since in them I have discussed how a benefit ought to be bestowed, and how it ought to be received. These are the limits of this action; when I dwell upon it further I am not obeying the orders, but the caprices of my subject which ought to be followed whither it leads, not whither it allures us to wander; for now and then something will arise, which, although it is all but unconnected with the subject, instead of being a necessary part of it, still thrills the mind with a certain charm. However, since you wish it to be so, let us go on, after having completed our discussion of the heads of the subject itself, to investigate those matters which, if you wish for truth, I must call adjacent to it, not actually connected with it; to examine which carefully is not one worth one's while, and yet is not labour in vain. No praise, however, which I can give to benefits does justice to you, Aebutius Liberalis, a man of excellent disposition and naturally inclined to bestow them. Never have I seen any one esteem even the most trifling services more kindly; indeed, your good-nature goes so far as to regard whatever benefit is bestowed upon anyone as bestowed upon yourself; you are prepared to pay even what is owed by the ungrateful, that no one may regret having bestowed benefits. You yourself are so far from any boastfulness, you are so eager at once to free those whom you serve from any feeling of obligation to you, that you like, when giving anything to any one, to seem not so much to be giving a present as returning one; and therefore what you give in this manner will all the more fully he repaid to you: for, as a rule, benefits come to one who does not demand repayment of them; and just as glory follows those who avoid it, so men receive a more plentiful harvest in return for benefits bestowed upon those who had it in their power to be ungrateful. With you there is no reason why those who have received benefits from you should not ask for fresh ones; nor would you refuse to bestow others, to overlook and conceal what you have given, and to add to it more and greater gifts, since it is the aim of all the best men and the noblest dispositions to bear with an ungrateful man until you make him grateful. Be not deceived in pursuing this plan; vice, if you do not too soon begin to hate it, will yield to virtue.

II

Thus it is that you are especially pleased with what you think the grandly-sounding phrase, "It is disgraceful to be worsted in a contest of benefits." Whether this be true or not deserves to be investigated, and it means something quite different from what you imagine; for it is never disgraceful to be worsted in any honourable contest, provided that you do not throw down your arms, and that even when conquered you wish to conquer. All men do not strive for a good object with the same strength, resources, and good fortune, upon which depend at all events the issues of the most admirable projects, though we ought to praise the will itself which makes an effort in the right direction. Even though another passes it by with swifter pace, yet the palm of victory does not, as in publicly-exhibited races, declare which is the better man; though even in the games chance frequently brings an inferior man to the front. As far as loyalty of feeling goes, which each man wishes to be possessed in the fullest measure on his own side, if one of the two be the more powerful, if he have at his disposal all the resources which he wishes to use, and be favoured by fortune in his most ambitious efforts, while the other, although equally willing, can only return less than he receives, or perhaps can make no return at all, but still wishes to do so and is entirely devoted to this object; then the latter is no more conquered than he who dies in arms, whom the enemy found it easier to slay than to turn back. To be conquered, which you consider disgraceful, cannot happen to a good man; for he will never surrender, never give up the contest, to the last day of his life he will stand prepared and in that posture he will die, testifying that though he has received much, yet that he had the will to repay as much as he had received.

III

The Lacedaemonians forbid their young men to contend in the pancratium, or with the caestus, in which games the defeated party has to acknowledge himself beaten. The winner of a race is he who first reaches the goal; he outstrips the others in swiftness, but not in courage. The wrestler who has been thrown three times loses the palm of victory, but does not yield it up. Since the Lacedaemonians thought it of great importance that their countrymen should be invincible, they kept them away from those contests in which victory is assigned, not by the judge, or by the issue of the contest itself, but by the voice of the vanquished begging the victor to spare him as he falls. This attribute of never being conquered, which they so jealously guard among their citizens, can be attained by all men through virtue and goodwill, because even when all else is vanquished, the mind remains unconquered. For this cause no one speaks of the three hundred Fabii as conquered, but slaughtered. Regulus was taken captive by the Carthaginians, not conquered; and so were all other men who have not yielded in spirit when overwhelmed by the strength and weight of angry fortune.

So is it with benefits. A man may have received more than he gave, more valuable ones, more frequently bestowed; yet is he not vanquished. It may be that, if you compare the benefits with one another, those which he has received will outweigh those which he has bestowed; but if you compare the giver and the receiver, whose intentions also ought to be considered apart, neither will prove the victor. It often happens that even when one combatant is pierced with many wounds, while the other is only slightly injured, yet they are said to have fought a drawn battle, although the former may appear to be the worse man.

IV

No one, therefore, can be conquered in a contest of benefits, if he knows how to owe a debt, if he wishes to make a return for what he has received, and raises himself to the same level with his friend in spirit, though he cannot do so in material gifts. As long as he remains in this temper of mind, as long as he has the wish to declare by proofs that he has a grateful mind, what difference does it make upon which side we can count the greater number of presents? You are able to give much; I can do nothing but receive. Fortune abides with you, goodwill alone with me; yet I am as much on an equality with you as naked or lightly armed men are with a large body armed to the teeth. No one, therefore, is worsted by benefits, because each man's gratitude is to be measured by his will. If it be disgraceful to be worsted in a contest of benefits, you ought not to receive a benefit from very powerful men whose kindness you cannot return, I mean such as princes and kings, whom fortune has placed in such a station that they can give away much, and can only receive very little and quite inadequate returns for what they give. I have spoken of kings and princes, who alone can cause works to be accomplished, and whose superlative power depends upon the obedience and services of inferiors; but some there are, free from all earthly lusts, who are scarcely affected by any human objects of desire, upon whom fortune herself could bestow nothing. I must be worsted in a contest of benefits with Socrates, or with Diogenes, who walked naked through the treasures of Macedonia, treading the king's wealth under his feet. In good sooth, he must then rightly have seemed, both to himself and to all others whose eyes were keen enough to perceive the real truth, to be superior even to him at whose feet all the world lay. He was far more powerful, far richer even than Alexander, who then possessed everything; for there was more that Diogenes could refuse to receive than that Alexander was able to give.

V

It is not disgraceful to be worsted by these men, for I am not the less brave because you pit me against an invulnerable enemy, nor does fire not burn because you throw into it something over which flames have no power, nor does iron lose its power of cutting, though you may wish to cut up a stone which is hard, impervious to blows, and of such a nature that hard tools are blunted upon it. I give you the same answer about gratitude. A man is not disgracefully worsted in a contest of benefits if he lays himself under an obligation to such persons as these, whose enormous wealth or admirable virtue shut out all possibility of their benefits being returned. As a rule we are worsted by our parents; for while we have them with us, we regard them as severe, and do not understand what they do for us. When our age begins to bring us a little sense, and we gradually perceive that they deserve our love for those very things which used to prevent our loving them, their advice, their punishments, and the careful watch which they used to keep over our youthful recklessness, they are taken from us. Few live to reap any real fruit from children; most men feel their sons only as a burden. Yet there is no disgrace in being worsted by one's parent in bestowing benefits; how should there be, seeing that there is no disgrace in being worsted by anyone. We are equal to some men, and yet not equal; equal in intention, which is all that they care for, which is all that we promise to be, but unequal in fortune. And if fortune prevents any one from repaying a kindness, he need not, therefore, blush, as though he were vanquished; there is no disgrace in failing to reach your object, provided you attempt to reach it. It often is necessary, that before making any return for the benefits which we have received, we should ask for new ones; yet, if so, we shall not refrain from asking for them, nor shall we do so as though disgraced by so doing, because, even if we do not repay the debt, we shall owe it; because, even if something from without befalls us to prevent our repaying it, it will not be our fault if we are not grateful. We can neither be conquered in intention, nor can we be disgraced by yielding to what is beyond our strength to contend with.

VI

Alexander, the king of the Macedonians, used to boast that he had never been worsted by anybody in a contest of benefits. If so, it was no reason why, in the fulness of his pride, he should despise the Macedonians, Greeks, Carians, Persians, and other tribes of whom his army was composed, nor need he imagine that it was this that gave him an empire reaching from a corner of Thrace to the shore of the unknown sea. Socrates could make the same boast, and so could Diogenes, by whom Alexander was certainly surpassed; for was he not surpassed on the day when, swelling as he was beyond the limits of merely human pride, he beheld one to whom he could give nothing, from whom he could take nothing? King Archelaus invited Socrates to come to him. Socrates is reported to have answered that he should be sorry to go to one who would bestow benefits upon him, since he should not be able to make him an adequate return for them. In the first place, Socrates was at liberty not to receive them; next, Socrates himself would have been the first to bestow a benefit, for he would have come when invited, and would have given to Archelaus that for which Archelaus could have made no return to Socrates. Even if Archelaus were to give Socrates gold and silver, if he learned in return for them to despise gold and silver, would not Socrates be able to repay Archelaus? Could Socrates receive from him as much value as he gave, in displaying to him a man skilled in the knowledge of life and of death, comprehending the true purpose of each? Suppose that he had found this king, as it were, groping his way in the clear sunlight, and had taught him the secrets of nature, of which he was so ignorant, that when there was an eclipse of the sun, he up his palace, and shaved his son's head,[1] which men are wont to do in times of mourning and distress. What a benefit it would have been if he had dragged the terror-stricken king out of his hiding-place, and bidden him be of good cheer, saying, "This is not a disappearance of the sun, but a conjunction of two heavenly bodies; for the moon, which proceeds along a lower path, has placed her disk beneath the sun, and hidden it by the interposition of her own mass. Sometimes she only hides a small portion of the sun's disk, because she only grazes it in passing; sometimes she hides more, by placing more of herself before it; and sometimes she shuts it out from our sight altogether, if she passes in an exactly even course between the sun and the earth. Soon, however, their own swift motion will draw these two bodies apart; soon the earth will receive back again the light of day. And this system will continue throughout centuries, having certain days, known beforehand, upon which the sun cannot display all rays, because of the

---

[1] Gertz very reasonably conjectures that he shaved his own head which reading would require a very trifling alteration of the text.

intervention of the moon. Wait only for a short time; he will soon emerge, he will soon leave that seeming cloud, and freely shed abroad his light without any hindrances." Could Socrates not have made an adequate return to Archelaus, if he had taught him to reign? as though Socrates would not benefit him sufficiently, merely by enabling him to bestow a benefit upon Socrates. Why, then, did Socrates say this? Being a joker and a speaker in parables--a man who turned all, especially the great, into ridicule--he preferred giving him a satirical refusal, rather than an obstinate or haughty one, and therefore said that he did not wish to receive benefits from one to whom he could not return as much as he received. He feared, perhaps, that he might be forced to receive something which he did not wish, he feared that it might be something unfit for Socrates to receive. Some one may say, "He ought to have said that he did not wish to go." But by so doing he would have excited against himself the anger of an arrogant king, who wished everything connected with himself to be highly valued. It makes no difference to a king whether you be unwilling to give anything to him or to accept anything from him; he is equally incensed at either rebuff, and to be treated with disdain is more bitter to a proud spirit than not to be feared. Do you wish to know what Socrates really meant? He, whose freedom of speech could not be borne even by a free state, was not willing of his own choice to become a slave.

VII

I think that we have sufficiently discussed this part of the subject, whether it be disgraceful to be worsted in a contest of benefits. Whoever asks this question must know that men are not wont to bestow benefits upon themselves, for evidently it could not be disgraceful to be worsted by oneself. Yet some of the Stoics debate this question, whether any one can confer a benefit upon himself, and whether one ought to return one's own kindness to oneself. This discussion has been raised in consequence of our habit of saying, "I am thankful to myself," "I can complain of no one but myself," "I am angry with myself," "I will punish myself," "I hate myself," and many other phrases of the same sort, in which one speaks of oneself as one would of some other person. "If," they argue, "I can injure myself, why should I not be able also to bestow a benefit upon myself? Besides this, why are those things not called benefits when I bestow them upon myself which would be called benefits if I bestowed them upon another? If to receive a certain thing from another would lay me under an obligation to him, how is it that if I give it to myself, I do not contract an obligation to myself? why should I be ungrateful to my own self, which is no less disgraceful than it is to be mean to oneself, or hard and cruel to oneself, or neglectful of oneself? The procurer is equally odious whether he prostitutes others or himself. We blame a flatterer, and one who imitates another man's mode of speech, or is prepared to give praise whether it be deserved or not; we ought equally to blame one who humours himself and looks up to himself, and so to speak is his own flatterer. Vices are not only hateful when outwardly practised, but also when they are repressed within the mind. Whom would you admire more than he who governs himself and has himself under command? It is easier to rule savage nations, impatient of foreign control, than to restrain one's own mind and keep it under one's own control. Plato, it is argued, was grateful to Socrates for having been taught by him; why should not Socrates be grateful to himself for having taught himself? Marcus Cato said, "Borrow from yourself whatever you lack;" why, then, if I can lend myself anything, should I be unable to give myself anything? The instances in which usage divides us into two persons are innumerable; we are wont to say, "Let me converse with myself," and, "I will give myself a twitch of the ear;"[2] and if it be true that one can do so, then a man ought to be grateful to himself, just as he is angry with himself; as he blames himself, so he ought to praise himself; since he can impoverish himself, he can also enrich himself. Injuries and benefits are the converse of one another: if we say of a man, 'he has done

---

[2] See book iv. ch. xxxvi.

himself an injury,' we can also say 'he has bestowed upon himself a benefit?'

VIII

It is natural that a man should first incur an obligation, and then that he should return gratitude for it; a debtor cannot exist without a creditor, any more than a husband without a wife, or a son without a father; someone must give in order that some one may receive. Just as no one carries himself, although he moves his body and transports it from place to place; as no one, though he may have made a speech in his own defence, is said to have stood by himself, or erects a statue to himself as his own patron; as no sick man, when by his own care he has regained his health, asks himself for a fee; so in no transaction, even when a man does what is useful to himself, need he return thanks to himself, because there is no one to whom he can return them. Though I grant that a man can bestow a benefit upon himself, yet at the same time that he gives it, he also receives it; though I grant that a man may receive a benefit from himself, yet he receives it at the same time that he gives it. The exchange takes place within doors, as they say, and the transfer is made at once, as though the debt were a fictitious one; for he who gives is not a different person to he who receives, but one and the same. The word "to owe" has no meaning except as between two persons; how then can it apply to one man who incurs an obligation, and by the same act frees himself from it? In a disk or a ball there is no top or bottom, no beginning or end, because the relation of the parts is changed when it moves, what was behind coming before, and what went down on one side coming up on the other, so that all the parts, in whatever direction they may move, come back to the same position. Imagine that the same thing takes place in a man; into however many pieces you may divide him, he remains one. If he strikes himself, he has no one to call to account for the insult; if he binds himself and locks himself up, he cannot demand damages; if he bestows a benefit upon himself, he straightway returns it to the giver. It is said that there is no waste in nature, because everything which is taken from nature returns to her again, and nothing can perish, because it cannot fall out of nature, but goes round again to the point from whence it started. You ask, "What connection has this illustration with the subject?" I will tell you. Imagine yourself to be ungrateful, the benefit bestowed upon you is not lost, he who gave it has it; suppose that you are unwilling to receive it, it still belongs to you before it is returned. You cannot lose anything, because what you take away from yourself, you nevertheless gain yourself. The matter revolves in a circle within yourself; by receiving you give, by giving you receive.

IX

"It is our duty," argues our adversary, "to bestow benefits upon ourselves, therefore we ought also to be grateful to ourselves." The original axiom, upon which the inference depends, is untrue, for no one bestows benefits upon himself, but obeys the dictates of his nature, which disposes him to affection for himself, and which makes him take the greatest pains to avoid hurtful things, and to follow after those things which are profitable to him. Consequently, the man who gives to himself is not generous, nor is he who pardons himself forgiving, nor is he who is touched by his own misfortunes tender-hearted; it is natural to do those things to oneself which when done to others become generosity, clemency, and tenderness of heart. A benefit is a voluntary act, but to do good to oneself is an instinctive one. The more benefits a man bestows, the more beneficent he is, yet who ever was praised for having been of service to himself? or for having rescued himself from brigands? No one bestows a benefit upon himself any more than he bestows hospitality upon himself; no one gives himself anything, any more than he lends himself anything. If each man bestows benefits upon himself, is always bestowing them, and bestows them without any cessation, then it is impossible for him to make any calculation of the number of his benefits; when then can he show his gratitude, seeing that by the very act of doing so he would bestow a benefit? for what distinction can you draw between giving himself a benefit or receiving a benefit for himself, when the whole transaction takes place in the mind of the same man? Suppose that I have freed myself from danger, then I have bestowed a benefit upon myself; suppose I free myself a second time, by so doing do I bestow or repay a benefit? In the next place, even if I grant the primary axiom, that we can bestow benefits upon ourselves, I do not admit that which follows; for even if we can do so, we ought not to do so. Wherefore? Because we receive a return for them at once. It is right for me to receive a benefit, then to lie under an obligation, then to repay it; now here there is no time for remaining under an obligation, because we receive the return without any delay. No one really gives except to another, no one owes except to another, no one repays except to another. An act which always requires two persons cannot take place within the mind of one.

X

A benefit means the affording of something useful, and the word AFFORDING implies other persons. Would not a man be thought mad if he said that he had sold something to himself, because selling means alienation, and the transferring of a thing and of one's rights in that thing to another person? Yet giving, like selling anything, consists in making it pass away from you, handing over what you yourself once owned into the keeping of some one else.

If this be so, no one ever gave himself a benefit, because no one gives to himself; if not, two opposites coalesce, so that it becomes the same thing to give and to receive. Yet there is a great difference between giving and receiving; how should there not be, seeing that these words are the converse of one another? Still, if any one can give himself a benefit, there can be no difference between giving and receiving. I said a little before that some words apply only to other persons, and are so constituted that their whole meaning lies apart from ourselves; for instance, I am a brother, but a brother of some other man, for no one is his own brother; I am an equal, but equal to somebody else, for who is equal to himself? A thing which is compared to another thing is unintelligible without that other thing; a thing which is joined to something else does not exist apart from it; so that which is given does not exist without the other person, nor can a benefit have any existence without another person. This is clear from the very phrase which describes it, 'to do good,' yet no one does good to himself, any more than he favours himself or is on his own side. I might enlarge further upon this subject and give many examples. Why should benefits not be included among those acts which require two persons to perform them? Many honourable, most admirable and highly virtuous acts cannot take place without a second person. Fidelity is praised and held to be one of the chief blessings known among men, yet was any one ever on that account said to have kept faith with himself?

XI

I come now to the last part of this subject. The man who returns a kindness ought to expend something, just as he who repays expends money; but the man who returns a kindness to himself expends nothing, just as he who receives a benefit from himself gains nothing. A benefit and gratitude for it must pass to and fro between two persons; their interchange cannot take place within one man. He who returns a kindness does good in his turn to him from whom he has received something; but the man who returns his own kindness, to whom does he do good? To himself? Is there any one who does not regard the returning of a kindness, and the bestowal of a benefit, as distinct acts? 'He who returns a kindness to himself does good to himself.' Was any man ever unwilling to do this, even though he were ungrateful? nay, who ever was ungrateful from any other motive than this? "If," it is argued, "we are right in thanking ourselves, we ought to return our own kindness;" yet we say, "I am thankful to myself for having refused to marry that woman," or "for having refused to join a partnership with that man." When we speak thus, we are really praising ourselves, and make use of the language of those who return thanks to approve our own acts. A benefit is something which, when given, may or may not be returned. Now, he who gives a benefit to himself must needs receive what he gives; therefore, this is not a benefit. A benefit is received at one time, and is returned at another; (but when a man bestows a benefit upon himself, he both receives it and returns it at the same time). In a benefit, too, what we commend and admire is, that a man has for the time being forgotten his own interests, in order that he may do good to another; that he has deprived himself of something, in order to bestow it upon another. Now, he who bestows a benefit upon himself does not do this. The bestowal of a benefit is an act of companionship--it wins some man's friendship, and lays some man under an obligation; but to bestow it upon oneself is no act of companionship--it wins no man's friendship, lays no man under an obligation, raises no man's hopes, or leads him to say, "This man must be courted; he bestowed a benefit upon that person, perhaps he will bestow one upon me also." A benefit is a thing which one gives not for one's own sake, but for the sake of him to whom it is given; but he who bestows a benefit upon himself, does so for his own sake; therefore, it is not a benefit.

XII

Now I seem to you not to have made good what I said at the beginning of this book. You say that I am far from doing what is worth any one's while; nay, that in real fact I have thrown away all my trouble. Wait, and soon you will be able to say this more truly, for I shall lead you into covert lurking-places, from which when you have escaped, you will have gained nothing except that you will have freed yourself from difficulties with which you need never have hampered yourself. What is the use of laboriously untying knots which you yourself have tied, in order that you might untie them? Yet, just as some knots are tied in fun and for amusement, so that a tyro may find difficulty in untying them, which knots he who tied them can loose without any trouble, because he knows the joinings and the difficulties of them, and these nevertheless afford us some pleasure, because they test the sharpness of our wits, and engross our attention; so also these questions, which seem subtle and tricky, prevent our intellects becoming careless and lazy, for they ought at one time to have a field given them to level, in order that they may wander about it, and at another to have some dark and rough passage thrown in their way for them to creep through, and make their way with caution. It is said by our opponent that no one is ungrateful; and this is supported by the following arguments: "A benefit is that which does good; but, as you Stoics say, no one can do good to a bad man; therefore, a bad man does not receive a benefit. (If he does not receive it, he need not return it; therefore, no bad man is ungrateful.) Furthermore, a benefit is an honourable and commendable thing. No honourable or commendable thing can find any place with a bad man; therefore, neither can a benefit. If he cannot receive one, he need not repay one; therefore, he does not become ungrateful. Moreover, as you say, a good man does everything rightly; if he does everything rightly, he cannot be ungrateful. A good man returns a benefit, a bad man does not receive one. If this be so, no man, good or bad, can be ungrateful. Therefore, there is no such thing in nature as an ungrateful man: the word is meaningless." We Stoics have only one kind of good, that which is honourable. This cannot come to a bad man, for he would cease to be bad if virtue entered into him; but as long as he is bad, no one can bestow a benefit upon him, because good and bad are contraries, and cannot exist together. Therefore, no one can do good to such a man, because whatever he receives is corrupted by his vicious way of using it. Just as the stomach, when disordered by disease and secreting bile, changes all the food which it receives, and turns every kind of sustenance into a source of pain, so whatever you entrust to an ill-regulated mind becomes to it a burden, an annoyance, and a source of misery. Thus the most prosperous and the richest men have the most trouble; and the more property they have to perplex them, the less likely they are to find out what they really are. Nothing, therefore, can reach bad men which would do them good; nay, nothing which would not do them harm. They change whatever falls to their lot into their own evil nature; and things which elsewhere would, if given to better men, be both beautiful and profitable, are ruinous to them. They cannot, therefore, bestow benefits, because no one can give what he does not possess, and, therefore, they lack the pleasure of doing good to others.

XIII

But, though this be so, yet even a bad man can receive some things which resemble benefits, and he will be ungrateful if he does not return them. There are good things belonging to the mind, to the body, and to fortune. A fool or a bad man is debarred from the first--those, that is, of the mind; but he is admitted to a share in the two latter, and, if he does not return them, he is ungrateful. Nor does this follow from our (Stoic) system alone the Peripatetics, also, who widely extend the boundaries of human happiness, declare that trifling benefits reach bad men, and that he who does not return them is ungrateful. We therefore do not agree that things which do not tend to improve the mind should be called benefits, yet do not deny that these things are convenient and desirable. Such things as these a bad man may bestow upon a good man, or may receive from him--such, for example, as money, clothes, public office, or life; and, if he makes no return for these, he will come under the denomination of ungrateful. "But how can you call a man ungrateful for not returning that which you say is not a benefit?" Some things, on account of their similarity, are included under the same designation, although they do not really deserve it. Thus we speak of a silver or golden box; ["The original word is 'pyx,' which means a box made of box-wood."] thus we call a man illiterate, although he may not be utterly ignorant, but only not acquainted with the higher branches of literature; thus, seeing a badly-dressed ragged man we say that we have seen a naked man. These things of which we spoke are not benefits, but they possess the appearance of benefits. "Then, just as they are quasi-benefits, so your man is quasi-ungrateful, not really ungrateful." This is untrue, because both he who gives and he who receives them speaks of them as benefits; so he who fails to return the semblance of a real benefit is as much an ungrateful man as he who mixes a sleeping draught, believing it to be poison, is a poisoner.

XIV

Cleanthes speaks more impetuously than this. "Granted," says he, "that what he received was not a benefit, yet he is ungrateful, because he would not have returned a benefit if he had received one." So he who carries deadly weapons and has intentions of robbing and murdering, is a brigand even before he has dipped his hands in blood; his wickedness consists and is shown in action, but does not begin thereby. Men are punished for sacrilege, although no one's hands can reach to the gods. "How," asks our opponent, "can any one be ungrateful to a bad man, since a bad man cannot bestow a benefit?" In the same way, I answer, because that which he received was not a benefit, but was called one; if any one receives from a bad man any of those things which are valued by the ignorant, and of which bad men often possess great store, it becomes his duty to make a return in the same kind, and to give back as though they were truly good those things which he received as though they were truly good. A man is said to be in debt, whether he owes gold pieces or leather marked with a state stamp, such as the Lacedaemonians used, which passes for coined money. Pay your debts in that kind in which you incurred them. You have nothing to do with the definition of benefits, or with the question whether so great and noble a name ought to be degraded by applying it to such vulgar and mean matters as these, nor do we seek for truth that we may use it to the disadvantage of others; do you adjust your minds to the semblance of truth, and while you are learning what is really honourable, respect everything to which the name of honour is applied.

XV

"In the same way," argues our adversary, "that your school proves that no one is ungrateful, you afterwards prove that all men are ungrateful. For, as you say, all fools are bad men; he who has one vice has all vices; all men are both fools and bad men; therefore all men are ungrateful." Well, what then? Are they not? Is not this the universal reproach of the human race? is there not a general complaint that benefits are thrown away, and that there are very few men who do not requite their benefactors with the basest ingratitude? Nor need you suppose that what we say is merely the grumbling of men who think every act wicked and depraved which falls short of an ideal standard of righteousness. Listen! I know not who it is who speaks, yet the voice with which he condemns mankind proceeds, not from the schools of philosophers, but from the midst of the crowd:

> "Host is not safe from guest;
> Father-in-law from son; but seldom love
> Exists 'twixt brothers; wives long to destroy
> Their husbands; husbands long to slay their wives."

This goes even further: according to this, crimes take the place of benefits, and men do not shrink from shedding the blood of those for whom they ought to shed their own; we requite benefits by steel and poison. We call laying violent hands upon our own country, and putting down its resistance by the fasces of its own lictors, gaining power and great place; every man thinks himself to be in a mean and degraded position if he has not raised himself above the constitution; the armies which are received from the state are turned against her, and a general now says to his men, "Fight against your wives, fight against your children, march in arms against your altars, your hearths and homes!" Yes,[3] you, who even when about to triumph ought not to enter the city at the command of the senate, and who have often, when bringing home a victorious army, been given an audience outside the walls, you now, after slaughtering your countrymen, stained with the blood of your kindred, march into the city with standards erect. "Let liberty," say you, "be silent amidst the ensigns of war, and now that wars are driven far away and no ground for terror remains, let that people which conquered and civilized all nations be beleaguered within its own walls, and shudder at the sight of its own eagles."

---

[3] I believe, in spite of Gertz, that this is part of the speech of the Roman general, and that the conjecture of Muretus, "without the command of the senate," gives better sense.

XVI

Coriolanus was ungrateful, and became dutiful late, and after repenting of his crime; he did indeed lay down his arms, but only in the midst of his unnatural warfare. Catilina was ungrateful; he was not satisfied with taking his country captive without overturning it, without despatching the hosts of the Allobroges against it, without bringing an enemy from beyond the Alps to glut his old inborn hatred, and to offer Roman generals as sacrifices which had been long owing to the tombs of the Gaulish dead. Caius Marius was ungrateful, when, after being raised from the ranks to the consulship, he felt that he would not have wreaked his vengeance upon fortune, and would sink to his original obscurity, unless he slaughtered Romans as freely as he had slaughtered the Cimbri, and not merely gave the signal, but was himself the signal for civil disasters and butcheries. Lucius Sulla was ungrateful, for he saved his country by using remedies worse than the perils with which it was threatened, when he marched through human blood all the way from the citadel of Praeneste to the Colline Gate, fought more battles and caused more slaughter afterwards within the city, and most cruelly after the victory was won, most wickedly after quarter had been promised them, drove two legions into a corner and put them to the sword, and, great gods! invented a proscription by which he who slew a Roman citizen received indemnity, a sum of money, everything but a civic crown! Cnaeus Pompeius was ungrateful, for the return which he made to his country for three consulships, three triumphs, and the innumerable public offices into most of which he thrust himself when under age, was to lead others also to lay hands upon her under the pretext of thus rendering his own power less odious; as though what no one ought to do became right if more than one person did it. Whilst he was coveting extraordinary commands, arranging the provinces so as to have his own choice of them, and dividing the whole state with a third person,[4] in such a manner as to leave two-thirds of it in the possession of his own family,[5] he reduced the Roman people to such a condition that they could only save themselves by submitting to slavery. The foe and conqueror[6] of Pompeius was himself ungrateful; he brought war from Gaul and Germany to Rome, and he, the friend of the populace, the champion of the commons,

---

[4] Crassus.

[5] Pompey was married to Caesar's daughter. Cf. Virg., "Aen.," vi., 831, sq., and Lucan's beautiful verses, "Phars.," i., 114.

[6] Seneca is careful to avoid the mention of Caesar's name, which might have given offence to the emperors under whom he lived, who used the name as a title.

pitched his camp in the Circus Flaminus, nearer to the city than Porsena's camp had been. He did, indeed, use the cruel privileges of victory with moderation; as was said at the time, he protected his countrymen, and put to death no man who was not in arms. Yet what credit is there in this? Others used their arms more cruelly, but flung them away when glutted with blood, while he, though he soon sheathed the sword, never laid it aside. Antonius was ungrateful to his dictator, who he declared was rightly slain, and whose murderers he allowed to depart to their commands in the provinces; as for his country, after it had been torn to pieces by so many proscriptions, invasions, and civil wars, he intended to subject it to kings, not even of Roman birth, and to force that very state to pay tribute to eunuchs,[7] which had itself restored sovereign rights, autonomy, and immunities, to the Achaeans, the Rhodians, and the people of many other famous cities.

---

[7] The allusion is to Antonius's connection with Cleopatra. Cf. Virg. "Aen.," viii., 688.

XVII

The day would not be long enough for me to enumerate those who have pushed their ingratitude so far as to ruin their native land. It would be as vast a task to mention how often the state has been ungrateful to its best and most devoted lovers, although it has done no less wrong than it has suffered. It sent Camillus and Scipio into exile; even after the death of Catiline it exiled Cicero, destroyed his house, plundered his property, and did everything which Catiline would have done if victorious; Rutilius found his virtue rewarded with a hiding-place in Asia; to Cato the Roman people refused the praetorship, and persisted in refusing the consulship. We are ungrateful in public matters; and if every man asks himself, you will find that there is no one who has not some private ingratitude to complain of. Yet it is impossible that all men should complain, unless all were deserving of complaint, therefore all men are ungrateful. Are they ungrateful alone? nay, they are also all covetous, all spiteful, and all cowardly, especially those who appear daring; and, besides this, all men fawn upon the great, and all are impious. Yet you need not be angry with them; pardon them, for they are all mad. I do not wish to recall you to what is not proved, or to say, "See how ungrateful is youth! what young man, even if of innocent life, does not long for his father's death? even if moderate in his desires, does not look forward to it? even if dutiful, does not think about it? How few there are who fear the death even of the best of wives, who do not even calculate the probabilities of it. Pray, what litigant, after having been successfully defended, retains any remembrance of so great a benefit for more than a few days?" All agree that no one dies without complaining. Who on his last day dares to say,

"I've lived, I've done the task which Fortune set me."

Who does not leave the world with reluctance, and with lamentations? Yet it is the part of an ungrateful man not to be satisfied with the past. Your days will always be few if you count them. Reflect that length of time is not the greatest of blessings; make the best of your time, however short it may be; even if the day of your death be postponed, your happiness will not be increased, for life is merely made longer, not pleasanter, by delay. How much better is it to be thankful for the pleasures which one has received, not to reckon up the years of others, but to set a high value upon one's own, and score them to one's credit, saying, "God thought me worthy of this; I am satisfied with it; he might have given me more, but this, too, is a benefit." Let us be grateful towards both gods and men, grateful to those who have given us anything, and grateful even to those who have given anything to our relatives.

XVIII

"You render me liable to an infinite debt of gratitude," says our opponent, "when you say 'even to those who have given any thing to our relations,' so fix some limit. He who bestows a benefit upon the son, according to you, bestows it likewise upon the father: this is the first question I wish to raise. In the next place I should like to have a clear definition of whether a benefit, if it be bestowed upon your friend's father as well as upon himself, is bestowed also upon his brother? or upon his uncle? or his grandfather? or his wife and his father-in-law? tell me where I am to stop, how far I am to follow out the pedigree of the family?"

SENECA. If I cultivate your land, I bestow a benefit upon you; if I extinguish your house when burning, or prop it so as to save it from falling, I shall bestow a benefit upon you; if I heal your slave, I shall charge it to you; if I save your son's life, will you not thereby receive a benefit from me?

XIX

THE ADVERSARY. Your instances are not to the purpose, for he who cultivates my land, does not benefit the land, but me; he who props my house so that it does not fall, does this service to me, for the house itself is without feeling, and as it has none, it is I who am indebted to him; and he who cultivates my land does so because he wishes to oblige me, not to oblige the land. I should say the same of a slave; he is a chattel owned by me; he is saved for my advantage, therefore I am indebted for him. My son is himself capable of receiving a benefit; so it is he who receives it; I am gratified at a benefit which comes so near to myself, but am not laid under any obligation.

SE. Still I should like you, who say that you are under no obligation, to answer me this. The good health, the happiness, and the inheritance of a son are connected with his father; his father will be more happy if he keeps his son safe, and more unhappy if he loses him. What follows, then? when a man is made happier by me and is freed from the greatest danger of unhappiness, does he not receive a benefit?

AD. No, because there are some things which are bestowed upon others, and yet flow from them so as to reach ourselves; yet we must ask the person upon whom it was bestowed for repayment; as for example, money must be sought from the man to whom it was lent, although it may, by some means, have come into my hands. There is no benefit whose advantages do not extend to the receiver's nearest friends, and sometimes even to those less intimately connected with him; yet we do not enquire whither the benefit has proceeded from him to whom it was first given, but where it was first placed. You must demand repayment from the defendant himself personally.

SE. Well, but I pray you, do you not say, "you have preserved my son for me; had he perished, I could not have survived him?" Do you not owe a benefit for the life of one whose safety you value above your own? Moreover, should I save your son's life, you would fall down before my knees, and would pay vows to heaven as though you yourself had been saved; you would say, "It makes no difference whether you have saved mine or me; you have saved us both, yet me more than him." Why do you say this, if you do not receive a benefit?

A.D. Because, if my son were to contract a loan, I should pay his creditor, yet I should not, therefore, be indebted to him; or if my son were taken in adultery, I should blush, yet I should not, therefore, be an adulterer. I say that I am under an obligation to you for saving my son, not because I really am, but because I am willing to constitute myself your debtor of my own free will. On the other hand I have derived from his safety the greatest possible pleasure and advantage, and I have escaped that most dreadful blow, the loss of my child. True, but we are not now discussing whether you have done me any good or not, but whether you have bestowed a benefit upon me; for animals, stones, and herbs can do one good, but do not bestow benefits, which can only be given by one who wishes well to the receiver. Now you do not wish well to the father, but only to the son; and sometimes you do not even know the father. So when you have said, "Have I not bestowed a benefit upon the father by saving the son?" you ought to meet this with, "Have I, then, bestowed a benefit upon a father whom I do not know, whom I never thought of?" And what will you say when, as is sometimes the case, you hate the father, and yet save his son? Can you be thought to have bestowed a benefit upon one whom you hated most bitterly while you were bestowing it?

However, if I were to lay aside the bickering of dialogue, and answer you as a lawyer, I should say that you ought to consider the intention of the giver, you must regard his benefit as bestowed upon the person upon whom he meant to bestow it. If he did it in honour of the father, then the father received the benefit; if he thought only of the son, then the father is not laid under any obligation: by the benefit which was conferred upon the son, even though the father derives pleasure from it. Should he, however, have an opportunity, he will himself wish to give you something, yet not as though he were forced to repay a debt, but rather as if he had grounds for beginning an exchange of favours. No return for a benefit ought to be demanded from the father of the receiver; if he does you any kindness in return for it, he should be regarded as, a righteous man, but not as a grateful one. For there is no end to it; if I bestow a benefit on the receiver's father, do I likewise bestow it upon his mother, his grandfather, his maternal uncle, his children, relations, friends, slaves, and country? Where, then, does a benefit begin to stop? for there follows it this endless chain of people, to whom it is hard to assign bounds, because they join it by degrees, and are always creeping on towards it.

XX

A common question is, "Two brothers are at variance. If I save the life of one, do I confer a benefit upon the other, who will be sorry that his hated brother did not perish?" There can be no doubt that it is a benefit to do good to a man, even against that man's will, just as he, who against his own will does a man good, does not bestow a benefit upon him. "Do you," asks our adversary, "call that by which he is displeased and hurt a benefit?" Yes; many benefits have a harsh and forbidding appearance, such as cutting or burning to cure disease, or confining with chains. We must not consider whether a man is grieved at receiving a benefit, but whether he ought to rejoice: a coin is not bad because it is refused by a savage who is unacquainted with its proper stamp. A man receives a benefit even though he hates what is done, provided that it does him good, and that the giver bestowed it in order to do him good. It makes no difference if he receives a good thing in a bad spirit. Consider the converse of this. Suppose that a man hates his brother, though it is to his advantage to have a brother, and I kill this brother, this is not a benefit, though he may say that it is, and be glad of it. Our most artful enemies are those whom we thank for the wrongs which they do us.

"I understand; a thing which does good is a benefit, a thing which does harm is not a benefit. Now I will suggest to you an act which neither does good nor harm, and yet is a benefit. Suppose that I find the corpse of some one's father in a wilderness, and bury it, then I certainly have done him no good, for what difference could it make to him in what manner his body decayed? Nor have I done any good to his son, for what advantage does he gain by my act?" I will tell you what he gains. He has by my means performed a solemn and necessary rite; I have performed a service for his father which he would have wished, nay, which it would have been his duty to have performed himself. Yet this act is not a benefit, if I merely yielded to those feelings of pity and kindliness which would make me bury any corpse whatever, but only if I recognized this body, and buried it, with the thought in my mind that I was doing this service to the son; but, by merely throwing earth over a dead stranger, I lay no one under an obligation for an act performed on general principles of humanity.

It may be asked, "Why are you so careful in inquiring upon whom you bestow benefits, as though some day you meant to demand repayment of them? Some say that repayment should never be demanded; and they give the following reasons. An unworthy man will not repay the benefit which he has received, even if it be demanded of him, while a worthy man will do so of his own accord. Consequently, if you have bestowed it upon a good man, wait; do not outrage him by asking him for it, as though of his own accord he never would repay it. If you have bestowed it upon a bad man, suffer for it, but do not spoil your benefit by turning it into a loan. Moreover the law, by not authorizing you, forbids you, by implication, to demand the repayment of a benefit." All this is nonsense. As long as I am in no pressing need, as long as I am not forced by poverty, I will lose my benefits rather than ask for repayment; but if the lives of my children were at stake, if my wife were in danger, if my regard for the welfare of my country and for my own liberty were to force me to adopt a course which I disliked, I should overcome my delicacy, and openly declare that I had done all that I could to avoid the necessity of receiving help from an ungrateful man; the necessity of obtaining repayment of one's benefit will in the end overcome one's delicacy about asking for it. In the next place, when I bestow a benefit upon a good man, I do so with the intention of never demanding repayment, except in case of absolute necessity.

XXI

"But," argues he, "by not authorizing you, the law forbids you to exact repayment." There are many things which are not enforced by any law or process, but which the conventions of society, which are stronger than any law, compel us to observe. There is no law forbidding us to divulge our friend's secrets; there is no law which bids us keep faith even with an enemy; pray what law is there which binds us to stand by what we have promised? There is none. Nevertheless I should remonstrate with one who did not keep a secret, and I should be indignant with one who pledged his word and broke it. "But," he argues, "you are turning a benefit into a loan." By no means, for I do not insist upon repayment, but only demand it; nay, I do not even demand it, but remind my friend of it. Even the direst need will not bring me to apply for help to one with whom I should have to undergo a long struggle.

If there be any one so ungrateful that it is not sufficient to remind him of his debt, I should pass him over, and think that he did not deserve to be made grateful by force. A money-lender does not demand repayment from his debtors if he knows they have become bankrupt, and, to their shame, have nothing but shame left to lose; and I, like him, should pass over those who are openly and obstinately ungrateful, and would demand repayment only from those who were likely to give it me, not from those from whom I should have to extort it by force.

XXII

There are many who cannot deny that they have received a benefit, yet cannot return it--men who are not good enough to be termed grateful, nor yet bad enough to be termed ungrateful; but who are dull and sluggish, backward debtors, though not defaulters. Such men as these I should not ask for repayment, but forcibly remind them of it, and, from a state of indifference, bring them back to their duty. They would at once reply, "Forgive me; I did not know, by Hercules, that you missed this, or I would have offered it of my own accord, I beg that you will not think me ungrateful; I remember your goodness to me." Why need I hesitate to make such men as these better to themselves and to me? I would prevent any one from doing wrong, if I were able; much more would I prevent a friend, both lest he should do wrong, and lest he should do wrong to me in particular. I bestow a second benefit upon him by not permitting him to be ungrateful; and I should not reproach him harshly with what I had done for him, but should speak as gently as I could. In order to afford him an opportunity of returning my kindness, I should refresh his remembrance of it, and ask for a benefit; he would understand that I was asking for repayment. Sometimes I would make use of somewhat severe language, if I had any hope that by it he might be amended; though I would not irritate a hopelessly ungrateful man, for fear that I might turn him into an enemy. If we spare the ungrateful even the affront of reminding them of their conduct, we shall render them' more backward in returning benefits; and although some might be cured of their evil ways, and be made into good men, if their consciences were stung by remorse, yet we shall allow them to perish for want of a word of warning, with which a father sometimes corrects his son, a wife brings back to herself an erring husband, or a man stimulates the wavering fidelity of his friend.

XXIII

To awaken some men, it is only necessary to stir them, not to strike them; in like manner, with some men, the feeling of honour about returning a benefit is not extinct, but slumbering. Let us rouse it. "Do not," they will say, "make the kindness you have done me into a wrong: for it is a wrong, if you do not demand some return from me, and so make me ungrateful. What if I do not know what sort of repayment you wish for? if I am so occupied by business, and my attention is so much diverted to other subjects that I have not been able to watch for an opportunity of serving you? Point out to me what I can do for you, what you wish me to do. Why do you despair, before making a trial of me? Why are you in such haste to lose both your benefit and your friend? How can you tell whether I do not wish, or whether I do not know how to repay you: whether it be in intention or in opportunity that I am wanting? Make a trial of me." I would therefore remind him of what I had done, without bitterness, not in public, or in a reproachful manner, but so that he may think that he himself has remembered it rather than that it has been recalled to him.

XXIV

One of Julius Caesar's veterans was once pleading before him against his neighbours, and the cause was going against him. "Do you remember, general," said he, "that in Spain you dislocated your ankle near the river Sucro[8]?" When Caesar said that he remembered it, he continued, "Do you remember that when, during the excessive heat, you wished to rest under a tree which afforded very little shade, as the ground in which that solitary tree grew was rough and rocky, one of your comrades spread his cloak under you?" Caesar answered, "Of course, I remember; indeed, I was perishing with thirst; and since was unable to walk to the nearest spring, I would have crawled thither on my hands and knees, had not my comrade, a brave and active man, brought me water in his helmet." "Could you, then, my general, recognize that man or that helmet?" Caesar replied that he could not remember the helmet, but that he could remember the man well; and he added, I fancy in anger at being led away to this old story in the midst of a judicial enquiry, "At any rate, you are not he." "I do not blame you, Caesar," answered the man, "for not recognizing me; for when this took place, I was unwounded; but afterwards, at the battle of Munda, my eye was struck out, and the bones of my skull crushed. Nor would you recognize that helmet if you saw it, for it was split by a Spanish sword." Caesar would not permit this man to be troubled with lawsuits, and presented his old soldier with the fields through which a village right of way had given rise to the dispute.

---

[8] Xucar

XXV

In this case, what ought he to have done? Because his commander's memory was confused by a multitude of incidents, and because his position as the leader of vast armies did not permit him to notice individual soldiers, ought the man not to have asked for a return for the benefit which he had conferred? To act as he did is not so much to ask for a return as to take it when it lies in a convenient position ready for us, although we have to stretch out our hands in order to receive it. I shall therefore ask for the return of a benefit, whenever I am either reduced to great straits, or where by doing so I shall act to the advantage of him from whom I ask it. Tiberius Caesar, when some one addressed him with the words, "Do you remember . . . .?" answered, before the man could mention any further proofs of former acquaintance, "I do not remember what I was." Why should it not be forbidden to demand of this man repayment of former favours? He had a motive for forgetting them: he denied all knowledge of his friends and comrades, and wished men only to see, to think, and to speak of him as emperor. He regarded his old friend as an impertinent meddler.

We ought to be even more careful to choose a favorable opportunity when we ask for a benefit to be repaid to us than when we ask for one to be bestowed upon us. We must be temperate in our language, so that the grateful may not take offence, or the ungrateful pretend to do so. If we lived among wise men, it would be our duty to wait in silence until our benefits were returned. Yet even to wise men it would be better to give some hint of what our position required. We ask for help even from the gods themselves, from whose knowledge nothing is hid, although our prayers cannot alter their intentions towards us, but can only recall them to their minds. Homer's priest, [Il. i. 39 sqq.] I say, recounts even to the gods his duteous conduct and his pious care of their altars. The second best form of virtue is to be willing and able to take advice.[Hes. Op. 291.] A horse who is docile and prompt to obey can be guided hither and thither by the slightest movement of the reins. Very few men are led by their own reason: those who come next to the best are those who return to the right path in consequence of advice; and these we must not deprive of their guide. When our eyes are covered they still possess sight; but it is the light of day which, when admitted to them, summons them to perform their duty: tools lie idle, unless the workman uses them to take part in his work. Similarly men's minds contain a good feeling, which, however, lies torpid, either through luxury and disuse, or through ignorance of its duties. This we ought to render useful, and not to get into a passion with it, and leave it in its wrong doing, but bear with it patiently, just as schoolmasters bear patiently with the blunders of forgetful scholars; for as by the prompting of a word or two their memory is often recalled to the text of the speech which they have to repeat, so men's goodwill can be brought to return kindness by reminding them of it.

On Benefits – Book VI

I

There are some things, my most excellent Liberalis, which lie completely outside of our actual life, and which we only inquire into in order to exercise our intellects, while others both give us pleasure while we are discovering them, and are of use when discovered. I will place all these in your hands; you, at your own discretion, may order them either to be investigated thoroughly, or to be reserved, and be used as agreeable interludes. Something will be gained even by those which you dismiss at once, for it is advantageous even to know what subjects are not worth learning. I shall be guided, therefore, by your face: according to its expression, I shall deal with some questions at greater length, and drive others out of court, and put an end to them at once.

II

It is a question whether a benefit can be taken away from one by force. Some say that it cannot, because it is not a thing, but an act. A gift is not the same as the act of giving, any more than a sailor is the same as the act of sailing. A sick man and a disease are not the same thing, although no one can be ill without disease; and, similarly, a benefit itself is one thing, and what any of us receive through a benefit is another. The benefit itself is incorporeal, and never becomes invalid; but its subject-matter changes owners, and passes from hand to hand. So, when you take away from anyone what you have given him, you take away the subject-matter only of the benefit, not the benefit itself. Nature herself cannot recall what she has given. She may cease to bestow benefits, but cannot take them away: a man who dies, yet has lived; a man who becomes blind, nevertheless has seen. She can cut off her blessings from us in the future, but she cannot prevent our having enjoyed them in the past. We are frequently not able to enjoy a benefit for long, but the benefit is not thereby destroyed. Let Nature struggle as hard as she please, she cannot give herself retrospective action. A man may lose his house, his money, his property--everything to which the name of benefit can be given-- yet the benefit itself will remain firm and unmoved; no power can prevent his benefactor's having bestowed them, or his having received them.

III

I think that a fine passage in Rabirius's poem, where M. Antonius, seeing his fortune deserting him, nothing left him except the privilege of dying, and even that only on condition that he used it promptly, exclaims,

"What I have given, that I now possess!"

How much he might have possessed, had he chosen! These are riches to be depended upon, which through all the turmoil of human life will remain steadfast; and the greater they are, the less envy they will attract. Why are you sparing of your property, as though it were your own? You are but the manager of it. All those treasures, which make you swell with pride, and soar above mere mortals, till you forget the weakness of your nature; all that which you lock up in iron-grated treasuries, and guard in arms, which you win from other men with their lives, and defend at the risk of your own; for which you launch fleets to dye the sea with blood, and shake the walls of cities, not knowing what arrows fortune may be preparing for you behind your back; to gain which you have so often violated all the ties of relationship, of friendship, and of colleagueship, till the whole world lies crushed between the two combatants: all these are not yours; they are a kind of deposit, which is on the point of passing into other hands: your enemies, or your heirs, who are little better, will seize upon them. "How," do you ask, "can you make them your own?" "By giving them away." Do, then, what is best for your own interests, and gain a sure enjoyment of them, which cannot be taken from you, making them at once more certainly yours, and more honorable to you. That which you esteem so highly, that by which you think that you are made rich and powerful, owns but the shabby title of "house," "slave," or "money;" but when you have given it away, it becomes a benefit.

IV

"You admit," says our adversary, "that we sometimes are under no obligation to him from whom we have received a benefit. In that case it has been taken by force." Nay, there are many things which would cause us to cease to feel gratitude for a benefit, not because the benefit has been taken from me, but because it has been spoiled. Suppose that a man has defended me in a lawsuit, but has forcibly outraged my wife; he has not taken away the benefit which he conferred upon me, but by balancing it with an equivalent wrong, he has set me free from my debt; indeed, if he has injured me more than he had previously benefited me, he not only puts an end to my gratitude, but makes me free to revenge myself upon him, and to complain of him, when the wrong outweighs the benefit; in such a case the benefit is not taken away, but is overcome. Why, are not some fathers so cruel and so wicked that it is right and proper for their sons to turn away from them, and disown them? Yet, pray, have they taken away the life which they gave? No, but their unnatural conduct in later years has destroyed all the gratitude which was due to them for their original benefit. In these cases it is not a benefit itself, but the gratitude owing for a benefit which is taken away, and the result is, not that one does not possess the benefit, but that one is not laid under any obligation by it. It is as though a man were to lend me money, and then burn my house down; the advantage of the loan is balanced by the damage which he has caused: I do not repay him, and yet I am not in his debt. In like manner any one who may have acted kindly and generously to me, and who afterwards has shown himself haughty, insulting, and cruel, places me in just the same position as though I never had received anything from him: he has murdered his own benefits. Though the lease may remain in force, still a man does not continue to be a tenant if his landlord tramples down his crops, or cuts down his orchard; their contract is at an end, not because the landlord has received the rent which was agreed upon, but because he has made it impossible that he should receive it. So, too, a creditor often has to pay money to his debtor, should he have taken more property from him in other transactions than he claims as having lent him. The judge does not sit merely to decide between debtor and creditor, when he says, "You did lend the man money; but then, what followed? You have driven away his cattle, you have murdered his slave, you have in your possession plate which you have not paid for. After valuing what each has received, I order you, who came to this court as a creditor, to leave it as a debtor." In like manner a balance is struck between benefits and injuries. In many cases, I repeat, a benefit is not taken away from him who receives it, and yet it lays him under no obligation, if the giver has repented of giving it, called himself unhappy because he gave it, sighed or made a wry face while he gave it; if he thought that he was throwing it away rather than giving it, if he gave it to please himself, or to please any one except me, the receiver; if he persistently makes himself offensive by boasting of what he has done, if he brags of his gift everywhere, and makes it a misery to me, then indeed the benefit remains in my hands, but I owe him nothing for it, just as sums of money to which a creditor has no legal right are owed to him, but cannot be claimed by him;

V

Though you have bestowed a benefit upon me, yet you have since done me a wrong; the benefit demanded gratitude, the wrong required vengeance: the result is that I do not owe you gratitude, nor do you owe me compensation--each is cancelled by the other. When we say, "I returned him his benefit," we do not mean that we restored to him the very thing which we had received, but something else in its place. To return is to give back one thing instead of another, because, of course, in all repayment it is not the thing itself, but its equivalent which is returned. We are said to have returned money even though we count out gold pieces instead of silver ones, or even if no money passes between us, but the transaction be effected verbally by the assignment of a debt.

I think I see you say, "You are wasting your time; of what use is it to me to know whether what I do not owe to another still remains in my hands or not? These are like the ingenious subtleties of the lawyers, who declare that one cannot acquire an inheritance by prescription, but can only acquire those things of which the inheritance consists, as though there were any difference between the heritage and the things of which it consists. Rather decide this point for me, which may be of use. If the same man confers a benefit upon me, and afterwards does me a wrong, is it my duty to return the benefit to him, and nevertheless to avenge myself upon him, having, as it were, two distinct accounts open with him, or to mix them both together, and do nothing, leaving the benefit to be wiped out by the injury, the injury by the benefit? I see that the former course is adopted by the law of the land; you know best what the law may be among you Stoic philosophers in such a case. I suppose that you keep the action which I bring against another distinct from that which he Strings against me, and the two processes are not merged into one? For instance, if a man entrusts me with money, and afterwards robs me, I shall bring an action against him for theft, and he will bring one against me for unlawfully detaining his property?"

VI

The cases which you have mentioned, my Liberalis, come under well-established laws, which it is necessary for us to follow. One law cannot be merged in another: each one proceeds its own way. There is a particular action which deals with deposits just as there is one which deals with theft. A benefit is subject to no law; it depends upon my own arbitration. I am at liberty to contrast the amount of good or harm which any one may have done me, and then to decide which of us is indebted to the other. In legal processes we ourselves have no power, we must go whither they lead us; in the case of a benefit the supreme power is mine, I pronounce sentence. Consequently I do not separate or distinguish between benefits and wrongs, but send them before the same judge. Unless I did so, you would bid me love and hate, give thanks and make complaints at the same time, which human nature does not admit of. I would rather compare the benefit and the injury with one another, and see whether there were any balance in my favour. If anybody puts lines of other writing upon my manuscript he conceals, though he does not take away, the letters which were there before, and in like manner a wrong coming after a benefit does not allow it to be seen.

VII

Your face, by which I have agreed to be guided, now becomes wrinkled with frowns, as though I were straying too widely from the subject. You seem to say to me:

"Why steer to seaward? Hither bend thy course, Hug close the shore..."

I do hug it as close as possible. So now, if you think that we have dwelt sufficiently upon this point, let us proceed to the consideration of the next-- that is, whether we are at all indebted to any one who does us good without wishing to do so. I might have expressed this more clearly, if it were not right that the question should be somewhat obscurely stated, in order that by the distinction immediately following it may be shown that we mean to investigate the case both of him who does us good against his will, and that of him who does us good without knowing it. That a man who does us good by acting under compulsion does not thereby lay us under any obligation, is so clear, that no words are needed to prove it. Both this question, and any other of the like character which may be raised, can easily be settled if in each case we bear in mind that, for anything to be a benefit, it must reach us in the first place through some thought, and secondly through the thought of a friend and well-wisher. Therefore we do not feel any gratitude towards rivers, albeit they may bear large ships, afford an ample and unvarying stream for the conveyance of merchandise, or flow beauteously and full of fish through fertile fields. No one conceives himself to be indebted for a benefit to the Nile, any more than he would owe it a grudge if its waters flooded his fields to excess, and retired more slowly than usual; the wind does not bestow benefits, gentle and favorable though it may be, nor does wholesome and useful food; for he who would bestow a benefit upon me, must not only do me good, but must wish to do so. No obligation can therefore be incurred towards dumb animals; yet how many men have been saved from peril by the swiftness of a horse!--nor yet towards trees--yet how many sufferers from summer heat have been sheltered by the thick foliage of a tree! What difference can it make, whether I have profited by the act of one who did not know that he was doing me good, or one who could not know it, when in each case the will to do me good was wanting? You might as well bid me be grateful to a ship, a carriage, or a lance for saving me from danger, as bid me be grateful to a man who may have done me good by chance, but with no more intention of doing me good than those things could have.

VIII

Some men may receive benefits without knowing it, but no man can bestow them without knowing it. Many sick persons have been cured by chance circumstances, which do not therefore become specific remedies; as, for instance, one man was restored to health by falling into a river during very cold weather, as another was set free from a quartan fever by means of a flogging, because the sudden terror turned his attention into a new channel, so that the dangerous hours passed unnoticed. Yet none of these are remedies, even though they may have been successful; and in like manner some men do us good, though they are unwilling--indeed, because they are unwilling to do so--yet we need not feel grateful to them as though we had received a benefit from them, because fortune has changed the evil which they intended into good. Do you suppose that I am indebted to a man who strikes my enemy with a blow which he aimed at me, who would have injured me had he not missed his mark? It often happens that by openly perjuring himself a man makes even trustworthy witnesses disbelieved, and renders his intended victim an object of compassion, as though he were being ruined by a conspiracy. Some have been saved by the very power which was exerted to crush them, and judges who would have condemned a man by law, have refused to condemn him by favour. Yet they did not confer a benefit upon the accused, although they rendered him a service, because we must consider at what the dart was aimed, not what it hits, and a benefit is distinguished from an injury not by its result, but by the spirit in which it was meant. By contradicting himself, by irritating the judge by his arrogance, or by rashly allowing his whole case to depend upon the testimony of one witness, my opponent may have saved my cause. I do not consider whether his mistakes benefited me or not, for he wished me ill.

IX

In order that I may be grateful, I must wish to do what my benefactor must have wished in order that he might bestow a benefit. Can anything be more unjust than to bear a grudge against a person who may have trodden upon one's foot in a crowd, or splashed one, or pushed one the way which one did not wish to go? Yet it was by his act that we were injured, and we only refrain from complaining of him, because he did not know what he was doing. The same reason makes it possible for men to do us good without conferring benefits upon us, or to harm us without doing us wrong, because it is intention which distinguishes our friends from our enemies. How many have been saved from service in the army by sickness! Some men have been saved from sharing the fall of their house, by being brought up upon their recognizances to a court of law by their enemies; some have been saved by ship-wreck from falling into the hands of pirates; yet we do not feel grateful to such things, because chance has no feeling of the service it renders, nor are we grateful to our enemy, though his lawsuit, while it harassed and detained us, still saved our lives. Nothing can be a benefit which does not proceed from good will, and which is not meant as such by the giver. If any one does me a service, without knowing it, I am under no obligation to him; should he do so, meaning to injure me, I shall imitate his conduct.

X

Let us turn our attention to the first of these. Can you desire me to do anything to express my gratitude to a man who did nothing in order to confer a benefit upon me? Passing on to the next, do you wish me to show my gratitude to such a man, and of my own will to return to him what I received from him against his will? What am I to say of the third, he who, meaning to do an injury, blunders into bestowing a benefit? That you should have wished to confer a benefit upon me is not sufficient to render me grateful; but that you should have wished not to do so is enough to set me free from any obligation to you. A mere wish does not constitute a benefit; and just as the best and heartiest wish is not a benefit when fortune prevents its being carried into effect, neither is what fortune bestows upon us a benefit, unless good wishes preceded it. In order to lay me under an obligation, you must not merely do me a service, but you must do so intentionally.

XI

Cleanthes makes use of the following example:--"I sent," says he, "two slaves to look for Plato and bring him to me from the Academy. One of them searched through the whole of the colonnade, and every other place in which he thought that he was likely to be found, and returned home alike weary and unsuccessful; the other sat down among the audience of a mountebank close by, and, while amusing himself in the society of other slaves like a careless vagabond as he was, found Plato, without seeking for him, as he happened to pass that way. We ought," says he, "to praise that slave who, as far as lay in his power, did what he was ordered, and we ought to punish the other whose laziness turned out so fortunate." It is goodwill alone which does one real service; let us then consider under what conditions it lays us under obligations. It is not enough to wish a man well, without doing him good; nor is it enough to do him good without wishing him well. Suppose that some one wished to give me a present, but did not give it; I have his good will, but I do not have his benefit, which consists of subject matter and goodwill together. I owe nothing to one who wished to lend me money but did not do so, and in like manner I shall be the friend of one who wished but was not able to bestow a benefit upon me, but I shall not be under any obligation to him. I also shall wish to bestow something upon him, even as he did upon me; but if fortune be more favorable to me than to him, and I succeed in bestowing something upon him, my doing so will be a benefit bestowed upon him, not a repayment out of gratitude for what he did for me. It will become his duty to be grateful to me; I shall have begun the interchange of benefits; the series must be counted from my act.

XII

I already understand what you wish to ask; there is no need for you to say anything, your countenance speaks for you. "If any one does us good for his own sake, are we," you ask, "under an obligation to him? I often hear you complain that there are some things which men make use of themselves, but which they put down to the account of others." I will tell you, my Liberalis; but first let me distinguish between the two parts of your question, and separate what is fair from what is unfair. It makes a great difference whether any one bestows a benefit upon us for his own sake, or whether he does so partly for his own sake and partly for ours. He who looks only to his own interests, and who does us good because he cannot otherwise make a profit for himself, seems to me to be like the farmer who provides winter and summer fodder for his flocks, or like the man who feeds up the captives whom he has bought in order that they may fetch a better price in the slave market, or who crams and curry-combs fat oxen for sale; or like the keeper of a school of arms, who takes great pains in exercising and equipping his gladiators. As Cleanthes says, there is a great difference between benefits and trade.

XIII

On the other hand, I am not so unjust as to feel no gratitude to a man, because, while helping me, he helped himself also; for I do not insist upon his consulting my interests to the exclusion of his own--nay, I should prefer that the benefit which I receive may be of even greater advantage to the giver, provided that he thought of us both when giving it, and meant to divide it between me and himself. Even should he possess the larger portion of it, still, if he admits me to a share, if he meant it for both of us, I am not only unjust but ungrateful, if I do not rejoice in what has benefited me benefiting him also. It is the essence of spitefulness to say that nothing can be a benefit which does not cause some inconvenience to the giver.

As for him who bestows a benefit for his own sake, I should say to him, "You have made use of me, and how can you say that you have bestowed a benefit upon me, rather than I upon you?" "Suppose," answers he, "that I cannot obtain a public office except by ransoming ten citizens out of a great number of captives, will you owe me nothing for setting you free from slavery and bondage? Yet I shall do so for my own sake." To this I should answer, "You do this partly for my sake, partly for your own. It is for your own sake that you ransom captives, but it is for my sake that you ransom me; for to serve your purpose it would be enough for you to ransom any one. I am therefore your debtor, not for ransoming me but for choosing me, since you might have attained the same result by ransoming some one else instead of me. You divide the advantages of the act between yourself and me, and you confer upon me a benefit by which both of us profit. What you do entirely for my sake is, that you choose me in preference to others. If therefore you were to be made praetor for ransoming ten captives, and there were only ten of us captives, none of us would be under any obligation to you, because there is nothing for which you can ask any one of us to give you credit apart from your own advantage. I do not regard a benefit jealously and wish it to be given to myself alone, but I wish to have a share in it."

XIV

"Well, then," says he, "suppose that I were to order all your names to be put into a ballot-box, and that your name was drawn among those who were to be ransomed, would you owe me nothing?" Yes, I should owe you something, but very little: how little, I will explain to you. By so doing you do something for my sake, in that you grant me the chance of being ransomed; I owe to fortune that my name was drawn, all I owe to you is that my name could be drawn. You have given me the means of obtaining your benefit. For the greater part of that benefit I am indebted to fortune; that I could be so indebted, I owe to you.

I shall take no notice whatever of those whose benefits are bestowed in a mercenary spirit, who do not consider to whom, but upon what terms they give, whose benefits are entirely selfish. Suppose that some one sells me corn; I cannot live unless I buy it; yet I do not owe my life to him because I have bought it. I do not consider how essential it was to me, and that I could not live without it; but how little thanks are due for it, since I could not have had it without paying for it, and since the merchant who imported it did not consider how much good he would do me, but how much he would gain for himself, I owe nothing for what I have bought and paid for.

XV

"According to this reasoning," says my opponent, "you would say that you owe nothing to a physician beyond his paltry fee, nor to your teacher, because you have paid him some money; yet these persons are all held very dear, and are very much respected." In answer to this I should urge that some things are of greater value than the price which we pay for them. You buy of a physician life and good health, the value of which cannot be estimated in money; from a teacher of the liberal sciences you buy the education of a gentleman and mental culture; therefore you pay these persons the price, not of what they give us, but of their trouble in giving it; you pay them for devoting their attention to us, for disregarding their own affairs to attend to us: they receive the price, not of their services, but of the expenditure of their time. Yet this may be more truly stated in another way, which I will at once lay before you, having first pointed out how the above may be confuted. Our adversary would say, "If some things are of greater value than the price which we pay for them, then, though you may have bought them, you still owe me something more for them." I answer, in the first place, what does their real value matter, since the buyer and seller have settled the price between them? Next, I did not buy it at it's own price, but at yours. "It is," you say, "worth more than its sale price." True, but it cannot be sold for more. The price of everything varies according to circumstances; after you have well praised your wares, they are worth only the highest price at which you can sell them; a man who buys things cheap is not on that account under any obligation to the seller. In the next place, even if they are worth more, there is no generosity in your letting them go for less, since the price is settled by custom and the rate of the market, not by the uses and powers of the merchandise. What would you state to be the proper payment of a man who crosses the seas, holding a true course through the midst of the waves after the land has sunk out of sight, who foresees coming storms, and suddenly, when no one expects danger, orders sails to be furled, yards to be lowered, and the crew to stand at their posts ready to meet the fury of the unexpected gale? and yet the price of such great skill is fully paid for by the passage money. At what sum can you estimate the value of a lodging in a wilderness, of a shelter in the rain, of a bath or fire in cold weather? Yet I know on what terms I shall be supplied with these when I enter an inn. How much the man does for us who props our house when it is about to fall, and who, with a skill beyond belief, suspends in the air a block of building which has begun to crack at the, foundation; yet we can contract for underpinning at a fixed and cheap rate. The city wall keeps us safe from our enemies, and from sudden inroads of brigands; yet it is, well known how much a day a smith would earn for erecting towers and scaffoldings[1] to provide for the public safety.

---

[1] See Viollet-le-Duc's "Dictionnaire d'Architecture," articles "Architecture Militaire" and "Hourds," for the probable meaning of "Propugnacula."

XVI

I might go on for ever collecting instances to prove that valuable things are sold at a low price. What then? why is it that I owe something extra both to my physician and to my teacher, and that I do not acquit myself of all obligation to them by paying them their fee? It is because they pass from physicians and teachers into friends, and lay us under obligations, not by the skill which they sell to us, but by kindly and familiar good will. If my physician does no more than feel my pulse and class me among those whom he sees in his daily rounds, pointing out what I ought to do or to avoid without any personal interest, then I owe him no more than his fee, because he views me with the eye not of a friend, but of a commander.[2] Neither have I any reason for loving my teacher, if he has regarded me merely as one of the mass of his scholars, and has not thought me worthy of taking especial pains with by myself, if he has never fixed his attention upon me, and if when he discharged his knowledge on the public, I might be said rather to have picked it up than to have learnt it from him. What then is our reason for owing them much? It is, not that what they have sold us is worth more than we paid for it, but that they have given something to us personally. Suppose that my physician has spent more consideration upon my case than was professionally necessary; that it was for me, not for his own credit, that he feared: that he was not satisfied with pointing out remedies, but himself applied them, that he sat by my bedside among my anxious friends, and came to see me at the crises of my disorder; that no service was too troublesome or too disgusting for him to perform; that he did not hear my groans unmoved; that among the numbers who called for him I was his favourite case; and that he gave the others only so much time as his care of my health permitted him: I should feel obliged to such a man not as to a physician, but as to a friend. Suppose again that my teacher endured labour and weariness in instructing me; that he taught me something more than is taught by all masters alike; that he roused my better feelings by his encouragement, and that at one time he would raise my spirits by praise, and at another warn me to shake off slothfulness: that he laid his hand, as it were, upon my latent and torpid powers of intellect and drew them out into the light of day; that he did not stingily dole out to me what he knew, in order that he might be wanted for a longer time, but was eager, if possible, to pour all his learning into me; then I am ungrateful, if I do not love him as much as I love my nearest relatives and my dearest friends.

---

[2] I read "Nbn tamquam amicus videt sed tamquam imperator."

XVII

We give something additional even to those who teach the meanest trades, if their efforts appear to be extraordinary; we bestow a gratuity upon pilots, upon workmen who deal with the commonest materials and hire themselves out by the day. In the noblest arts, however, those which either preserve or beautify our lives, a man would be ungrateful who thinks he owes the artist no more than he bargained for. Besides this, the teaching of such learning as we have spoken of blends mind with mind; now when this takes place, both in the case of the physician and of the teacher the price of his work is paid, but that of his mind remains owing.

XVIII

Plato once crossed a river, and as the ferryman did not ask him for anything, he supposed that he had let him pass free out of respect, and said that the ferryman had laid Plato under an obligation. Shortly afterwards, seeing the ferryman take one person after another across the river with the same pains, and without charging anything, Plato declared that the ferryman had not laid him under an obligation. If you wish me to be grateful for what you give, you must not merely give it to me, but show that you mean it specially for me; you cannot make any claim upon one for having given him what you fling away broad-cast among the crowd. What then? shall I owe you nothing for it? Nothing, as an individual; I will pay, when the rest of mankind do, what I owe no more than they.

XIX

"Do you say," inquires my opponent, "that he who carries me gratis in a boat across the river Po, does not bestow any benefit upon me?" I do. He does me some good, but he does not bestow a benefit upon me; for he does it for his own sake, or at any rate not for mine; in short, he himself does not imagine that he is bestowing a benefit upon me, but does it for the credit of the State, or of the neighbourhood, or of himself, and expects some return for doing so, different from what he would receive from individual passengers. "Well," asks my opponent, "if the emperor were to grant the franchise to all the Gauls, or exemption, from taxes to all the Spaniards, would each individual of them owe him nothing on that account?" Of course he would: but he would be indebted to him, not as having personally received a benefit intended for himself alone, but as a partaker in one conferred upon his nation. He would argue, "The emperor had no thought of me at the time when he benefited us all; he did not care to give me the franchise separately, he did not fix his attention upon me; why then should I be grateful to one who did not have me in his mind when he was thinking of doing what he did? In answer to this, I say that when he thought of doing good to all the Gauls, he thought of doing good to me also, for I was a Gaul, and he included me under my national, if not under my personal appellation. In like manner, I should feel grateful to him, not as for a personal, but for a general benefit; being only one of the people, I should regard the debt of gratitude as incurred, not by myself, but by my country, and should not pay it myself, but only contribute my share towards doing so. I do not call a man my creditor because he has lent money to my country, nor should I include that money in a schedule of my debts were I either a candidate for a public office, or a defendant in the courts; yet I would pay my share towards extinguishing such a debt. Similarly, I deny that I am laid under an obligation by a gift bestowed upon my entire nation, because although the giver gave it to me, yet he did not do so for my sake, but gave it without knowing whether he was giving it to me or not: nevertheless I should feel that I owed something for the gift, because it did reach me, though not directly. To lay me under an obligation, a thing must be done for my sake alone.

XX

"According to this," argues our opponent, "you are under no obligation to the sun or the moon; for they do not move for your sake alone." No, but since they move with the object of preserving the balance of the universe, they move for my sake also, seeing that I am a fraction of the universe. Besides, our position and theirs is not the same, for he who does me good in order that he may by my means do good to himself, does not bestow a benefit upon me, because he merely makes use of me as an instrument for his own advantage; whereas the sun and the moon, even if they do us good for their own sakes, still cannot do good to us in order that by our means they may do good to themselves, for what is there which we can bestow upon them?

XXI

"I should be sure," replies he, "that the sun and the moon wished to do us good, if they were able to refuse to do so; but they cannot help moving as they do. In short, let them stop and discontinue their work."

See now, in how many ways this argument may be refuted. One who cannot refuse to do a thing may nevertheless wish to do it; indeed there is no greater proof of a fixed desire to do anything, than not to be able to alter one's determination. A good man cannot leave undone what he does: for unless he does it he will not be a good man. Is a good man, then, not able to bestow a benefit, because he does what he ought to do, and is not able not to do what he ought to do? Besides this, it makes a great difference whether you say, "He is not able not to do this, because he is forced to do it," or "He is not able to wish not to do it;" for, if he could not help doing it, then I am not indebted for it to him, but to the person who forced him to do it; if he could not help wishing for it because he had nothing better to wish for, then it is he who forces himself to do it, and in this case the debt which as acting under compulsion he could not claim, is due to him as compelling himself.

"Let the sun and moon cease to wish to benefit us," says our adversary. I answer, "Remember what has been said. Who can be so crazy as to refuse the name of free-will to that which has no danger of ceasing to act, and of adopting the opposite course, since, on the contrary, he whose will is fixed for ever, must be thought to wish more earnestly than any one else. Surely if he, who may at any moment change his mind, can be said to wish, we must not deny the existence of will in a being whose nature does not admit of change of mind.

XXII

"Well," says he "let them stop, if it be possible." What you say is this:--Let all those heavenly bodies, placed as they are at vast distances from each other, and arranged to preserve the balance of the universe, leave their appointed posts: let sudden confusion arise, so that constellations may collide with constellations, that the established harmony of all things may be destroyed and the works of God be shaken into ruin; let the whole frame of the rapidly moving heavenly bodies abandon in mid career those movements which we were assured would endure for ages, and let those which now by their regular advance and retreat keep the world at a moderate temperature, be instantly consumed by fire, so that instead of the infinite variety of the seasons all may be reduced to one uniform condition; let fire rage everywhere, followed by dull night, and let the bottomless abyss swallow up all the gods." Is it worth while to destroy all this merely in order to refute you? Even though you do not wish it, they do you good, and they wheel in their courses for your sake, though their motion may be due to some earlier and more important cause.

XXIII

Besides this, the gods act under no external constraint, but their own will is a law to them for all time. They have established an order which is not to be changed, and consequently it is impossible that they should appear to be likely to do anything against their will, since they wish to continue doing whatever they cannot cease from doing, and they never regret their original decision, No doubt it is impossible for them to stop short, or to desert to the other side, but it is so for no other reason than that their own force holds them to their purpose. It is from no weakness that they persevere; no, they have no mind to leave the best course, and by this it is fated that they should proceed. When, at the time of the original creation, they arranged the entire universe, they paid attention to us as well as to the rest, and took thought about the human race; and for this reason we cannot suppose that it is merely for their own pleasure that they move in their orbits and display their work since we also are a part of that work. We are, therefore; under an obligation to the sun and moon and the rest of the heavenly host, because, although they may rise in order to bestow more important benefits than those which we receive from them, yet they do bestow these upon us as they pass on their way to greater things. Besides this, they assist us of set purpose, and, therefore, lay us under an obligation, because we do not in their case stumble by chance upon a benefit bestowed by one who knew not what he was doing, but they knew that we should receive from them the advantages which we do; so that, though they may have some higher aim, though the result of their movements may be something of greater importance than the preservation of the human race, yet from the beginning thought has been directed to our comforts, and the scheme of the world has been arranged in a fashion which proves that our interests were neither their least nor last concern. It is our duty to show filial love for our parents, although many of them had no thought of children when they married. Not so with the gods: they cannot but have known what they were doing when they furnished mankind with food and comforts. Those for whose advantage so much was created, could not have been created without design. Nature conceived the idea of us before she formed us, and, indeed, we are no such trifling piece of work as could have fallen from her hands unheeded. See how great privileges she has bestowed upon us, how far beyond the human race the empire of mankind extends; consider how widely she allows us to roam, not having restricted us to the land alone, but permitted us to traverse every part of herself; consider, too, the audacity of our intellect, the only one which knows of the gods or seeks for them, and how we can raise our mind high above the earth, and commune with those divine influences: you will perceive that man is not a hurriedly put together, or an unstudied piece of work.

Among her noblest products nature has none of which she can boast more than man, and assuredly no other which can comprehend her boast. What madness is this, to call the gods in question for their bounty? If a man declares that he has received nothing when he is receiving all the while, and from those who will always be giving without ever receiving anything in return, how will he be grateful to those whose kindness cannot be returned without expense? and how great a mistake is it not to be thankful to a giver, because he is good even to him who disowns him, or to use the fact of his bounty being poured upon us in an uninterrupted stream, as an argument to prove that he cannot help bestowing it. Suppose that such men as these say, "I do not want it," "Let him keep it to himself," "Who asks him for it?" and so forth, with all the other speeches of insolent minds: still, he whose bounty reaches you, although you say that it does not, lays you under an obligation nevertheless; indeed, perhaps the greatest part of the benefit which he bestows is that he is ready to give even when you are complaining against him.

XXIV

Do you not see how parents force children during their infancy to undergo what is useful for their health? Though the children cry and struggle, they swathe them and bind their limbs straight lest premature liberty should make them grow crooked, afterwards instill into them a liberal education, threatening those who are unwilling to learn, and finally, if spirited young men do not conduct themselves frugally, modestly, and respectably, they compel them to do so. Force and harsh measures are used even to youths who have grown up and are their own masters, if they, either from fear or from insolence, refuse to take what is good for them. Thus the greatest benefits that we receive, we receive either without knowing it, or against our will, from our parents.

XXV

Those persons who are ungrateful and repudiate benefits, not because they do not wish to receive them, but in order that they may not be laid under an obligation for them, are like those who fall into the opposite extreme, and are over grateful, who pray that some trouble or misfortune may befall their benefactors to give them an opportunity of proving how gratefully they remember the benefit which they have received. It is a question whether they are right, and show a truly dutiful feeling; their state of mind is morbid, like that of frantic lovers who long for their mistress to be exiled, that they may accompany her when she leaves her country forsaken by all her friends, or that she may be poor in order that she may the more need what they give her, or who long that she may be ill in order that they may sit by her bedside, and who, in short, out of sheer love form the same wishes as her enemies would wish for her. Thus the results of hatred and of frantic love are very nearly the same; and these lovers are very like those who hope that their friends may meet with difficulties which they may remove, and who thus do a wrong that they may bestow a benefit, whereas it would have been much better for them to do nothing, than by a crime to gain an opportunity of doing good service. What should we say of a pilot who prayed to the gods for dreadful storms and tempests, in order that danger might make his skill more highly esteemed? what of a general who should pray that a vast number of the enemy surround his camp, fill the ditches by a sudden charge, tear down the rampart round his panic-stricken army, and plant its hostile standards at the very gates, in order that he might gain more glory by restoring his broken ranks and shattered fortunes? All such men confer their benefits upon us by odious means, for they beg the gods to harm those whom they mean to help, and wish them to be struck down before they raise them up; it is a cruel feeling, brought about by a distorted sense of gratitude, to wish evil to befall one whom one is bound in honour to succour.

XXVI

"My wish," argues our opponent, "does him no harm, because when I wish for the danger I wish for the rescue at the same time." What you mean by this is not that you do no wrong, but that you do less than if you wished that the danger might befall him, without wishing for the rescue. It is wicked to throw a man into the water in order that you may pull him out, to throw him down that you may raise him up, or to shut him up that you may release him. You do not bestow a benefit upon a man by ceasing to wrong him, nor can it ever be a piece of good service to anyone to remove from him a burden which you yourself imposed on him. True, you may cure the hurt which you inflict, but I had rather that you did not hurt me at all. You may gain my gratitude by curing me because I am wounded, but not by wounding me in order that you may cure me: no man likes scars except as compared with wounds, which he is glad to see thus healed, though he had rather not have received them. It would be cruel to wish such things to befall one from whom you had never received a kindness; how much more cruel is it to wish that they may befall one in whose debt you are.

XXVII

"I pray," replies he, "at the same time, that I may be able to help him." In the first place, if I stop you short in the middle of your prayer, it shows at once that you are ungrateful: I have not yet heard what you wish to do for him; I have heard what you wish him to suffer. You pray that anxiety and fear and even worse evil than this may come upon him. You desire that he may need aid: this is to his disadvantage; you desire that he may need your aid: this is to your advantage. You do not wish to help him, but to be set free from your obligation to him: for when you are eager to repay your debt in such a way as this, you merely wish to be set free from the debt, not to repay it. So the only part of your wish that could be thought honourable proves to be the base and ungrateful feeling of unwillingness to lie under an obligation: for what you wish for is, not that you may have an opportunity of repaying his kindness, but that he may be forced to beg you to do him a kindness. You make yourself the superior, and you wickedly degrade beneath your feet the man who has done you good service. How much better would it be to remain in his debt in an honourable and friendly manner, than to seek to discharge the debt by these evil means! You would be less to blame if you denied that you had received it, for your benefactor would then lose nothing more than what he gave you, whereas now you wish him to be rendered inferior to you, and brought by the loss of his property and social position into a condition below his own benefits. Do you think yourself grateful? Just utter your wishes in the hearing of him to whom you wish to do good. Do you call that a prayer for his welfare, which can be divided between his friend and his enemy, which, if the last part were omitted, you would not doubt was pronounced, by one who opposed and hated him? Enemies in war have sometimes wished to capture certain towns in order to spare them, or to conquer certain persons in order to pardon, them, yet these were the wishes of enemies, and what was the kindest part of them began by cruelty. Finally, what sort of prayers do you think those can be which he, on whose behalf they are made, hopes more earnestly than any one else may not be granted? In hoping that the gods may injure a man, and that you may help him, you deal most dishonourably with him, and you do not treat the gods themselves fairly, for you give them the odious part to play, and reserve the generous one for yourself: the gods must do him wrong in order that you may do him a service. If you were to suborn an informer to accuse a man, and afterwards withdrew him, if you engaged a man in a law suit and afterwards gave it up, no one would hesitate to call you a villain: what difference does it make, whether you attempt to do this by chicanery or by prayer, unless it be that by prayer you raise up more powerful enemies to him than by the other means? You cannot say "Why, what harm do I do him?" your prayer is either futile or harmful, indeed it is harmful even though nothing comes of it. You do your friend wrong by wishing him harm: you must thank the gods that you do him no harm. The fact of your wishing it is enough: we ought to be just as angry with you as if you had effected it.

XXVIII

"If," argues our adversary, "my prayers had any efficacy, they would also have been efficacious to save him from danger." In the first place, I reply, the danger into which you wish me to fall is certain, the help which I should receive is uncertain. Or call them both certain; it is that which injures me that comes first. Besides, YOU understand the terms of your wish; _I_ shall be tossed by the storm without being sure that I have a haven of rest at hand.

Think what torture it must have been to me, even if I receive your help, to have stood in need of it: if I escape safely, to have trembled for myself; if I be acquitted, to have had to plead my cause. To escape from fear, however great it may be, can never be so pleasant as to live in sound unassailable safety. Pray that you may return my kindnesses when I need their return, but do not pray that I may need them. You would have done what you prayed for, had it been in your power.

XXIX

How far more honourable would a prayer of this sort be: "I pray that he may remain in such a position as that he may always bestow benefits and never need them: may he be attended by the means of giving and helping, of which he makes such a bountiful use; may he never want benefits to bestow, or be sorry for any which he has bestowed; may his nature, fitted as it is for acts of pity, goodness, and clemency, be stimulated and brought out by numbers of grateful persons, whom I trust he will find without needing to make trial of their gratitude; may he refuse to be reconciled to no one, and may no one require to be reconciled to him: may fortune so uniformly continue to favour him that no one may be able to return his kindness in any way except by feeling grateful to him."

How far more proper are such prayers as these, which do not put you off to some distant opportunity, but express your gratitude at once? What is there to prevent your returning your benefactor's kindness, even while he is in prosperity? How many ways are there by which we can repay what we owe even to the affluent--for instance, by honest advice, by constant intercourse, by courteous conversation, pleasing him without flattering him, by listening attentively to any subject which he may wish to discuss, by keeping safe any secret that he may impart to us, and by social intercourse. There is no one so highly placed by fortune as not to want a friend all the more because he wants nothing.

XXX

The other is a melancholy opportunity, and one which we ought always to pray may be kept far from us: must the gods be angry with a man in order that you may prove your gratitude to him? Do you not perceive that you are doing wrong, from the very fact that those to whom you are ungrateful fare better? Call up before your mind dungeons, chains, wretchedness, slavery, war, poverty: these are the opportunities for which you pray; if any one has any dealings with you, it is by means of these that you square your account. Why not rather wish that he to whom you owe most may be powerful and happy? for, as I have just said, what is there to prevent your returning the kindness even of those who enjoy the greatest prosperity? to do which, ample and various opportunities will present themselves to you, What! do you not know that a debt can be paid even to a rich man? Nor will I trouble you with many instances of what you may do. Though a man's riches and prosperity may prevent your making him any other repayment, I will show you what the highest in the land stand in need of, what is wanting to those who possess everything. They want a man to speak the truth, to save them from the organized mass of falsehood by which they are beset, which so bewilders them with lies that the habit of hearing only what is pleasant instead of what is true, prevents their knowing what truth really is. Do you not see how such persons are driven to ruin by the want of candour among their friends, whose loyalty has degenerated into slavish obsequiousness? No one, when giving them his advice, tells them what he really thinks, but each vies with the other in flattery; and while the man's friends make it their only object to see who can most pleasantly deceive him, he himself is ignorant of his real powers, and, believing himself to be as great a man as he is told that he is, plunges the State in useless wars, which bring disasters upon it, breaks off a useful and necessary peace, and, through a passion of anger which no one checks, spills the blood of numbers of people, and at last sheds his own. Such persons assert what has never been investigated as certain facts, consider that to modify their opinion is as dishonourable as to be conquered, believe that institutions which are just flickering out of existence will last for ever, and, thus overturn great States, to the destruction of themselves and all who are connected with them. Living as they do in a fool's paradise, resplendent with unreal and short-lived advantages, they forget that, as soon as they put it out of their power to hear the truth, there is no limit to the misfortunes which they may expect.

XXXI

When Xerxes declared war against Greece, all his courtiers encouraged his boastful temper, which forgot how unsubstantial his grounds for confidence were. One declared that the Greeks would not endure to hear the news of the declaration of war, and would take to flight at the first rumour of his approach; another, that with such a vast army Greece could not only be conquered, but utterly overwhelmed, and that it was rather to be feared that they would find the Greek cities empty and abandoned, and that the panic flight of the enemy would leave them only vast deserts, where no use could be made of their enormous forces. Another told him that the world was hardly large enough to contain him, that the seas were too narrow for his fleets, the camps would not take in his armies, the plains were not wide enough to deploy his cavalry in, and that the sky itself was scarcely large enough to enable all his troops to hurl their darts at once. While much boasting of this sort was going on around him, raising his already overweening self-confidence to a frantic pitch, Demaratus, the Lacedaemonian, alone told him that the disorganized and unwieldy multitude in which he trusted, was in itself a danger to its chief, because it possessed only weight without strength; for an army which is too large cannot be governed, and one which cannot be governed, cannot long exist. "The Lacedaemonians," said he, "will meet you upon the first mountain in Greece, and will give you a taste of their quality. All these thousands of nations of yours will be held in check by three hundred men: they will stand firm at their posts, they will defend the passes entrusted to them with their weapons, and block them up with their bodies: all Asia will not force them to give way; few as they are, they will stop all this terrible invasion, attempted though it be by nearly the whole human race. Though the laws of nature may give way to you, and enable you to pass from Europe to Asia, yet you will stop short in a bypath; consider what your losses will be afterwards, when you have reckoned up the price which you have to pay for the pass of Thermopylae; when you learn that your march can be stayed, you will discover that you may be put to flight. The Greeks will yield up many parts of their country to you, as if they were swept out of them by the first terrible rush of a mountain torrent; afterwards they will rise against you from all quarters and will crush you by means of your own strength. What people say, that your warlike preparations are too great to be contained in the countries which you intend to attack, is quite true; but this is to our disadvantage. Greece will conquer you for this very reason, that she cannot contain you; you cannot make use of the whole of your force. Besides this, you will not be able to do what is essential to victory--that is, to meet the manoeuvres of the enemy at once, to support your own men if they give way, or to confirm and strengthen them when their ranks are wavering; long before you know it, you will be defeated. Moreover, you should not think that because your army is so large that its own chief does not know its numbers, it is therefore irresistible; there is nothing so great that it cannot perish; nay, without any other cause, its own excessive size may prove its ruin." What Demaratus predicted came to pass. He whose power gods and men obeyed, and who swept away all that opposed him, was bidden to halt by three hundred men, and the Persians, defeated in every part of Greece, learned how great a difference there is between a mob and an army. Thus it came to pass that Xerxes, who suffered more from the shame of his failure than from the losses which he sustained, thanked Demaratus for having been the only man who told him the truth, and permitted him to ask what boon he pleased. He asked to be allowed to drive a chariot into Sardis, the largest city in Asia, wearing a tiara erect upon his head, a privilege which was enjoyed by kings alone. He deserved his reward before he asked for it, but how wretched must the nation have been, in which there was no one who would speak the truth to the king except one man. who did not speak it to himself.

XXXII

The late Emperor Augustus banished his daughter, whose conduct went beyond the shame of ordinary immodesty, and made public the scandals of the imperial house

Led away by his passion, he divulged all these crimes which, as emperor, he ought to have kept secret with as much care as he punished them, because the shame of some deeds asperses even him who avenges them. Afterwards, when by lapse of time shame took the place of anger in his mind, he lamented that he had not kept silence about matters which he had not learned until it was disgraceful to speak of them, and often used to exclaim, "None of these things would have happened to me, if either Agrippa or Maecenas had lived!" So hard was it for the master of so many thousands of men to repair the loss of two. When his legions were slaughtered, new ones were at once enrolled; when his fleet was wrecked, within a few days another was afloat; when the public buildings were consumed by fire, finer ones arose in their stead; but the places of Agrippa and Maecenas remained unfilled throughout his life. What am I to imagine? that there were not any men like these, who could take their place, or that it was the fault of Augustus himself, who preferred mourning for them to seeking for their likes? We have no reason for supposing that it was the habit of Agrippa or Maecenas to speak the truth to him; indeed, if they had lived they would have been as great dissemblers as the rest. It is one of the habits of kings to insult their present servants by praising those whom they have lost, and to attribute the virtue of truthful speaking to those from whom there is no further risk of hearing it.

XXXIII

However, to return to my subject, you see how easy it is to return the kindness of the prosperous, and even of those who occupy the highest places of all mankind. Tell them, not what they wish to hear, but what they will wish that they always had heard; though their ears be stopped by flatteries, yet sometimes truth may penetrate them; give them useful advice. Do you ask what service you can render to a prosperous man? Teach him not to rely upon his prosperity, and to understand that it ought to be supported by the hands of many trusty friends. Will you not have done much for him, if you take away his foolish belief that his influence will endure for ever, and teach him that what we gain by chance passes away soon, and at a quicker rate than it came; that we cannot fall by the same stages by which we rose to the height of good fortune, but that frequently between it and ruin there is but one step? You do not know how great is the value of friendship, if you do not understand how much you give to him to whom you give a friend, a commodity which is scarce not only in men's houses, but in whole centuries, and which is nowhere scarcer than in the places where it is thought to be most plentiful. Pray, do you suppose that those books of names, which your nomenclator[3] can hardly carry or remember, are those of friends? It is not your friends who crowd to knock at your door, and who are admitted to your greater or lesser levees.

---

[3] The nomenclator was a slave who attended his master in canvassing and on similar occasions, for the purpose of telling him the names of whom he met in the street.

XXXIV

To divide one's friends into classes is an old trick of kings and their imitators; it shows great arrogance to think that to touch or to pass one's threshold can be a valuable privilege, or to grant as an honour that you should sit nearer one's front door than others, or enter house before them, although within the house there are many more doors, which shut out even those who have been admitted so far. With us Gaius Gracchus, and shortly after him Livius Drusus, were the first to keep themselves apart from the mass of their adherents, and to admit some to their privacy, some to their more select, and others to their general receptions. These men consequently had friends of the first and second rank, and so on, but in none had they true friends. Can you apply the name of friend to one who is admitted in his regular order to pay his respects to you? or can you expect perfect loyalty from one who is forced to slip into your presence through a grudgingly-opened door? How can a man arrive at using bold freedom of speech with you, if he is only allowed in his proper turn to make use of the common phrase, "Hail to you," which is used by perfect strangers? Whenever you go to any of these great men, whose levees interest the whole city, though you find all the streets beset with throngs of people, and the passers-by hardly able to make their way through the crowd, you may be sure that you have come to a place where there are many men, but no friends of their patron. We must not seek our friends in our entrance hall, but in our own breast; it is there that he ought to be received, there retained, and hoarded up in our minds. Teach this, and you will have repaid your debt of gratitude.

XXXV

If you are useful to your friend only when he is in distress, and are superfluous when all goes well with him, you form a mean estimate of your own value. As you can bear yourself wisely both in doubtful, in prosperous, and in adverse circumstances, by showing prudence in doubtful cases, courage in misfortune, and self-restraint in good fortune, so in all circumstances you can make yourself useful to your friend. Do not desert him in adversity, but do not wish that it may befall him: the various incidents of human life will afford you many opportunities of proving your loyalty to him without wishing him evil. He who prays that another may become rich, in order that he may share his riches, really has a view to his own advantage, although his prayers are ostensibly offered in behalf of his friend; and similarly he who wishes that his friend may get into some trouble from which his own friendly assistance may extricate him--a most ungrateful wish--prefers himself to his friend, and thinks it worthwhile that his friend should be unhappy, in order that he may prove his gratitude. This very wish makes him ungrateful, for he wishes to rid himself of his gratitude as though it were a heavy burden. In returning a kindness it makes a great difference whether you are eager to bestow a benefit, or merely to free yourself from a debt. He who wishes to return a benefit will study his friend's interests, and will hope that a suitable occasion will arise; he who only wishes to free himself from an obligation will be eager to do so by any means whatever, which shows very bad feeling. "Do you say," we may be asked, "that eagerness to repay kindness belongs to a morbid feeling of gratitude?" I cannot explain my meaning more clearly than by repeating what I have already said. You do not want to repay, but to escape from the benefit which you have received. You seem to say, "When shall I get free from this obligation? I must strive by any means in my power to extinguish my debt to him." You would be thought to be far from grateful, if you wished to pay a debt to him with his own money; yet this wish of yours is even more unjust; for you invoke curses upon him, and call down terrible imprecations upon the head of one who ought to be held sacred by you. No one, I suppose, would have any doubt of your wickedness if you were openly to pray that he might suffer poverty, captivity, hunger, or fear; yet what is the difference between openly praying for some of these things, and silently wishing for them? for you do wish for some of these. Go, and enjoy your belief that this is gratitude, to do what not even an ungrateful man would do, supposing he confined himself to repudiating the benefit, and did not go so far as to hate his benefactor.

XXXVI

Who would call Aeneas pious, if he wished that his native city might be captured, in order that he might save his father from captivity? Who would point to the Sicilian youths as good examples for his children, if they had prayed that Aetna might flame with unusual heat and pour forth a vast mass of fire in order to afford them an opportunity of displaying their filial affection by rescuing their parents from the midst of the conflagration? Rome owes Scipio nothing if he kept the Punic War alive in order that he might have the glory of finishing it; she owes nothing to the Decii if they prayed for public disasters, to give themselves an opportunity of displaying their brave self-devotion. It is the greatest scandal for a physician to make work for himself; and many who have aggravated the diseases of their patients that they may have the greater credit for curing them, have either failed to cure them, at all or have done so at the cost of the most terrible suffering to their victims.

XXXVII

It is said (at any rate Hecaton tells us) that when Callistratus with many others was driven into exile by his factious and licentiously free country, some one prayed that such trouble might befall the Athenians that they would be forced to recall the exiles, on hearing which, he prayed that God might forbid his return upon such terms. When some one tried to console our own countryman, Rutilius, for his exile, pointing out that civil war was at hand, and that all exiles would soon be restored to Rome, he answered with even greater spirit, "What harm have I done you, that you should wish that I may return to my country more unhappily than I quit it? My wish is, that my country should blush at my being banished, rather than that she should mourn at my having returned." An exile, of which every one is more ashamed than the sufferer, is not exile at all. These two persons, who did not wish to be restored to their homes at the cost of a public disaster, but preferred that two should suffer unjustly than that all should suffer alike, are thought to have acted like good citizens; and in like manner it does not accord with the character of a grateful man, to wish that his benefactor may fall into troubles which he may dispel; because, even though he may mean well to him, yet he wishes him evil. To put out a fire which you yourself have lighted, will not even gain acquittal for you, let alone credit.

XXXVIII

In some states an evil wish was regarded as a crime. It is certain that at Athens Demades obtained a verdict against one who sold furniture for funerals, by proving that he had prayed for great gains, which he could not obtain without the death of many persons. Yet it is a stock question whether he was rightly found guilty. Perhaps he prayed, not that he might sell his wares to many persons, but that he might sell them dear, or that he might procure what he was going to sell, cheaply. Since his business consisted of buying and selling, why should you consider his prayer to apply to one branch of it only, although he made profit from both? Besides this, you might find every one of his trade guilty, for they all wish, that is, secretly pray, as he did. You might, moreover, find a great part of the human race guilty, for who is there who does not profit by his neighbour's wants? A soldier, if he wishes for glory, must wish for war; the farmer profits by corn being dear; a large number of litigants raises the price of forensic eloquence; physicians make money by a sickly season; dealers in luxuries are made rich by the effeminacy of youth; suppose that no storms and no conflagrations injured our dwellings, the builder's trade would be at a standstill. The prayer of one man was detected, but it was just like the prayers of all other men. Do you imagine that Arruntius and Haterius, and all other professional legacy-hunters do not put up the same prayers as undertakers and grave-diggers? though the latter know not whose death it is that they wish for, while the former wish for the death of their dearest friends, from whom, on account of their intimacy, they have most hopes of inheriting a fortune. No one's life does the undertaker any harm, whereas these men starve if their friends are long about dying; they do not, therefore, merely wish for their deaths in order that they may receive what they have earned by a disgraceful servitude, but in order that they may be set free from a heavy tax. There can, therefore, be no doubt that such persons repeat with even greater earnestness the prayer for which the undertaker was condemned, for whoever is likely to profit such men by dying, does them an injury by living. Yet the wishes of all these are alike well known and unpunished. Lastly, let every man examine his own self, let him look into the secret thoughts of his heart and consider what it is that he silently hopes for; how many of his prayers he would blush to acknowledge, even to himself; how few there are which we could repeat in the presence of witnesses!

XXXIX

Yet we must not condemn every thing which we find worthy of blame, as, for instance, this wish about our friends which we have been discussing, arises from a misdirected feeling of affection, and falls into the very error which it strives to avoid, for the man is ungrateful at the very time when he hurries to prove his gratitude. He prays aloud, "May he fall into my power, may he need my influence, may not be able to be safe and respectable without my aid, may he be so unfortunate that whatever return I make to him may be regarded as a benefit." To the gods alone he adds, "May domestic treasons encompass him, which can be quelled by me alone; may some powerful and virulent enemy, some excited and armed mob, assail him; may he be set upon by a creditor or an informer."

XL

See, how just you are; you would never have wished any of these misfortunes to befall him, if he had not bestowed a benefit upon you. Not to speak of the graver guilt which you incur by returning evil for good, you distinctly do wrong in not waiting for the fitting time for each action, for it is as wrong to anticipate this as it is not to take it when it comes. A benefit ought not always to be accepted, and ought not in all cases to be returned. If you were to return it to me against my will, you would be ungrateful, how much more ungrateful are you, if you force me to wish for it? Wait patiently; why are you unwilling to let my bounty abide with you? Why do you chafe at being laid under an obligation? why, as though you were dealing with a harsh usurer, are you in such a hurry to sign and seal an equivalent bond? Why do you wish me to get into trouble? Why do you call upon the gods to ruin me? If this is your way of returning a kindness, what would you do if you were exacting repayment of a debt?

XLI

Above all, therefore, my Liberalis, let us learn to live calmly under an obligation to others, and watch for opportunities of repaying our debt without manufacturing them. Let us remember that this anxiety to seize the first opportunity of setting ourselves free shows ingratitude; for no one repays with good will that which he is unwilling to owe, and his eagerness to get it out of his hands shows that he regards it as a burden rather than as a favour. How much better and more righteous is it to bear in mind what we owe to our friends, and to offer repayment, not to obtrude it, nor to think ourselves too much indebted; because a benefit is a common bond which connects two persons. Say "I do not delay to repay your kindness to me; I hope that you will accept my gratitude cheerfully. If irresistible fate hangs over either of us, and destiny rules either that you must receive your benefit back again, or that I must receive a second benefit, why then, of us two, let him give that was wont to give. I am ready to receive it.

"'Tis not the part of Turnus to delay."

That is the spirit which I shall show whenever the time comes; in the meanwhile the gods shall be my witnesses.

XLII

I have noted in you, my Liberalis, and as it were touched with my hand a feeling of fussy anxiety not to be behindhand in doing what is your duty. This anxiety is not suitable to a grateful mind, which, on the contrary, produces the utmost confidence in oneself, and which drives away all trouble by the consciousness of real affection towards one's benefactor. To say "Take back what you gave me," is no less a reproach than to say "You are in my debt." Let this be the first privilege of a benefit, that he who bestowed it may choose the time when he will have it returned. "But I fear that men may speak ill of me." You do wrong if you are grateful only for the sake of your reputation, and not to satisfy your conscience. You have in this matter two judges, your benefactor, whom you ought not, and yourself, whom you cannot deceive. "But," say you, "if no occasion of repayment offers, am I always to remain in his debt?" Yes; but you should do so openly, and willingly, and should view with great pleasure what he has entrusted to you. If you are vexed at not having yet returned a benefit, you must be sorry that you ever received it; but if he deserved that you should receive a benefit from him, why should he not deserve that you should long remain in his debt?

XLIII

Those persons are much mistaken who regard it as a proof of a great mind to make offers to give, and to fill many men's pockets and houses with their presents, for sometimes these are due not to a great mind, but to a great fortune; they do not know how far more great and more difficult it sometimes is to receive than to lavish gifts. I must disparage neither act; it is as proper to a noble heart to owe as to receive, for both are of equal value when done virtuously; indeed, to owe is the more difficult, because it requires more pains to keep a thing safe than to give it away. We ought not therefore to be in a hurry to repay, nor need we seek to do so out of due season, for to hasten to make repayment at the wrong time is as bad as to be slow to do so at the right time. My benefactor has entrusted his bounty to me: I ought not to have any fears either on his behalf or on my own. He has a sufficient security; he cannot lose it except he loses me--nay, not even if he loses me. I have returned thanks to him for it--that is, I have requited him. He who thinks too much about repaying a benefit must suppose that his friend thinks too much about receiving repayment. Make no difficulty about either course. If he wishes to receive his benefit back again, let us return it cheerfully; if he prefers to leave it in our hands, why should we dig up his treasure? why should we decline to be its guardians? he deserves to be allowed to do whichever he pleases. As for fame and reputation, let us regard them as matters which ought to accompany, but which ought not to direct our actions.

On Benefits – Book VII

I

Be of good cheer, my Liberalis:

"Our port is close, and I will not delay,
Nor by digressions wander from the way."

This book collects together all that has been omitted, and in it, having exhausted my subject, I shall consider not what I am to say, but what there is which I have not yet said. If there be anything superfluous in it, I pray you take it in good part, since it is for you that it is superfluous. Had I wished to set off my work to the best advantage, I ought to have added to it by degrees, and to have kept for the last that part which would be eagerly perused even by a sated reader. However, instead of this, I have collected together all that was essential in the beginning; I am now collecting together whatever then escaped me; nor, by Hercules, if you ask me, do I think that, after the rules which govern our conduct have been stated, it is very much to the purpose to discuss the other questions which have been raised more for the exercise of our intellects than for the health of our minds. The cynic Demetrius, who in my opinion was a great man even if compared with the greatest philosophers, had an admirable saying about this, that one gained more by having a few wise precepts ready and in common use than by learning many without having them at hand. "The best wrestler," he would say, "is not he who has learned thoroughly all the tricks and twists of the art, which are seldom met with in actual wrestling, but he who has well and carefully trained himself in one or two of them, and watches keenly for an opportunity of practising them. It does not matter how many of them he knows, if he knows enough to give him the victory; and so in this subject of ours there are many points of interest, but few of importance. You need not know what is the system of the ocean tides, why each seventh year leaves its mark upon the human body, why the more distant parts of a long portico do not keep their true proportion, but seem to approach one another until at last the spaces between the columns disappear, how it can be that twins are conceived separately, though they are born together, whether both result from one, or each from a separate act, why those whose birth was the same should have such different fates in life, and dwell at the greatest possible distance from one another, although they were born touching one another; it will not do you much harm to pass over matters which we are not permitted to know, and which we should not profit by knowing. Truths so obscure may be neglected with impunity.[1] Nor can we complain that nature deals hardly with us, for there is nothing which is hard to discover except those things by which we gain nothing beyond the credit of having discovered them; whatever things tend to make us better or happier are either obvious or easily discovered. Your mind can rise superior to the accidents of life, if it can raise itself above fears and not greedily covet boundless wealth, but has learned to seek for riches within itself; if it has cast out the fear of men and gods, and has learned that it has not much to fear from man, and nothing to fear from God; if by scorning all those things which make life miserable while they adorn it, the mind can soar to such a height as to see clearly that death cannot be the beginning of any trouble, though it is the end of many; if it can dedicate itself to righteousness and think any path easy which leads to it; if, being a gregarious creature, and born for the common good, it regards the world as the universal home, if it keeps its conscience clear towards God and lives always as though in public, fearing itself more than other men, then it avoids all storms, it stands on firm ground in fair daylight, and has brought to perfection its knowledge of all that is useful and essential. All that remains serves merely to amuse our leisure; yet, when once anchored in safety, the mind may consider these matters also, though it can derive no strength, but only culture from their discussion."

---

[1] The old saying, 'Truth lurks deep in a well (or abyss).'

II

The above are the rules which my friend Demetrius bids him who would make progress in philosophy to clutch with both hands, never to let go, but to cling to them, and make them a part of himself, and by daily meditation upon them to bring himself into such a state of mind, that these wholesome maxims occur to him of their own accord, that wherever he may be, they may straightway be ready for use when required, and that the criterion of right and wrong may present itself to him without delay. Let him know that nothing is evil except what is base, and nothing good except what is honourable: let him guide his life by this rule: let him both act and expect others to act in accordance with this law, and let him regard those whose minds are steeped in indolence, and who are given up to lust and gluttony, as the most pitiable of mankind, no matter how splendid their fortunes may be. Let him say to himself, "Pleasure is uncertain, short, apt to pall upon us, and the more eagerly we indulge in it, the sooner we bring on a reaction of feeling against it; we must necessarily afterwards blush for it, or be sorry for it, there is nothing grand about it, nothing worthy of man's nature, little lower as it is than that of the gods; pleasure is a low act, brought about by the agency of our inferior and baser members, and shameful in its result. True pleasure, worthy of a human being and of a man, is, not to stuff or swell his body with food and drink, nor to excite lusts which are least hurtful when they are most quiet, but to be free from all forms of mental disturbance, both those which arise from men's ambitious struggles with one another, and those which come from on high and are more difficult to deal with, which flow from our taking the traditional view of the gods, and estimating them by the analogy of our own vices." This equable, secure, uncloying pleasure is enjoyed by the man now described; a man skilled, so to say, in the laws of gods and men alike. Such a man enjoys the present without anxiety for the future: for he who depends upon what is uncertain can rely confidently upon nothing. Thus he is free from all those great troubles which unhinge the mind, he neither hopes for, nor covets anything, and engages in no uncertain adventures, being satisfied with what he has. Do not suppose that he is satisfied with a little; for everything is his, and that not in the sense in which all was Alexander's, who, though he reached the shore of the Red Sea, yet wanted more territory than that through which he had come. He did not even own those countries which he held or had conquered, while Onesicritus, whom he had sent on before him to discover new countries, was wandering about the ocean and engaging in war in unknown seas. Is it clear that he who pushed his armies beyond the bounds of the universe, who with reckless greed dashed headlong into a boundless and unexplored sea, must in reality have been full of wants? It matters not how many kingdoms he may have seized or given away, or how great a part of the world may pay him tribute; such a man must be in need of as much as he desires.

III

This was not the vice of Alexander alone, who followed with a fortunate audacity in the footsteps of Bacchus and Hercules, but it is common to all those whose covetousness is whetted rather than appeased by good fortune. Look at Cyrus and Cambyses and all the royal house of Persia: can you find one among them who thought his empire large enough, or was not at the last gasp still aspiring after further conquests? We need not wonder at this, for whatever is obtained by covetousness is simply swallowed up and lost, nor does it matter how much is poured into its insatiable maw. Only the wise man possesses everything without having to struggle to retain it; he alone does not need to send ambassadors across the seas, measure out camps upon hostile shores, place garrisons in commanding forts, or manoeuvre legions and squadrons of cavalry. Like the immortal gods, who govern their realm without recourse to arms, and from their serene and lofty heights protect their own, so the wise man fulfils his duties, however far-reaching they may be, without disorder, and looks down upon the whole human race, because he himself is the greatest and most powerful member thereof. You may laugh at him, but if you in your mind survey the east and the west, reaching even to the regions separated from us by vast wildernesses, if you think of all the creatures of the earth, all the riches which the bounty of nature lavishes, it shows a great spirit to be able to say, as though you were a god, "All these are mine." Thus it is that he covets nothing, for there is nothing which is not contained in everything, and everything is his.

IV

"This," say you, "is the very thing that I wanted! I have caught you! I shall be glad to see how you will extricate yourself from the toils into which you have fallen of your own accord. Tell me, if the wise man possesses everything, how can one give anything to a wise man? for even what you give him is his already. It is impossible, therefore, to bestow a benefit upon a wise man, if whatever is given him comes from his own store; yet you Stoics declare that it is possible to give to a wise man. I make the same inquiry about friends as well: for you say that friends own everything in common, and if so, no one can give anything to his friend, for he gives what his friend owned already in common with himself."

There is nothing to prevent a thing belonging to a wise man, and yet being the property of its legal owner. According to law everything in a state belongs to the king, yet all that property over which the king has rights of possession is parcelled out among individual owners, and each separate thing belongs to somebody: and so one can give the king a house, a slave, or a sum of money without being said to give him what was his already; for the king has rights over all these things, while each citizen has the ownership of them. We speak of the country of the Athenians, or of the Campanians, though the inhabitants divide them amongst themselves into separate estates; the whole region belongs to one state or another, but each part of it belongs to its own individual proprietor; so that we are able to give our lands to the state, although they are reckoned as belonging to the state, because we and the state own them in different ways. Can there be any doubt that all the private savings of a slave belong to his master as well as he himself? yet he makes his master presents. The slave does not therefore possess nothing, because if his master chose he might possess nothing; nor does what he gives of his own free will cease to be a present, because it might have been wrung from him against his will. As for how we are to prove that the wise man possesses all things, we shall see afterwards; for the present we are both agreed to regard this as true; we must gather together something to answer the question before us, which is, how any means remain of acting generously towards one who already possesses all things? All things that a son has belong to his father, yet who does not know that in spite of this a son can make presents to his father? All things belong to the gods; yet we make presents and bestow alms even upon the gods. What I have is not necessarily not mine because it belongs to you; for the same thing may belong both to me and to you.

"He to whom courtezans belong," argues our adversary, "must be a procurer: now courtezans are included in all things, therefore courtezans belong to the wise man. But he to whom courtezans belong is a procurer;

therefore the wise man is a procurer." Yes! by the same reasoning, our opponents would forbid him to buy anything, arguing, "No man buys his own property. Now all things are the property of the wise man; therefore the wise man buys nothing." By the same reasoning they object to his borrowing, because no one pays interest for the use of his own money. They raise endless quibbles, although they perfectly well understand what we say.

V

For, when I say that the wise man possesses everything, I mean that he does so without thereby impairing each man's individual rights in his own property, in the same way as in a country ruled by a good king, everything belongs to the king, by the right of his authority, and to the people by their several rights of ownership. This I shall prove in its proper place; in the mean time it is a sufficient answer to the question to declare that I am able to give to the wise man that which is in one way mine, and in another way his. Nor is it strange that I should be able to give anything to one who possesses everything. Suppose I have hired a house from you: some part of that house is mine, some is yours; the house itself is yours, the use of your house belongs to me. Crops may ripen upon your land, but you cannot touch them against the will of your tenant; and if corn be dear, or at famine price, you will

"In vain another's mighty store behold,"

grown upon your land, lying upon your land, and to be deposited in your own barns. Though you be the landlord, you must not enter my hired house, nor may you take away your own slave from me if I have contracted for his services; nay, if I hire a carriage from you, I bestow a benefit by allowing you to take your seat in it, although it is your own. You see, therefore, that it is possible for a man to receive a present by accepting what is his own.

VI

In all the cases which I have mentioned, each party is the owner of the same thing. How is this? It is because the one owns the thing, the other owns the use of the thing. We speak of the books of Cicero. Dorus, the bookseller, calls these same books his own; the one claims them because he wrote them, the other because he bought them; so that they may quite correctly be spoken of as belonging to either of the two, for they do belong to each, though in a different manner. Thus Titus Livius may receive as a present, or may buy his own books from Dorus. Although the wise man possesses everything, yet I can give him what I individually possess; for though, king-like, he in his mind possesses everything, yet the ownership of all things is divided among various individuals, so that he can both receive a present and owe one; can buy, or hire things. Everything belongs to Caesar; yet he has no private property beyond his own privy purse; as Emperor all things are his, but nothing is his own except what he inherits. It is possible, without treason, to discuss what is and what is not his; for even what the court may decide not to be his, from another point of view is his. In the same way the wise man in his mind possesses everything, in actual right and ownership he possesses only his own property.

VII

Bion is able to prove by argument at one time that everyone is sacrilegious, at another that no one is. When he is in a mood for casting all men down the Tarpeian rock, he says, "Whosoever touches that which belongs to the gods, and consumes it or converts it to his own uses, is sacrilegious; but all things belong to the gods, so that whatever thing any one touches belongs to them to whom all belongs; whoever, therefore, touches anything is sacrilegious." Again, when he bids men break open temples and pillage the Capitol without fear of the wrath of heaven, he declares that no one can be sacrilegious; because, whatever a man takes away, he takes from one place which belongs to the gods into another place which belongs to the gods. The answer to this is that all places do indeed belong to the gods, but all are not consecrated to them, and that sacrilege can only be done in places solemnly dedicated to heaven. Thus, also, the whole world is a temple of the immortal gods, and, indeed, the only one worthy of their greatness and splendour, and yet there is a distinction between things sacred and profane; all things which it is lawful to do under the sky and the stars are not lawful to do within consecrated walls. The sacrilegious man cannot do God any harm, for He is placed beyond his reach by His divine nature; yet he is punished because he seems to have done Him harm: his punishment is demanded by our feeling on the matter, and even by his own. In the same way, therefore, as he who carries off any sacred things is regarded as sacrilegious, although that which he stole is nevertheless within the limits of the world, so it is possible to steal from a wise man: for in that case it will be some, not of that universe which he possesses, but some of those things of which he is the acknowledged owner, and which are severally his own property, which will be stolen from him. The former of these possessions he will recognize as his own, the latter he will be unwilling, even if he be able to possess; he will say, as that Roman commander said, when, to reward his courage and good service to the state, he was assigned as much land as he could inclose in one day's ploughing. "You do not," said he, "want a citizen who wants more than is enough for one citizen." Do you not think that it required a much greater man to refuse this reward than to earn it? for many have taken away the landmarks of other men's property, but no one sets up limits to his own.

VIII

When, then, we consider that the mind of the truly wise man has power over all things and pervades all things, we cannot help declaring that everything is his, although, in the estimation of our common law, it may chance that he may be rated as possessing no property whatever. It makes a great difference whether we estimate what he owns by the greatness of his mind, or by the public register. He would pray to be delivered from that possession of everything of which you speak. I will not remind you of Socrates, Chrysippus, Zeno, and other great men, all the greater, however, because envy prevents no one from praising the ancients. But a short time ago I mentioned Demetrius, who seems to have been placed by nature in our times that he might prove that we could neither corrupt him nor be corrected by him; a man of consummate wisdom, though he himself disclaimed it, constant to the principles which he professed, of an eloquence worthy to deal with the mightiest subjects, scorning mere prettinesses and verbal niceties, but expressing with infinite spirit, the ideas which inspired it. I doubt not that he was endowed by divine providence with so pure a life and such power of speech in order that our age might neither be without a model nor a reproach. Had some god wished to give all our wealth to Demetrius on the fixed condition that he should not be permitted to give it away, I am sure that he would have refused to accept it, and would have said,

IX

"I do not intend to fasten upon my back a burden like this, of which I never can rid myself, nor do I, nimble and lightly equipped as I am, mean to hinder my progress by plunging into the deep morass of business transactions. Why do you offer to me what is the bane of all nations? I would not accept it even if I meant to give it away, for I see many things which it would not become me to give. I should like to place before my eyes the things which fascinate both kings and peoples, I wish to behold the price of your blood and your lives. First bring before me the trophies of Luxury, exhibiting them as you please, either in succession, or, which is better, in one mass. I see the shell of the tortoise, a foul and slothful brute, bought for immense sums and ornamented with the most elaborate care, the contrast of colours which is admired in it being obtained by the use of dyes resembling the natural tints. I see tables and pieces of wood valued at the price of a senator's estate, which are all the more precious, the more knots the tree has been twisted into by disease. I see crystal vessels, whose price is enhanced by their fragility, for among the ignorant the risk of losing things increases their value instead of lowering it, as it ought. I see murrhine cups, for luxury would be too cheap if men did not drink to one another out of hollow gems the wine to be afterwards thrown up again. I see more than one large pearl placed in each ear; for now our ears are trained to carry burdens, pearls are hung from them in pairs, and each pair has other single ones fastened above it. This womanish folly is not exaggerated enough for the men of our time, unless they hang two or three estates upon each ear. I see ladies' silk dresses, if those deserve to be called dresses which can neither cover their body or their shame; when wearing which, they can scarcely with a good conscience, swear that they are not naked. These are imported at a vast expense from nations unknown even to trade, in order that our matrons may show as much of their persons in public as they do to their lovers in private."

X

What are you doing, Avarice? see how many things there are whose price exceeds that of your beloved gold: all those which I have mentioned are more highly esteemed and valued. I now wish to review your wealth, those plates of gold and silver which dazzle our covetousness. By Hercules, the very earth, while she brings forth upon the surface every thing that is of use to us, has buried these, sunk them deep, and rests upon them with her whole weight, regarding them as pernicious substances, and likely to prove the ruin of mankind if brought into the light of day. I see that iron is brought out of the same dark pits as gold and silver, in order that we may lack neither the means nor the reward of murder. Thus far we have dealt with actual substances; but some forms of wealth deceive our eyes and minds alike. I see there letters of credit, promissory notes, and bonds, empty phantoms of property, ghosts of sick Avarice, with which she deceives our minds, which delight in unreal fancies; for what are these things, and what are interest, and account books, and usury, except the names of unnatural developments of human covetousness? I might complain of nature for not having hidden gold and silver deeper, for not having laid over it a weight too heavy to be removed: but what are your documents, your sale of time, your blood-sucking twelve per cent. interest? these are evils which we owe to our own will, which flow merely from our perverted habit, having nothing about them which can be seen or handled, mere dreams of empty avarice. Wretched is he who can take pleasure in the size of the audit book of his estate, in great tracts of land cultivated by slaves in chains, in huge flocks and herds which require provinces and kingdoms for their pasture ground, in a household of servants, more in number than some of the most warlike nations, or in a private house whose extent surpasses that of a large city! After he has carefully reviewed all his wealth, in what it is invested, and on what it is spent, and has rendered himself proud by the thoughts of it, let him compare what he has with what he wants: he becomes a poor man at once. Let me go: restore me to those riches of mine. I know the kingdom of wisdom, which is great and stable: I possess every thing, and in such a manner that it belongs to all men nevertheless."

XI

When, therefore, Gaius Caesar offered him two hundred thousand sesterces, he laughingly refused it, thinking it unworthy of himself to boast of having refused so small a sum. Ye gods and goddesses, what a mean mind must the emperor have had, if he hoped either to honour or to corrupt him. I must here repeat a proof of his magnanimity. I have heard that when he was expressing his wonder at the folly of Gaius at supposing that he could be influenced by such a bribe, he said, "If he meant to tempt me, he ought to have tried to do so by offering his entire kingdom."

XII

It is possible, then, to give something to the wise man, although all things belong to the wise man. Similarly, though we declare that friends have all things in common, it is nevertheless possible to give something to a friend: for I have not everything in common with a friend in the same manner as with a partner, where one part belongs to him, and another to me, but rather as a father and a mother possess their children in common when they have two, not each parent possessing one child, but each possessing both. First of all I will prove that any chance would-be partner of mine has nothing in common with me: and why? Because this community of goods can only exist between wise men, who are alone capable of friendship: other men can neither be friends nor partners one to another. In the next place, things may be owned in common in various ways. The knights' seats in the theatre belong to all the Roman knights; yet of these the seat which I occupy becomes my own, and if I yield it up to any one, although I only yield him a thing which we own in common, still I appear to have given him something. Some things belong to certain persons under particular conditions. I have a place among the knights, not to sell, or to let, or to dwell in, but simply to see the spectacle from, wherefore I do not tell an untruth when I say that I have a place among the knights' seats. Yet if, when I come into the theatre, the knights' seats are full, I both have a seat there by right, because I have the privilege of sitting there, and I have not a seat there, because my seat is occupied by those who share my right to those places. Suppose that the same thing takes place between friends; whatever our friend possesses, is common to us, but is the property of him who owns it; I cannot make use of it against his will. "You are laughing at me," say you; "if what belongs to my friend is mine, I am able to sell it." You are not able; for you are not able to sell your place among the knights' seats, and yet they are in common between you and the other knights. Consequently, the fact that you cannot sell a thing, or consume it, or exchange it for the better or the worse does not prove that it is not yours; for that which is yours under certain conditions is yours nevertheless.

XIII

I have received, but certainly not less. Not to detain you longer than is necessary, a benefit can be no more than a benefit; but the means employed to convey benefits may be both greater and more numerous. I mean those things by which kindness expresses and gives vent to itself, like lovers, whose many kisses and close embraces do not increase their love but give it play.

XIV

The next question which arises has been thoroughly threshed out in the former books, so here it shall only be touched on shortly; for the arguments which have been used for other cases can be transferred to it.

The question is, whether one who has done everything in his power to return a benefit, has returned it. "You may know," says our adversary, "that he has not returned it, because he did everything in his power to return it; it is evident, therefore, that he did not not do that which he did not have an opportunity of doing. A man who searches everywhere for his creditor without finding him does not thereby pay him what he owes." Some are in such a position that it is their duty to effect something material; in the case of others to have done all in their power to effect it is as good as effecting it. If a physician has done all in his power to heal his patient he has performed his duty; an advocate who employs his whole powers of eloquence on his client's behalf, performs his duty even though his client be convicted; the generalship even of a beaten commander is praised if he has prudently, laboriously, and courageously exercised his functions. Your friend has done all in his power to return your kindness, but your good fortune stood in his way; no adversity befell you in which he could prove the truth of his friendship; he could not give you money when you were rich, or nurse you when you were in health, or help you when you were succeeding; yet he repaid your kindness, even though you did not receive a benefit from him. Moreover, this man, being always eager, and on the watch for an opportunity of doing this, as he has expended much anxiety and much trouble upon it, has really done more than he who quickly had an opportunity of repaying your kindness. The case of a debtor is not the same, for it is not enough for him to have tried to find the money unless he pays it; in his case a harsh creditor stands over him who will not let a single day pass without charging him interest; in yours there is a most kind friend, who seeing you busy, troubled, and anxious would say.

"'Dismiss this trouble from thy breast;'

leave off disturbing yourself; I have received from you all that I wish; you wrong me, if you suppose that I want anything further; you have fully repaid me in intention."

"Tell me," says our adversary, "if he had repaid the benefit you would say that he had returned your kindness: is, then, he who repays it in the same position as he who does not repay it?"

On the other hand, consider this: if he had forgotten the benefit which he had received, if he had not even attempted to be grateful, you would say that he had not returned the kindness; but this man has laboured day and night to the neglect of all his other duties in his devoted care to let no opportunity of proving his gratitude escape him; is then he who took no pains to return a kindness to be classed with this man who never ceased to take pains? you are unjust, if you require a material payment from me when you see that I am not wanting in intention.

XV

In short, suppose that when you are taken captive, I have borrowed money, made over my property as security to my creditor, that I have sailed in a stormy winter season along coasts swarming with pirates, that I have braved all the perils which necessarily attend a voyage even on a peaceful sea, that I have wandered through all wildernesses seeking for those men whom all others flee from, and that when I have at length reached the pirates, someone else has already ransomed you: will you say that I have not returned your kindness? Even if during this voyage I have lost by shipwreck the money that I had raised to save you, even if I myself have fallen into the prison from which I sought to release you, will you say that I have not returned your kindness? No, by Hercules! the Athenians call Harmodius and Aristogiton, tyrannicides; the hand of Mucius which he left on the enemy's altar was equivalent to the death of Porsena, and valour struggling against fortune is always illustrious, even if it falls short of accomplishing its design. He who watches each opportunity as it passes, and tries to avail himself of one after another, does more to show his gratitude than he whom the first opportunity enabled to be grateful without any trouble whatever. "But," says our adversary, "he gave you two things, material help and kindly feeling; you, therefore, owe him two." You might justly say this to one who returns your kindly feeling without troubling himself further; this man is really in your debt; but you cannot say so of one who wishes to repay you, who struggles and leaves no stone unturned to do so; for, as far as in him lies, he repays you in both kinds; in the next place, counting is not always a true test, sometimes one thing is equivalent to two; consequently so intense and ardent a wish to repay takes the place of a material repayment. Indeed, if a feeling of gratitude has no value in repaying a kindness without giving something material, then no one can be grateful to the gods, whom we can repay by gratitude alone. "We cannot," says our adversary, "give the gods anything else." Well, but if I am not able to give this man, whose kindness I am bound to return, anything beside my gratitude, why should that which is all that I can bestow on a god be insufficient to prove my gratitude towards a man?

XVI

If, however, you ask me what I really think, and wish me to give a definite answer, I should say that the one party ought to consider his benefit to have been returned, while the other ought to feel that he has not returned it; the one should release his friend from the debt, the other should hold himself bound to pay it; the one should say, "I have received;" the other should answer, "I owe." In our whole investigation, we ought to look entirely to the public good; we ought to prevent the ungrateful having any excuses in which they can take refuge, and under cover of which they can disown their debts. "I have done all in my power," say you. Well, keep on doing so still. Do you suppose that our ancestors were so foolish, as not to understand that it is most unjust that the man who has wasted the money which he received from his creditor on debauchery, or gambling, should be classed with one who has lost his own property as well as that of others in a fire, by robbery, or some sadder mischance? They would take no excuse, that men might understand that they were always bound to keep their word; it was thought better that even a good excuse should not be accepted from a few persons, than that all men should be led to try to make excuses. You say that you have done all in your power to repay your debt; this ought to be enough for your friend, but not enough for you. He to whom you owe a kindness, is unworthy of gratitude if he lets all your anxious care and trouble to repay it go for nothing; and so, too, if your friend takes your good will as a repayment, you are ungrateful if you are not all the more eager to feel the obligation of the debt which he has forgiven you. Do not snap up his receipt, or call witnesses to prove it; rather seek opportunities for repaying not less than before; repay the one man because he asks for repayment, the other because he forgives you your debt; the one because he is good, the other because he is bad. You, need not, therefore, think that you have anything to do with the question whether a man be bound to repay the benefit which he has received from a wise man, if that man has ceased to be wise and has turned into a bad man. You would return a deposit which you had received from a wise man; you would return a loan even to a bad man; what grounds have you for not returning a benefit also? Because he has changed, ought he to change you? What? if you had received anything from a man when healthy, would you not return it to him when he was sick, though we always are more bound to treat our friends with more kindness when they are ailing? So, too, this man is sick in his mind; we ought to help him, and bear with him; folly is a disease of the mind.

XVII

I think here we ought to make a distinction, in order to render this point more intelligible. Benefits are of two kinds: one, the perfect and true benefit, which can only be bestowed by one wise man upon another; the other, the common vulgar form which ignorant men like ourselves interchange. With regard to the latter, there is no doubt that it is my duty to repay it whether my friend turns out to be a murderer, a thief, or an adulterer. Crimes have laws to punish them; criminals are better reformed by judges than by ingratitude; a man ought not to make you bad by being so himself. I will fling a benefit back to a bad man, I will return it to a good man; I do so to the latter, because I owe it to him; to the former, that I may not be in his debt.

XVIII

With regard to the other class of benefit, the question arises whether if I was not able to take it without being a wise man, I am able to return it, except to a wise man. For suppose I do return it to him, he cannot receive it, he is not any longer able to receive such a thing, he has lost the knowledge of how to use it. You would not bid me throw back[2] a ball to a man who has lost his hand; it is folly to give any one what he cannot receive. If I am to begin to reply to the last argument, I say that I should not give him what he is unable to take; but I would return it, even though he is not able to receive it. I cannot lay him under an obligation unless he takes my bounty; but by returning it I can free myself from my obligations to him. You say, "he will not be able to use it." Let him see to that; the fault will lie with him, not with me.

---

[2] i.e. in the game of ball.

XIX

"To return a thing," says our adversary, "is to hand it over to one who can receive it. Why, if you owed some wine to any man, and he bade you pour it into a net or a sieve, would you say that you had returned it? or would you be willing to return it in such a way that in the act of returning it was lost between you?" To return is to give that which you owe back to its owner when he wishes for it. It is not my duty to perform more than this; that he should possess what he has received from me is a matter for further consideration; I do not owe him the safe-keeping of his property, but the honourable payment of my debt, and it is much better that he should not have it, than that I should not return it to him. I would repay my creditor, even though he would at once take what I paid him to the market; even if he deputed an adulteress to receive the money from me, I would pay it to her; even if he were to pour the coins which he receives into a loose fold of his cloak, I would pay it. It is my business to return it to him, not to keep it and save it for him after I have returned it; I am bound to take care of his bounty when I have received it, but not when I have returned it to him. While it remains with me, it must be kept safe; but when he asks for it again I must give it to him, even though it slips out of his hands as he takes it. I will repay a good man when it is convenient; I will repay a bad man when he asks me to do so.

"You cannot," argues our adversary, "return him a benefit of the same kind as that which you received; for you received it from a wise man, and you are returning it to a fool." Do I not return to him such a benefit, as he is now able to receive? It is not my fault if I return it to him worse than I received it, the fault lies with him, and so, unless he regains his former wisdom, I shall return it in such a form as he in his fallen condition is able to receive. "But what," asks he, "if he become not only bad, but savage and ferocious, like Apollodorus or Phalaris, would you return even to such a man as this a benefit which you had received from him?" I answer, Nature does not admit of so great a change in a wise man. Men do not change from the best to the worst; even in becoming bad, he would necessarily retain some traces of goodness; virtue is never so utterly quenched as not to imprint on the mind marks which no degradation can efface. If wild animals bred in captivity escape into the woods, they still retain something of their original tameness, and are as remote from the gentlest in the one extreme as they are in the other from those which have always been wild, and have never endured to be touched by man's hand. No one who has ever applied himself to philosophy ever becomes completely wicked; his mind becomes so deeply coloured with it, that its tints can never be entirely spoiled and blackened. In the next place, I ask whether this man of yours be ferocious merely in intent, or whether he breaks out into actual outrages upon mankind? You have instanced the tyrants Apollodorus and Phalaris; if the bad man restrains their evil likeness within himself, why should I not return his benefit to him, in order to set myself free from any further dealings with him? If, however, he not only delights in human blood, but feeds upon it; if he exercises his insatiable cruelty in the torture of persons of all ages, and his fury is not prompted by anger, but by a sort of delight in cruelty, if he cuts the throats of children before the eyes of their parents; if, not satisfied with merely killing his victims, he tortures them, and not only burns but actually roasts them; if his castle is always wet with freshly shed blood; then it is not enough not to return his benefits. All connexion between me and such a man has been broken off by his destruction of the bonds of human society. If he had bestowed something upon me, but were to invade my native country, he would have lost all claim to my gratitude, and it would be counted a crime to make him any return; if he does not attack my country, but is the scourge of his own; if he has nothing to do with my nation, but torments and cuts to pieces his own, then in the same manner such depravity, though it does not render him my personal enemy, yet renders him hateful to me, and the duty which I owe to the human race is anterior to and more important than that which I owe to him as an individual.

XX

However, although this be so, and although I am freed from all obligation towards him, from the moment when, by outraging all laws, he rendered it impossible for any man to do him a wrong, nevertheless, I think I ought to make the following distinction in dealing with him. If my repayment of his benefit will neither increase nor maintain his powers of doing mischief to mankind, and is of such a character that I can return it to him without disadvantage to the public, I would return it: for instance, I would save the life of his infant child; for what harm can this benefit do to any of those who suffer from his cruelty? But I would not furnish him with money to pay his bodyguard. If he wishes for marbles, or fine clothes, the trappings of his luxury will harm no one; but with soldiers and arms I would not furnish him. If he demands, as a great boon, actors and courtesans and such things as will soften his savage nature, I would willingly bestow them upon him. I would not furnish him with triremes and brass-beaked ships of war, but I would send him fast sailing and luxuriously-fitted vessels, and all the toys of kings who take their pleasure on the sea. If his health was altogether despaired of, I would by the same act bestow a benefit on all men and return one to him; seeing that for such characters death is the only remedy, and that he who never will return to himself, had best leave himself. However, such wickedness as this is uncommon, and is always regarded as a portent, as when the earth opens, or when fires break forth from caves under the sea; so let us leave it, and speak of those vices which we can hate without shuddering at them. As for the ordinary bad man, whom I can find in the marketplace of any town, who is feared only by individuals, I would return to him a benefit which I had received from him. It is not right that I should profit by his wickedness; let me return what is not mine to its owner. Whether he be good or bad makes no difference; but I would consider the matter most carefully, if I were not returning but bestowing it.

XXI

This point requires to be illustrated by a story. A certain Pythagoraean bought a fine pair of shoes from a shoemaker; and as they were an expensive piece of work, he did not pay ready money for them. Some time afterwards he came to the shop to pay for them, and after he had long been knocking at the closed door, some one said to him, "Why do you waste your time? The shoemaker whom you seek has been carried out of his house and buried; this is a grief to us who lose our friends for ever, but by no means so to you, who know that he will be born again," jeering at the Pythagoraean. Upon this our philosopher not unwillingly carried his three or four denarii home again, shaking them every now and then; afterwards, blaming himself for the pleasure which he had secretly felt at not paying his debt, and perceiving that he enjoyed having made this trifling gain, he returned to the shop, and saying, "the man lives for you, pay him what you owe," he passed four denarii into the shop through the crack of the closed door, and let them fall inside, punishing himself for his unconscionable greediness that he might not form the habit of appropriating that which is not his own.

XXII

If you owe anything, seek for some one to whom you may repay it, and if no one demands it, dun your own self; whether the man be good or bad is no concern of yours; repay him, and then blame him. You have forgotten, how your several duties are divided: it is right for him to forget it, but we have bidden you bear it in mind. When, however, we say that he who bestows a benefit ought to forget it, it is a mistake to suppose that we rob him of all recollection of the business, though it is most creditable to him; some of our precepts are stated over strictly in order to reduce them to their true proportions. When we say that he ought not to remember it, we mean he ought not to speak publicly, or boast of it offensively. There are some, who, when they have bestowed a benefit, tell it in all societies, talk of it when sober, cannot be silent about it when drunk, force it upon strangers, and communicate it to friends; it is to quell this excessive and reproachful consciousness that we bid him who gave it forget it, and by commanding him to do this, which is more than he is able, encourage him to keep silence.

XXIII

When you distrust those whom you order to do anything, you ought to command them to do more than enough in order that they may do what is enough. The purpose of all exaggeration is to arrive at the truth by falsehood. Consequently, he who spoke of horses as being:

"Whiter than snows and swifter than the winds,"

said what could not possibly be in order that they might be thought to be as much so as possible. And he who said:

"More firm than crags, more headlong than the stream,"

did not suppose that he should make any one believe that a man could ever be as firm as a crag. Exaggeration never hopes all its daring flights to be believed, but affirms what is incredible, that thereby it may convey what is credible. When we say, "let the man who has bestowed a benefit, forget it," what we mean is, "let him be as though he had forgotten it; let not his remembrance of it appear or be seen." When we say that repayment of a benefit ought not to be demanded, we do not utterly forbid its being demanded; for repayment must often be extorted from bad men, and even good men require to be reminded of it. Am I not to point out a means of repayment to one who does not perceive it? Am I not to explain my wants to one does not know them? Why should he (if a bad man) have the excuse, or (if a good man) have the sorrow of not knowing them? Men ought sometimes to be reminded of their debts, though with modesty, not in the tone of one demanding a legal right.

XXIV

Socrates once said in the hearing of his friends: "I would have bought a cloak, if I had had the money for it." He asked no one for money, but he reminded them all to give it. There was a rivalry between them, as to who should give it; and how should there not be? Was it not a small thing which Socrates received? Yes, but it was a great thing to be the man from whom Socrates received it. Could he blame them more gently? "I would," said he, "have bought a cloak if I had had the money for it." After this, however eager any one was to give, he gave too late; for he had already been wanting in his duty to Socrates. Because some men harshly demand repayment of debts, we forbid it, not in order that it may never be done, but that it may be done sparingly.

XXV

Aristippus once, when enjoying a perfume, said: "Bad luck to those effeminate persons who have brought so nice a thing into disrepute." We also may say, "Bad luck to those base extortioners who pester us for a fourfold return of their benefits, and have brought into disrepute so nice a thing as reminding our friends of their duty." I shall nevertheless make use of this right of friendship, and I shall demand the return of a benefit from any man from whom I would not have scrupled to ask for one, such a man as would regard the power of returning a benefit as equivalent to receiving a second one. Never, not even when complaining of him, would I say,

"A wretch forlorn upon the shore he lay,
His ship, his comrades, all were swept away;
Fool that I was, I pitied his despair,
And even gave him of my realm a share."

This is not to remind, but to reproach; this is to make one's benefits odious to enable him, or even to make him wish to be ungrateful. It is enough, and more than enough, to remind him of it gently and familiarly:

"If aught of mine hath e'er deserved thy thanks."

To this his answer would be, "Of course you have deserved my thanks; you took me up, 'a wretch forlorn upon the shore.'"

XXVI

"But," says our adversary, "suppose that we gain nothing by this; suppose that he pretends that he has forgotten it, what ought I to do?" You now ask a very necessary question, and one which fitly concludes this branch of the subject, how, namely, one ought to bear with the ungrateful. I answer, calmly, gently, magnanimously. Never let any one's discourtesy, forgetfulness, or ingratitude, enrage you so much that you do not feel any pleasure at having bestowed a benefit upon him; never let your wrongs drive you into saying, "I wish I had not done it." You ought to take pleasure even in the ill-success of your benefit; he will always be sorry for it, even though you are not even now sorry for it. You ought not to be indignant, as if something strange had happened; you ought rather to be surprised if it had not happened. Some are prevented by difficulties, some by expense, and some by danger from returning your bounty; some are hindered by a false shame, because by returning it, they would confess that they had received it; with others ignorance of their duty, indolence, or excess of business, stands in the way. Reflect upon the insatiability of men's desires. You need not be surprised if no one repays you in a world in which no one ever gains enough. What man is there of so firm and trustworthy a mind that you can safely invest your benefits in him? One man is crazed with lust, another is the slave of his belly, another gives his whole soul to gain, caring nothing for the means by which he amasses it; some men's minds are disturbed by envy, some blinded by ambition till they are ready to fling themselves on the sword's point. In addition to this, one must reckon sluggishness of mind and old age; and also the opposites of these, restlessness and disturbance of mind, also excessive self-esteem and pride in the very things for which a man ought to be despised. I need not mention obstinate persistence in wrong-doing, or frivolity which cannot remain constant to one point; besides all this, there is headlong rashness, there is timidity which never gives us trustworthy counsel, and the numberless errors with which we struggle, the rashness of the most cowardly, the quarrels of our best friends, and that most common evil of trusting in what is most uncertain, and of undervaluing, when we have obtained it, that which we once never hoped to possess. Amidst all these restless passions, how can you hope to find a thing so full of rest as good faith?

XXVII

If a true picture of our life were to rise before your mental vision, you would, I think, behold a scene like that of a town just taken by storm, where decency and righteousness were no longer regarded, and no advice is heard but that of force, as if universal confusion were the word of command. Neither fire nor sword are spared; crime is unpunished by the laws; even religion, which saves the lives of suppliants in the very midst of armed enemies, does not check those who are rushing to secure plunder. Some men rob private houses, some public buildings; all places, sacred or profane, are alike stripped; some burst their way in, others climb over; some open a wider path for themselves by overthrowing the walls that keep them out, and make their way to their booty over ruins; some ravage without murdering, others brandish spoils dripping with their owner's blood; everyone carries off his neighbours' goods. In this greedy struggle of the human race surely you forget the common lot of all mankind, if you seek among these robbers for one who will return what he has got. If you are indignant at men being ungrateful, you ought also to be indignant at their being luxurious, avaricious and lustful; you might as well be indignant with sick men for being ugly, or with old men for being pale. It is, indeed, a serious vice, it is not to be borne, and sets men at variance with one another; nay, it rends and destroys that union by which alone our human weakness can be supported; yet it is so absolutely universal, that even those who complain of it most are not themselves free from it.

XXVIII

Consider within yourself, whether you have always shown gratitude to those to whom you owe it, whether no one's kindness has ever been wasted upon you, whether you constantly bear in mind all the benefits which you have received. You will find that those which you received as a boy were forgotten before you became a man; that those bestowed upon you as a young man slipped from your memory when you became an old one. Some we have lost, some we have thrown away, some have by degrees passed out of our sight, to some we have wilfully shut our eyes. If I am to make excuses for your weakness, I must say in the first place that human memory is a frail vessel, and is not large enough to contain the mass of things placed in it; the more it receives, the more it must necessarily lose; the oldest things in it give way to the newest. Thus it comes to pass that your nurse has hardly any influence with you, because the lapse of time has set the kindness which you received from her at so great a distance; thus it is that you no longer look upon your teacher with respect; and that now when you are busy about your candidature for the consulate or the priesthood, you forget those who supported you in your election to the quaestorship. If you carefully examine yourself, perhaps you will find the vice of which you complain in your own bosom; you are wrong in being angry with a universal failing, and foolish also, for it is your own as well; you must pardon others, that you may yourself be acquitted. You will make your friend a better man by bearing with him, you will in all cases make him a worse one by reproaching him. You can have no reason for rendering him shameless; let him preserve any remnants of modesty which he may have. Too loud reproaches have often dispelled a modesty which might have borne good fruit. No man fears to be that which all men see that he is; when his fault is made public, he loses his sense of shame.

XXIX

You say, "I have lost the benefit which I bestowed." Yet do we say that we have lost what we consecrate to heaven, and a benefit well bestowed, even though we get an ill return for it, is to be reckoned among things consecrated. Our friend is not such a man as we hoped he was; still, let us, unlike him, remain the same as we were. The loss did not take place when he proved himself so; his ingratitude cannot be made public without reflecting some shame upon us, since to complain of the loss of a benefit is a sign that it was not well bestowed. As far as we are able we ought to plead with ourselves on his behalf: "Perhaps he was not able to return it, perhaps he did not know of it, perhaps he will still do so." A wise and forbearing creditor prevents the loss of some debts by encouraging his debtor and giving him time. We ought to do the same, we ought to deal tenderly with a weakly sense of honour.

XXX

"I have lost," say you, "the benefit which I bestowed." You are a fool, and do not understand when your loss took place; you have indeed lost it, but you did so when you gave it, the fact has only now come to light. Even in the case of those benefits which appear to be lost, gentleness will do much good; the wounds of the mind ought to be handled as tenderly as those of the body. The string, which might be disentangled by patience, is often broken by a rough pull. What is the use of abuse, or of complaints? why do you overwhelm him with reproaches? why do you set him free from his obligation? even if he be ungrateful he owes you nothing after this. What sense is there in exasperating a man on whom you have conferred great favours, so as out of a doubtful friend to make a certain enemy, and one, too, who will seek to support his own cause by defaming you, or to make men say, "I do not know what the reason is that he cannot endure a man to whom he owes so much; there must be something in the background?" Any man can asperse, even if he does not permanently stain the reputation of his betters by complaining of them; nor will any one be satisfied with imputing small crimes to them, when it is only by the enormity of his falsehood that he can hope to be believed.

XXXI

What a much better way is that by which the semblance of friendship, and, indeed, if the other regains to his right mind, friendship itself is preserved! Bad men are overcome by unwearying goodness, nor does any one receive kindness in so harsh and hostile a spirit as not to love good men even while he does them wrong, when they lay him under the additional obligation of requiring no return for their kindness. Reflect, then, upon this: you say, "My kindness has met with no return, what am I to do? I ought to imitate the gods, those noblest disposers of all events, who begin to bestow their benefits on those who know them not, and persist in bestowing them on those who are ungrateful for them. Some reproach them with neglect of us, some with injustice towards us; others place them outside of their own world, in sloth and indifference, without light, and without any functions; others declare that the sun itself, to whom we owe the division of our times of labour and of rest, by whose means we are saved from being plunged in the darkness of eternal night; who, by his circuit, orders the seasons of the year, gives strength to our bodies, brings forth our crops and ripens our fruits, is merely a mass of stone, or a fortuitous collection of fiery particles, or anything rather than a god. Yet, nevertheless, like the kindest of parents, who only smile at the spiteful words of their children, the gods do not cease to heap benefits upon those who doubt from what source their benefits are derived, but continue impartially distributing their bounty among all the peoples and nations of the earth. Possessing only the power of doing good, they moisten the land with seasonable showers, they put the seas in movement by the winds, they mark time by the course of the constellations, they temper the extremes of heat and cold, of summer and winter, by breathing a milder air upon us; and they graciously and serenely bear with the faults of our erring spirits. Let us follow their example; let us give, even if much be given to no purpose, let us, in spite of this, give to others; nay, even to those upon whom our bounty has been wasted. No one is prevented by the fall of a house from building another; when one home has been destroyed by fire, we lay the foundations of another before the site has had time to cool; we rebuild ruined cities more than once upon the same spots, so untiring are our hopes of success. Men would undertake no works either on land or sea if they were not willing to try again what they have failed in once.

XXXII

Suppose a man is ungrateful, he does not injure me, but himself; I had the enjoyment of my benefit when I bestowed it upon him. Because he is ungrateful, I shall not be slower to give but more careful; what I have lost with him, I shall receive back from others. But I will bestow a second benefit upon this man himself, and will overcome him even as a good husbandman overcomes the sterility of the soil by care and culture; if I do not do so my benefit is lost to me, and he is lost to mankind. It is no proof of a great mind to give and to throw away one's bounty; the true test of a great mind is to throw away one's bounty and still to give."

Made in United States
Orlando, FL
13 June 2024

47831067R00355